Ouran High School
Host Club

Vol. 14
Bisco Hatori

Ouran High School
Host Club
Vol. 14

CONTENTS

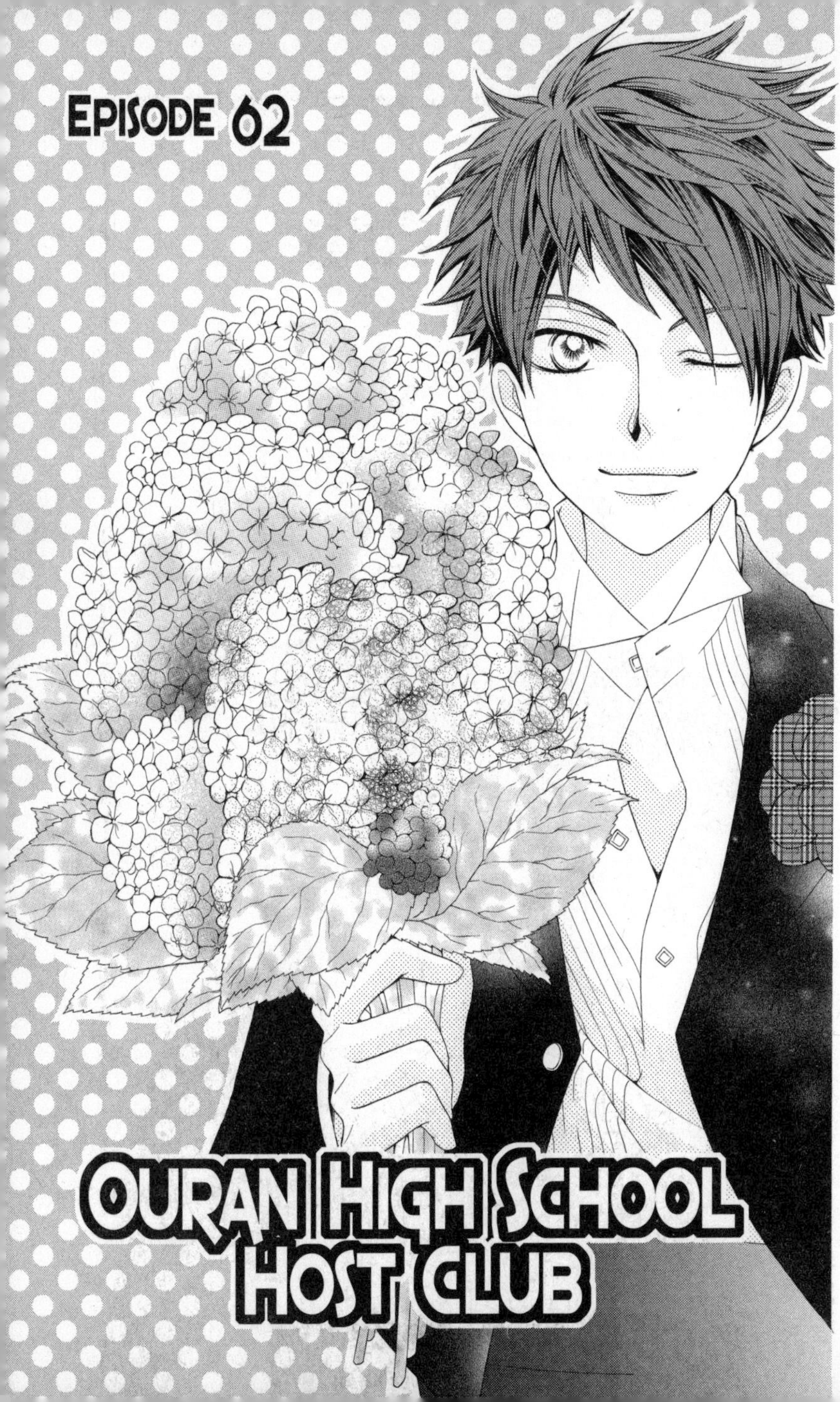
EPISODE 62
OURAN HIGH SCHOOL
HOST CLUB

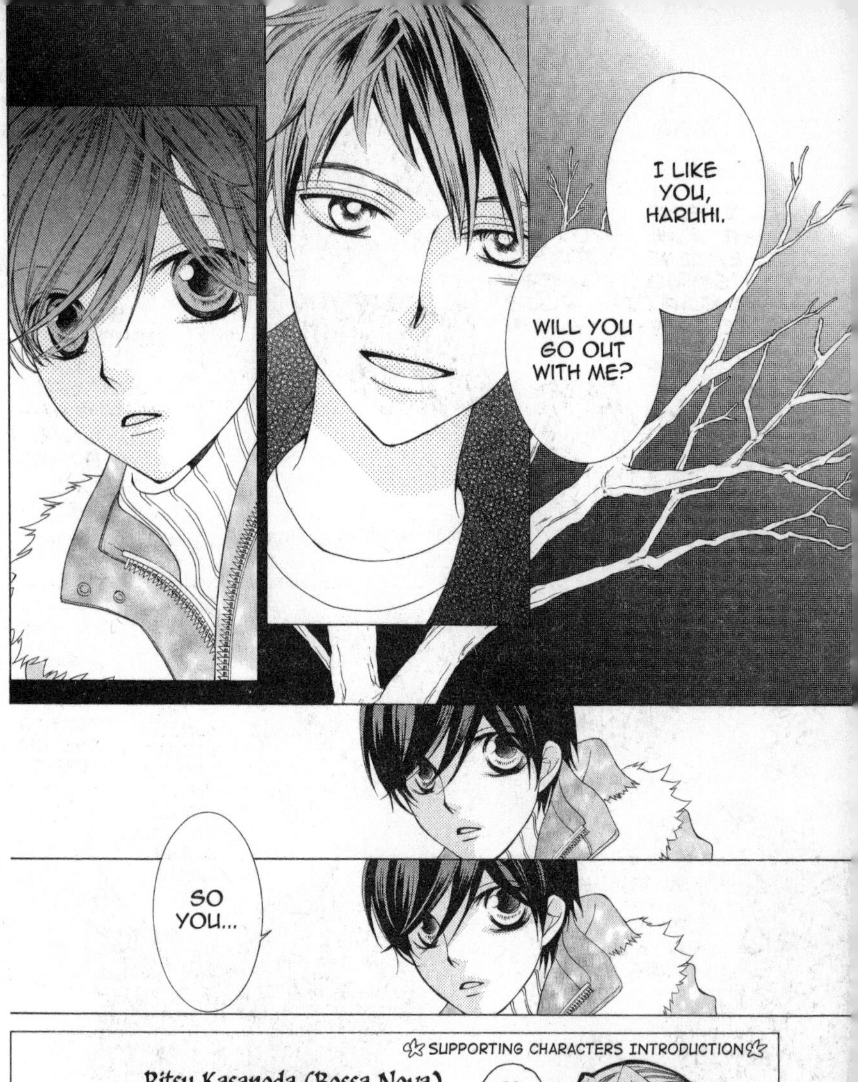
I LIKE YOU, HARUHI.
WILL YOU GO OUT WITH ME?
SO YOU...

SUPPORTING CHARACTERS INTRODUCTION

Ritsu Kasanoda (Bossa Nova)

FIRST-YEAR, CLASS D
GARDENING CLUB MEMBER

CURRENTLY VERY PASSIONATE ABOUT GROWING VEGETABLES. THOUGH HE ORIGINALLY STARTED IN ORDER TO GIVE THEM TO HARUHI, HE ENDED UP DEVELOPING A SINCERE LOVE OF GARDENING. BECAUSE OF HIS EARNEST NATURE, THE OTHER GARDENING CLUB MEMBERS HAVE TAKEN TO DOTING ON HIM.

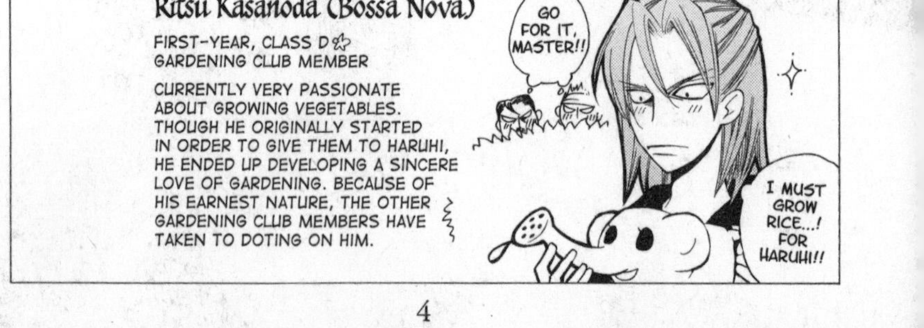
GO FOR IT, MASTER!!
I MUST GROW RICE...! FOR HARUHI!!

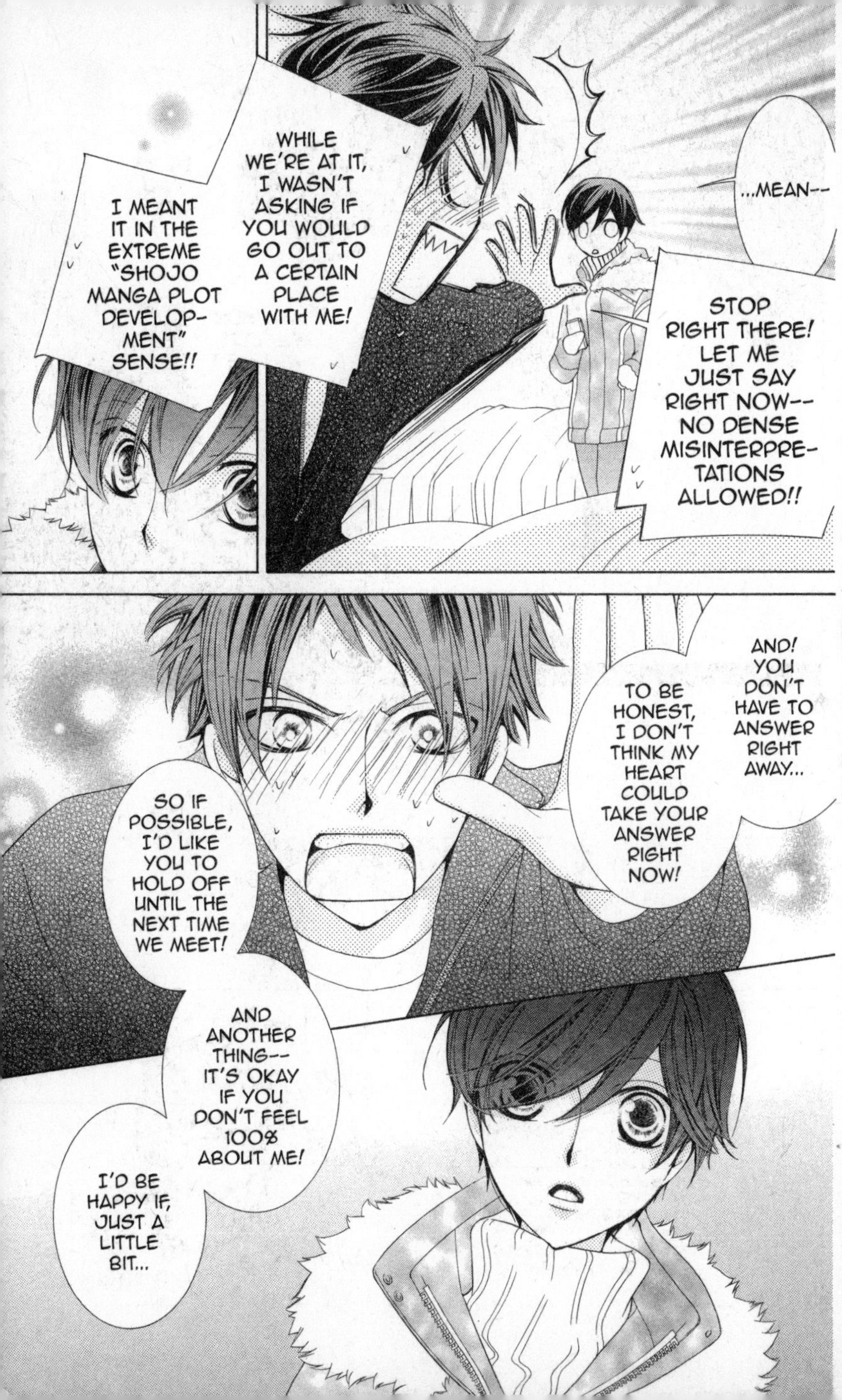
...MEAN--
STOP RIGHT THERE! LET ME JUST SAY RIGHT NOW-- NO DENSE MISINTERPRETATIONS ALLOWED!!
WHILE WE'RE AT IT, I WASN'T ASKING IF YOU WOULD GO OUT TO A CERTAIN PLACE WITH ME!
I MEANT IT IN THE EXTREME "SHOJO MANGA PLOT DEVELOPMENT" SENSE!!
AND! YOU DON'T HAVE TO ANSWER RIGHT AWAY...
TO BE HONEST, I DON'T THINK MY HEART COULD TAKE YOUR ANSWER RIGHT NOW!
SO IF POSSIBLE, I'D LIKE YOU TO HOLD OFF UNTIL THE NEXT TIME WE MEET!
AND ANOTHER THING-- IT'S OKAY IF YOU DON'T FEEL 100% ABOUT ME!
I'D BE HAPPY IF, JUST A LITTLE BIT...

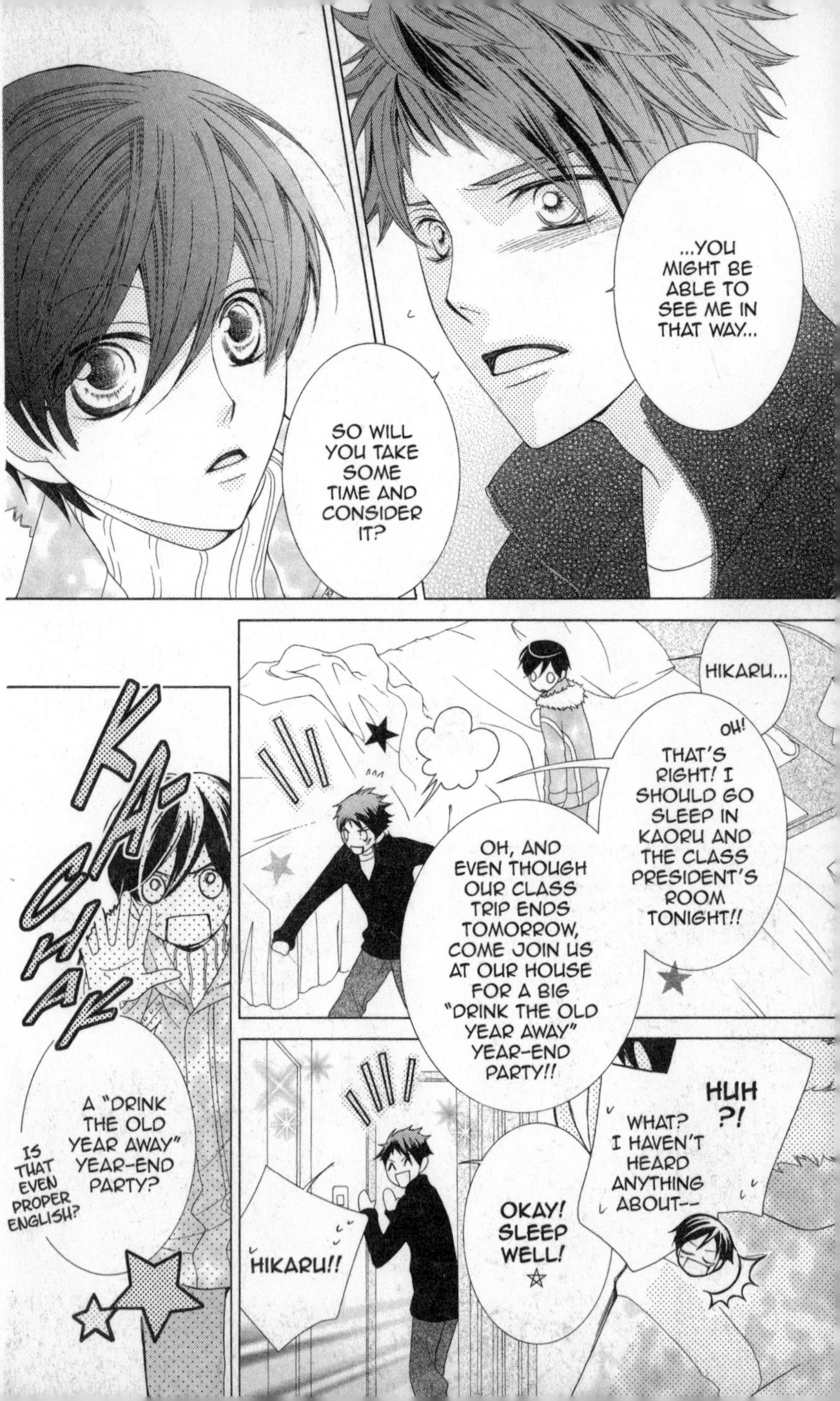
...YOU MIGHT BE ABLE TO SEE ME IN THAT WAY...
SO WILL YOU TAKE SOME TIME AND CONSIDER IT?
HIKARU...
OH!
THAT'S RIGHT! I SHOULD GO SLEEP IN KAORU AND THE CLASS PRESIDENT'S ROOM TONIGHT!!
OH, AND EVEN THOUGH OUR CLASS TRIP ENDS TOMORROW, COME JOIN US AT OUR HOUSE FOR A BIG "DRINK THE OLD YEAR AWAY" YEAR-END PARTY!!
HUH ?!
WHAT? I HAVEN'T HEARD ANYTHING ABOUT--
OKAY! SLEEP WELL!
HIKARU!!
KA-CHAK
A "DRINK THE OLD YEAR AWAY" YEAR-END PARTY?
IS THAT EVEN PROPER ENGLISH?

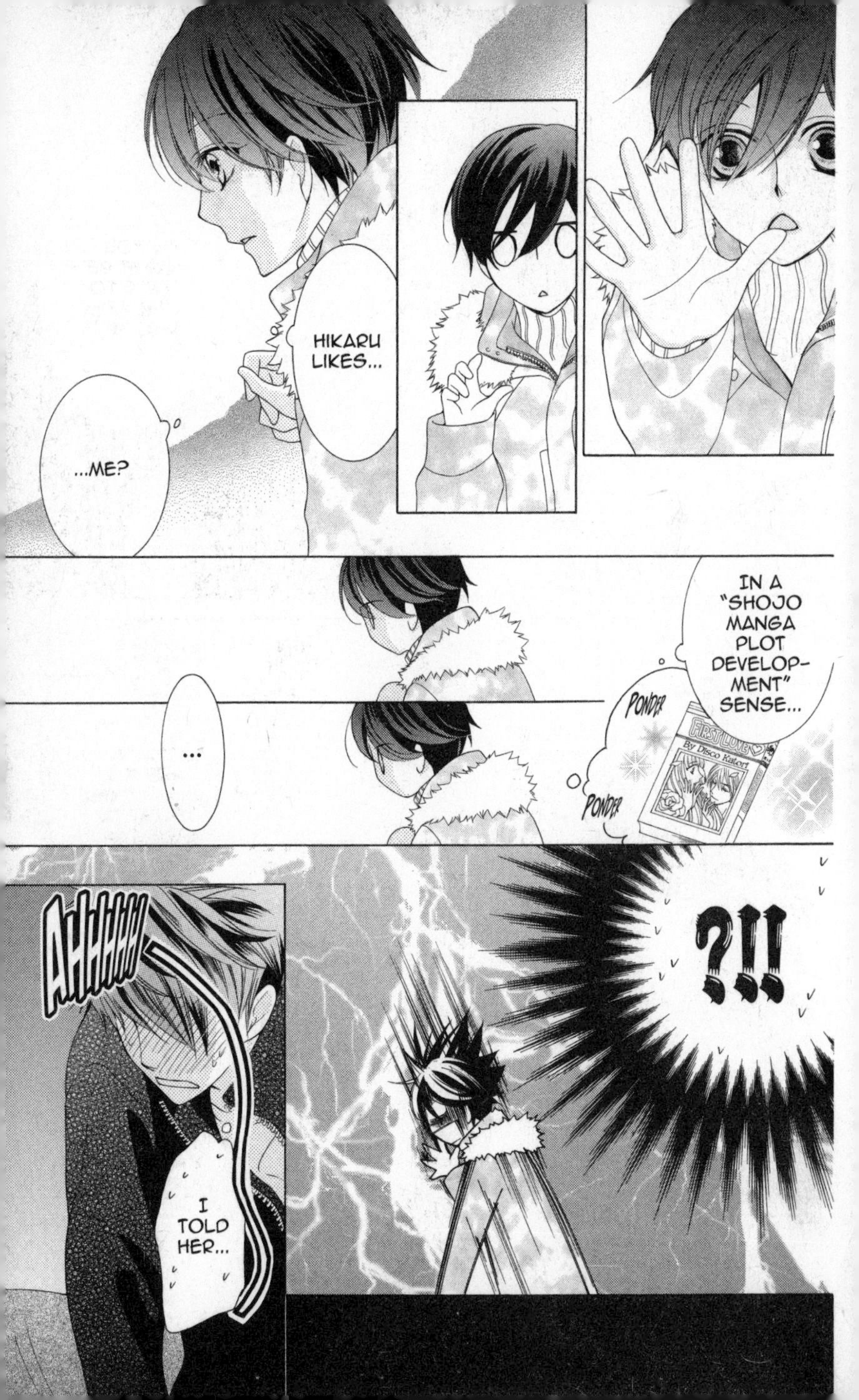
HIKARU LIKES...
...ME?
IN A "SHOJO MANGA PLOT DEVELOPMENT" SENSE...
PONDER
PONDER
FIRST LOVE
By Disco Katori
...
?!!
AHHHH!
I TOLD HER...

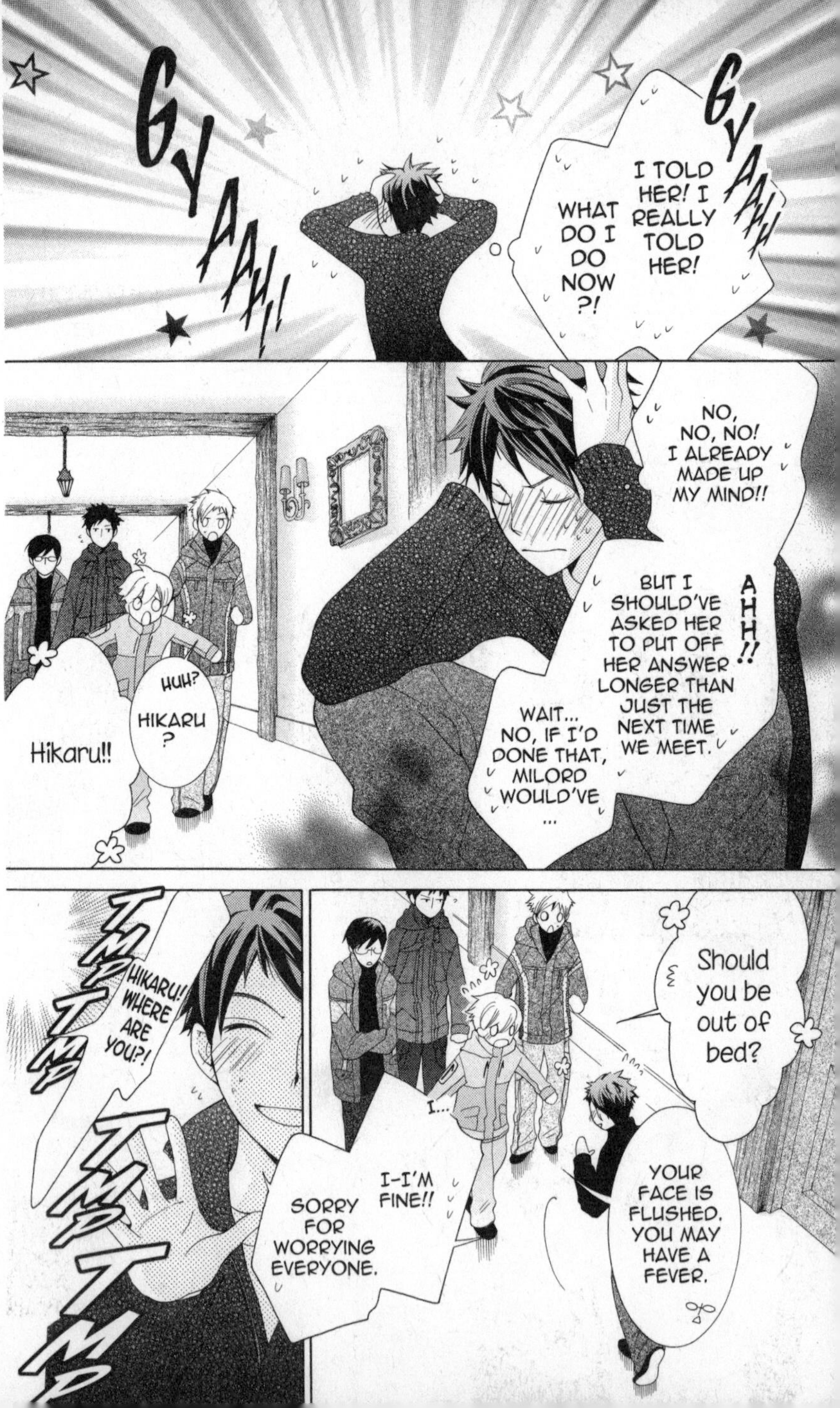
GYAAAH
I TOLD HER! I REALLY TOLD HER!
WHAT DO I DO NOW?!
GYAAH!!
NO, NO, NO! I ALREADY MADE UP MY MIND!!
AHH!!
BUT I SHOULD'VE ASKED HER TO PUT OFF HER ANSWER LONGER THAN JUST THE NEXT TIME WE MEET.
WAIT... NO, IF I'D DONE THAT, MILORD WOULD'VE ...
HUH? HIKARU?
Hikaru!!
Should you be out of bed?
YOUR FACE IS FLUSHED. YOU MAY HAVE A FEVER.
I...
I-I'M FINE!!
SORRY FOR WORRYING EVERYONE.
HIKARU! WHERE ARE YOU?!
TMP TMP
TMP TMP TMP

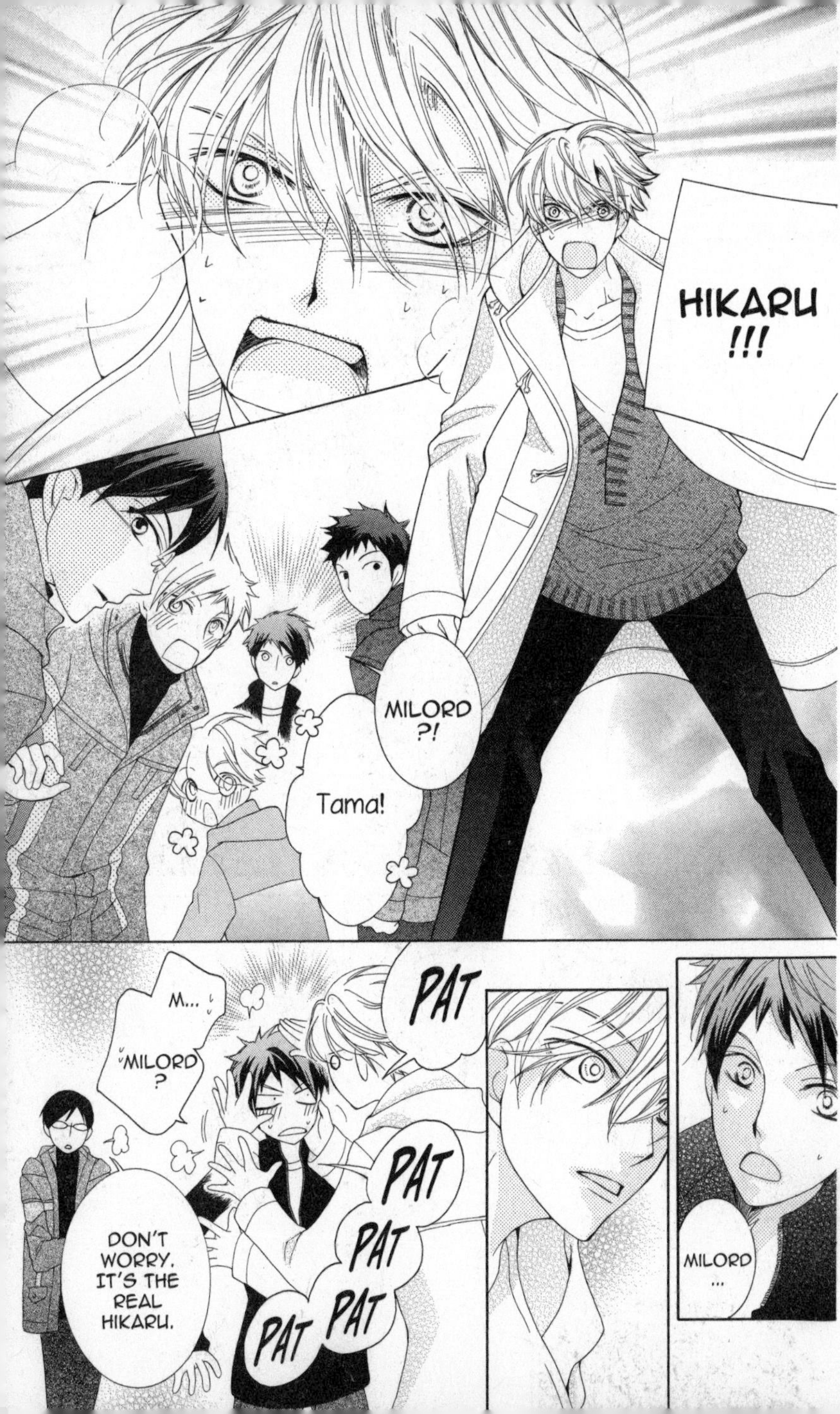
HIKARU !!!
MILORD ?!
Tama!
MILORD ...
PAT
M...
MILORD ?
PAT
PAT
PAT
DON'T WORRY. IT'S THE REAL HIKARU.
PAT

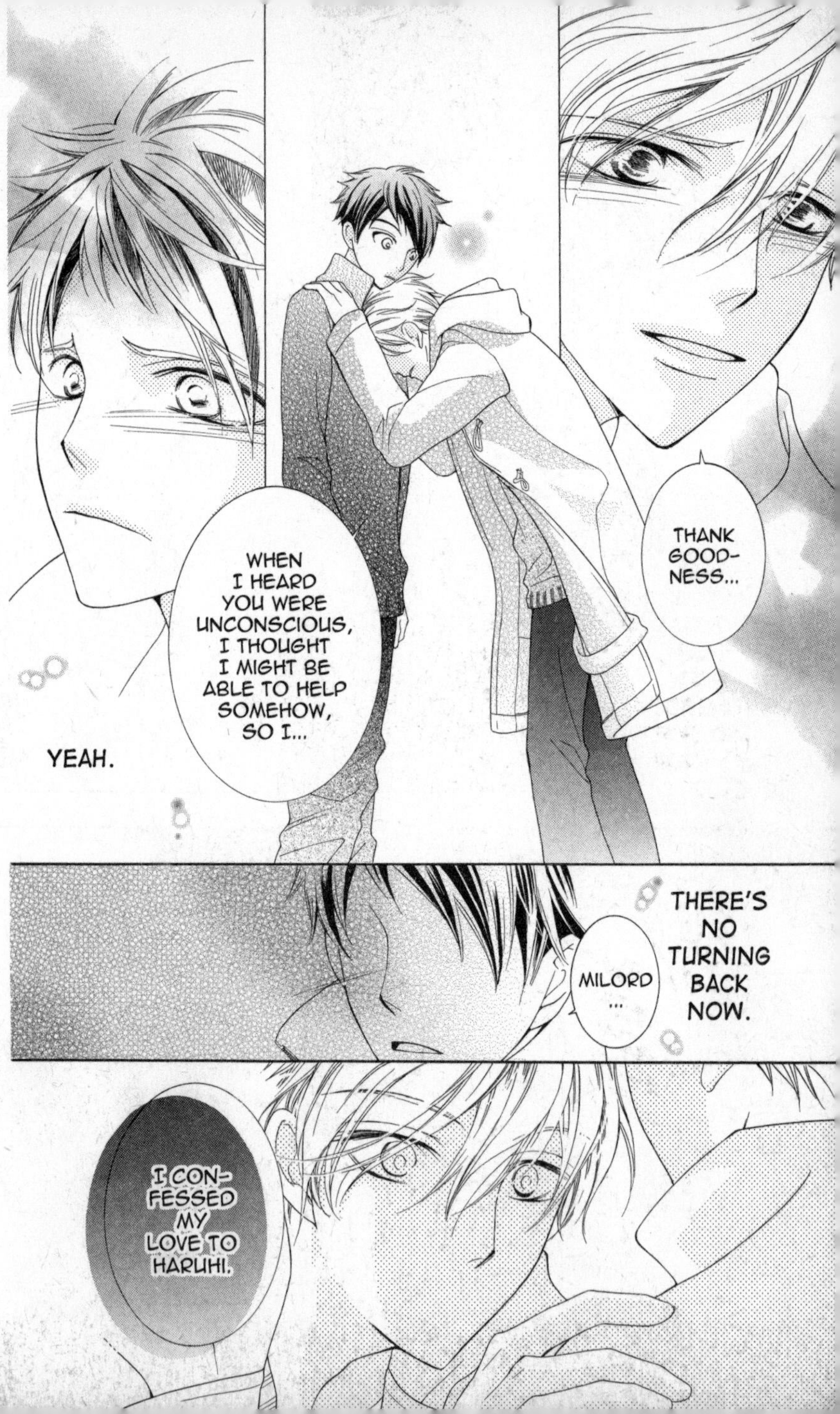
THANK GOOD-NESS...
WHEN I HEARD YOU WERE UNCONSCIOUS, I THOUGHT I MIGHT BE ABLE TO HELP SOMEHOW, SO I...
YEAH.
THERE'S NO TURNING BACK NOW.
MILORD ...
I CON-FESSED MY LOVE TO HARUHI.

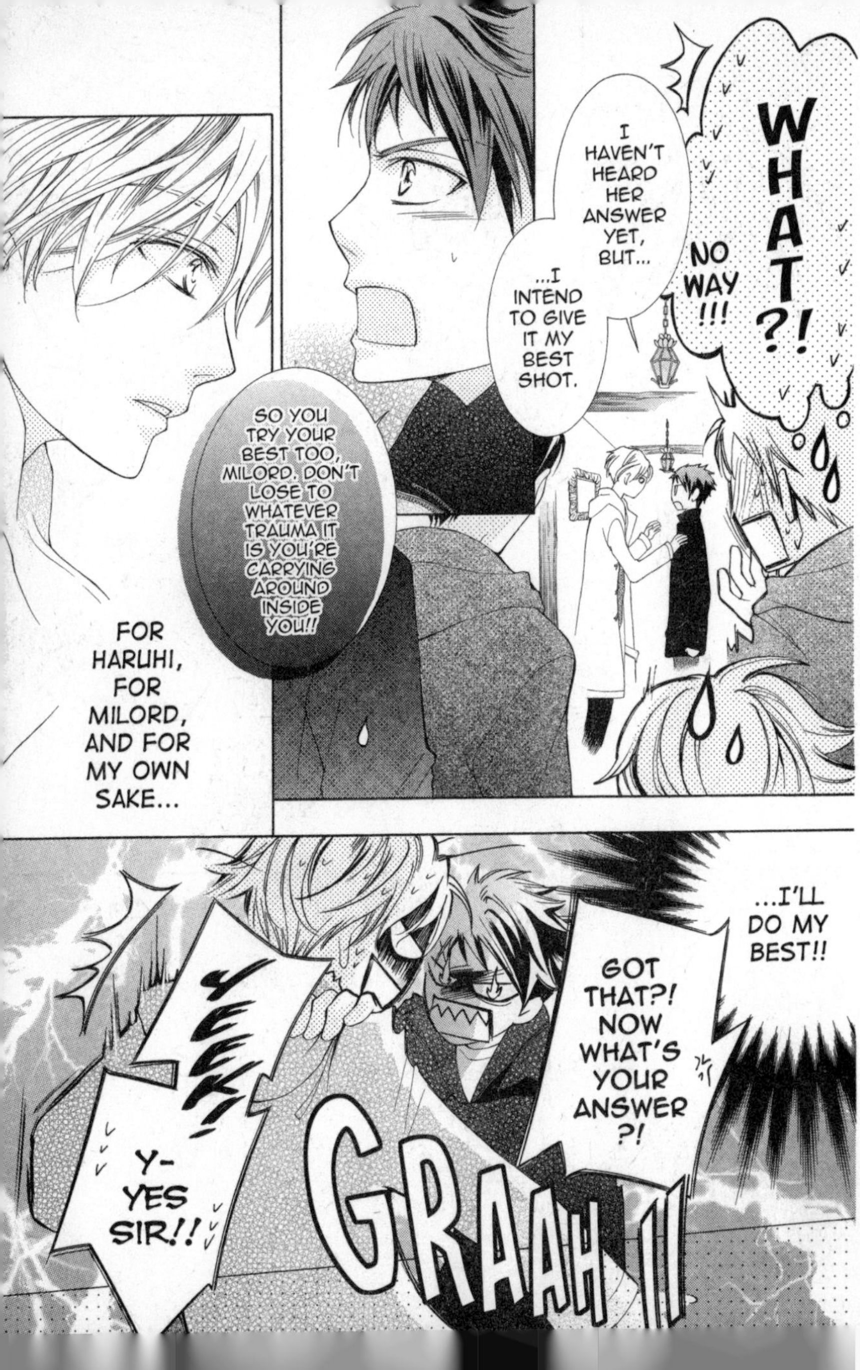
I HAVEN'T HEARD HER ANSWER YET, BUT...
...I INTEND TO GIVE IT MY BEST SHOT.
WHAT?!
NO WAY!!!
SO YOU TRY YOUR BEST TOO, MILORD. DON'T LOSE TO WHATEVER TRAUMA IT IS YOU'RE CARRYING AROUND INSIDE YOU!!
FOR HARUHI, FOR MILORD, AND FOR MY OWN SAKE...
...I'LL DO MY BEST!!
GOT THAT?! NOW WHAT'S YOUR ANSWER?!
GRAAH!!
YEEK!
Y-YES SIR!!

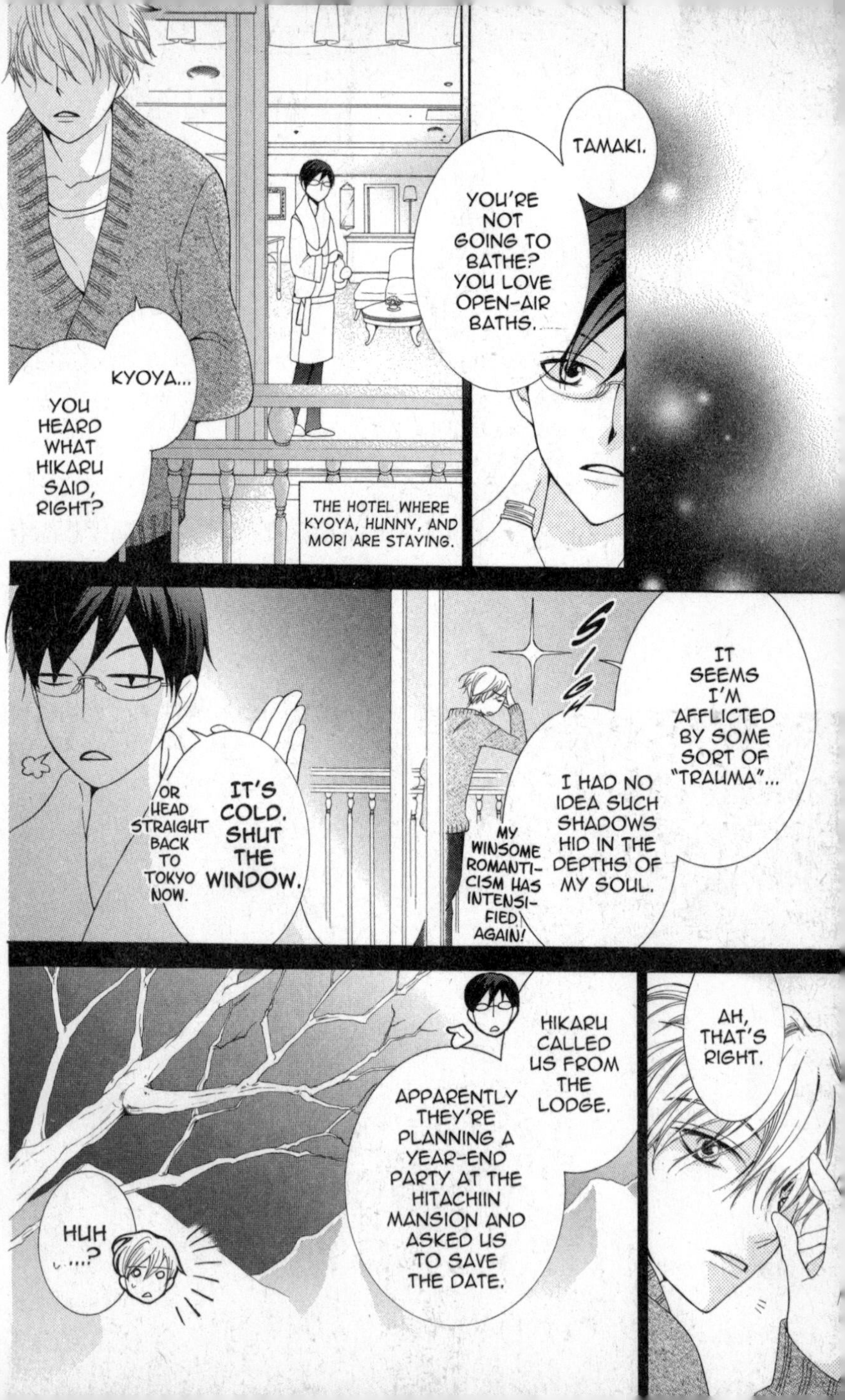
TAMAKI.
YOU'RE NOT GOING TO BATHE? YOU LOVE OPEN-AIR BATHS.
THE HOTEL WHERE KYOYA, HUNNY, AND MORI ARE STAYING.
KYOYA...
YOU HEARD WHAT HIKARU SAID, RIGHT?
SIGH
IT SEEMS I'M AFFLICTED BY SOME SORT OF "TRAUMA"...
I HAD NO IDEA SUCH SHADOWS HID IN THE DEPTHS OF MY SOUL.
MY WINSOME ROMANTICISM HAS INTENSIFIED AGAIN!
IT'S COLD. SHUT THE WINDOW.
OR HEAD STRAIGHT BACK TO TOKYO NOW.
AH, THAT'S RIGHT.
HIKARU CALLED US FROM THE LODGE.
APPARENTLY THEY'RE PLANNING A YEAR-END PARTY AT THE HITACHIIN MANSION AND ASKED US TO SAVE THE DATE.
HUH ...?

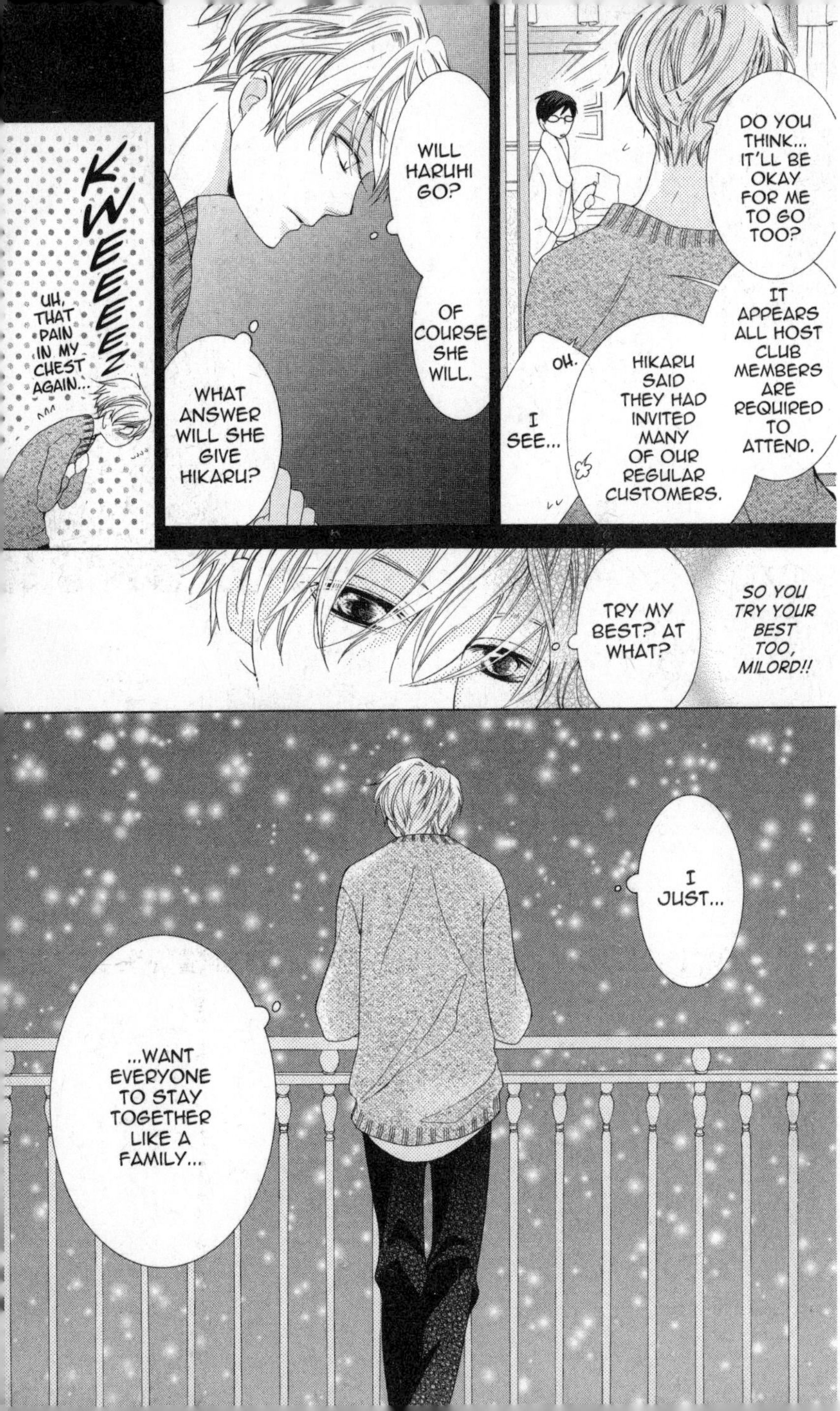
DO YOU THINK... IT'LL BE OKAY FOR ME TO GO TOO?
IT APPEARS ALL HOST CLUB MEMBERS ARE REQUIRED TO ATTEND.
HIKARU SAID THEY HAD INVITED MANY OF OUR REGULAR CUSTOMERS.
OH.
I SEE...
WILL HARUHI GO?
OF COURSE SHE WILL.
WHAT ANSWER WILL SHE GIVE HIKARU?
KWEEEEZ
UH, THAT PAIN IN MY CHEST AGAIN...
SO YOU TRY YOUR BEST TOO, MILORD!!
TRY MY BEST? AT WHAT?
I JUST...
...WANT EVERYONE TO STAY TOGETHER LIKE A FAMILY...

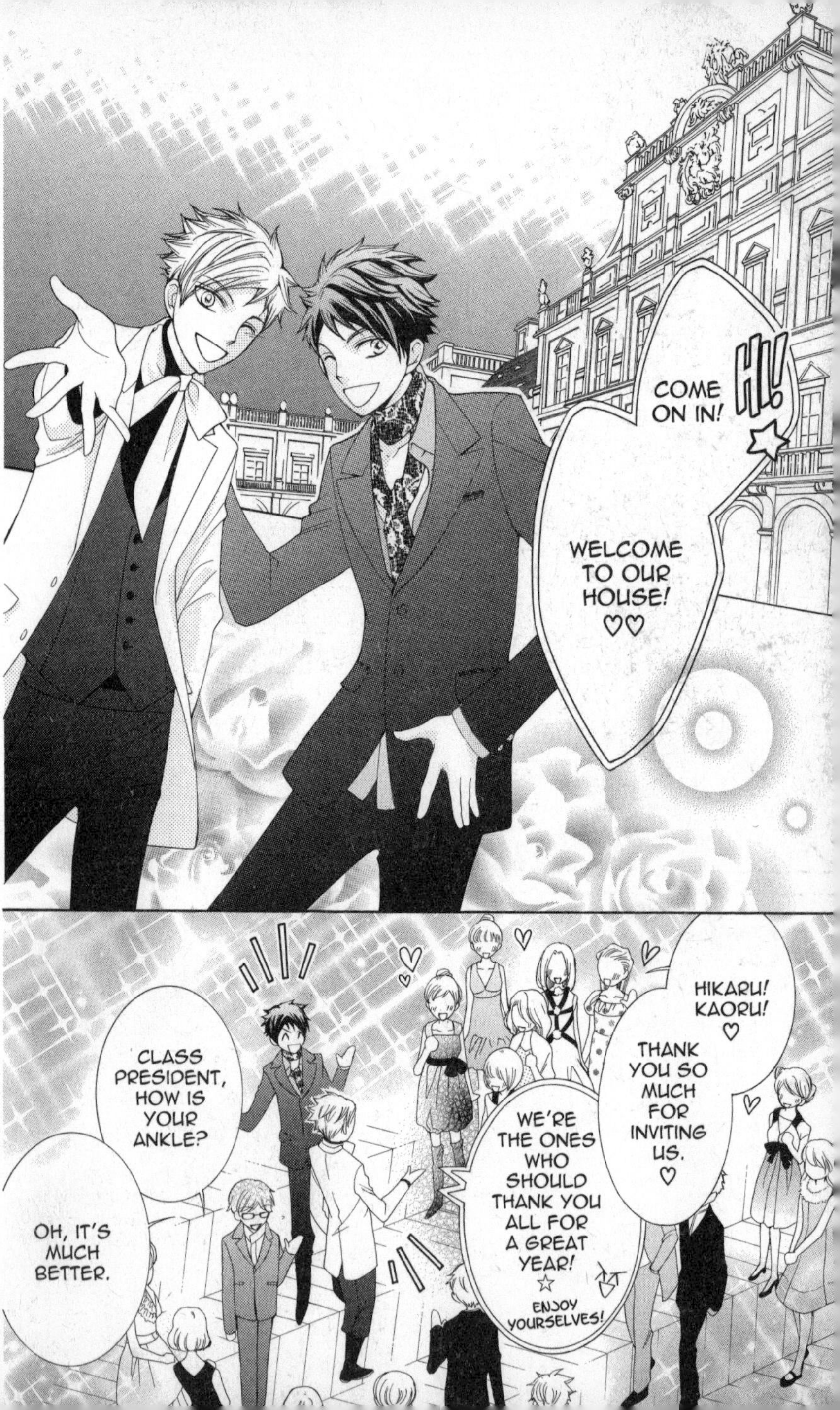
HI! ☆
COME ON IN!
WELCOME TO OUR HOUSE! ♡♡
HIKARU! KAORU! ♡
THANK YOU SO MUCH FOR INVITING US. ♡
WE'RE THE ONES WHO SHOULD THANK YOU ALL FOR A GREAT YEAR! ☆
ENJOY YOURSELVES!
CLASS PRESIDENT, HOW IS YOUR ANKLE?
OH, IT'S MUCH BETTER.

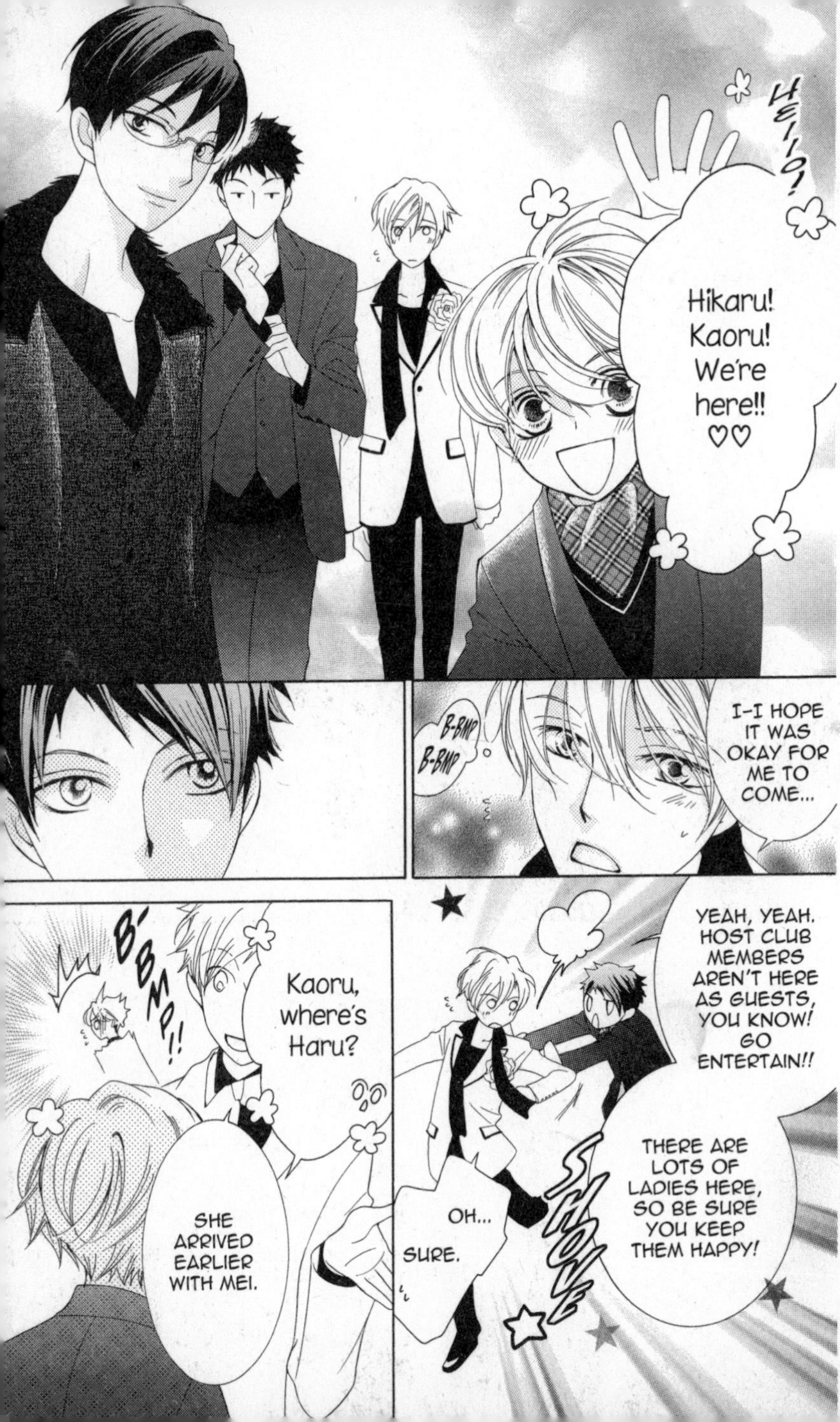
HELLO!
Hikaru! Kaoru! We're here!! ♡♡
B-BMP B-BMP
I-I HOPE IT WAS OKAY FOR ME TO COME...
YEAH, YEAH. HOST CLUB MEMBERS AREN'T HERE AS GUESTS, YOU KNOW! GO ENTERTAIN!!
THERE ARE LOTS OF LADIES HERE, SO BE SURE YOU KEEP THEM HAPPY!
SHOVE
OH... SURE.
B-BMP!!
Kaoru, where's Haru?
SHE ARRIVED EARLIER WITH MEI.

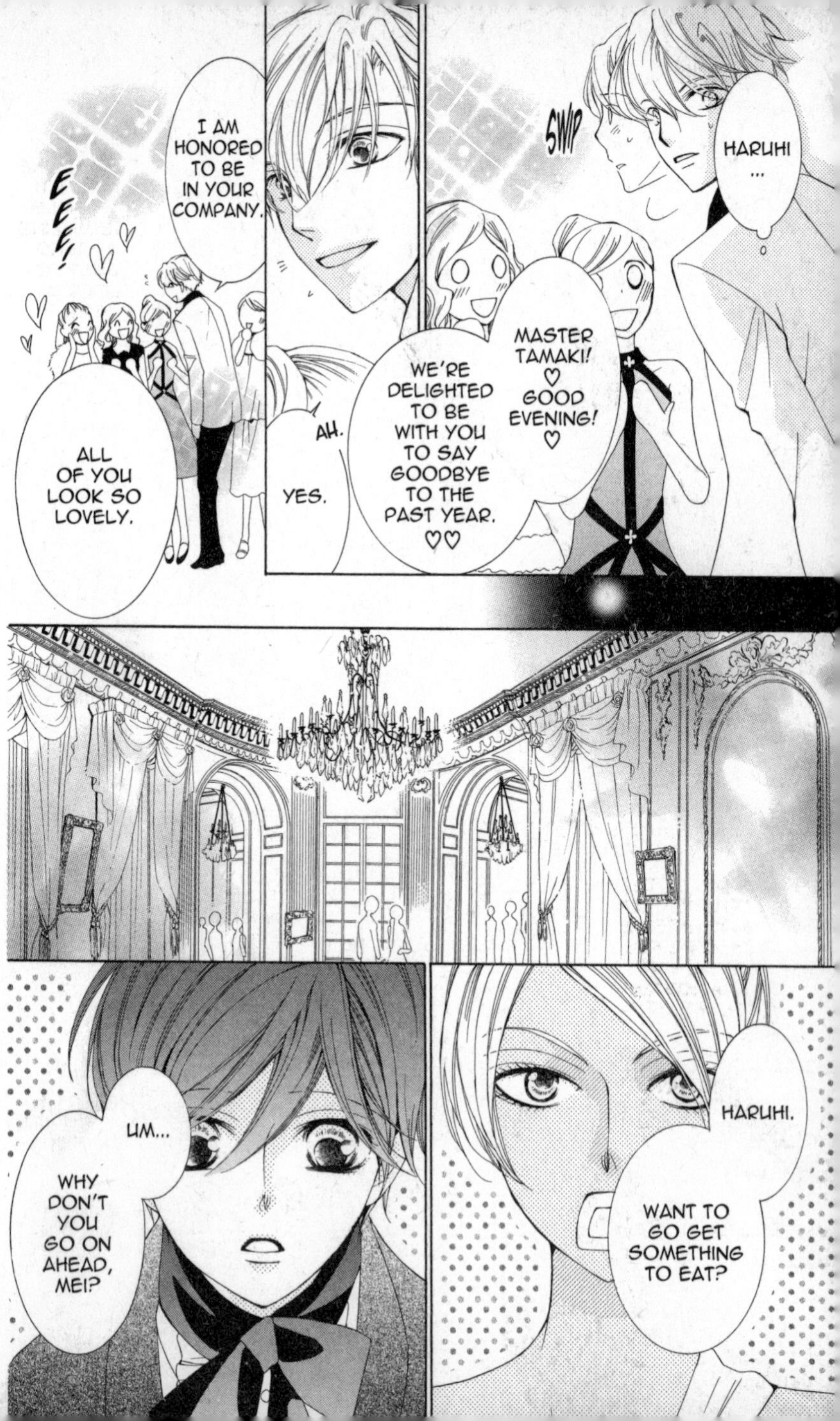
SWIP
HARUHI ...
MASTER TAMAKI! ♡ GOOD EVENING! ♡
WE'RE DELIGHTED TO BE WITH YOU TO SAY GOODBYE TO THE PAST YEAR. ♡♡
AH.
YES.
I AM HONORED TO BE IN YOUR COMPANY.
EEE!
ALL OF YOU LOOK SO LOVELY.
HARUHI.
WANT TO GO GET SOMETHING TO EAT?
UM...
WHY DON'T YOU GO ON AHEAD, MEI?

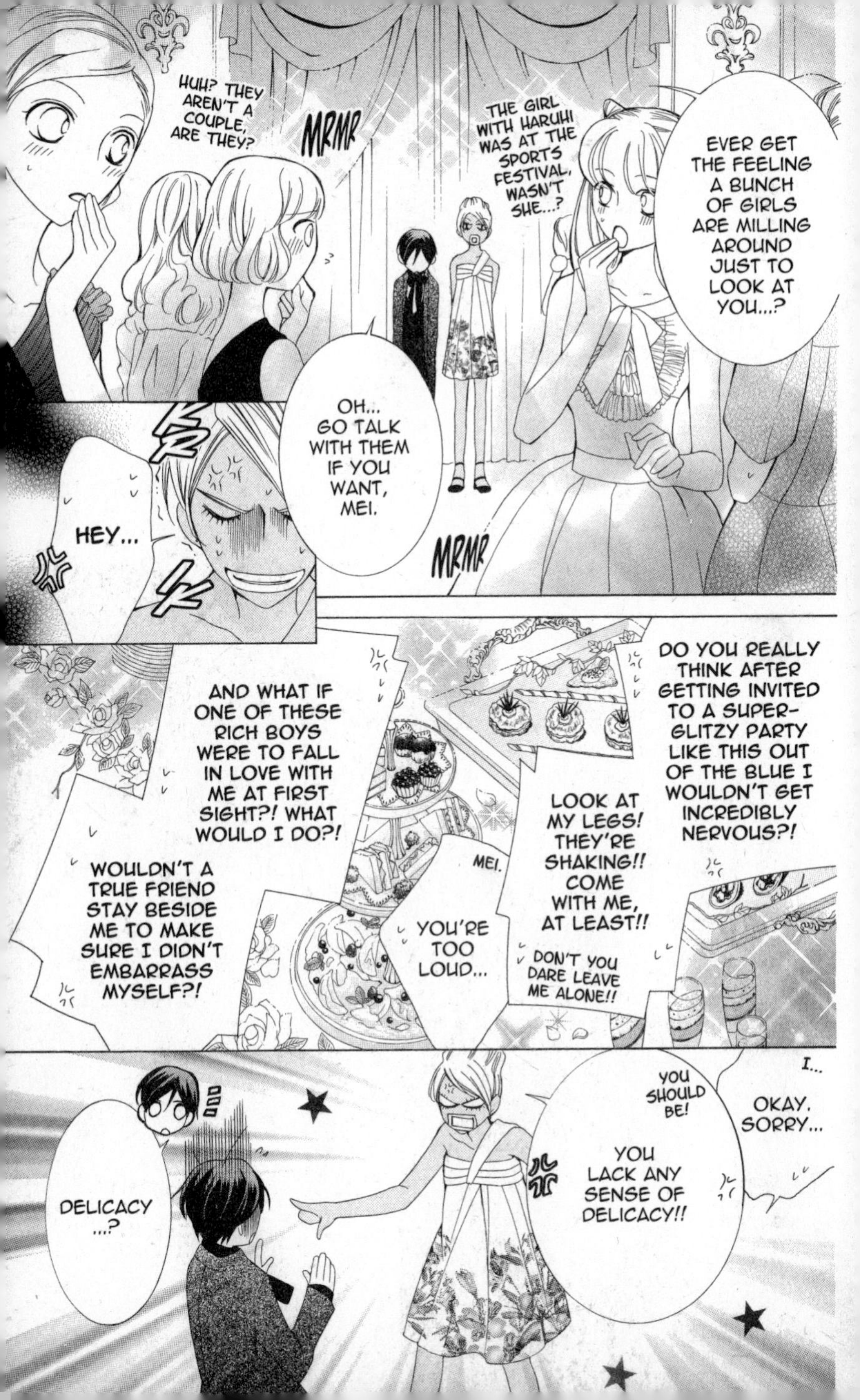
EVER GET THE FEELING A BUNCH OF GIRLS ARE MILLING AROUND JUST TO LOOK AT YOU...?
THE GIRL WITH HARUHI WAS AT THE SPORTS FESTIVAL, WASN'T SHE...?
MRMR
HUH? THEY AREN'T A COUPLE, ARE THEY?
OH... GO TALK WITH THEM IF YOU WANT, MEI.
MRMR
HEY...
DO YOU REALLY THINK AFTER GETTING INVITED TO A SUPER-GLITZY PARTY LIKE THIS OUT OF THE BLUE I WOULDN'T GET INCREDIBLY NERVOUS?!
LOOK AT MY LEGS! THEY'RE SHAKING!! COME WITH ME, AT LEAST!!
DON'T YOU DARE LEAVE ME ALONE!!
MEI.
YOU'RE TOO LOUD...
AND WHAT IF ONE OF THESE RICH BOYS WERE TO FALL IN LOVE WITH ME AT FIRST SIGHT?! WHAT WOULD I DO?!
WOULDN'T A TRUE FRIEND STAY BESIDE ME TO MAKE SURE I DIDN'T EMBARRASS MYSELF?!
I...
OKAY. SORRY...
YOU SHOULD BE!
YOU LACK ANY SENSE OF DELICACY!!
DELICACY ...?

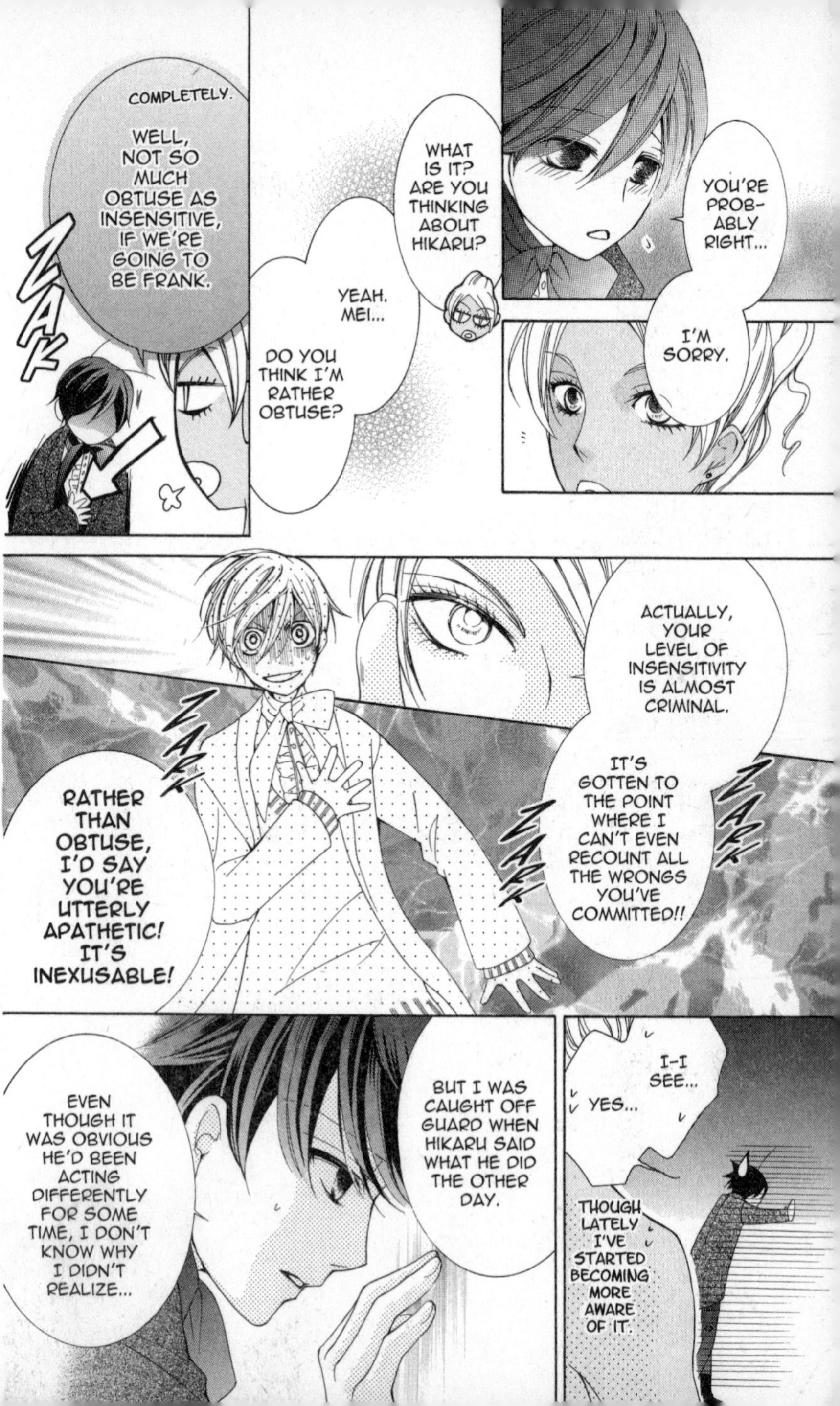

YOU'RE PROB-ABLY RIGHT...
I'M SORRY.
WHAT IS IT? ARE YOU THINKING ABOUT HIKARU?
YEAH. MEI...
DO YOU THINK I'M RATHER OBTUSE?
COMPLETELY.
WELL, NOT SO MUCH OBTUSE AS INSENSITIVE, IF WE'RE GOING TO BE FRANK.
ZAK
ACTUALLY, YOUR LEVEL OF INSENSITIVITY IS ALMOST CRIMINAL.
ZARK
IT'S GOTTEN TO THE POINT WHERE I CAN'T EVEN RECOUNT ALL THE WRONGS YOU'VE COMMITTED!!
ZARK
ZARK
RATHER THAN OBTUSE, I'D SAY YOU'RE UTTERLY APATHETIC! IT'S INEXUSABLE!
I-I SEE...
YES...
THOUGH LATELY I'VE STARTED BECOMING MORE AWARE OF IT.
BUT I WAS CAUGHT OFF GUARD WHEN HIKARU SAID WHAT HE DID THE OTHER DAY.
EVEN THOUGH IT WAS OBVIOUS HE'D BEEN ACTING DIFFERENTLY FOR SOME TIME, I DON'T KNOW WHY I DIDN'T REALIZE...

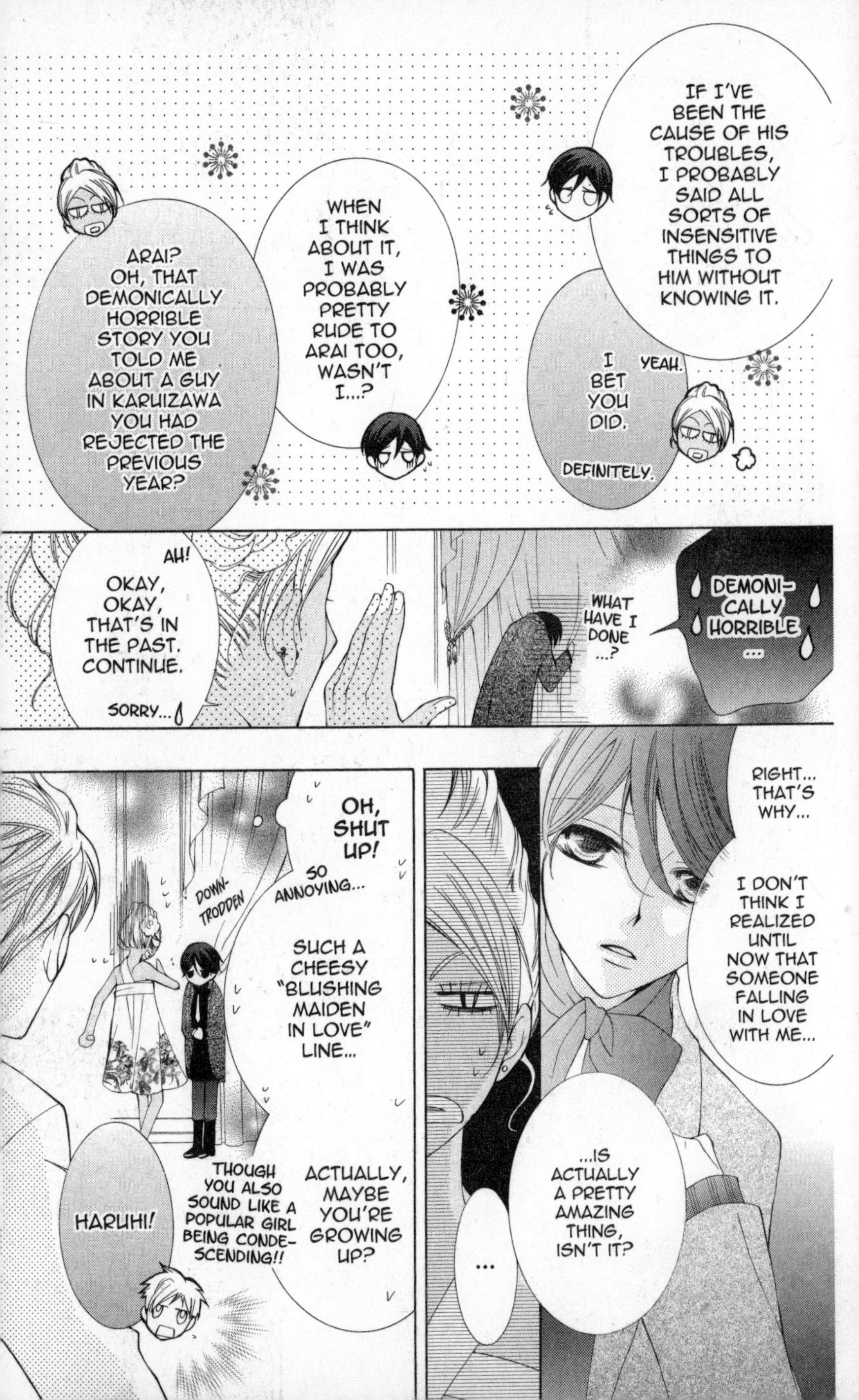
IF I'VE BEEN THE CAUSE OF HIS TROUBLES, I PROBABLY SAID ALL SORTS OF INSENSITIVE THINGS TO HIM WITHOUT KNOWING IT.
YEAH.
I BET YOU DID.
DEFINITELY.
WHEN I THINK ABOUT IT, I WAS PROBABLY PRETTY RUDE TO ARAI TOO, WASN'T I...?
ARAI? OH, THAT DEMONICALLY HORRIBLE STORY YOU TOLD ME ABOUT A GUY IN KARUIZAWA YOU HAD REJECTED THE PREVIOUS YEAR?
DEMONI-CALLY HORRIBLE...
WHAT HAVE I DONE...?
AH!
OKAY, OKAY, THAT'S IN THE PAST. CONTINUE.
SORRY...
RIGHT... THAT'S WHY...
I DON'T THINK I REALIZED UNTIL NOW THAT SOMEONE FALLING IN LOVE WITH ME...
...IS ACTUALLY A PRETTY AMAZING THING, ISN'T IT?
...
OH, SHUT UP!
SO ANNOYING...
DOWN-TRODDEN
SUCH A CHEESY "BLUSHING MAIDEN IN LOVE" LINE...
ACTUALLY, MAYBE YOU'RE GROWING UP?
THOUGH YOU ALSO SOUND LIKE A POPULAR GIRL BEING CONDE-SCENDING!!
HARUHI!

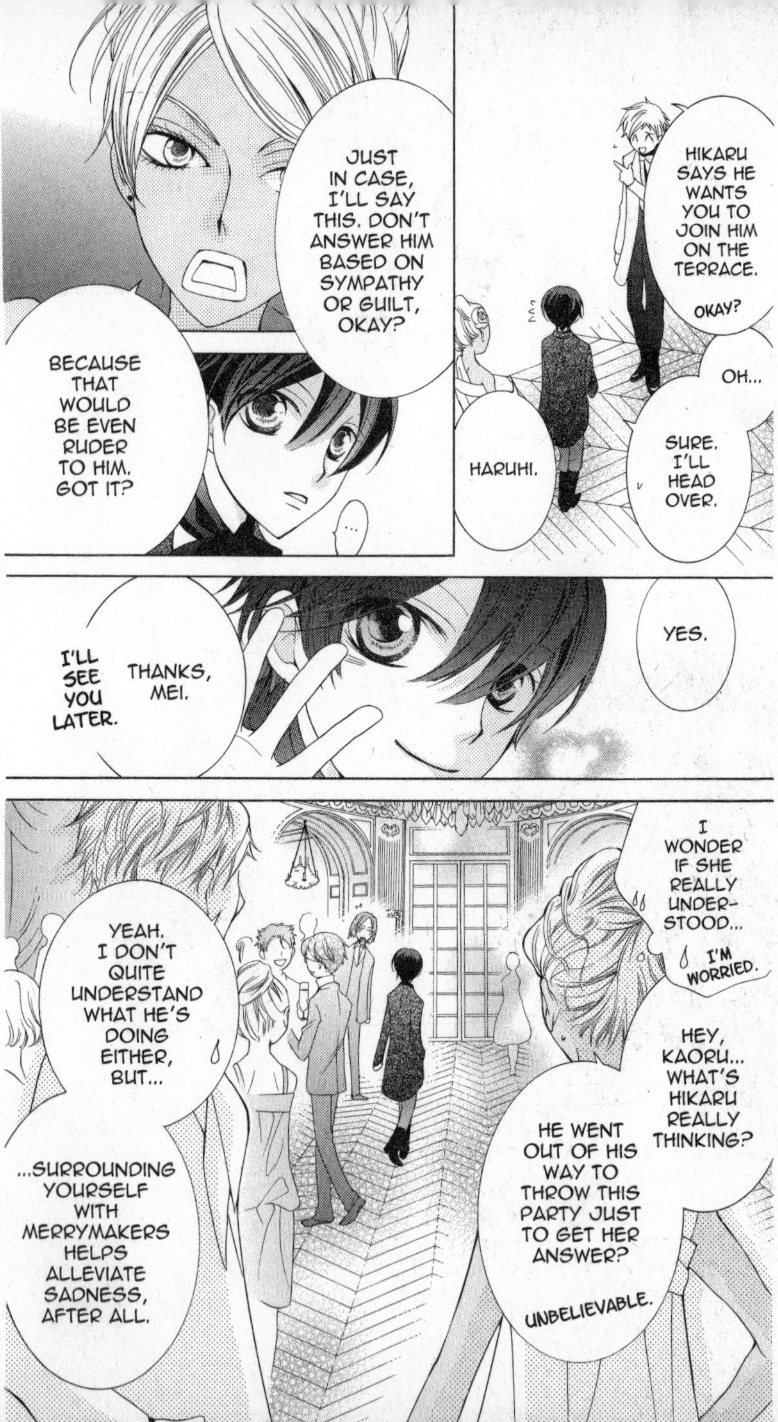
HIKARU SAYS HE WANTS YOU TO JOIN HIM ON THE TERRACE.
OKAY?
OH...
SURE. I'LL HEAD OVER.
HARUHI.
JUST IN CASE, I'LL SAY THIS. DON'T ANSWER HIM BASED ON SYMPATHY OR GUILT, OKAY?
BECAUSE THAT WOULD BE EVEN RUDER TO HIM. GOT IT?
...
YES.
THANKS, MEI.
I'LL SEE YOU LATER.
I WONDER IF SHE REALLY UNDER-STOOD...
I'M WORRIED.
HEY, KAORU... WHAT'S HIKARU REALLY THINKING?
HE WENT OUT OF HIS WAY TO THROW THIS PARTY JUST TO GET HER ANSWER?
UNBELIEVABLE.
YEAH. I DON'T QUITE UNDERSTAND WHAT HE'S DOING EITHER, BUT...
...SURROUNDING YOURSELF WITH MERRYMAKERS HELPS ALLEVIATE SADNESS, AFTER ALL.

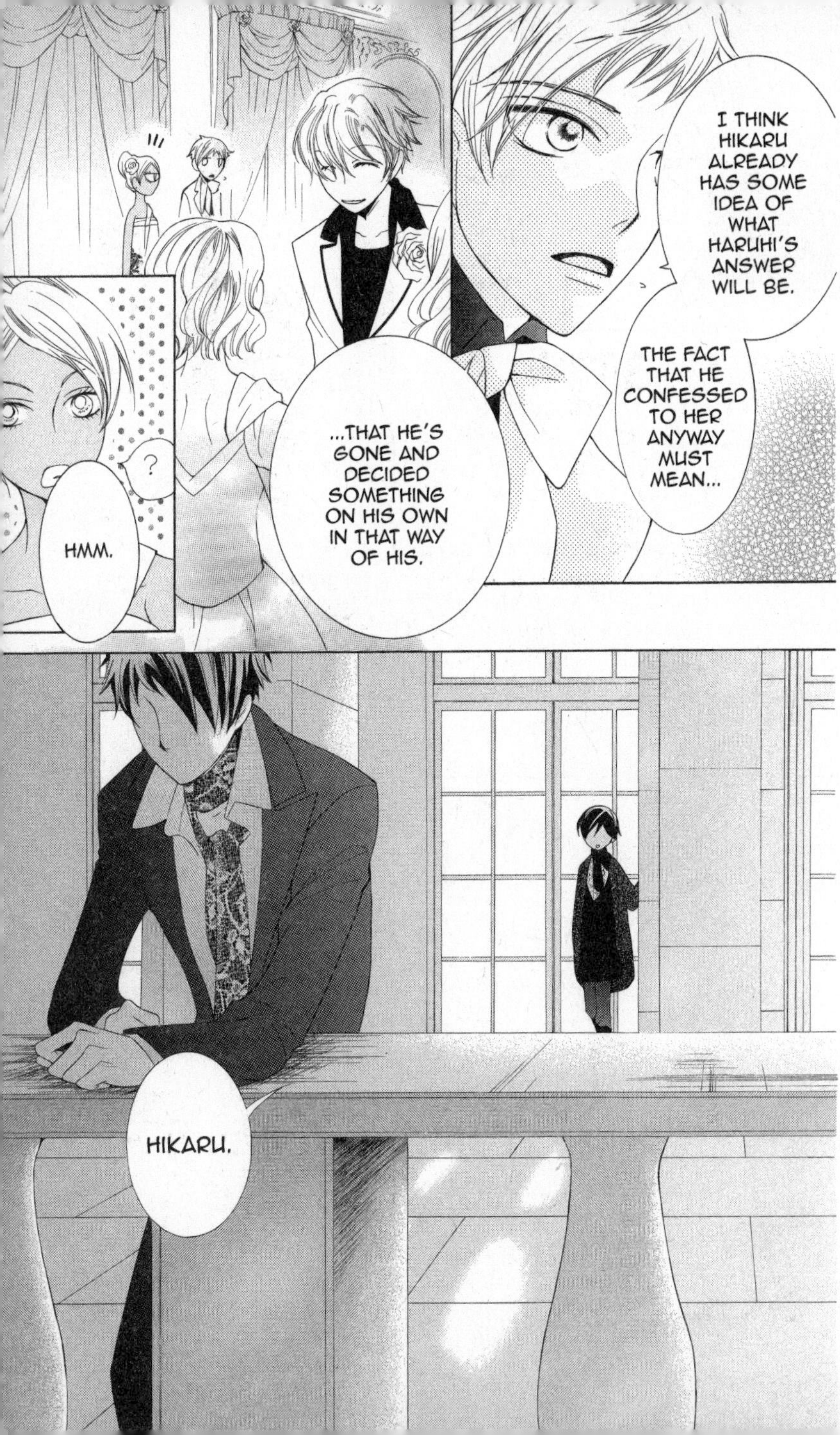
I THINK HIKARU ALREADY HAS SOME IDEA OF WHAT HARUHI'S ANSWER WILL BE.
THE FACT THAT HE CONFESSED TO HER ANYWAY MUST MEAN...
...THAT HE'S GONE AND DECIDED SOMETHING ON HIS OWN IN THAT WAY OF HIS.
?
HMM.
HIKARU.

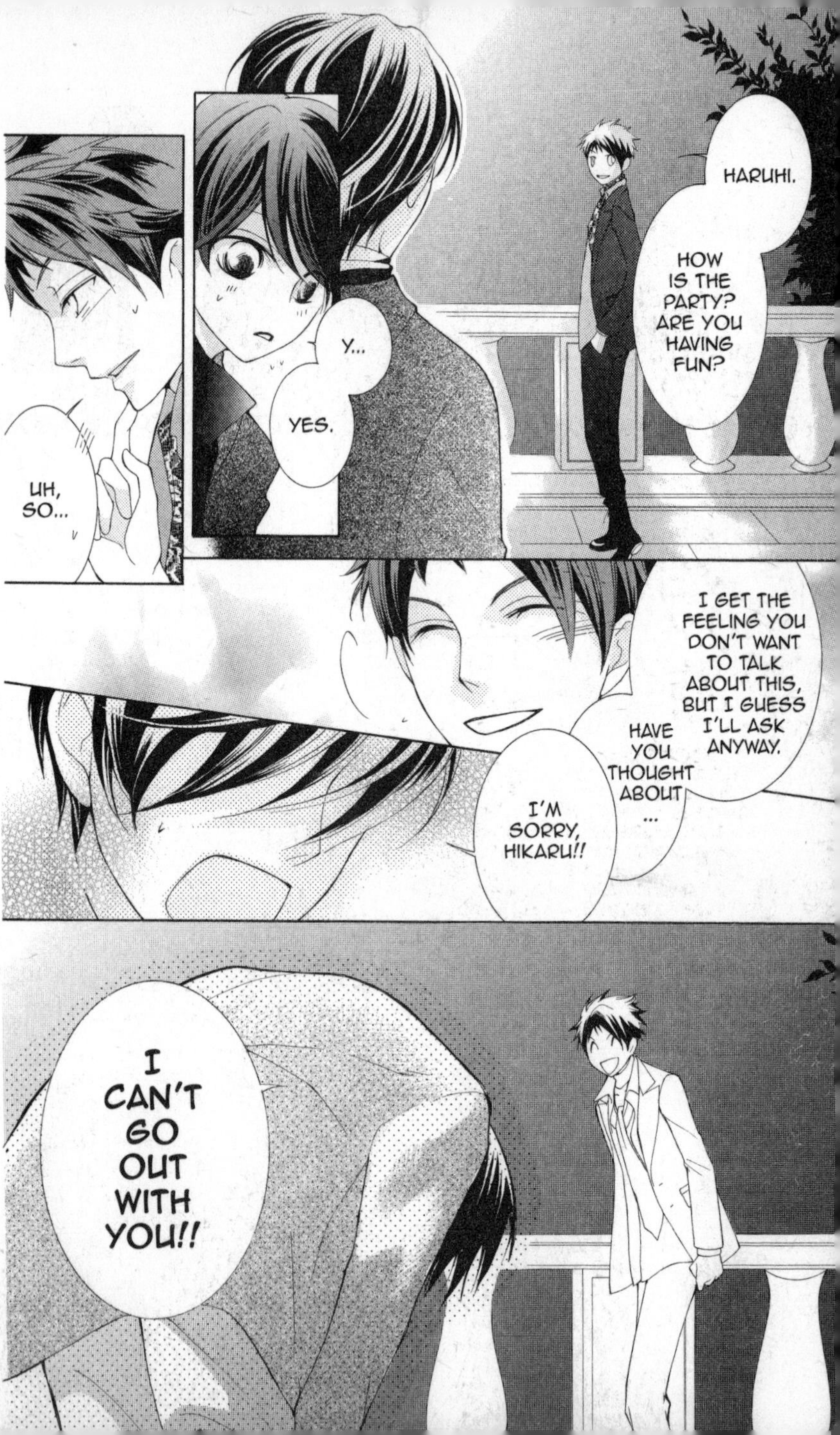
HARUHI.
HOW IS THE PARTY? ARE YOU HAVING FUN?
Y...
YES.
UH, SO...
I GET THE FEELING YOU DON'T WANT TO TALK ABOUT THIS, BUT I GUESS I'LL ASK ANYWAY.
HAVE YOU THOUGHT ABOUT ...
I'M SORRY, HIKARU!!
I CAN'T GO OUT WITH YOU!!

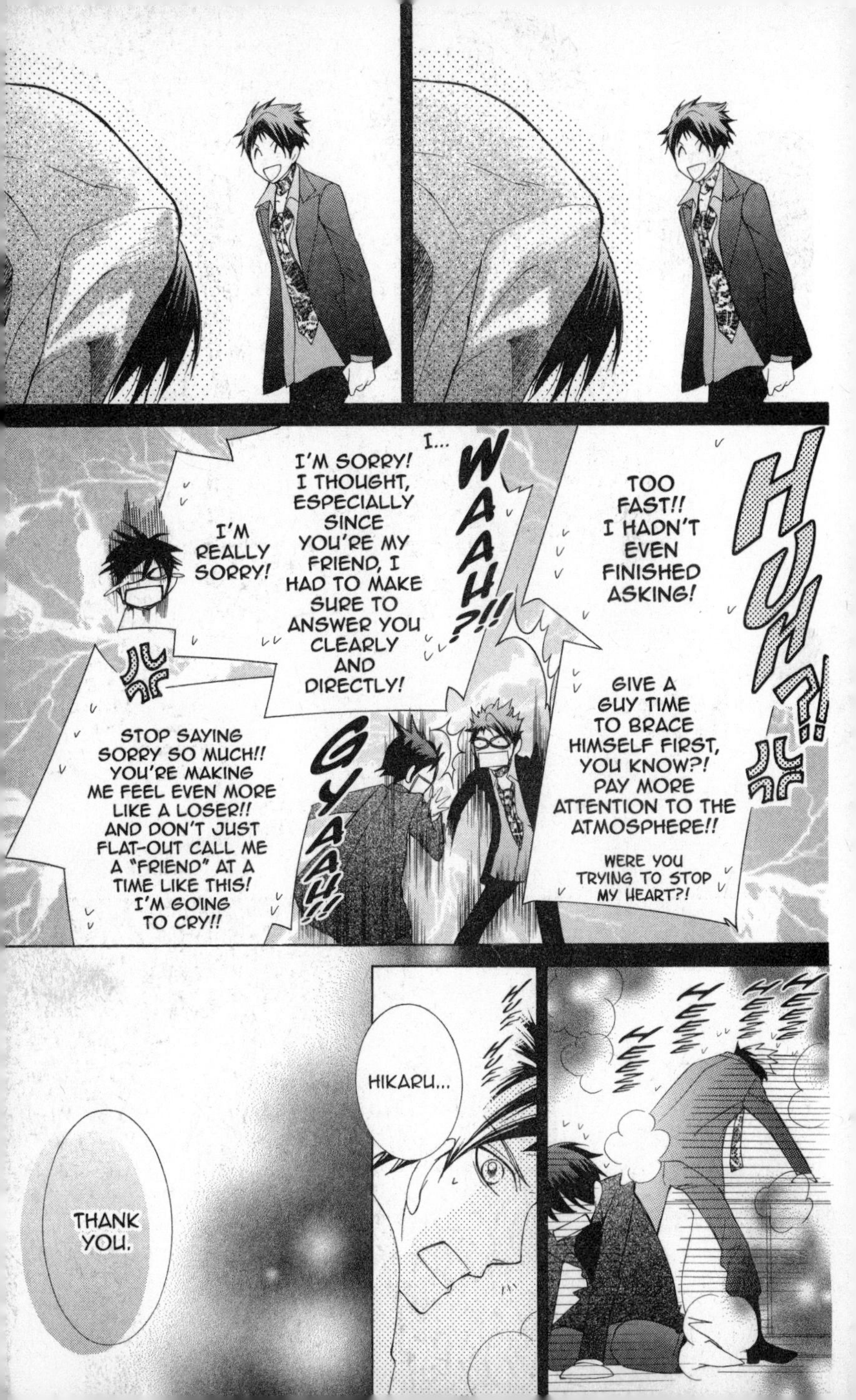
HUH?!!
TOO FAST!! I HADN'T EVEN FINISHED ASKING!
GIVE A GUY TIME TO BRACE HIMSELF FIRST, YOU KNOW?! PAY MORE ATTENTION TO THE ATMOSPHERE!!
WERE YOU TRYING TO STOP MY HEART?!
WAAAH?!!
I...
I'M SORRY! I THOUGHT, ESPECIALLY SINCE YOU'RE MY FRIEND, I HAD TO MAKE SURE TO ANSWER YOU CLEARLY AND DIRECTLY!
I'M REALLY SORRY!
GYAAAH!!
STOP SAYING SORRY SO MUCH!! YOU'RE MAKING ME FEEL EVEN MORE LIKE A LOSER!! AND DON'T JUST FLAT-OUT CALL ME A "FRIEND" AT A TIME LIKE THIS! I'M GOING TO CRY!!
HIKARU...
THANK YOU.

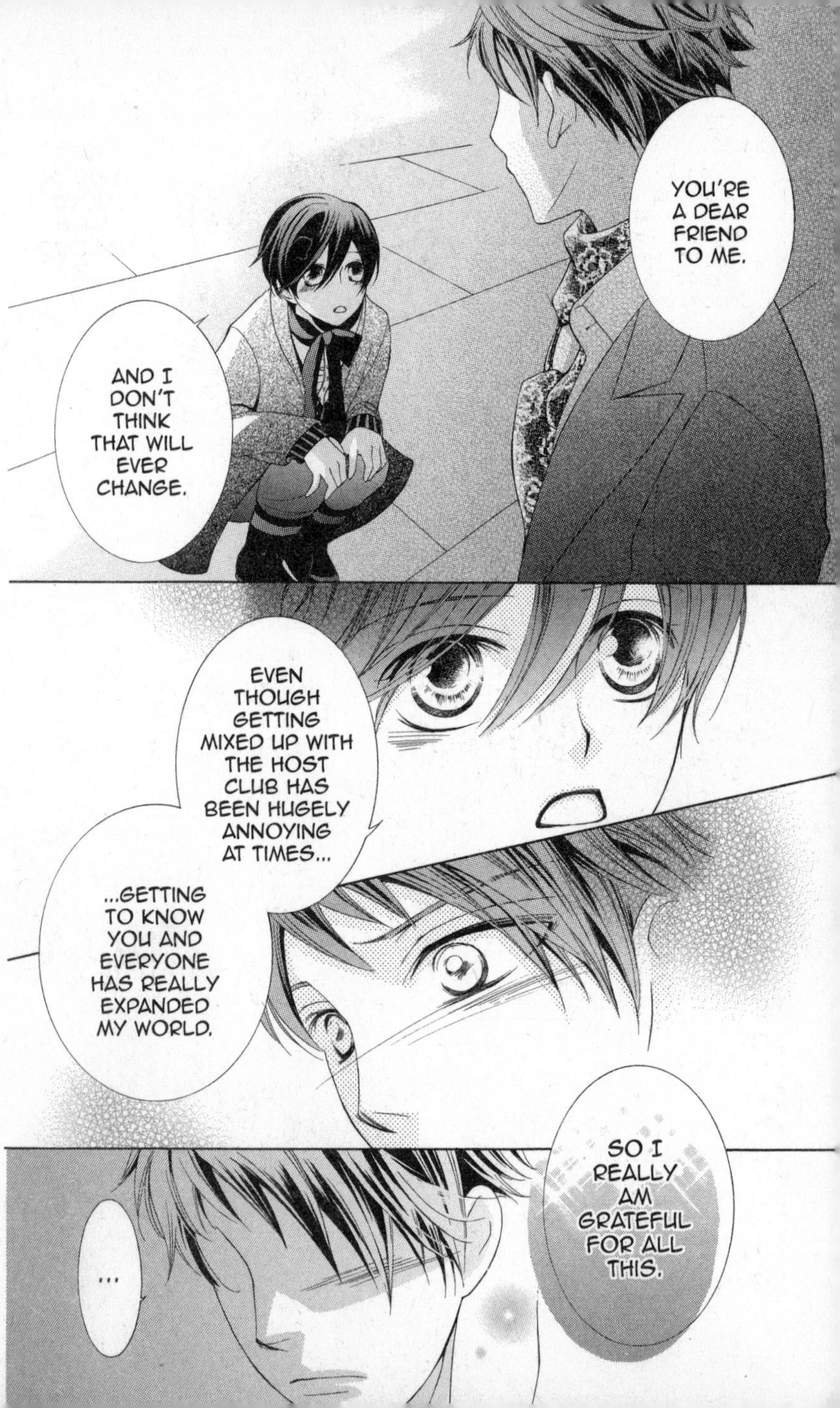
YOU'RE A DEAR FRIEND TO ME.
AND I DON'T THINK THAT WILL EVER CHANGE.
EVEN THOUGH GETTING MIXED UP WITH THE HOST CLUB HAS BEEN HUGELY ANNOYING AT TIMES...
...GETTING TO KNOW YOU AND EVERYONE HAS REALLY EXPANDED MY WORLD.
SO I REALLY AM GRATEFUL FOR ALL THIS.
...

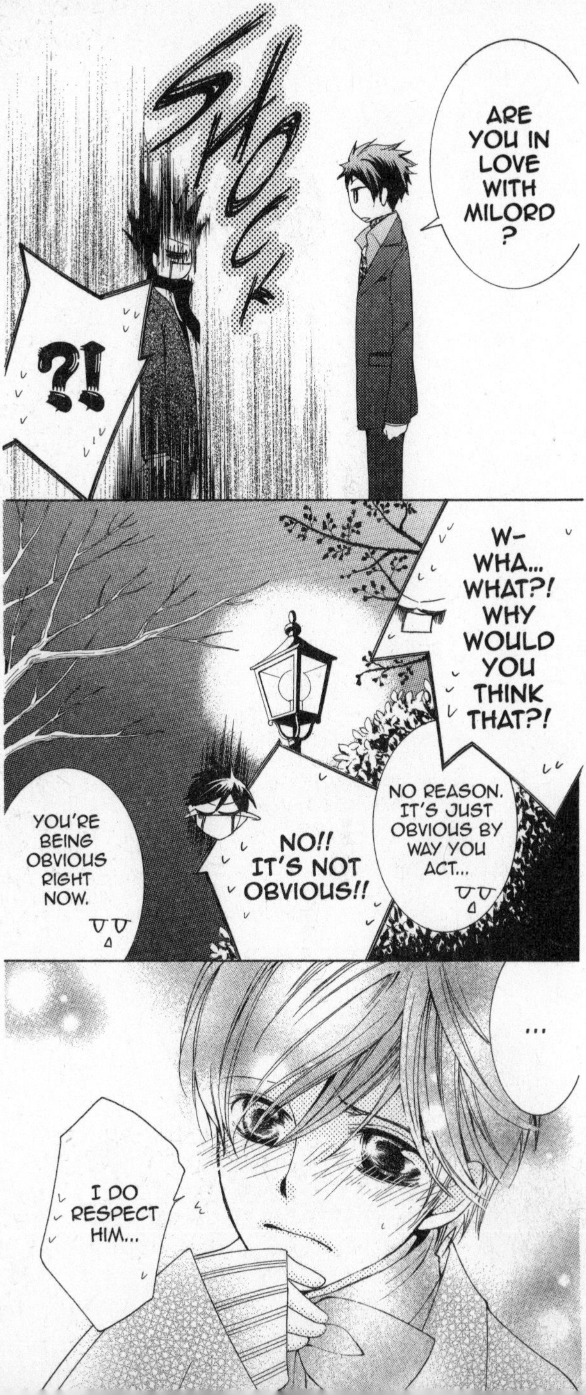
ARE YOU IN LOVE WITH MILORD?
SHOCK
?!
W-WHA... WHAT?! WHY WOULD YOU THINK THAT?!
NO REASON. IT'S JUST OBVIOUS BY WAY YOU ACT...
NO!! IT'S NOT OBVIOUS!!
YOU'RE BEING OBVIOUS RIGHT NOW.
...
I DO RESPECT HIM...

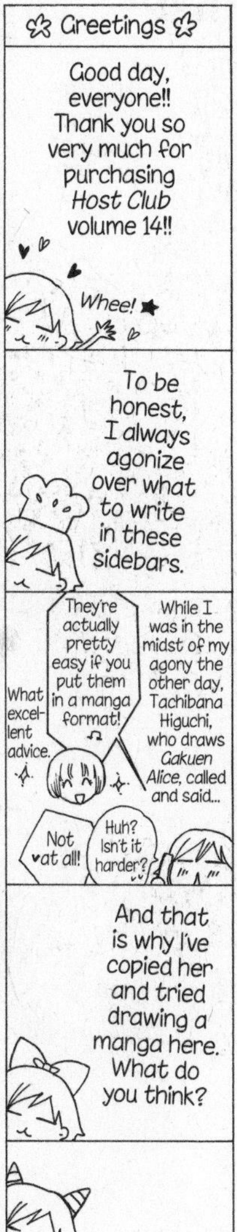
Greetings
Good day, everyone!! Thank you so very much for purchasing *Host Club* volume 14!!
Whee!
To be honest, I always agonize over what to write in these sidebars.
While I was in the midst of my agony the other day, Tachibana Higuchi, who draws *Gakuen Alice*, called and said...
They're actually pretty easy if you put them in a manga format! ♫
What excel-lent advice.
Huh? Isn't it harder?
Not at all!
And that is why I've copied her and tried drawing a manga here. What do you think?
Apparently it's lack of content that's my real problem.
Back to agonizing...

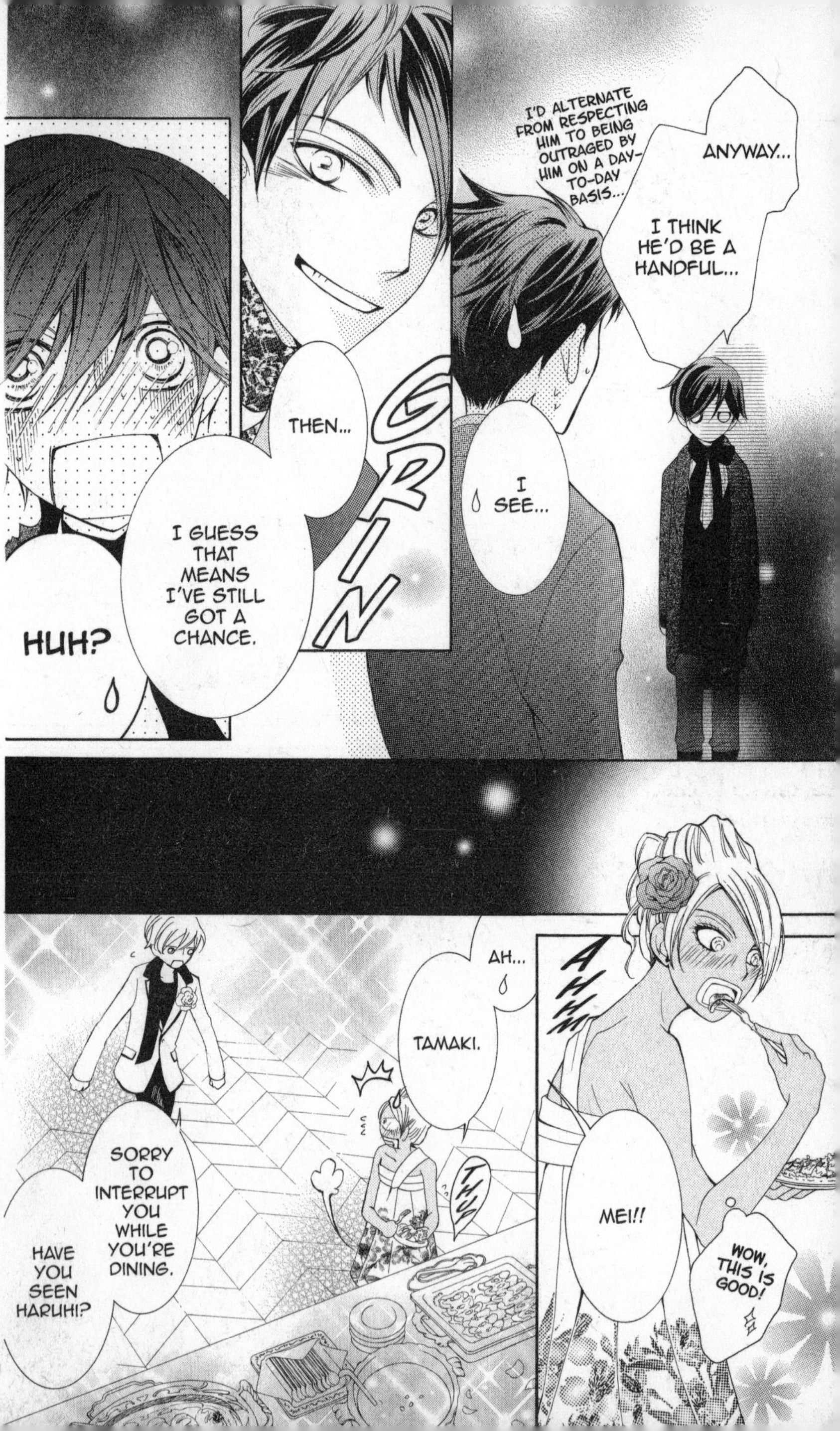
ANYWAY...
I THINK HE'D BE A HANDFUL...
I'D ALTERNATE FROM RESPECTING HIM TO BEING OUTRAGED BY HIM ON A DAY-TO-DAY BASIS...
I SEE...
THEN...
GRIN
I GUESS THAT MEANS I'VE STILL GOT A CHANCE.
HUH?
WOW, THIS IS GOOD!
MEI!!
AH...
TAMAKI.
SORRY TO INTERRUPT YOU WHILE YOU'RE DINING.
HAVE YOU SEEN HARUHI?

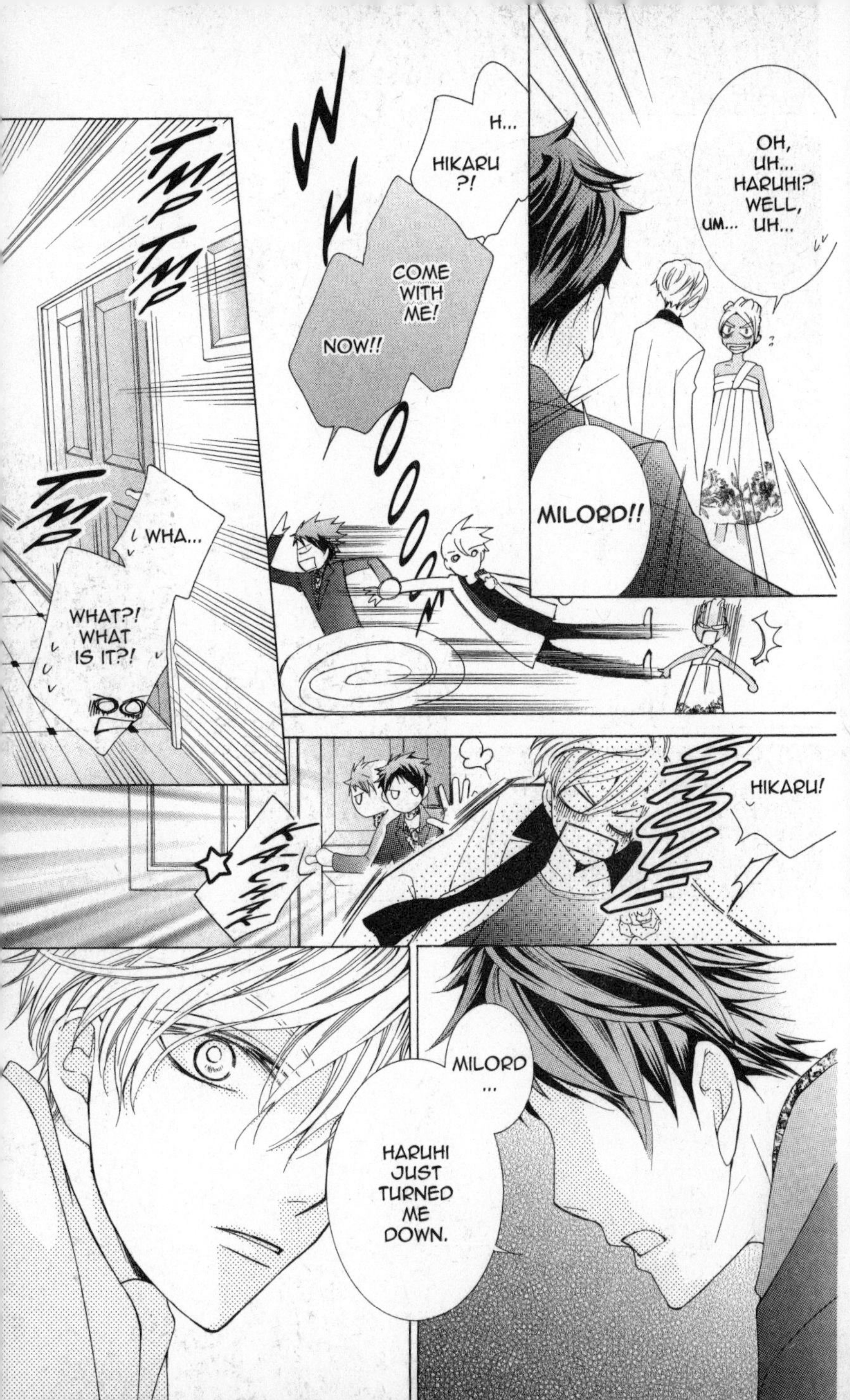
OH, UH... HARUHI? WELL, UM... UH...
MILORD!!
H... HIKARU?!
COME WITH ME! NOW!!
TMP TMP TMP
TMP
WHA...
WHAT?! WHAT IS IT?!
HIKARU!
KA-CHUNK
MILORD...
HARUHI JUST TURNED ME DOWN.

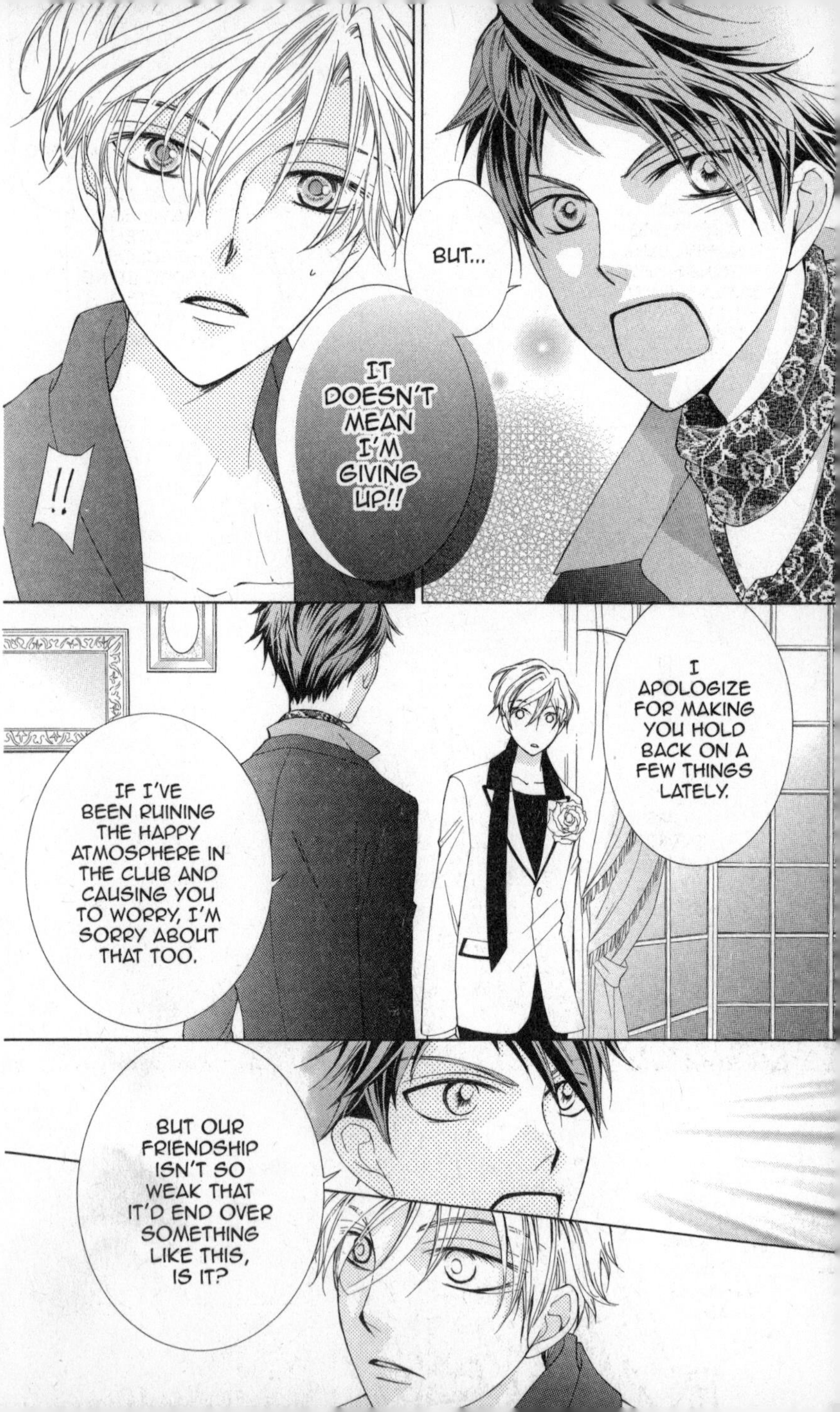
BUT...
IT DOESN'T MEAN I'M GIVING UP!!
!!
I APOLOGIZE FOR MAKING YOU HOLD BACK ON A FEW THINGS LATELY.
IF I'VE BEEN RUINING THE HAPPY ATMOSPHERE IN THE CLUB AND CAUSING YOU TO WORRY, I'M SORRY ABOUT THAT TOO.
BUT OUR FRIENDSHIP ISN'T SO WEAK THAT IT'D END OVER SOMETHING LIKE THIS, IS IT?

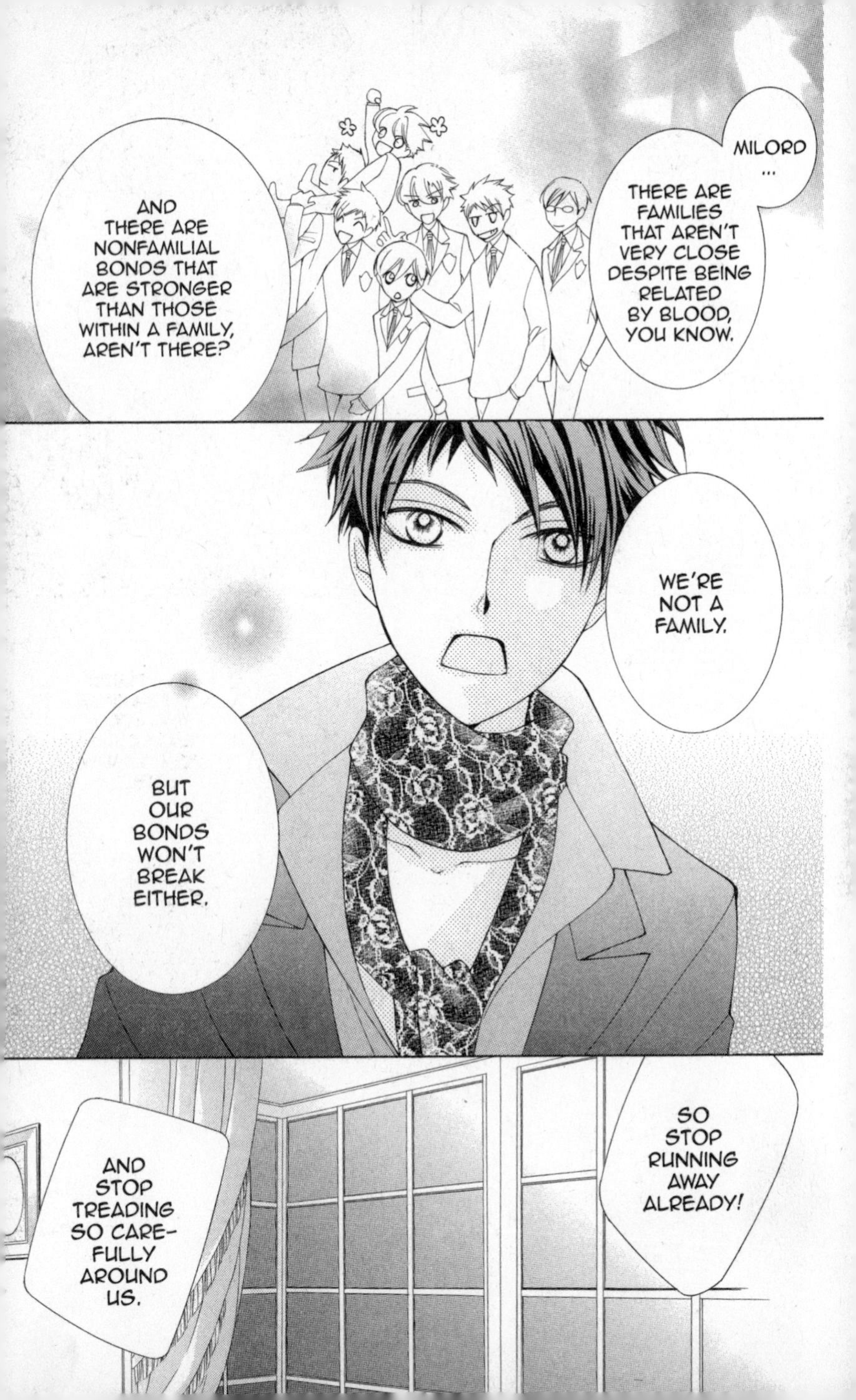
MILORD ...
THERE ARE FAMILIES THAT AREN'T VERY CLOSE DESPITE BEING RELATED BY BLOOD, YOU KNOW.
AND THERE ARE NONFAMILIAL BONDS THAT ARE STRONGER THAN THOSE WITHIN A FAMILY, AREN'T THERE?
WE'RE NOT A FAMILY.
BUT OUR BONDS WON'T BREAK EITHER.
SO STOP RUNNING AWAY ALREADY!
AND STOP TREADING SO CARE-FULLY AROUND US.

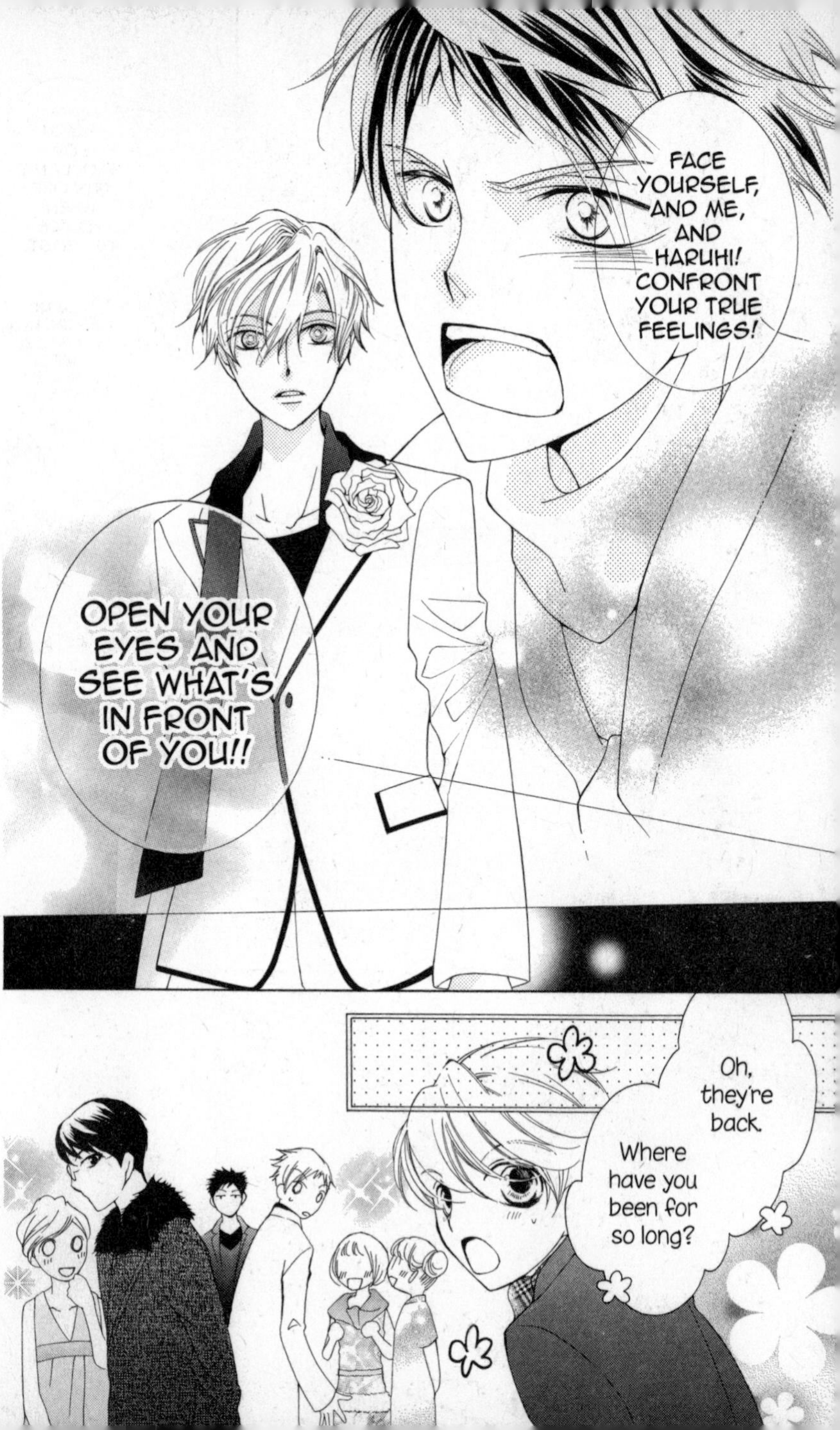
FACE YOURSELF, AND ME, AND HARUHI! CONFRONT YOUR TRUE FEELINGS!
OPEN YOUR EYES AND SEE WHAT'S IN FRONT OF YOU!!
Oh, they're back.
Where have you been for so long?

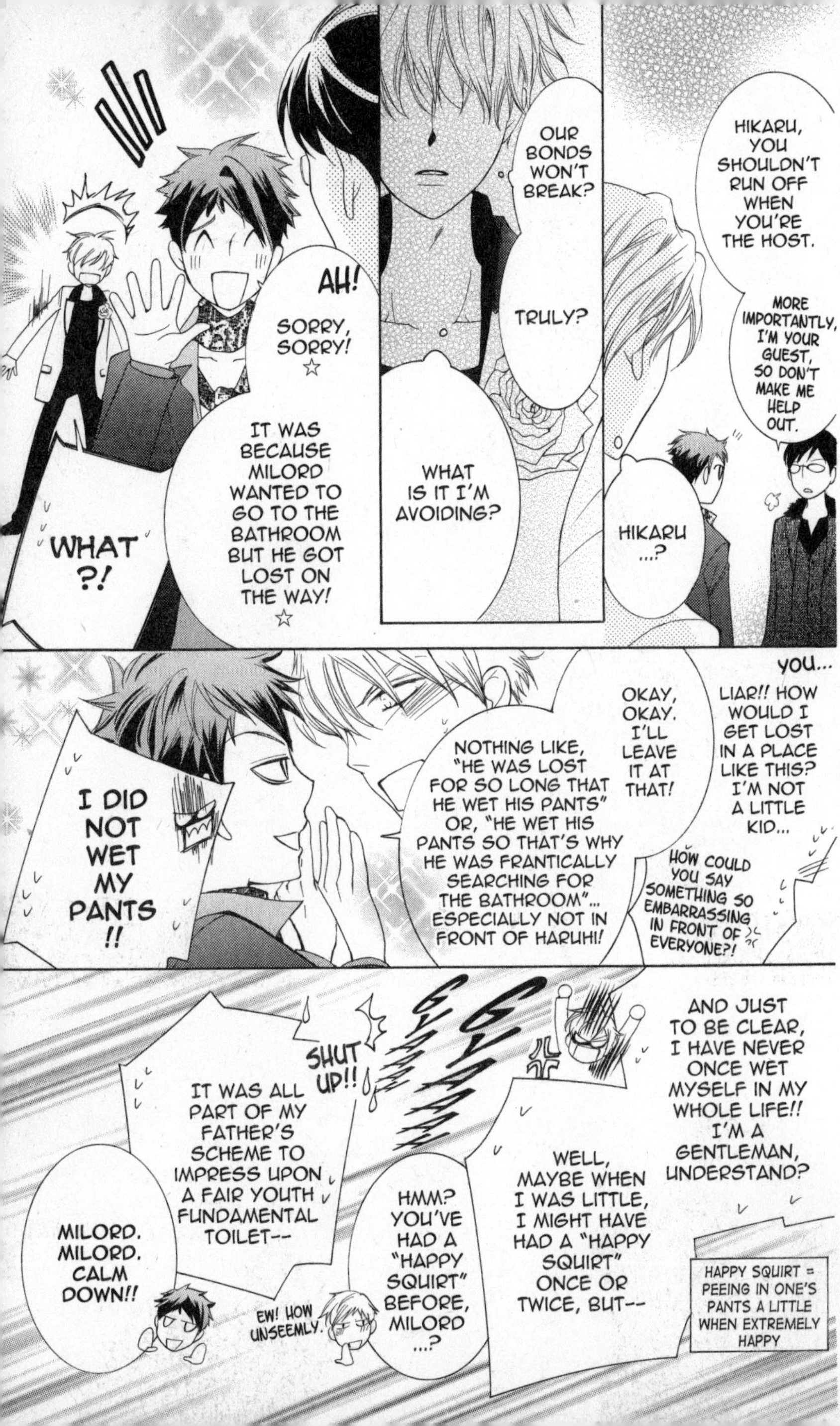
HIKARU, YOU SHOULDN'T RUN OFF WHEN YOU'RE THE HOST.
MORE IMPORTANTLY, I'M YOUR GUEST, SO DON'T MAKE ME HELP OUT.
HIKARU ...?
OUR BONDS WON'T BREAK?
TRULY?
WHAT IS IT I'M AVOIDING?
AH!
SORRY, SORRY! ☆
IT WAS BECAUSE MILORD WANTED TO GO TO THE BATHROOM BUT HE GOT LOST ON THE WAY! ☆
WHAT ?!
YOU...
LIAR!! HOW WOULD I GET LOST IN A PLACE LIKE THIS? I'M NOT A LITTLE KID...
HOW COULD YOU SAY SOMETHING SO EMBARRASSING IN FRONT OF EVERYONE?!
OKAY, OKAY. I'LL LEAVE IT AT THAT!
NOTHING LIKE, "HE WAS LOST FOR SO LONG THAT HE WET HIS PANTS" OR, "HE WET HIS PANTS SO THAT'S WHY HE WAS FRANTICALLY SEARCHING FOR THE BATHROOM"... ESPECIALLY NOT IN FRONT OF HARUHI!
I DID NOT WET MY PANTS !!
AND JUST TO BE CLEAR, I HAVE NEVER ONCE WET MYSELF IN MY WHOLE LIFE!! I'M A GENTLEMAN, UNDERSTAND?
HAPPY SQUIRT = PEEING IN ONE'S PANTS A LITTLE WHEN EXTREMELY HAPPY
WELL, MAYBE WHEN I WAS LITTLE, I MIGHT HAVE HAD A "HAPPY SQUIRT" ONCE OR TWICE, BUT--
HMM? YOU'VE HAD A "HAPPY SQUIRT" BEFORE, MILORD ...?
EW! HOW UNSEEMLY.
SHUT UP!!
IT WAS ALL PART OF MY FATHER'S SCHEME TO IMPRESS UPON A FAIR YOUTH FUNDAMENTAL TOILET--
MILORD. MILORD. CALM DOWN!!

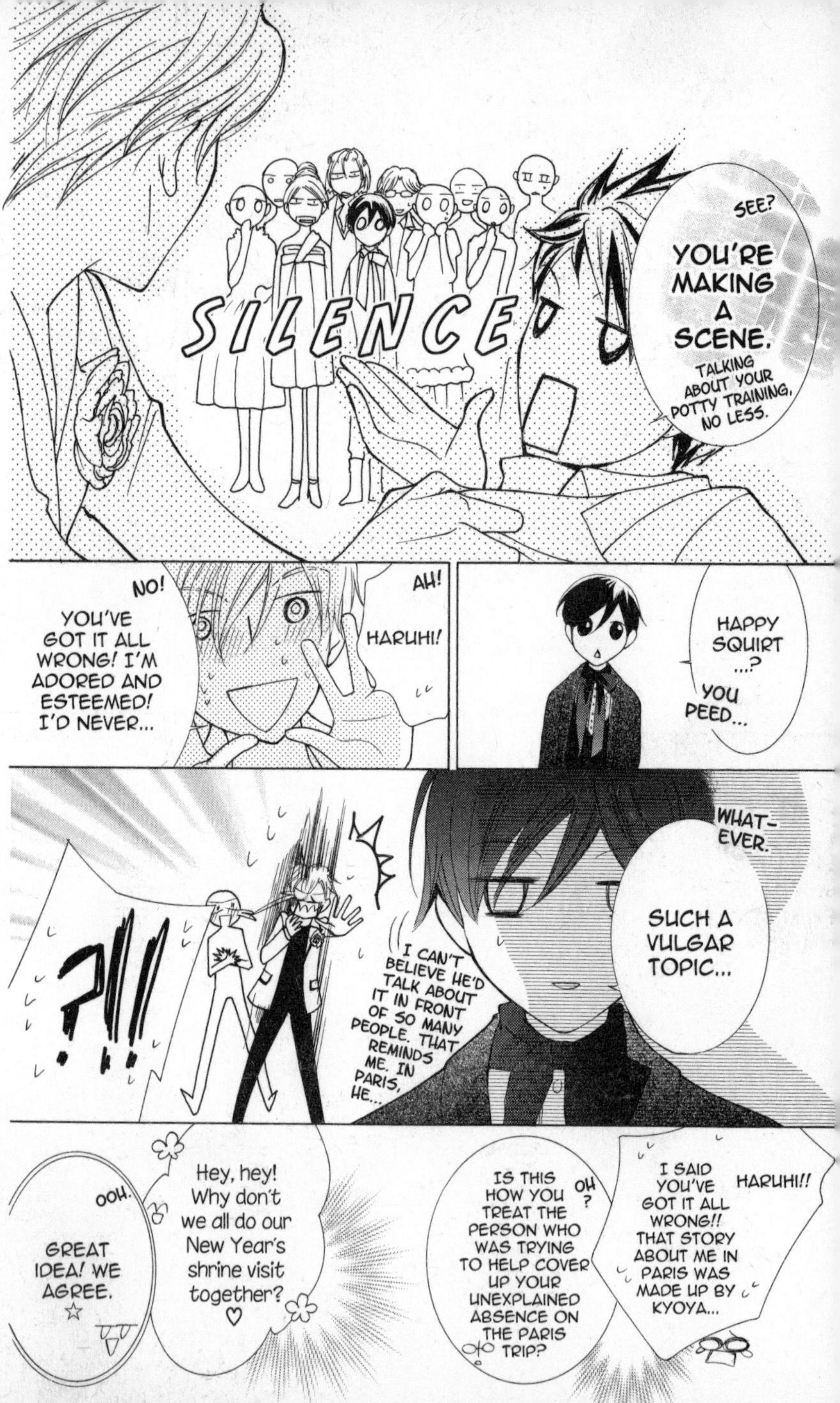
SEE?
YOU'RE MAKING A SCENE.
TALKING ABOUT YOUR POTTY TRAINING, NO LESS.
SILENCE
HAPPY SQUIRT ...?
YOU PEED...
AH!
HARUHI!
NO!
YOU'VE GOT IT ALL WRONG! I'M ADORED AND ESTEEMED! I'D NEVER...
WHAT-EVER.
SUCH A VULGAR TOPIC...
I CAN'T BELIEVE HE'D TALK ABOUT IT IN FRONT OF SO MANY PEOPLE. THAT REMINDS ME. IN PARIS, HE...
?!!
HARUHI!!
I SAID YOU'VE GOT IT ALL WRONG!! THAT STORY ABOUT ME IN PARIS WAS MADE UP BY KYOYA...
OH?
IS THIS HOW YOU TREAT THE PERSON WHO WAS TRYING TO HELP COVER UP YOUR UNEXPLAINED ABSENCE ON THE PARIS TRIP?
Hey, hey! Why don't we all do our New Year's shrine visit together? ♡
OOH.
GREAT IDEA! WE AGREE. ☆

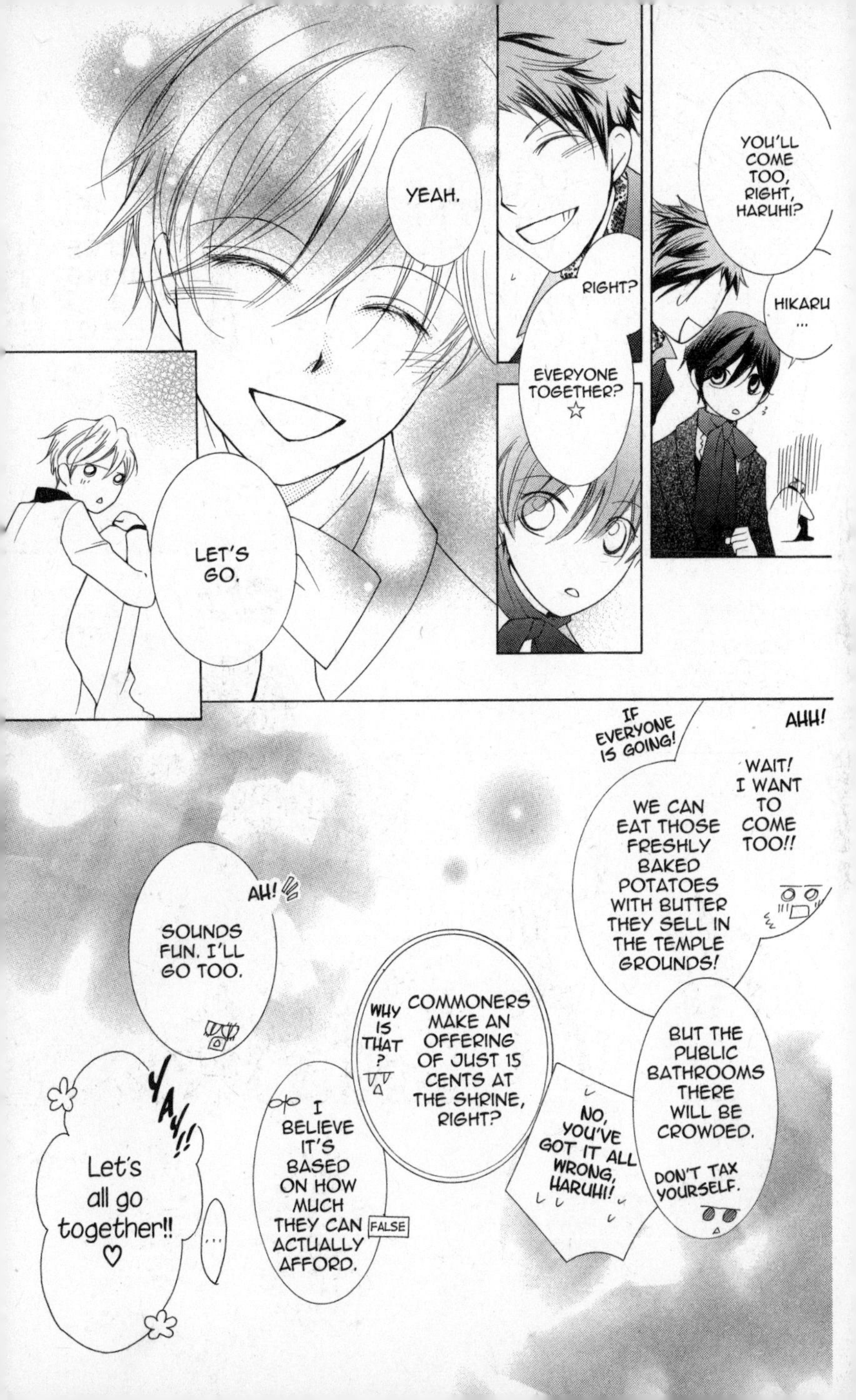
YOU'LL COME TOO, RIGHT, HARUHI?
HIKARU ...
RIGHT?
EVERYONE TOGETHER? ☆
YEAH.
LET'S GO.
AHH!
WAIT! I WANT TO COME TOO!!
IF EVERYONE IS GOING!
WE CAN EAT THOSE FRESHLY BAKED POTATOES WITH BUTTER THEY SELL IN THE TEMPLE GROUNDS!
BUT THE PUBLIC BATHROOMS THERE WILL BE CROWDED.
DON'T TAX YOURSELF.
NO, YOU'VE GOT IT ALL WRONG, HARUHI!
COMMONERS MAKE AN OFFERING OF JUST 15 CENTS AT THE SHRINE, RIGHT?
WHY IS THAT ?
I BELIEVE IT'S BASED ON HOW MUCH THEY CAN ACTUALLY AFFORD.
FALSE
AH!
SOUNDS FUN. I'LL GO TOO.
YAY!!
Let's all go together!! ♡
...

GUEST ROOM: FAXES

SPECIAL THANKS TO NATSUMI SATOU!!

THE MULTI-TALENTED "NATTSUN," WHO IS A
MANGAKA, A SUPER STAFF MEMBER WORKING
ON *LA CORDA D'ORO*, AND A SUPER HELPER ON
HOST CLUB, GRACIOUSLY DREW THIS LOVELY HARUHI
AND KYOYA WHILE SHE WAS WAITING FOR ME.♡
IT'S SO CUTE... NATTSUN IS A DOG LOVER
AND A *MEGANE* FAN. THANK YOU SO MUCH
FOR YOUR CONTINUING HELP AND SUPPORT!!
AND PLEASE SHOW ME MORE PHOTOS OF YOUR
ADORABLE DOGGIE TOO.♡

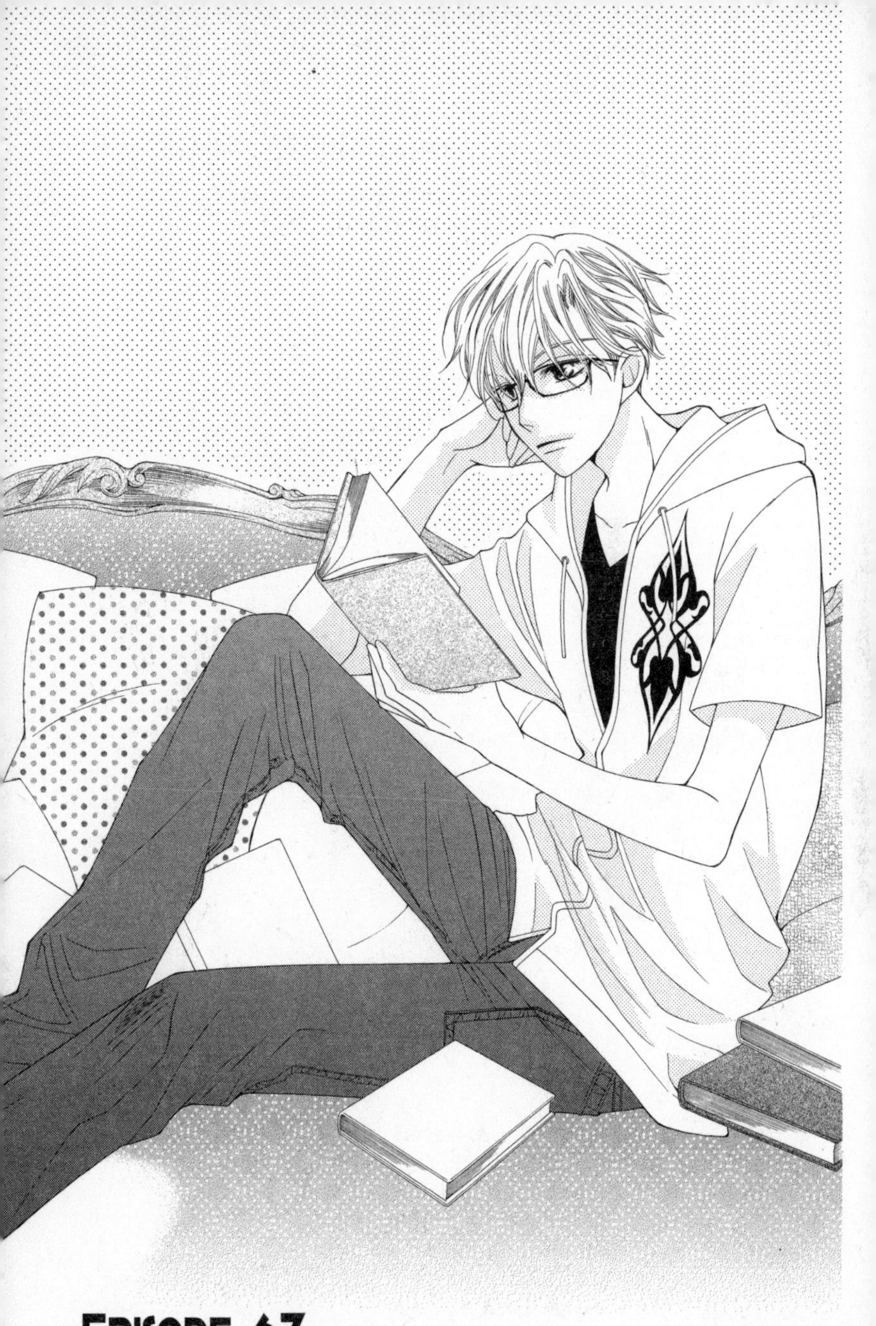

EPISODE 63

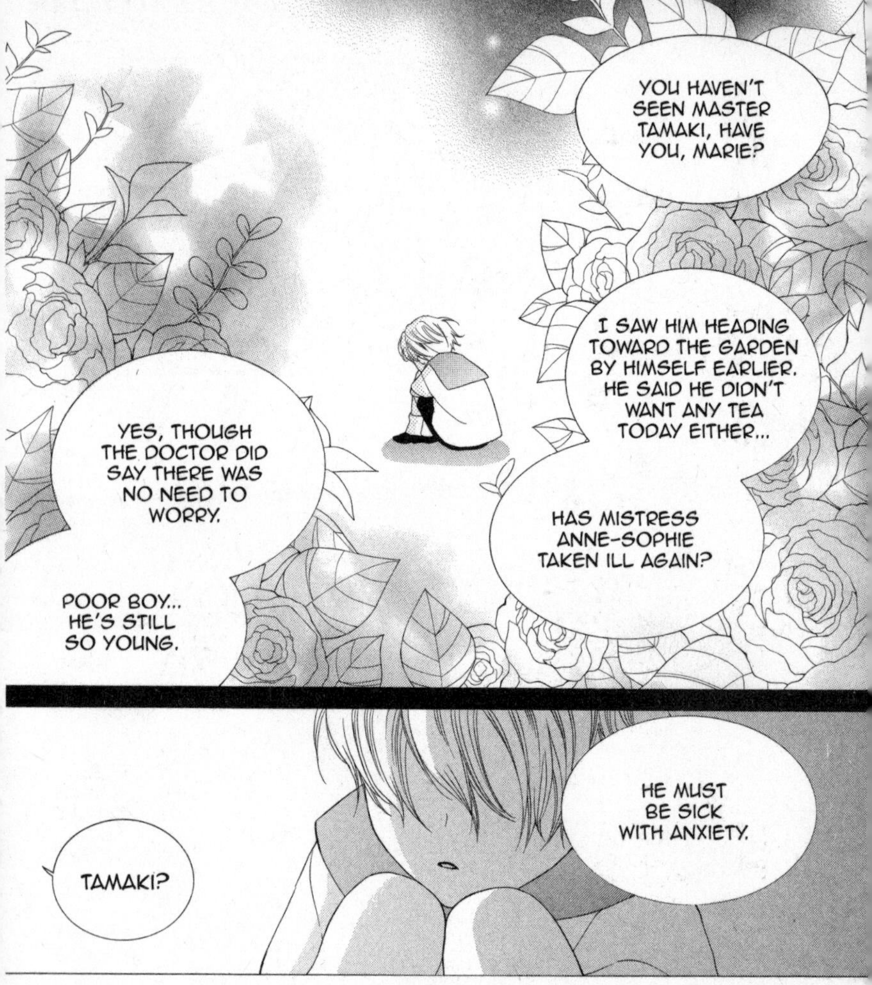
YOU HAVEN'T SEEN MASTER TAMAKI, HAVE YOU, MARIE?
I SAW HIM HEADING TOWARD THE GARDEN BY HIMSELF EARLIER. HE SAID HE DIDN'T WANT ANY TEA TODAY EITHER...
HAS MISTRESS ANNE-SOPHIE TAKEN ILL AGAIN?
YES, THOUGH THE DOCTOR DID SAY THERE WAS NO NEED TO WORRY.
POOR BOY... HE'S STILL SO YOUNG.
HE MUST BE SICK WITH ANXIETY.
TAMAKI?

SUPPORTING CHARACTERS INTRODUCTION

Tetsuya Sendo

AGE 22. BOSSA NOVA'S UNDERLING. HE IS METICULOUS. EVEN A SINGLE BUTTON MISSING FROM ONE OF THE MASTER'S SHIRTS WOULDN'T GO UNDETECTED BY HIM. YET UNEXPECTEDLY HE'S ALSO THE TYPE OF PERSON WHO'D SWEEP A SQUARE-SHAPED ROOM IN A CIRCLE, OR WHO'D GET SO CAUGHT UP PULLING WEEDS THAT HE'D ACCIDENTALLY UPROOT THE MASTER'S PRECIOUS SAPLINGS TOO. I INADVERTENTLY ENDED UP MAKING HIM A STRONG FIGHTER. AS FOR WHY HE KEEPS HIS HAIR SO LONG--THAT'S A MYSTERY.

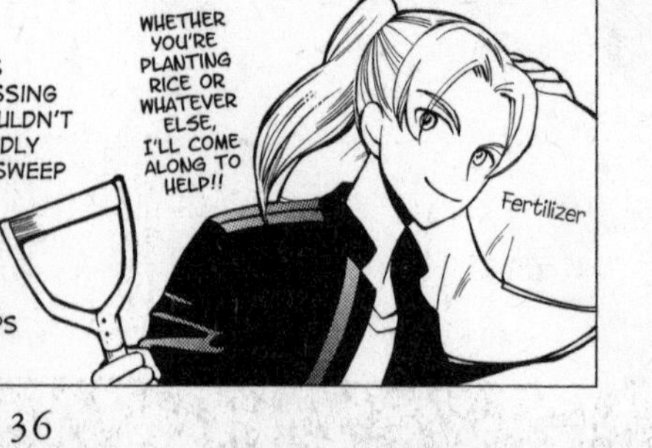
WHETHER YOU'RE PLANTING RICE OR WHATEVER ELSE, I'LL COME ALONG TO HELP!!
Fertilizer

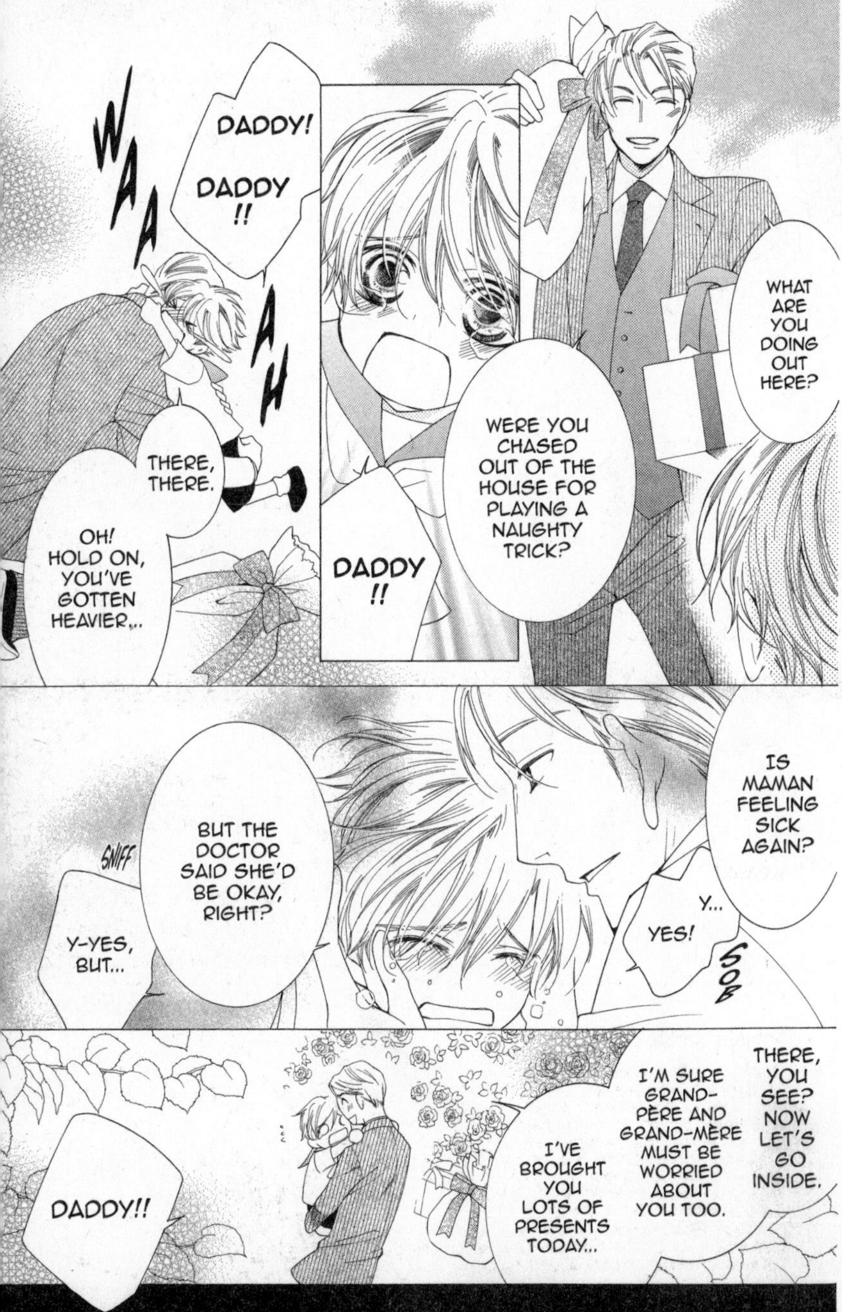
WHAT ARE YOU DOING OUT HERE?
WERE YOU CHASED OUT OF THE HOUSE FOR PLAYING A NAUGHTY TRICK?
DADDY !!
DADDY! DADDY !!
WAAAAH
THERE, THERE.
OH! HOLD ON, YOU'VE GOTTEN HEAVIER...
IS MAMAN FEELING SICK AGAIN?
Y... YES!
SOB
BUT THE DOCTOR SAID SHE'D BE OKAY, RIGHT?
SNIFF
Y-YES, BUT...
THERE, YOU SEE? NOW LET'S GO INSIDE.
I'M SURE GRAND-PÈRE AND GRAND-MÈRE MUST BE WORRIED ABOUT YOU TOO.
I'VE BROUGHT YOU LOTS OF PRESENTS TODAY...
DADDY!!

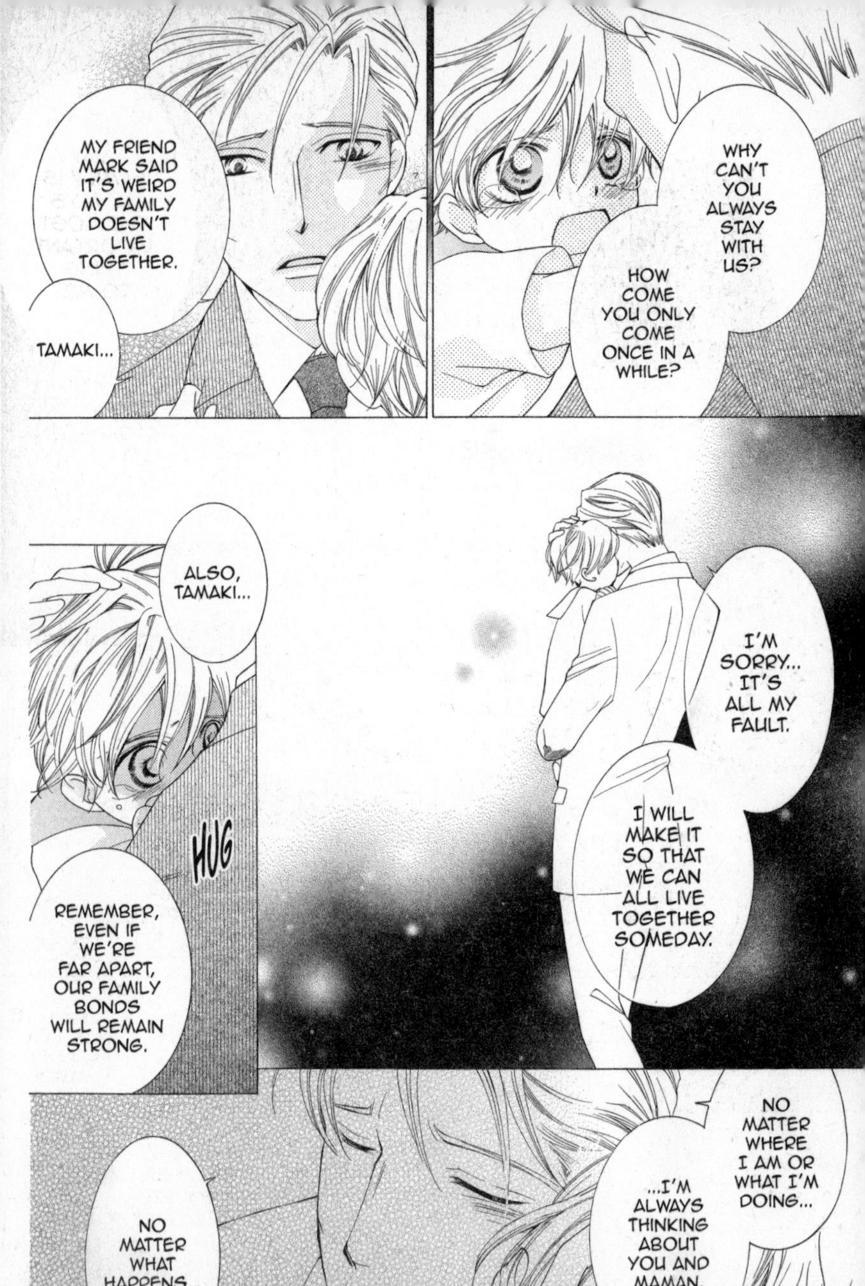
WHY CAN'T YOU ALWAYS STAY WITH US?
HOW COME YOU ONLY COME ONCE IN A WHILE?
MY FRIEND MARK SAID IT'S WEIRD MY FAMILY DOESN'T LIVE TOGETHER.
TAMAKI...
I'M SORRY... IT'S ALL MY FAULT.
I WILL MAKE IT SO THAT WE CAN ALL LIVE TOGETHER SOMEDAY.
ALSO, TAMAKI...
HUG
REMEMBER, EVEN IF WE'RE FAR APART, OUR FAMILY BONDS WILL REMAIN STRONG.
NO MATTER WHERE I AM OR WHAT I'M DOING...
...I'M ALWAYS THINKING ABOUT YOU AND MAMAN.
NO MATTER WHAT HAPPENS...

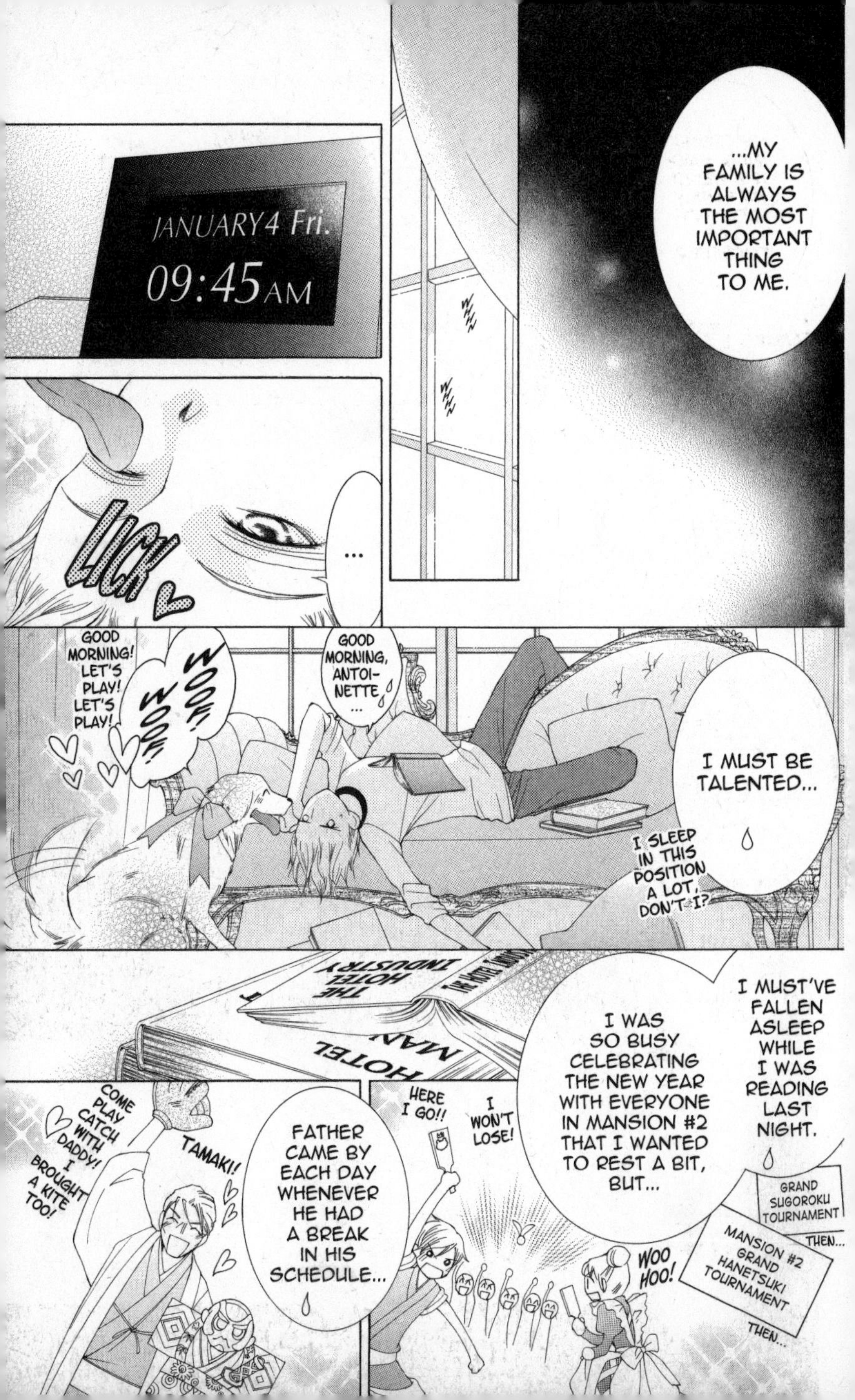
...MY FAMILY IS ALWAYS THE MOST IMPORTANT THING TO ME.
JANUARY4 Fri.
09:45AM
LICK
...
I MUST BE TALENTED...
I SLEEP IN THIS POSITION A LOT, DON'T I?
GOOD MORNING, ANTOI-NETTE ...
WOOF! WOOF!
GOOD MORNING! LET'S PLAY! LET'S PLAY!
I MUST'VE FALLEN ASLEEP WHILE I WAS READING LAST NIGHT.
THE HOTEL INDUSTRY
THE HOTEL INDUSTRY
HOTEL MAN
I WAS SO BUSY CELEBRATING THE NEW YEAR WITH EVERYONE IN MANSION #2 THAT I WANTED TO REST A BIT, BUT...
GRAND SUGOROKU TOURNAMENT
THEN...
MANSION #2 GRAND HANETSUKI TOURNAMENT
THEN...
WOO HOO!
I WON'T LOSE!
HERE I GO!!
FATHER CAME BY EACH DAY WHENEVER HE HAD A BREAK IN HIS SCHEDULE...
TAMAKI!
COME PLAY CATCH WITH DADDY! I BROUGHT A KITE TOO!

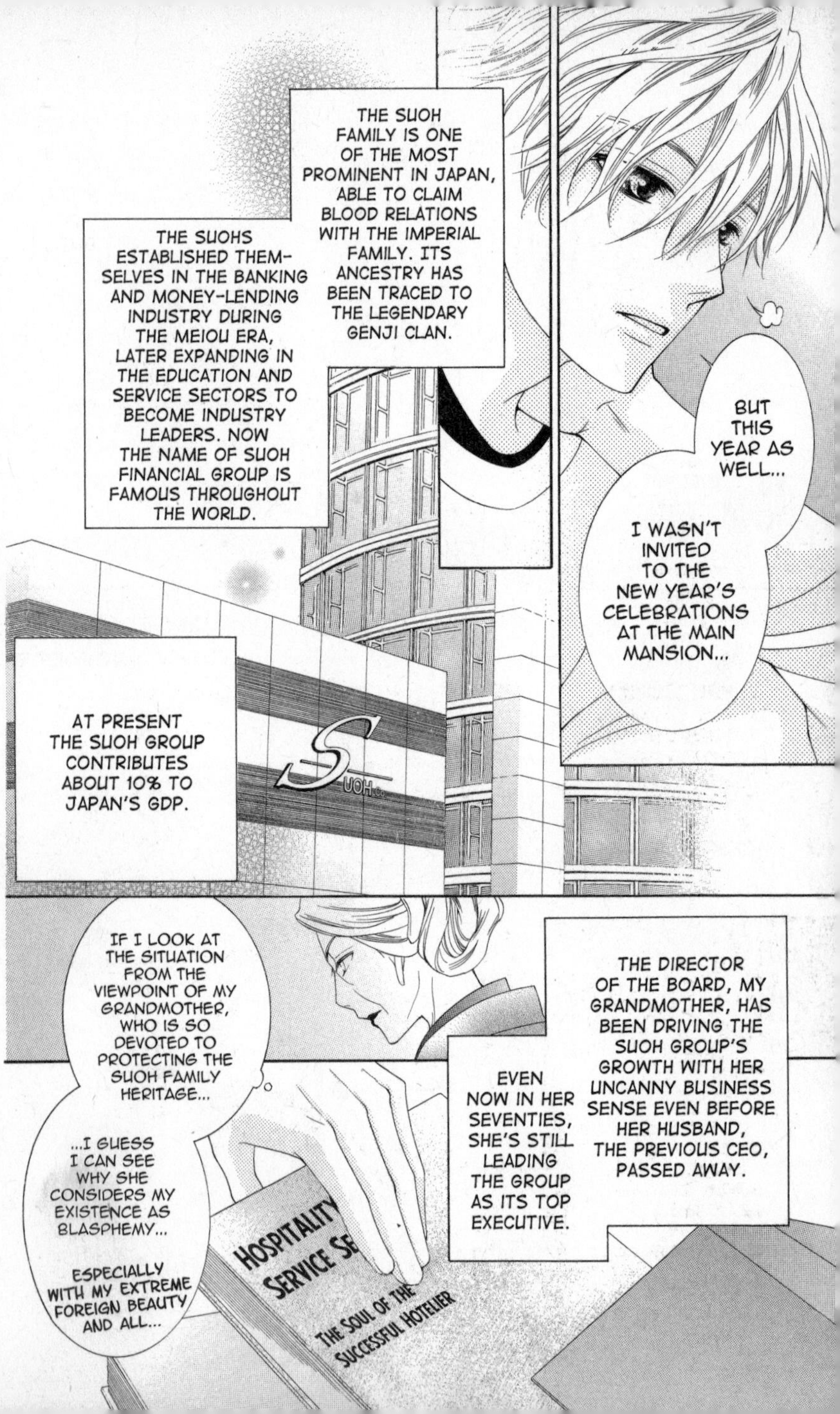
BUT THIS YEAR AS WELL...
I WASN'T INVITED TO THE NEW YEAR'S CELEBRATIONS AT THE MAIN MANSION...
THE SUOH FAMILY IS ONE OF THE MOST PROMINENT IN JAPAN, ABLE TO CLAIM BLOOD RELATIONS WITH THE IMPERIAL FAMILY. ITS ANCESTRY HAS BEEN TRACED TO THE LEGENDARY GENJI CLAN.
THE SUOHS ESTABLISHED THEM-SELVES IN THE BANKING AND MONEY-LENDING INDUSTRY DURING THE MEIOU ERA, LATER EXPANDING IN THE EDUCATION AND SERVICE SECTORS TO BECOME INDUSTRY LEADERS. NOW THE NAME OF SUOH FINANCIAL GROUP IS FAMOUS THROUGHOUT THE WORLD.
AT PRESENT THE SUOH GROUP CONTRIBUTES ABOUT 10% TO JAPAN'S GDP.
S UOH.Co
THE DIRECTOR OF THE BOARD, MY GRANDMOTHER, HAS BEEN DRIVING THE SUOH GROUP'S GROWTH WITH HER UNCANNY BUSINESS SENSE EVEN BEFORE HER HUSBAND, THE PREVIOUS CEO, PASSED AWAY.
EVEN NOW IN HER SEVENTIES, SHE'S STILL LEADING THE GROUP AS ITS TOP EXECUTIVE.
IF I LOOK AT THE SITUATION FROM THE VIEWPOINT OF MY GRANDMOTHER, WHO IS SO DEVOTED TO PROTECTING THE SUOH FAMILY HERITAGE...
...I GUESS I CAN SEE WHY SHE CONSIDERS MY EXISTENCE AS BLASPHEMY...
ESPECIALLY WITH MY EXTREME FOREIGN BEAUTY AND ALL...
HOSPITALITY SERVICE SE
THE SOUL OF THE SUCCESSFUL HOTELIER

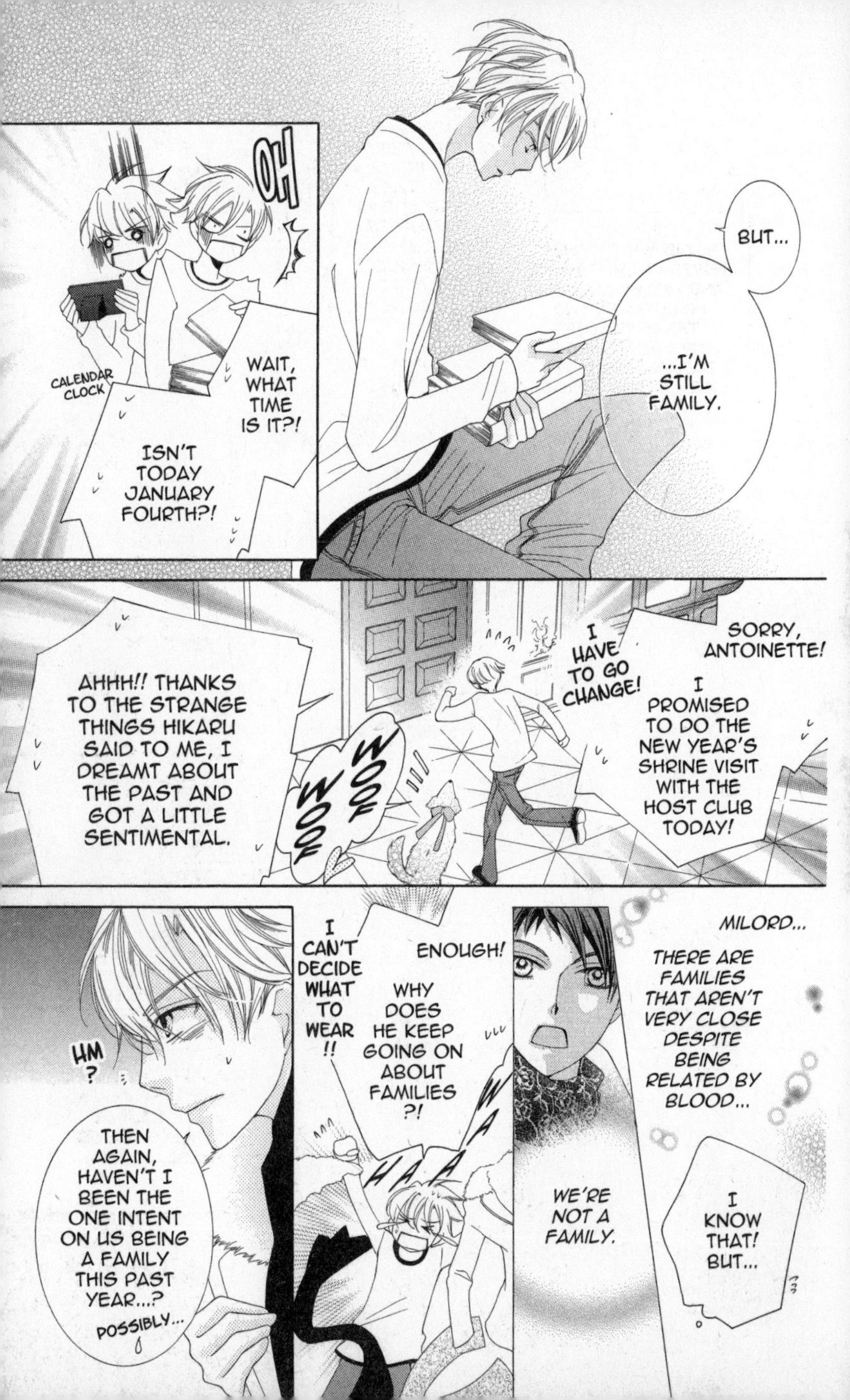
BUT...
...I'M STILL FAMILY.
OH
WAIT, WHAT TIME IS IT?!
CALENDAR CLOCK
ISN'T TODAY JANUARY FOURTH?!
SORRY, ANTOINETTE!
I PROMISED TO DO THE NEW YEAR'S SHRINE VISIT WITH THE HOST CLUB TODAY!
I HAVE TO GO CHANGE!
WOOF WOOF
AHHH!! THANKS TO THE STRANGE THINGS HIKARU SAID TO ME, I DREAMT ABOUT THE PAST AND GOT A LITTLE SENTIMENTAL.
MILORD...
THERE ARE FAMILIES THAT AREN'T VERY CLOSE DESPITE BEING RELATED BY BLOOD...
WE'RE NOT A FAMILY.
I KNOW THAT! BUT...
ENOUGH!
I CAN'T DECIDE WHAT TO WEAR!!
WHY DOES HE KEEP GOING ON ABOUT FAMILIES?!
HM?
THEN AGAIN, HAVEN'T I BEEN THE ONE INTENT ON US BEING A FAMILY THIS PAST YEAR...?
POSSIBLY...

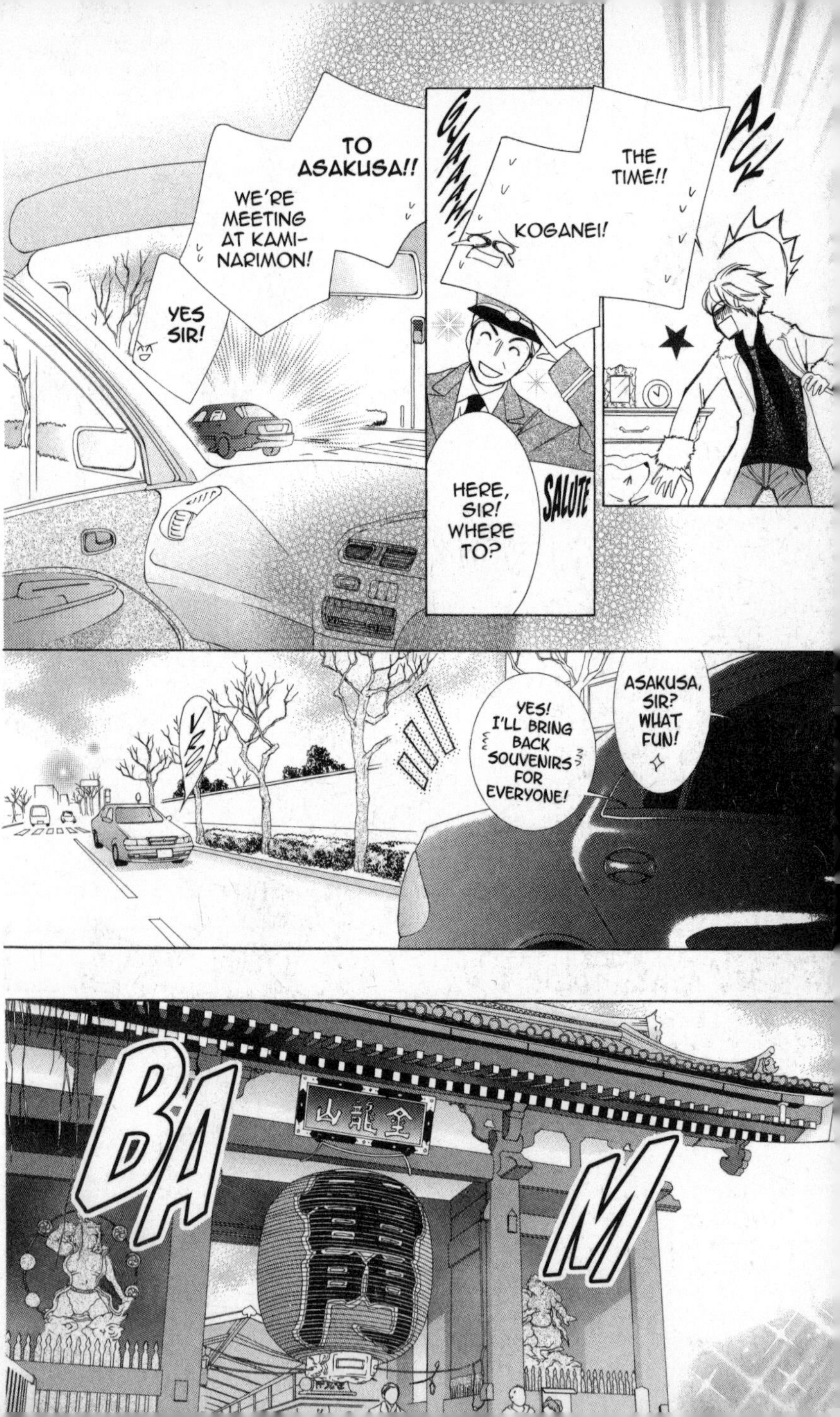
ACK
THE TIME!!
KOGANEI!
SALUTE
HERE, SIR! WHERE TO?
TO ASAKUSA!!
WE'RE MEETING AT KAMI-NARIMON!
YES SIR!
ASAKUSA, SIR? WHAT FUN!
YES! I'LL BRING BACK SOUVENIRS FOR EVERYONE!
BAM

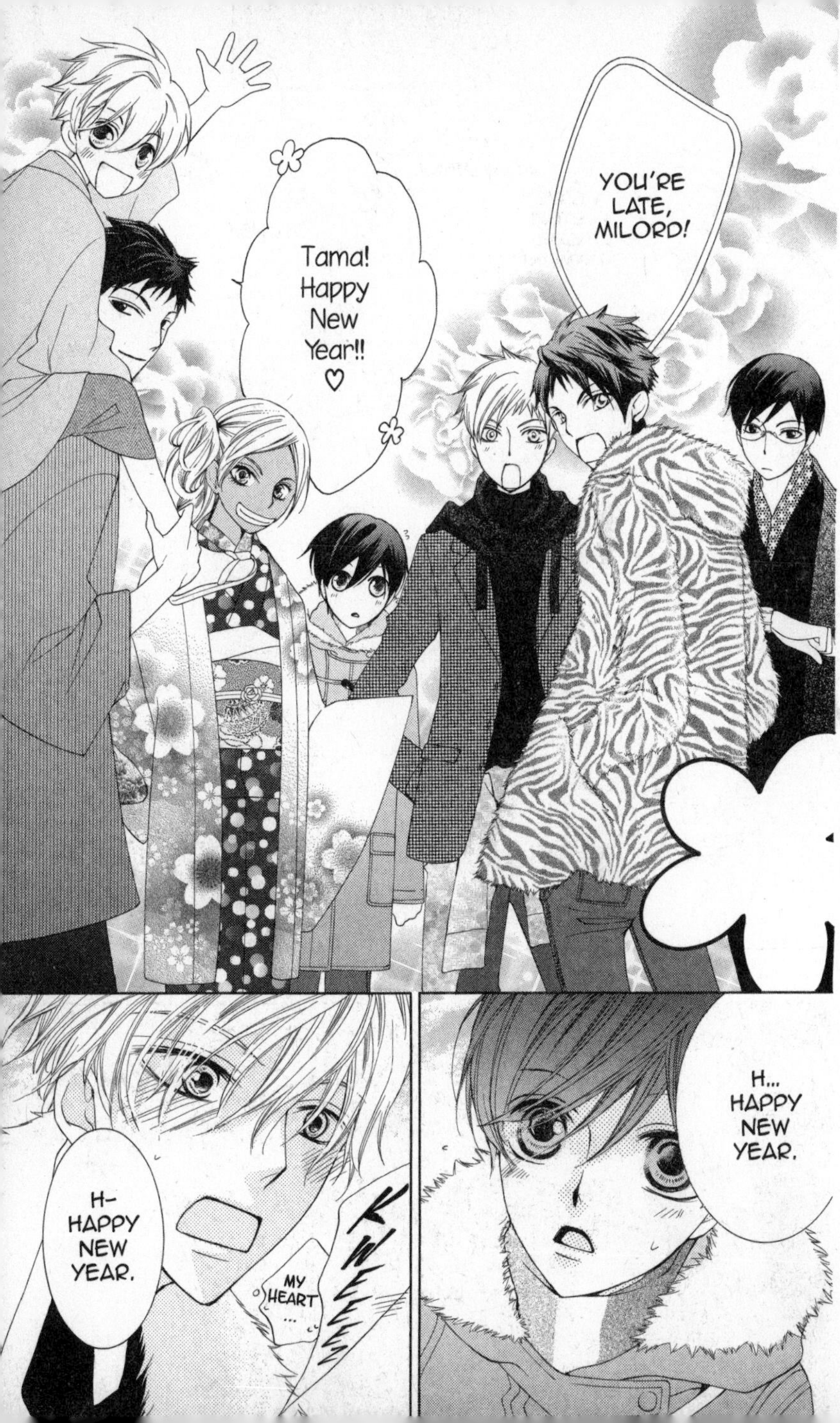
YOU'RE LATE, MILORD!
Tama! Happy New Year!! ♡
H... HAPPY NEW YEAR.
H- HAPPY NEW YEAR.
MY HEART ...

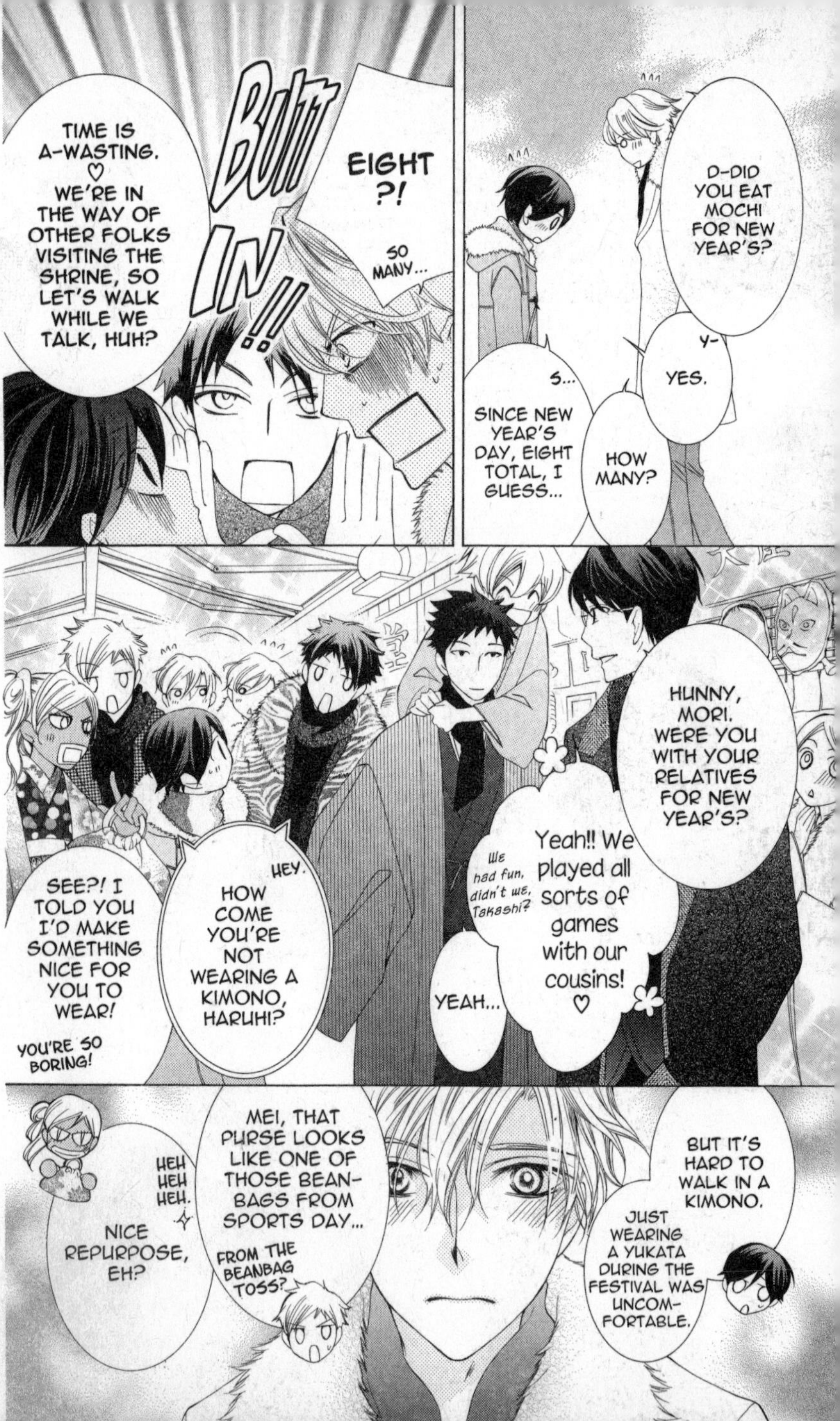
D-DID YOU EAT MOCHI FOR NEW YEAR'S?
Y- YES.
HOW MANY?
S... SINCE NEW YEAR'S DAY, EIGHT TOTAL, I GUESS...
EIGHT?!
SO MANY...
BUTT IN!!
TIME IS A-WASTING. ♡ WE'RE IN THE WAY OF OTHER FOLKS VISITING THE SHRINE, SO LET'S WALK WHILE WE TALK, HUH?
HUNNY, MORI. WERE YOU WITH YOUR RELATIVES FOR NEW YEAR'S?
Yeah!! We played all sorts of games with our cousins! ♡
We had fun, didn't we, Takashi?
YEAH...
HEY. HOW COME YOU'RE NOT WEARING A KIMONO, HARUHI?
SEE?! I TOLD YOU I'D MAKE SOMETHING NICE FOR YOU TO WEAR!
YOU'RE SO BORING!
BUT IT'S HARD TO WALK IN A KIMONO.
JUST WEARING A YUKATA DURING THE FESTIVAL WAS UNCOMFORTABLE.
MEI, THAT PURSE LOOKS LIKE ONE OF THOSE BEAN-BAGS FROM SPORTS DAY...
FROM THE BEANBAG TOSS?
HEH HEH HEH.
NICE REPURPOSE, EH?

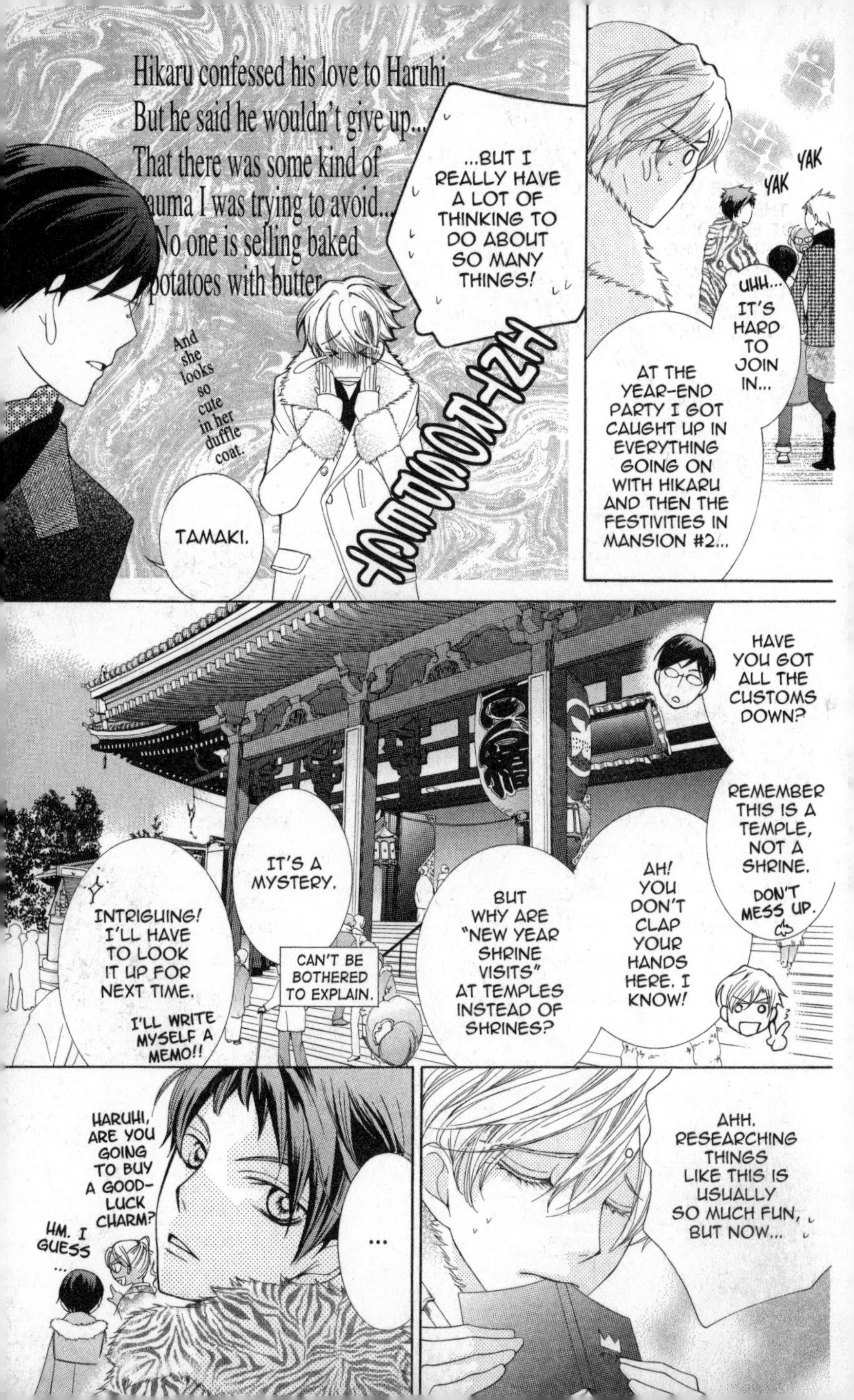
YAK
YAK
UHH... IT'S HARD TO JOIN IN...
AT THE YEAR-END PARTY I GOT CAUGHT UP IN EVERYTHING GOING ON WITH HIKARU AND THEN THE FESTIVITIES IN MANSION #2...
Hikaru confessed his love to Haruhi. But he said he wouldn't give up... That there was some kind of auma I was trying to avoid... No one is selling baked potatoes with butter.
...BUT I REALLY HAVE A LOT OF THINKING TO DO ABOUT SO MANY THINGS!
And she looks so cute in her duffle coat.
TAMAKI.
HAVE YOU GOT ALL THE CUSTOMS DOWN?
REMEMBER THIS IS A TEMPLE, NOT A SHRINE.
DON'T MESS UP.
AH! YOU DON'T CLAP YOUR HANDS HERE. I KNOW!
BUT WHY ARE "NEW YEAR SHRINE VISITS" AT TEMPLES INSTEAD OF SHRINES?
CAN'T BE BOTHERED TO EXPLAIN.
IT'S A MYSTERY.
INTRIGUING! I'LL HAVE TO LOOK IT UP FOR NEXT TIME.
I'LL WRITE MYSELF A MEMO!!
AHH. RESEARCHING THINGS LIKE THIS IS USUALLY SO MUCH FUN, BUT NOW...
...
HARUHI, ARE YOU GOING TO BUY A GOOD-LUCK CHARM?
HM. I GUESS ...

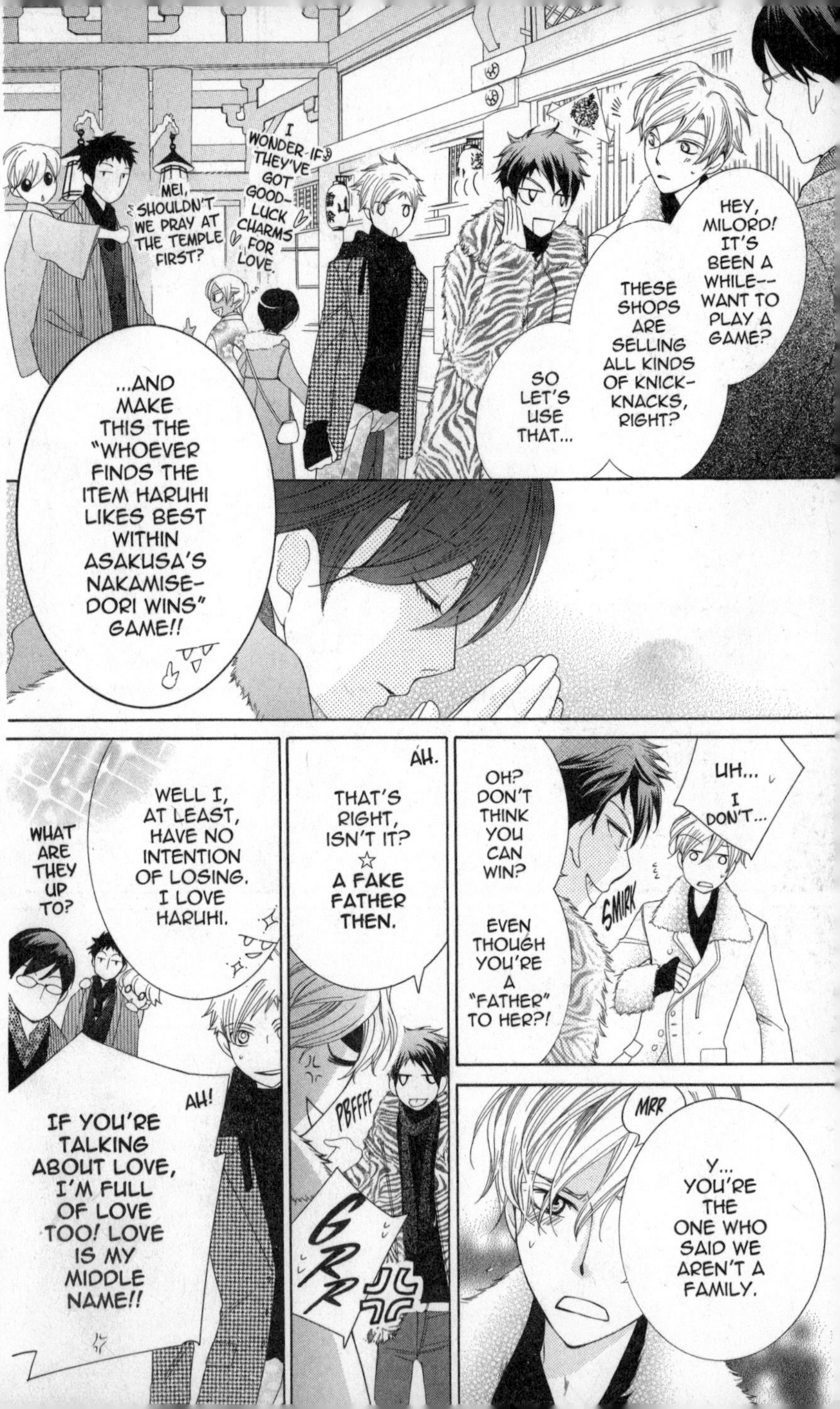
HEY, MILORD! IT'S BEEN A WHILE--WANT TO PLAY A GAME?
THESE SHOPS ARE SELLING ALL KINDS OF KNICK-KNACKS, RIGHT?
SO LET'S USE THAT...
I WONDER IF THEY'VE GOT GOOD-LUCK CHARMS FOR LOVE.
MEI, SHOULDN'T WE PRAY AT THE TEMPLE FIRST?
...AND MAKE THIS THE "WHOEVER FINDS THE ITEM HARUHI LIKES BEST WITHIN ASAKUSA'S NAKAMISE-DORI WINS" GAME!!
UH... I DON'T...
OH? DON'T THINK YOU CAN WIN?
SMIRK
EVEN THOUGH YOU'RE A "FATHER" TO HER?!
MRR
Y... YOU'RE THE ONE WHO SAID WE AREN'T A FAMILY.
AH.
THAT'S RIGHT, ISN'T IT? ☆ A FAKE FATHER THEN.
PBFFFF
GRR
WELL I, AT LEAST, HAVE NO INTENTION OF LOSING. I LOVE HARUHI.
WHAT ARE THEY UP TO?
AH!
IF YOU'RE TALKING ABOUT LOVE, I'M FULL OF LOVE TOO! LOVE IS MY MIDDLE NAME!!

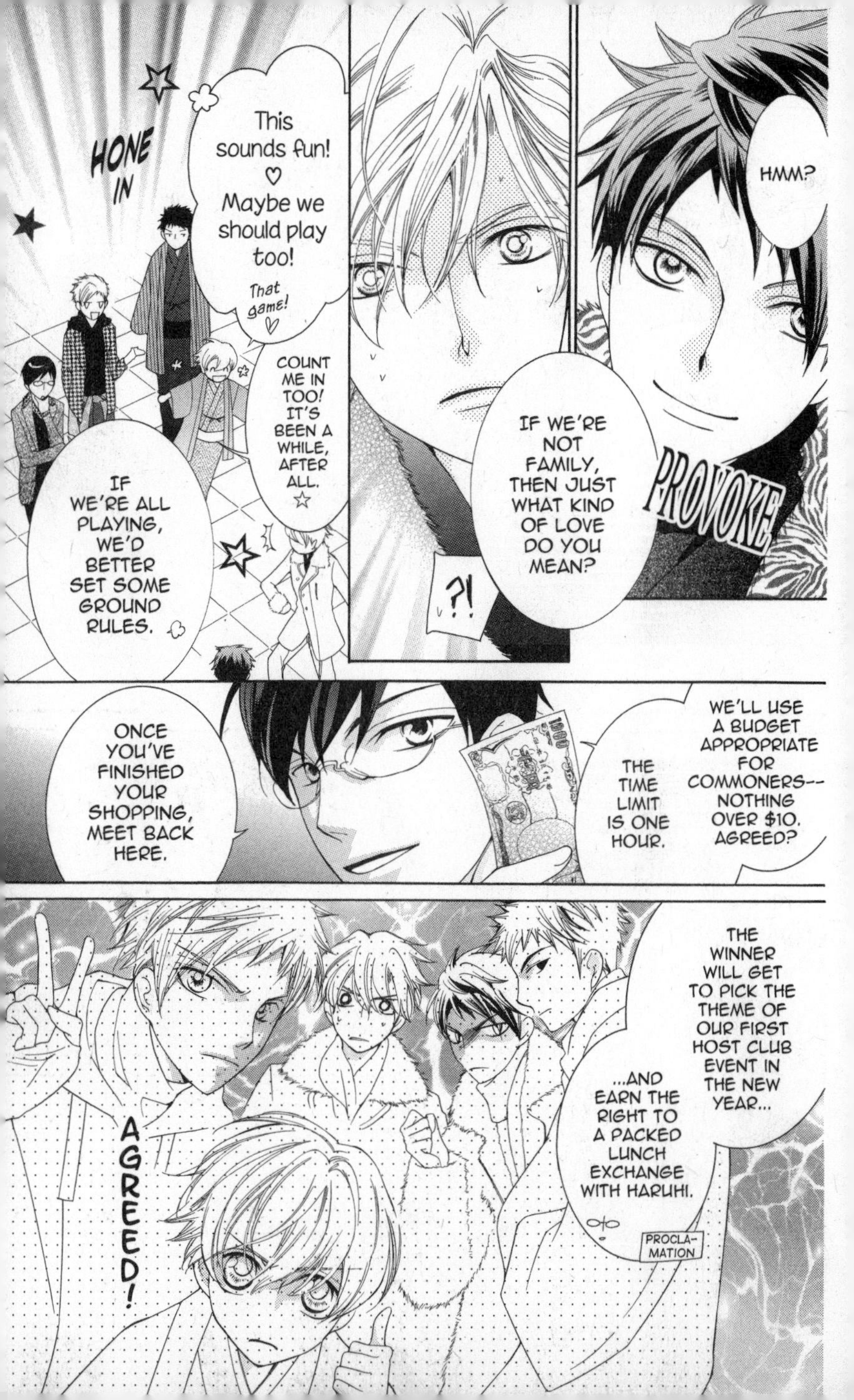
HMM?
PROVOKE
IF WE'RE NOT FAMILY, THEN JUST WHAT KIND OF LOVE DO YOU MEAN?
?!
This sounds fun! ♡ Maybe we should play too!
That game! ♡
HONE IN
COUNT ME IN TOO! IT'S BEEN A WHILE, AFTER ALL. ☆
IF WE'RE ALL PLAYING, WE'D BETTER SET SOME GROUND RULES.
WE'LL USE A BUDGET APPROPRIATE FOR COMMONERS--NOTHING OVER $10. AGREED?
THE TIME LIMIT IS ONE HOUR.
ONCE YOU'VE FINISHED YOUR SHOPPING, MEET BACK HERE.
THE WINNER WILL GET TO PICK THE THEME OF OUR FIRST HOST CLUB EVENT IN THE NEW YEAR...
...AND EARN THE RIGHT TO A PACKED LUNCH EXCHANGE WITH HARUHI.
PROCLAMATION
AGREED!

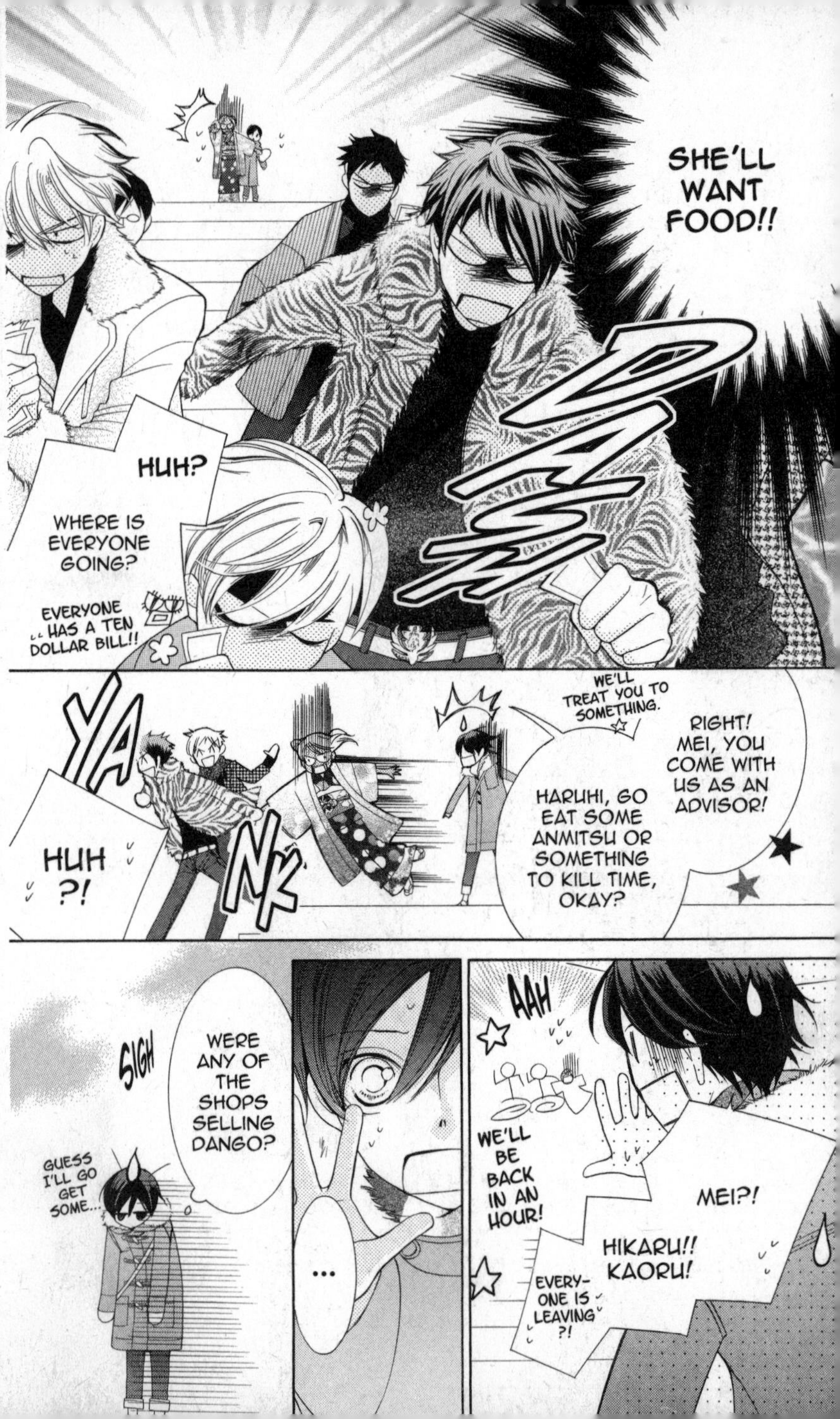
SHE'LL WANT FOOD!!
DASH
HUH?
WHERE IS EVERYONE GOING?
EVERYONE HAS A TEN DOLLAR BILL!!
RIGHT! MEI, YOU COME WITH US AS AN ADVISOR!
WE'LL TREAT YOU TO SOMETHING.
HARUHI, GO EAT SOME ANMITSU OR SOMETHING TO KILL TIME, OKAY?
YANK
HUH ?!
MEI?!
AAH
HIKARU!! KAORU!
WE'LL BE BACK IN AN HOUR!
EVERY-ONE IS LEAVING ?!
...
WERE ANY OF THE SHOPS SELLING DANGO?
SIGH
GUESS I'LL GO GET SOME...

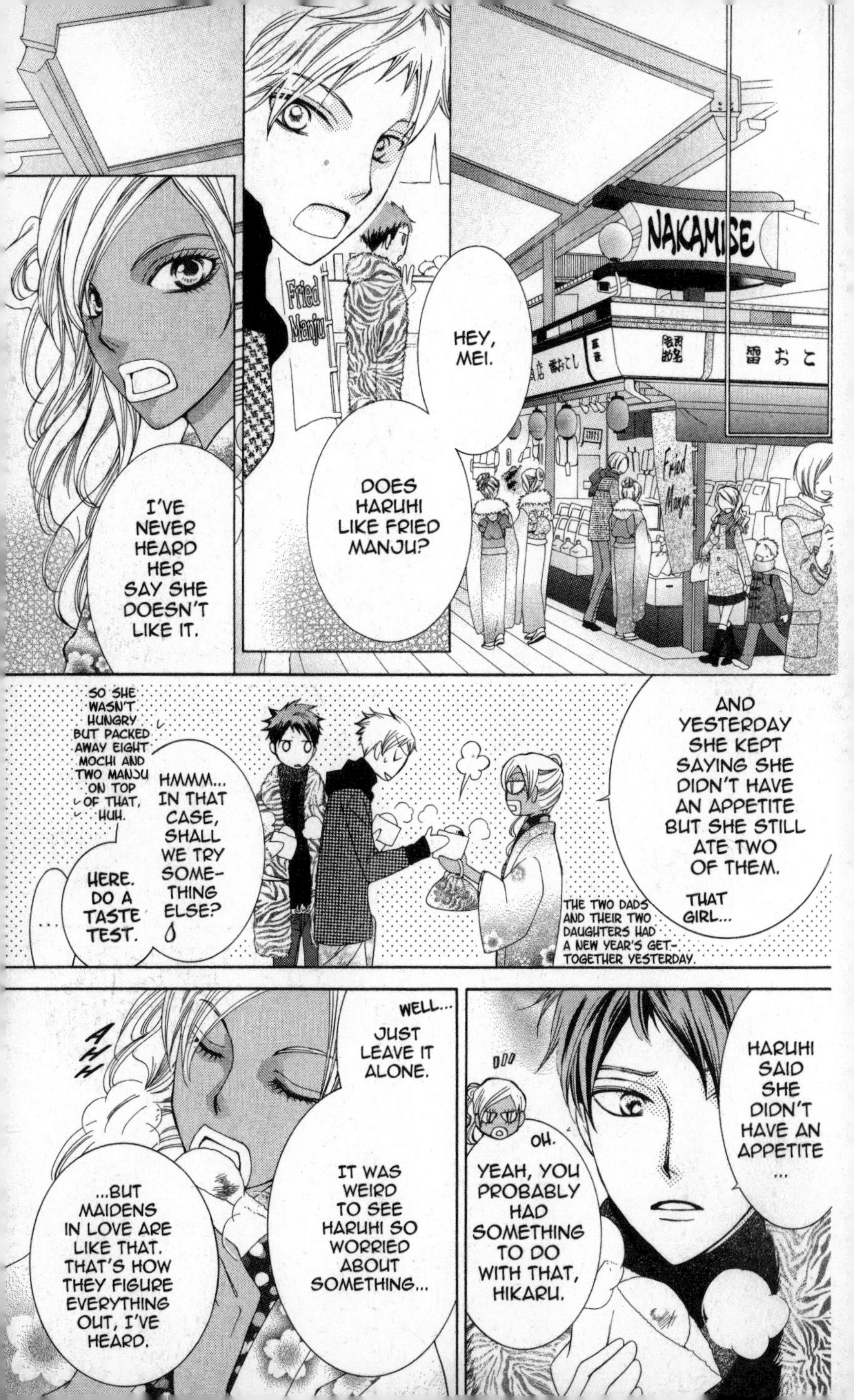
NAKAMISE
Fried Manju
Fried Manju
HEY, MEI.
DOES HARUHI LIKE FRIED MANJU?
I'VE NEVER HEARD HER SAY SHE DOESN'T LIKE IT.
AND YESTERDAY SHE KEPT SAYING SHE DIDN'T HAVE AN APPETITE BUT SHE STILL ATE TWO OF THEM.
THAT GIRL...
THE TWO DADS AND THEIR TWO DAUGHTERS HAD A NEW YEAR'S GET-TOGETHER YESTERDAY.
HMMM... IN THAT CASE, SHALL WE TRY SOME-THING ELSE?
SO SHE WASN'T HUNGRY BUT PACKED AWAY EIGHT MOCHI AND TWO MANJU ON TOP OF THAT, HUH.
HERE. DO A TASTE TEST.
...
HARUHI SAID SHE DIDN'T HAVE AN APPETITE ...
OH.
YEAH, YOU PROBABLY HAD SOMETHING TO DO WITH THAT, HIKARU.
WELL...
JUST LEAVE IT ALONE.
IT WAS WEIRD TO SEE HARUHI SO WORRIED ABOUT SOMETHING...
AHH
...BUT MAIDENS IN LOVE ARE LIKE THAT. THAT'S HOW THEY FIGURE EVERYTHING OUT, I'VE HEARD.

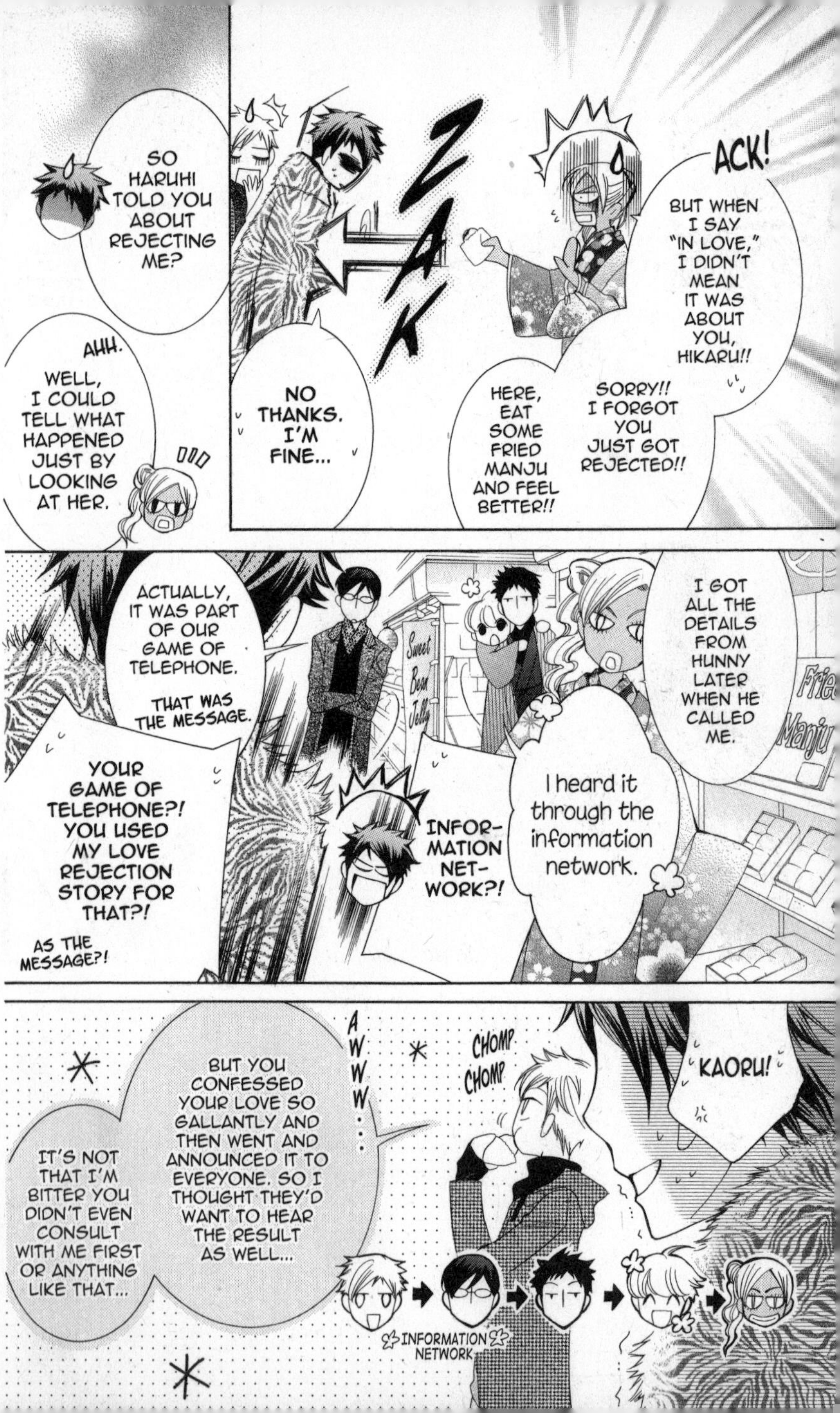
ACK!
BUT WHEN I SAY "IN LOVE," I DIDN'T MEAN IT WAS ABOUT YOU, HIKARU!!
SORRY!! I FORGOT YOU JUST GOT REJECTED!!
HERE, EAT SOME FRIED MANJU AND FEEL BETTER!!
ZAK
NO THANKS. I'M FINE...
SO HARUHI TOLD YOU ABOUT REJECTING ME?
AHH.
WELL, I COULD TELL WHAT HAPPENED JUST BY LOOKING AT HER.
I GOT ALL THE DETAILS FROM HUNNY LATER WHEN HE CALLED ME.
Sweet Bean Jelly
ACTUALLY, IT WAS PART OF OUR GAME OF TELEPHONE.
THAT WAS THE MESSAGE.
I heard it through the information network.
INFORMATION NETWORK?!
YOUR GAME OF TELEPHONE?! YOU USED MY LOVE REJECTION STORY FOR THAT?!
AS THE MESSAGE?!
KAORU!
CHOMP CHOMP
AWWW...
BUT YOU CONFESSED YOUR LOVE SO GALLANTLY AND THEN WENT AND ANNOUNCED IT TO EVERYONE. SO I THOUGHT THEY'D WANT TO HEAR THE RESULT AS WELL...
IT'S NOT THAT I'M BITTER YOU DIDN'T EVEN CONSULT WITH ME FIRST OR ANYTHING LIKE THAT...
INFORMATION NETWORK

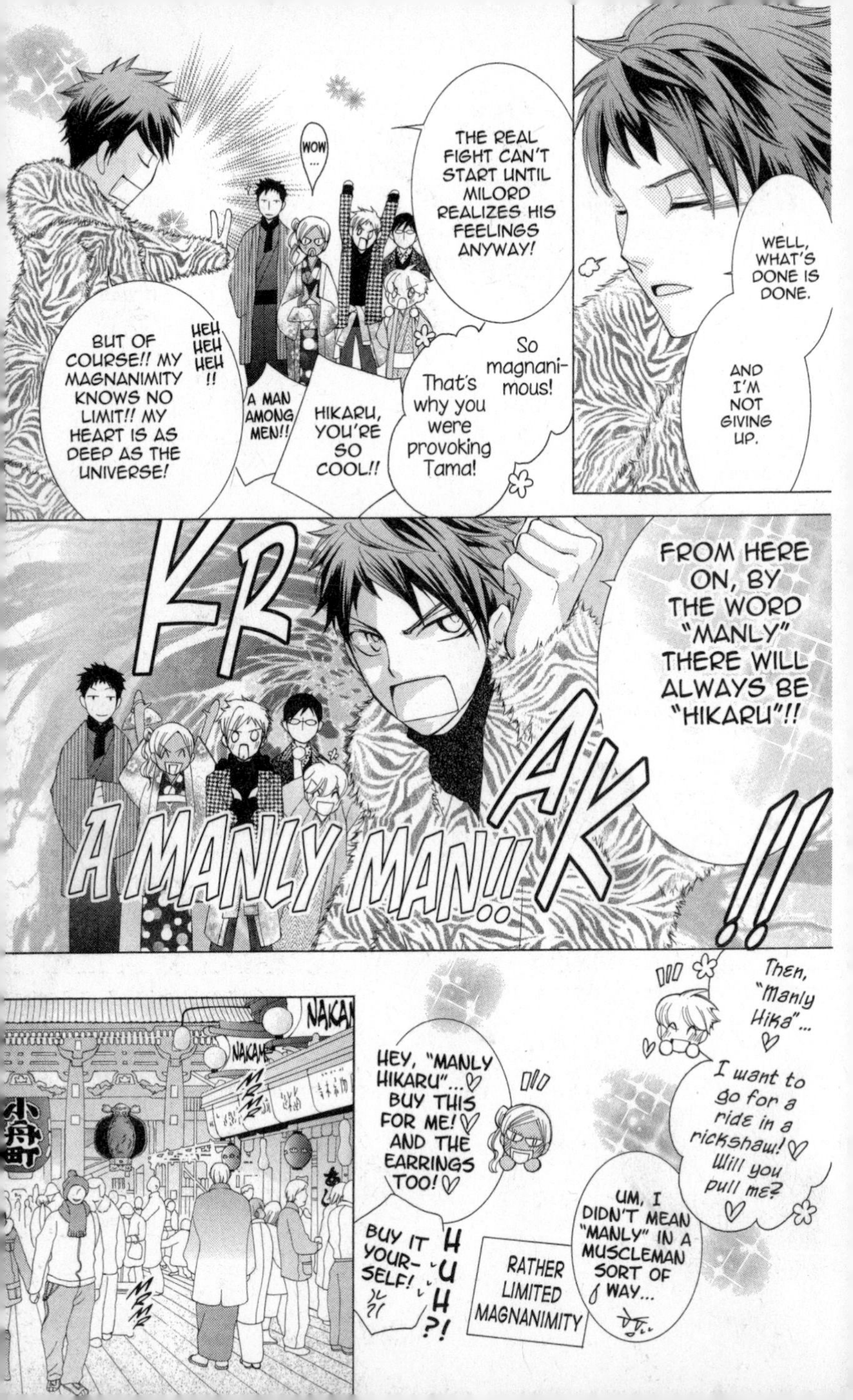
WELL, WHAT'S DONE IS DONE.
AND I'M NOT GIVING UP.
THE REAL FIGHT CAN'T START UNTIL MILORD REALIZES HIS FEELINGS ANYWAY!
WOW...
So magnanimous!
That's why you were provoking Tama!
HIKARU, YOU'RE SO COOL!!
A MAN AMONG MEN!!
HEH HEH HEH !!
BUT OF COURSE!! MY MAGNANIMITY KNOWS NO LIMIT!! MY HEART IS AS DEEP AS THE UNIVERSE!
FROM HERE ON, BY THE WORD "MANLY" THERE WILL ALWAYS BE "HIKARU"!!
KRAK!!
A MANLY MAN!!
Then, "Manly Hika"...
I want to go for a ride in a rickshaw! Will you pull me?
UM, I DIDN'T MEAN "MANLY" IN A MUSCLEMAN SORT OF WAY...
HEY, "MANLY HIKARU"... BUY THIS FOR ME! AND THE EARRINGS TOO!
HUH?!
BUY IT YOURSELF!
RATHER LIMITED MAGNANIMITY
小舟町

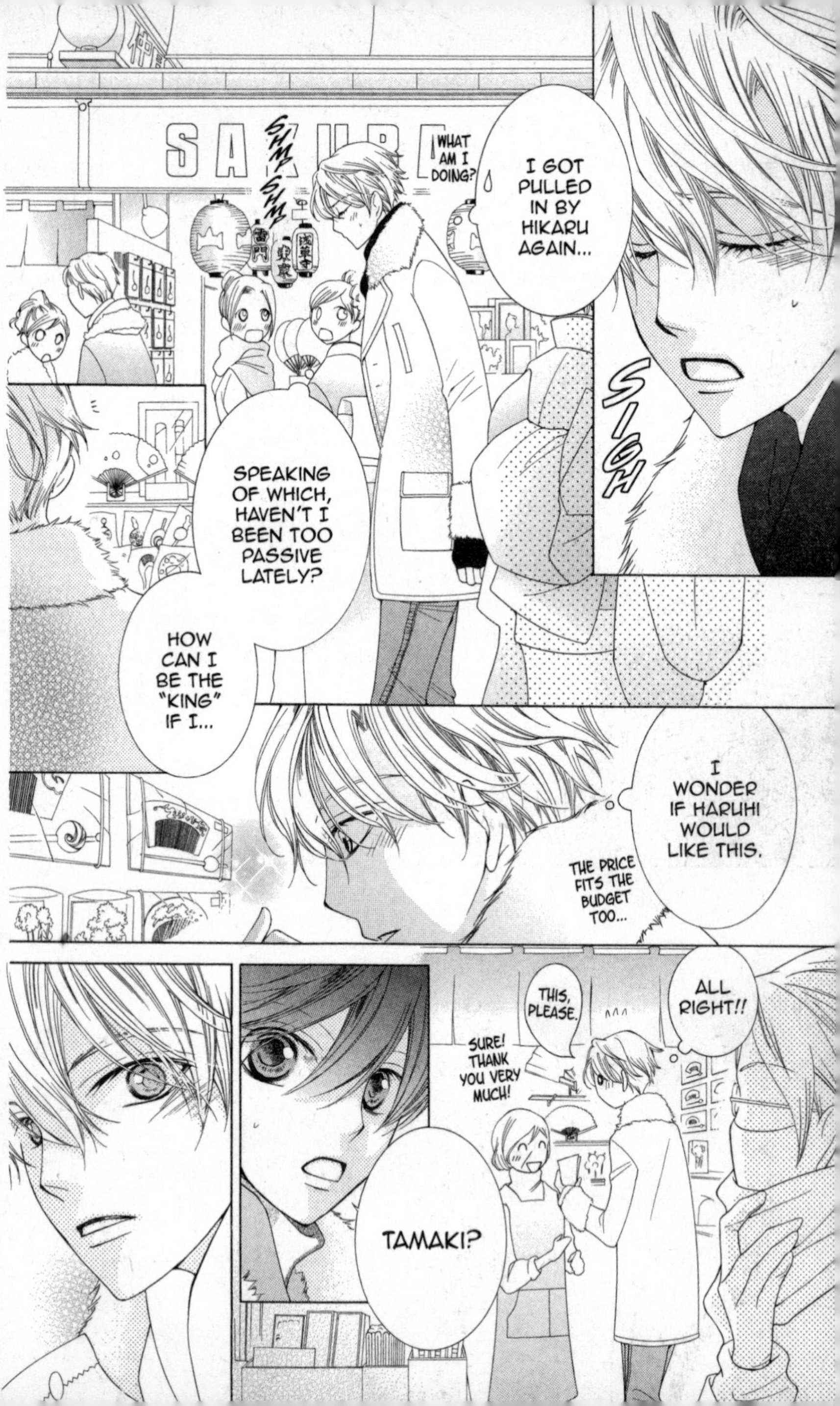
I GOT PULLED IN BY HIKARU AGAIN...
SIGH
SHMP SHMP
WHAT AM I DOING?
SPEAKING OF WHICH, HAVEN'T I BEEN TOO PASSIVE LATELY?
HOW CAN I BE THE "KING" IF I...
I WONDER IF HARUHI WOULD LIKE THIS.
THE PRICE FITS THE BUDGET TOO...
ALL RIGHT!!
THIS, PLEASE.
SURE! THANK YOU VERY MUCH!
TAMAKI?

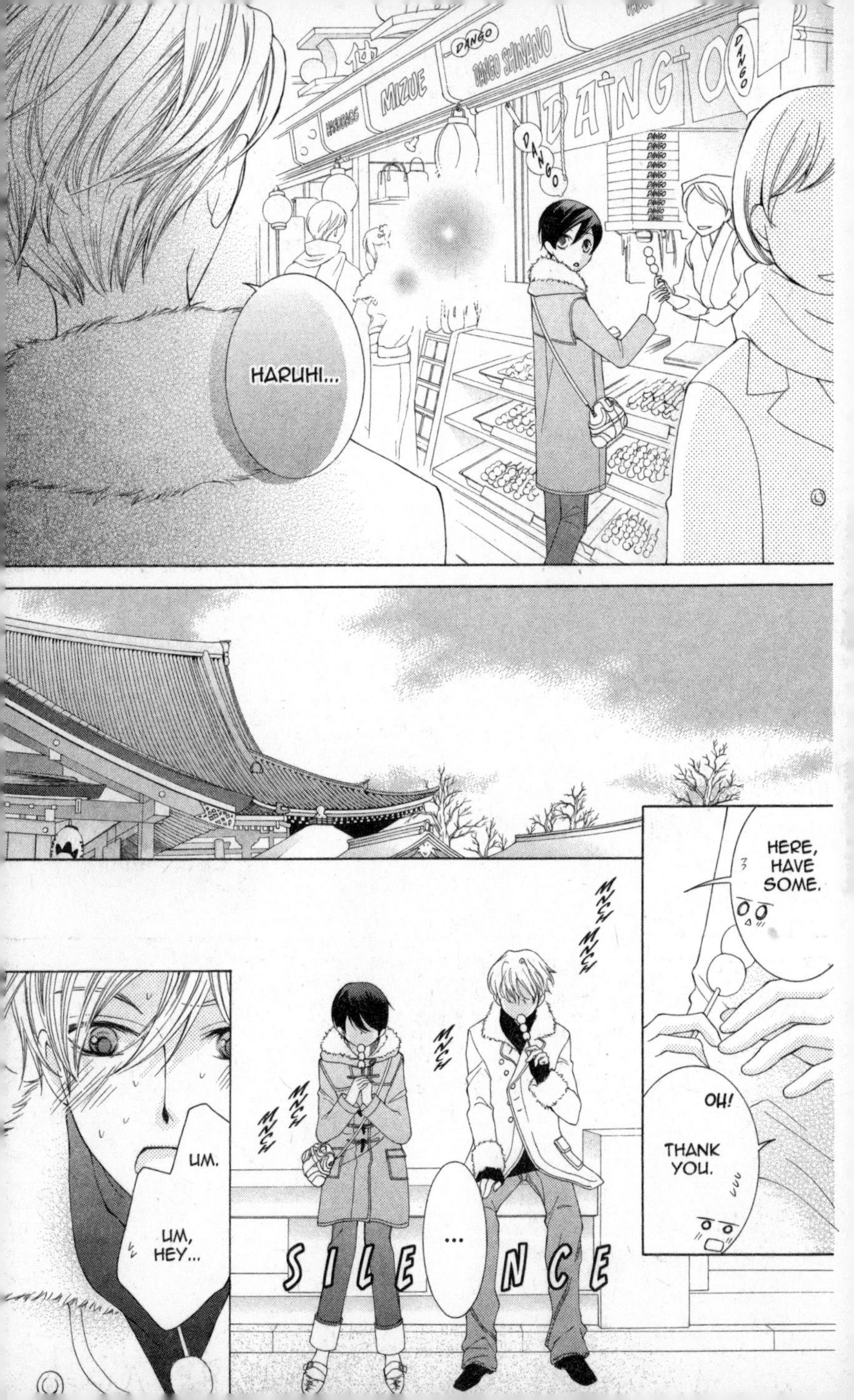
DANGO
DANGO SHINANO
MIZUE
DANGO
DANGO
DANGO
HARUHI...
HERE, HAVE SOME.
OH!
THANK YOU.
MNCH MNCH
MNCH
MNCH MNCH
...
SILENCE
UM.
UM, HEY...

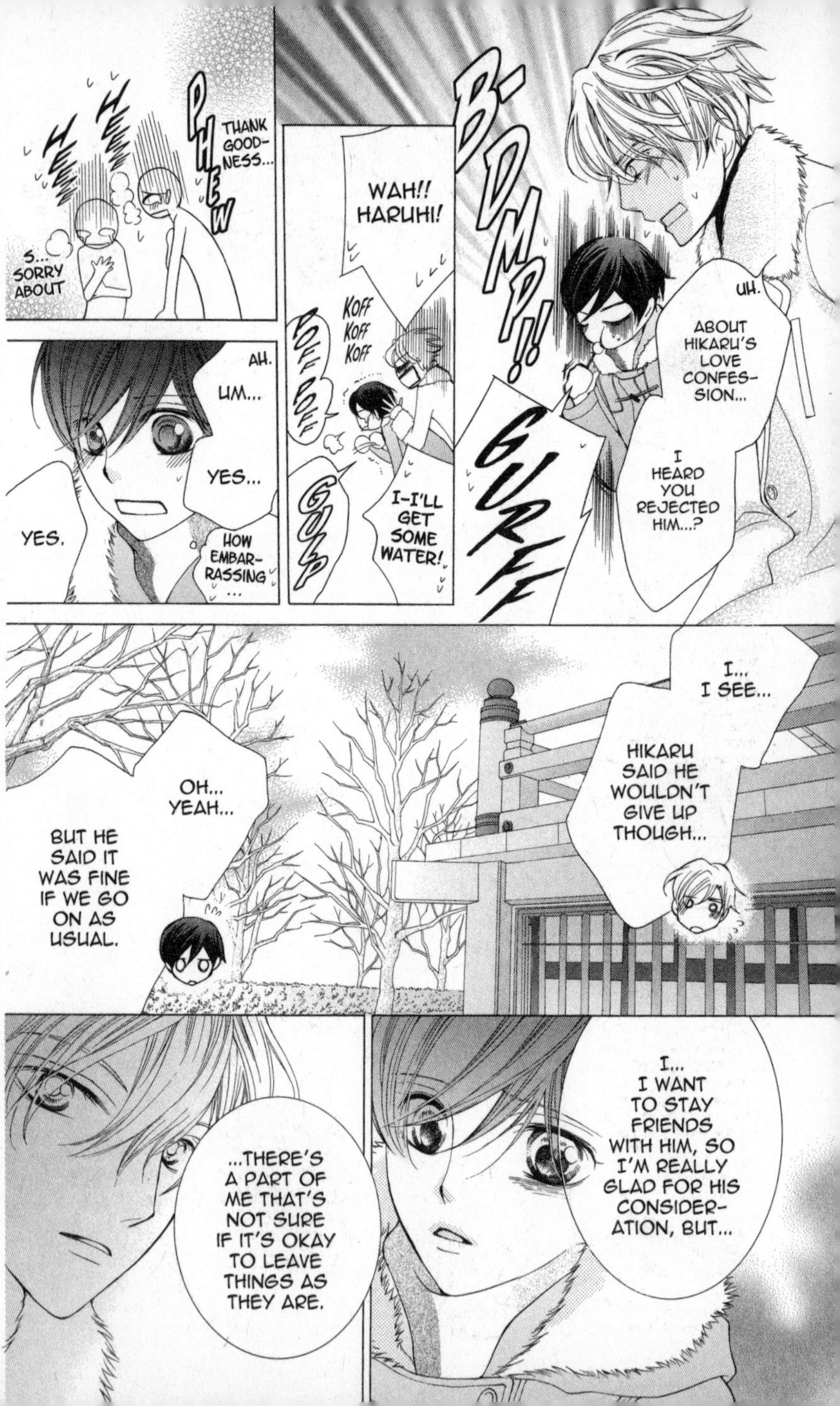
UH.
ABOUT HIKARU'S LOVE CONFES-SION...
I HEARD YOU REJECTED HIM...?
B-DUMP!!
GUFF
WAH!! HARUHI!
KOFF KOFF KOFF
KOFF KOFF
I-I'LL GET SOME WATER!
GULP
PHEW
THANK GOODNESS...
HEE HEE
S... SORRY ABOUT
AH.
UM...
YES...
YES.
HOW EMBAR-RASSING...
I... I SEE...
HIKARU SAID HE WOULDN'T GIVE UP THOUGH...
OH... YEAH...
BUT HE SAID IT WAS FINE IF WE GO ON AS USUAL.
I... I WANT TO STAY FRIENDS WITH HIM, SO I'M REALLY GLAD FOR HIS CONSIDER-ATION, BUT...
...THERE'S A PART OF ME THAT'S NOT SURE IF IT'S OKAY TO LEAVE THINGS AS THEY ARE.

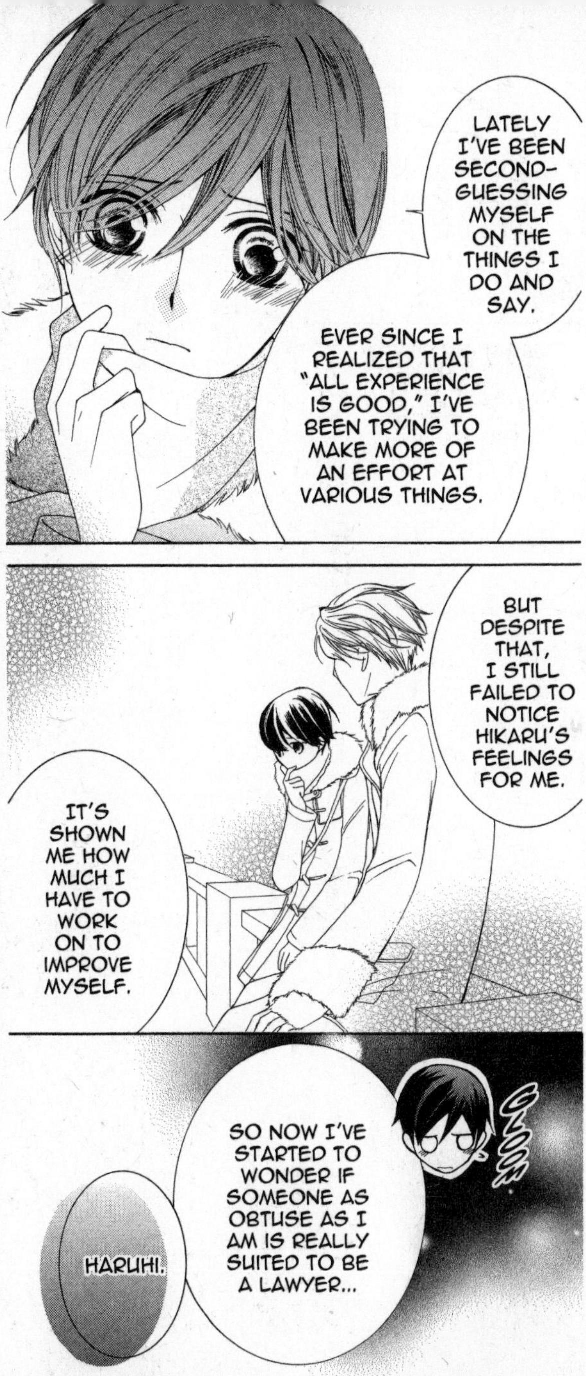
LATELY I'VE BEEN SECOND-GUESSING MYSELF ON THE THINGS I DO AND SAY.
EVER SINCE I REALIZED THAT "ALL EXPERIENCE IS GOOD," I'VE BEEN TRYING TO MAKE MORE OF AN EFFORT AT VARIOUS THINGS.
BUT DESPITE THAT, I STILL FAILED TO NOTICE HIKARU'S FEELINGS FOR ME.
IT'S SHOWN ME HOW MUCH I HAVE TO WORK ON TO IMPROVE MYSELF.
GLOOM
SO NOW I'VE STARTED TO WONDER IF SOMEONE AS OBTUSE AS I AM IS REALLY SUITED TO BE A LAWYER...
HARUHI.

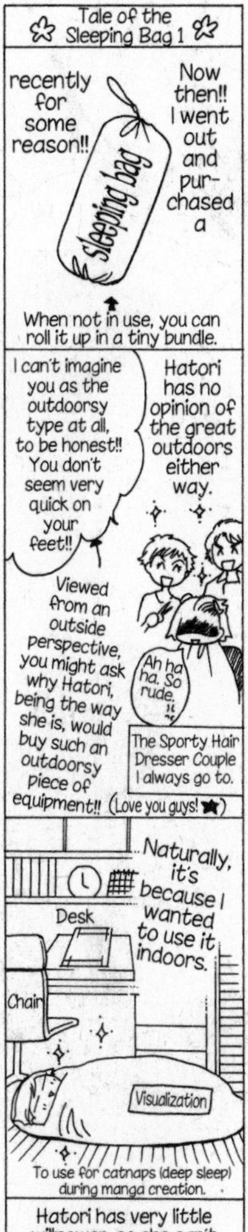
Tale of the Sleeping Bag 1
Now then!! I went out and purchased a
sleeping bag
recently for some reason!!
When not in use, you can roll it up in a tiny bundle.
Hatori has no opinion of the great outdoors either way.
I can't imagine you as the outdoorsy type at all, to be honest!! You don't seem very quick on your feet!!
Ah ha ha. So rude.
Viewed from an outside perspective, you might ask why Hatori, being the way she is, would buy such an outdoorsy piece of equipment!!
The Sporty Hair Dresser Couple I always go to.
(Love you guys! ★)
...Naturally, it's because I wanted to use it indoors.
Desk
Chair
Visualization
To use for catnaps (deep sleep) during manga creation.
Hatori has very little willpower, so she can't allow herself to go to her bedroom during deadlines. Which is why, every month during manga deadlines, she ends up sleeping in her chair a lot.
Variations

If I sleep in my bed, I won't get up again...

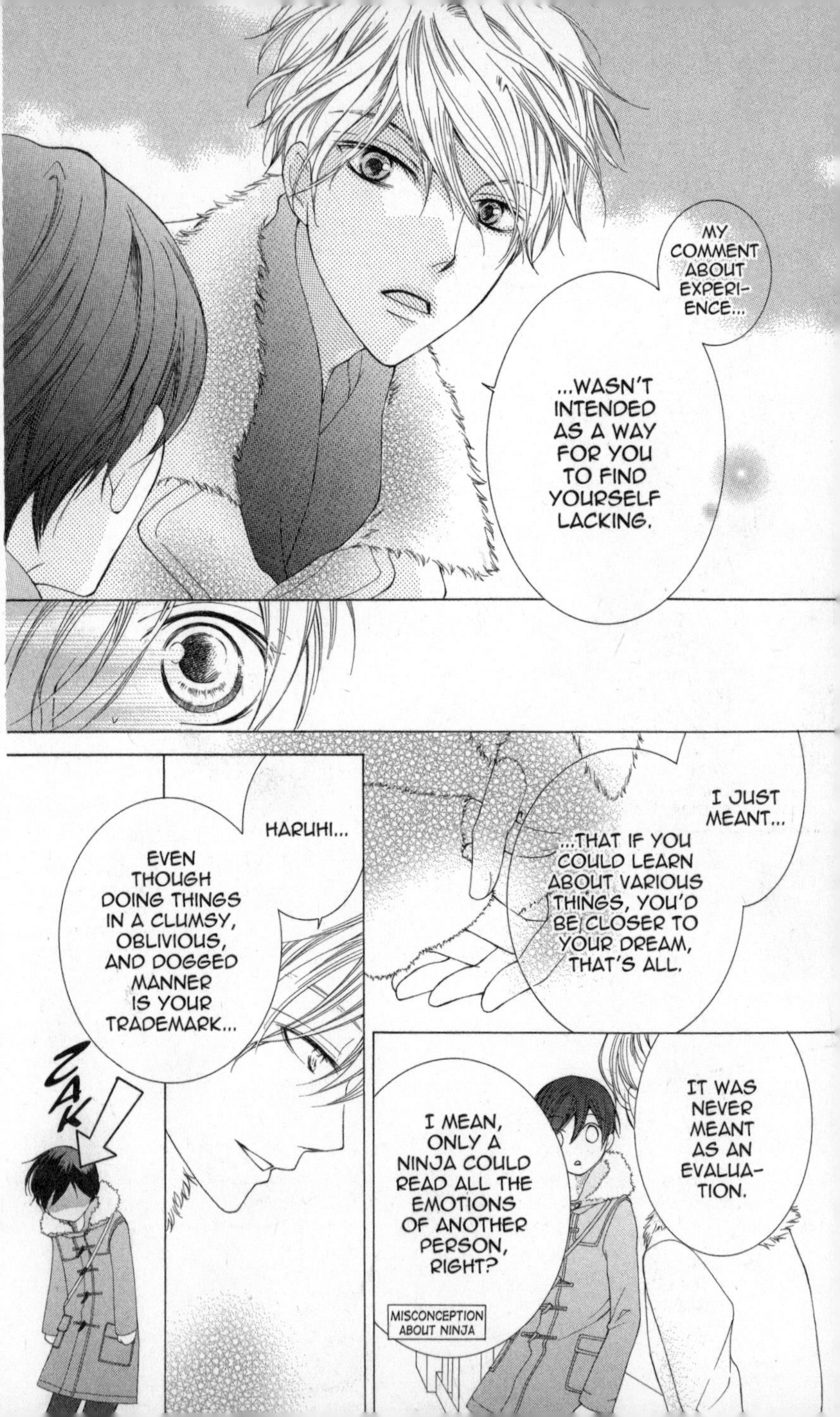

MY COMMENT ABOUT EXPERIENCE...
...WASN'T INTENDED AS A WAY FOR YOU TO FIND YOURSELF LACKING.
I JUST MEANT...
...THAT IF YOU COULD LEARN ABOUT VARIOUS THINGS, YOU'D BE CLOSER TO YOUR DREAM, THAT'S ALL.
IT WAS NEVER MEANT AS AN EVALUATION.
I MEAN, ONLY A NINJA COULD READ ALL THE EMOTIONS OF ANOTHER PERSON, RIGHT?
MISCONCEPTION ABOUT NINJA
HARUHI...
EVEN THOUGH DOING THINGS IN A CLUMSY, OBLIVIOUS, AND DOGGED MANNER IS YOUR TRADEMARK...
ZAK

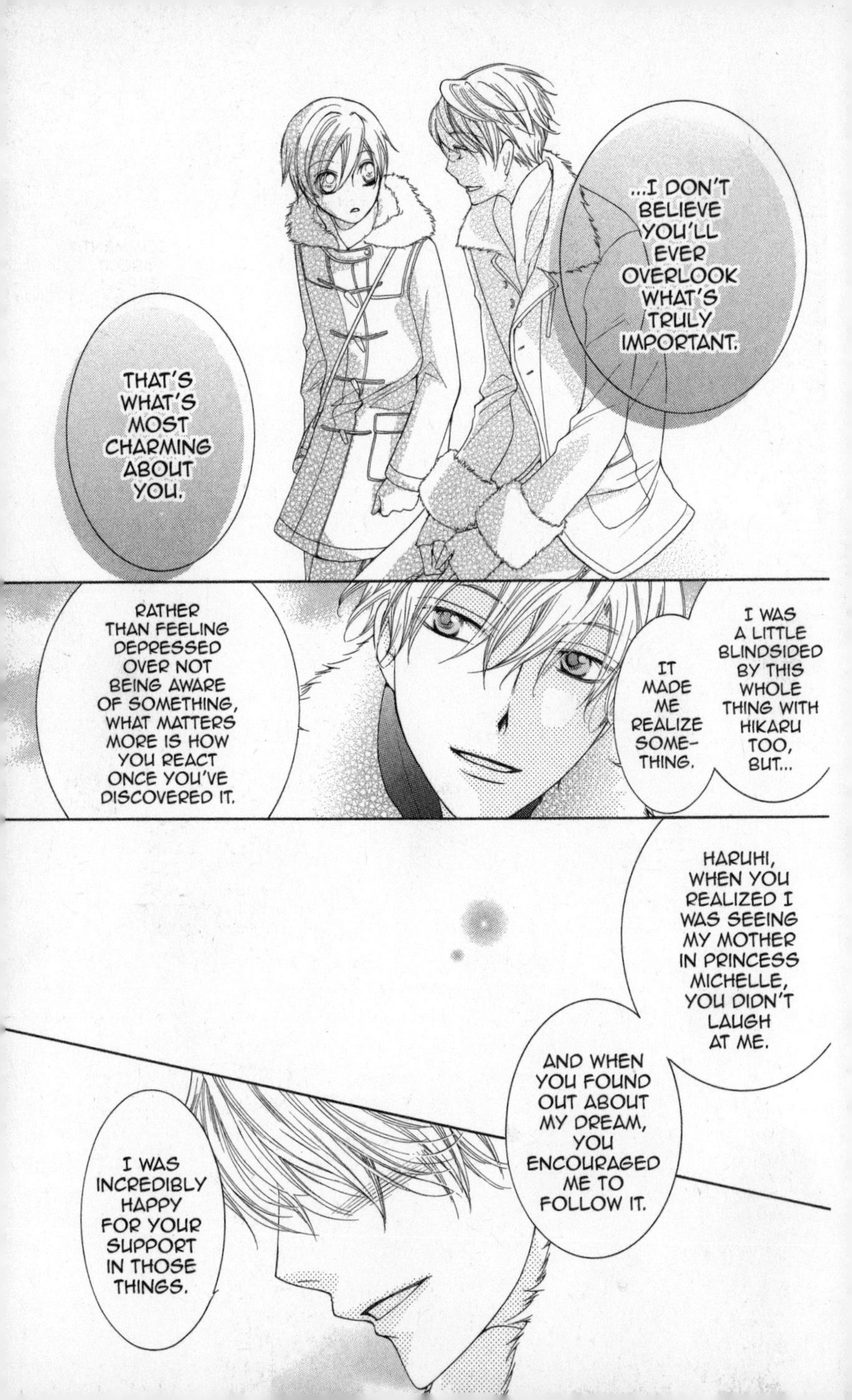
...I DON'T BELIEVE YOU'LL EVER OVERLOOK WHAT'S TRULY IMPORTANT.
THAT'S WHAT'S MOST CHARMING ABOUT YOU.
I WAS A LITTLE BLINDSIDED BY THIS WHOLE THING WITH HIKARU TOO, BUT...
IT MADE ME REALIZE SOME-THING.
RATHER THAN FEELING DEPRESSED OVER NOT BEING AWARE OF SOMETHING, WHAT MATTERS MORE IS HOW YOU REACT ONCE YOU'VE DISCOVERED IT.
HARUHI, WHEN YOU REALIZED I WAS SEEING MY MOTHER IN PRINCESS MICHELLE, YOU DIDN'T LAUGH AT ME.
AND WHEN YOU FOUND OUT ABOUT MY DREAM, YOU ENCOURAGED ME TO FOLLOW IT.
I WAS INCREDIBLY HAPPY FOR YOUR SUPPORT IN THOSE THINGS.

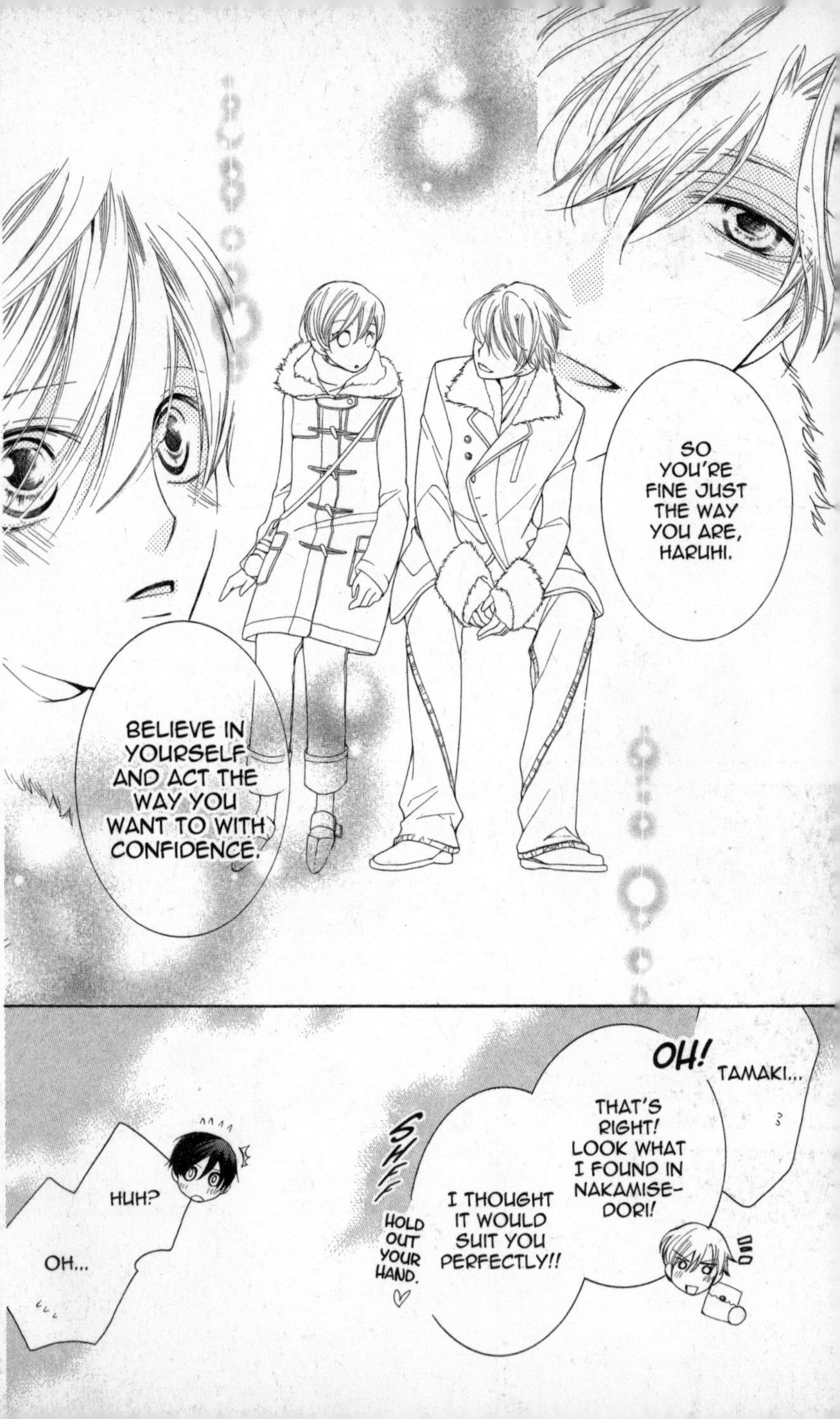
SO YOU'RE FINE JUST THE WAY YOU ARE, HARUHI.
BELIEVE IN YOURSELF AND ACT THE WAY YOU WANT TO WITH CONFIDENCE.
TAMAKI...
OH!
THAT'S RIGHT! LOOK WHAT I FOUND IN NAKAMISE-DORI!
I THOUGHT IT WOULD SUIT YOU PERFECTLY!!
SHFF
HOLD OUT YOUR HAND.
HUH?
OH...

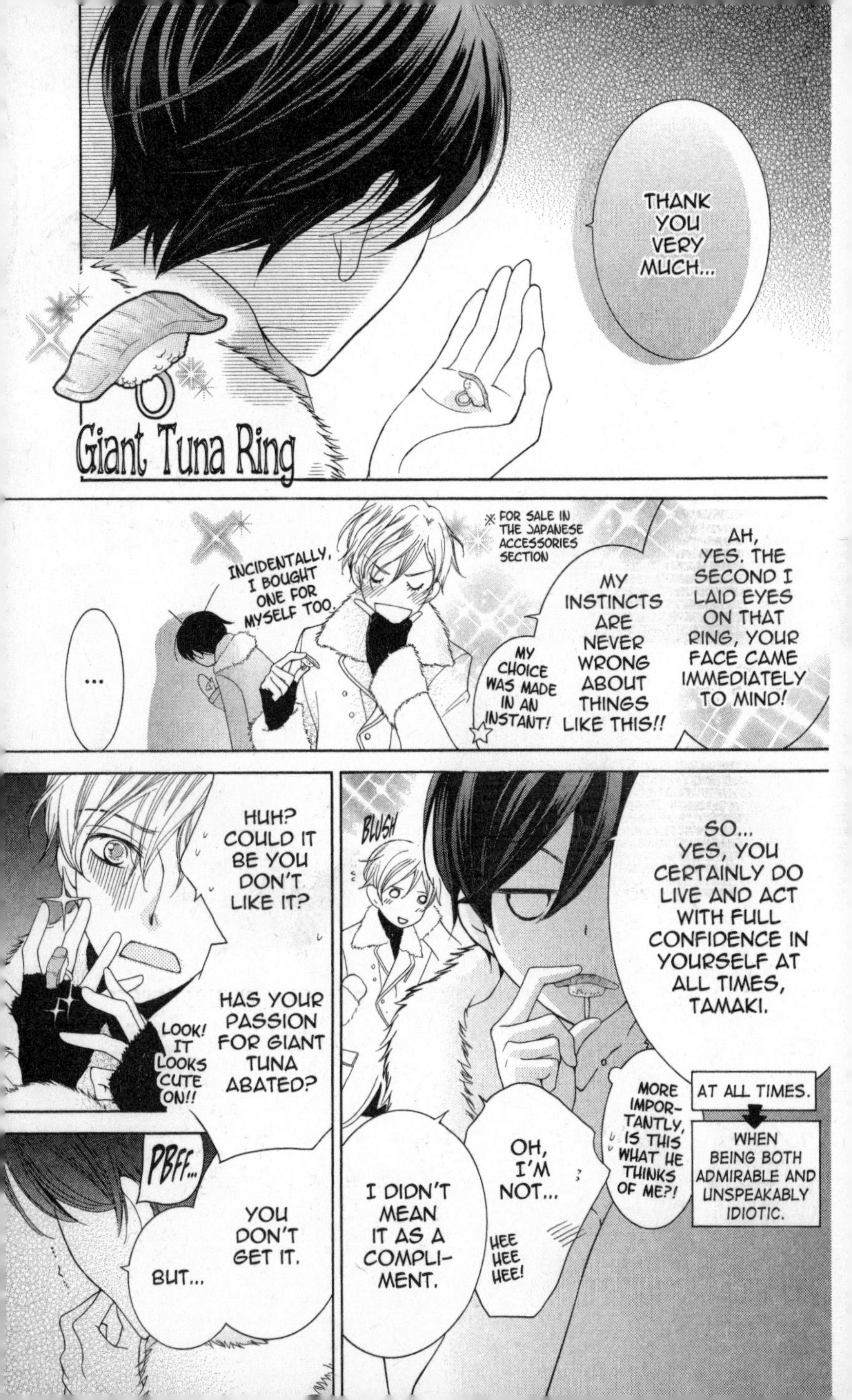
THANK YOU VERY MUCH...
Giant Tuna Ring
AH, YES. THE SECOND I LAID EYES ON THAT RING, YOUR FACE CAME IMMEDIATELY TO MIND!
MY INSTINCTS ARE NEVER WRONG ABOUT THINGS LIKE THIS!!
MY CHOICE WAS MADE IN AN INSTANT!
※ FOR SALE IN THE JAPANESE ACCESSORIES SECTION
INCIDENTALLY, I BOUGHT ONE FOR MYSELF TOO.
...
SO... YES, YOU CERTAINLY DO LIVE AND ACT WITH FULL CONFIDENCE IN YOURSELF AT ALL TIMES, TAMAKI.
BLUSH
AT ALL TIMES.
WHEN BEING BOTH ADMIRABLE AND UNSPEAKABLY IDIOTIC.
MORE IMPORTANTLY, IS THIS WHAT HE THINKS OF ME?!
OH, I'M NOT...
HEE HEE HEE!
I DIDN'T MEAN IT AS A COMPLIMENT.
HUH? COULD IT BE YOU DON'T LIKE IT?
HAS YOUR PASSION FOR GIANT TUNA ABATED?
LOOK! IT LOOKS CUTE ON!!
PBFF...
YOU DON'T GET IT.
BUT...

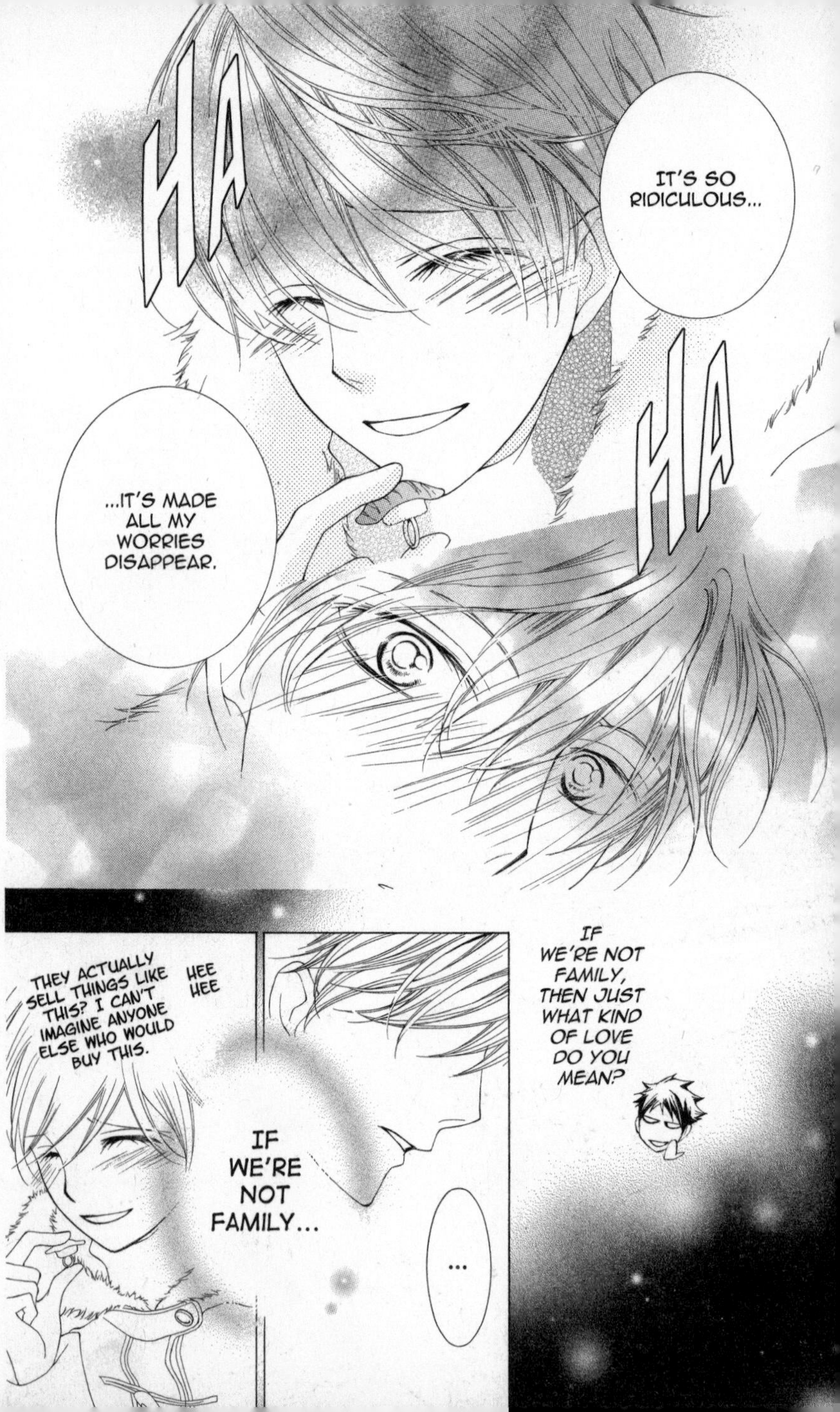
IT'S SO RIDICULOUS...
HA
HA
...IT'S MADE ALL MY WORRIES DISAPPEAR.
IF WE'RE NOT FAMILY, THEN JUST WHAT KIND OF LOVE DO YOU MEAN?
IF WE'RE NOT FAMILY...
...
THEY ACTUALLY SELL THINGS LIKE THIS? I CAN'T IMAGINE ANYONE ELSE WHO WOULD BUY THIS.
HEE HEE

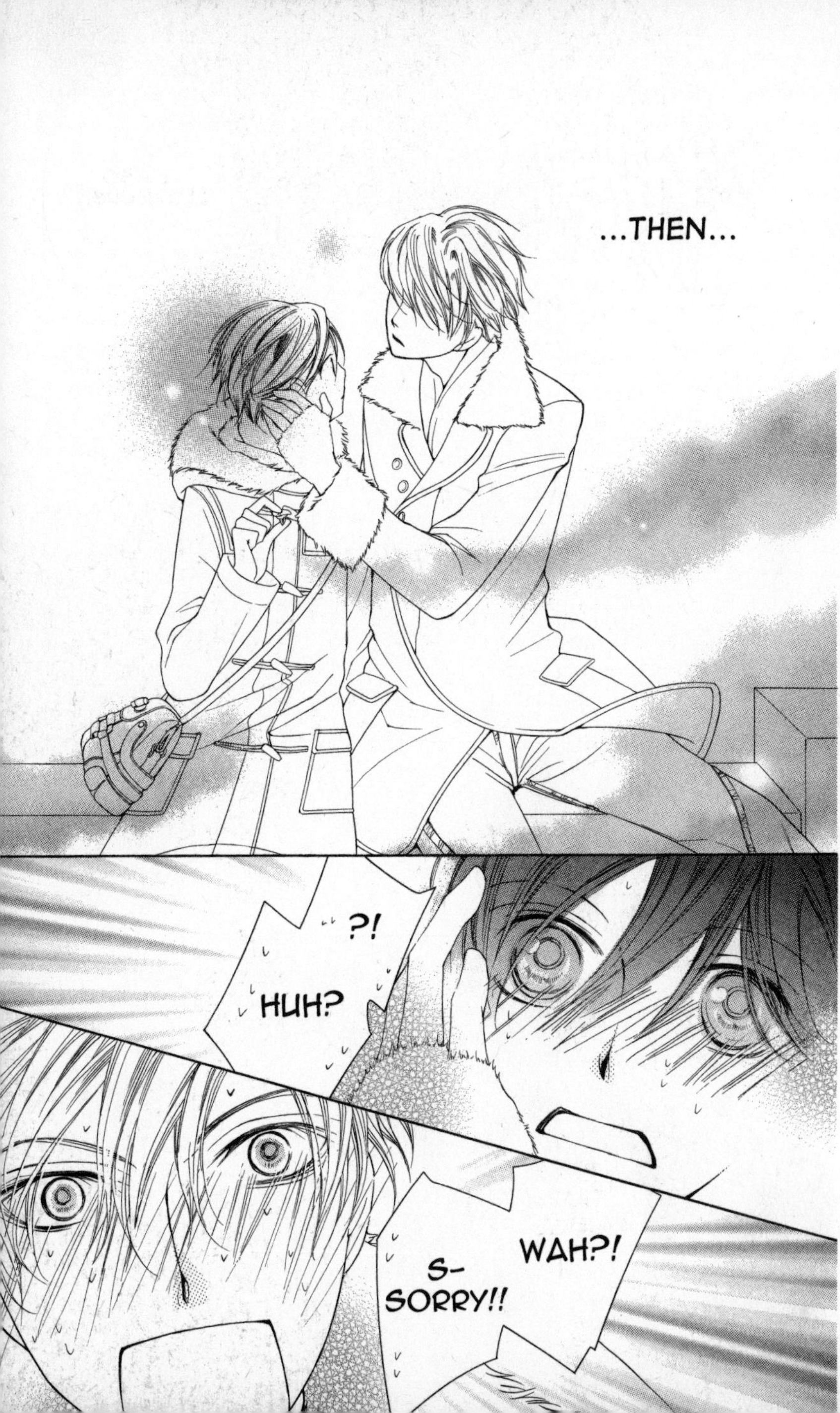
...THEN...
?!
HUH?
WAH?!
S- SORRY!!

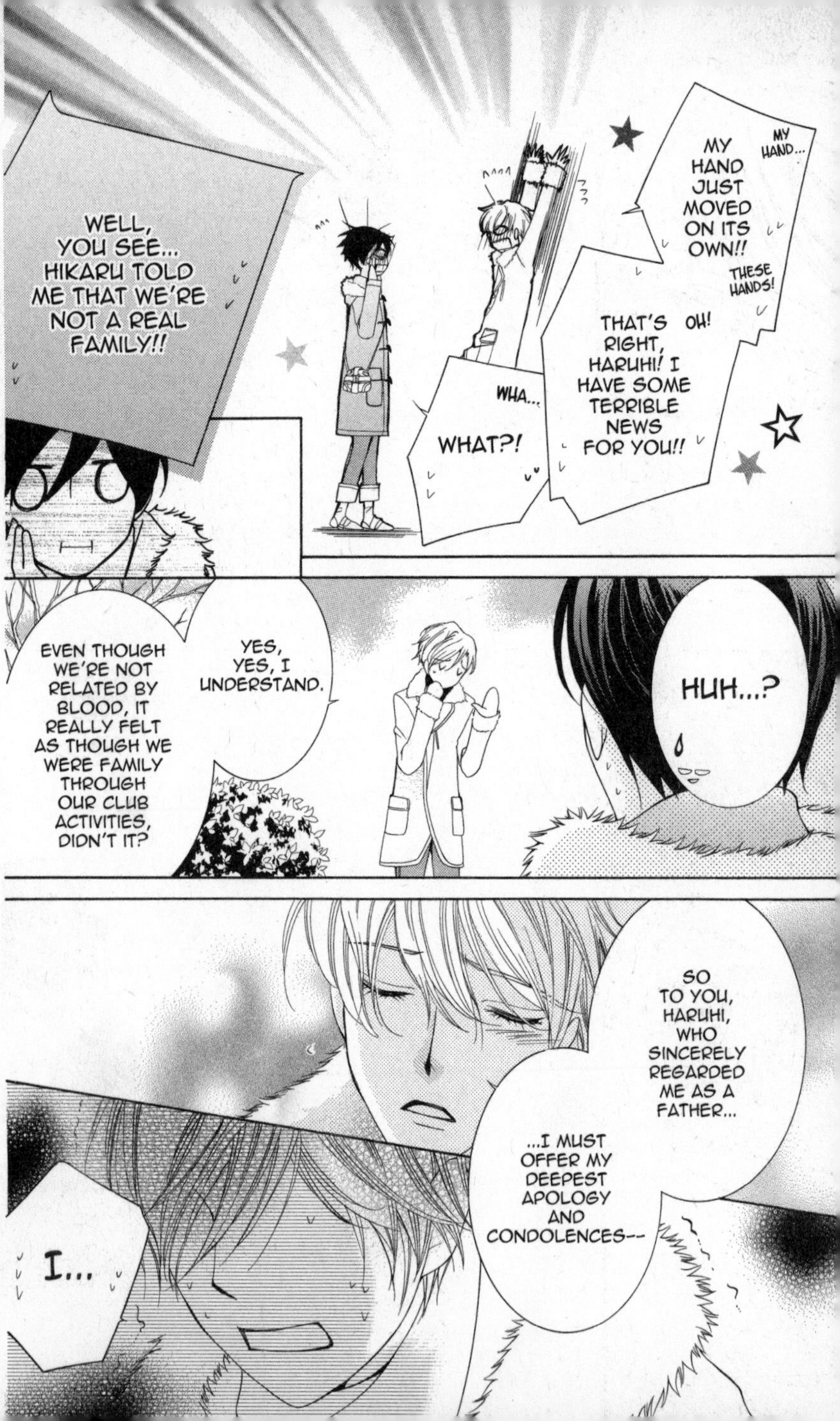
MY HAND JUST MOVED ON ITS OWN!!
MY HAND...
THESE HANDS!
OH!
THAT'S RIGHT, HARUHI! I HAVE SOME TERRIBLE NEWS FOR YOU!!
WHA...
WHAT?!
WELL, YOU SEE... HIKARU TOLD ME THAT WE'RE NOT A REAL FAMILY!!
HUH...?
YES, YES, I UNDERSTAND.
EVEN THOUGH WE'RE NOT RELATED BY BLOOD, IT REALLY FELT AS THOUGH WE WERE FAMILY THROUGH OUR CLUB ACTIVITIES, DIDN'T IT?
SO TO YOU, HARUHI, WHO SINCERELY REGARDED ME AS A FATHER...
...I MUST OFFER MY DEEPEST APOLOGY AND CONDOLENCES--
I...

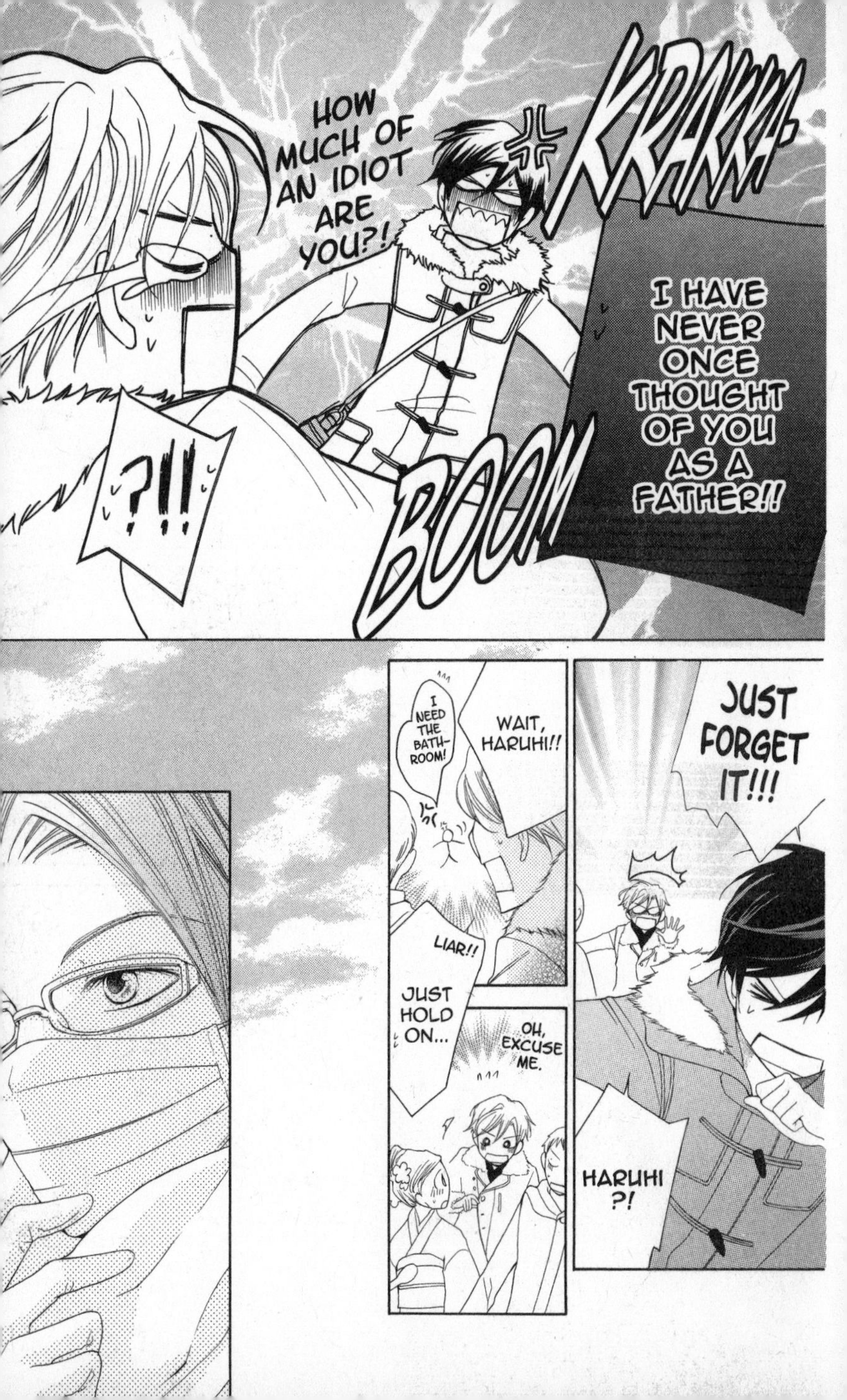
KRAKKA
I HAVE NEVER ONCE THOUGHT OF YOU AS A FATHER!!
HOW MUCH OF AN IDIOT ARE YOU?!
BOOM
?!!
JUST FORGET IT!!!
HARUHI ?!
WAIT, HARUHI!!
I NEED THE BATH-ROOM!
LIAR!!
JUST HOLD ON...
OH, EXCUSE ME.

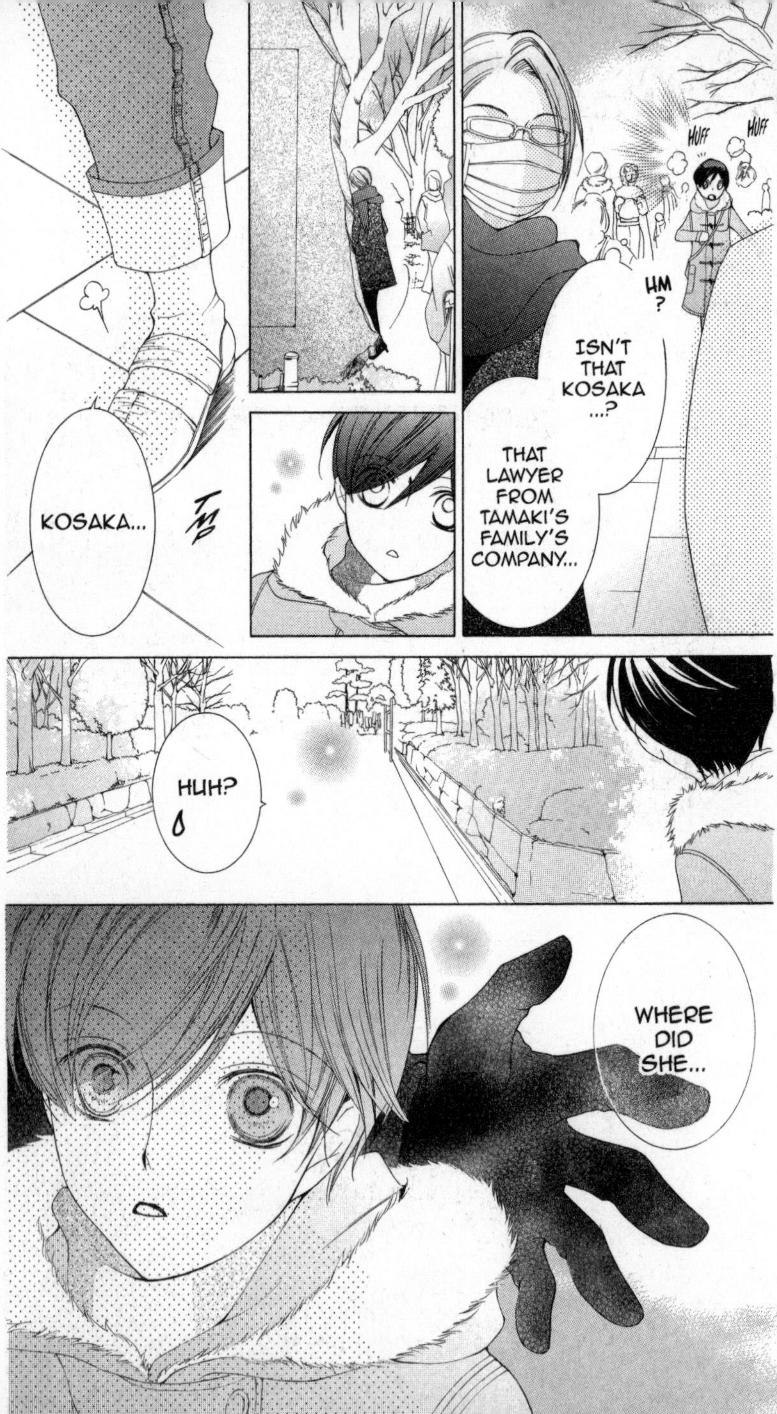
HUFF
HUFF
HM?
ISN'T THAT KOSAKA ...?
THAT LAWYER FROM TAMAKI'S FAMILY'S COMPANY...
TMP
KOSAKA...
HUH?
WHERE DID SHE...

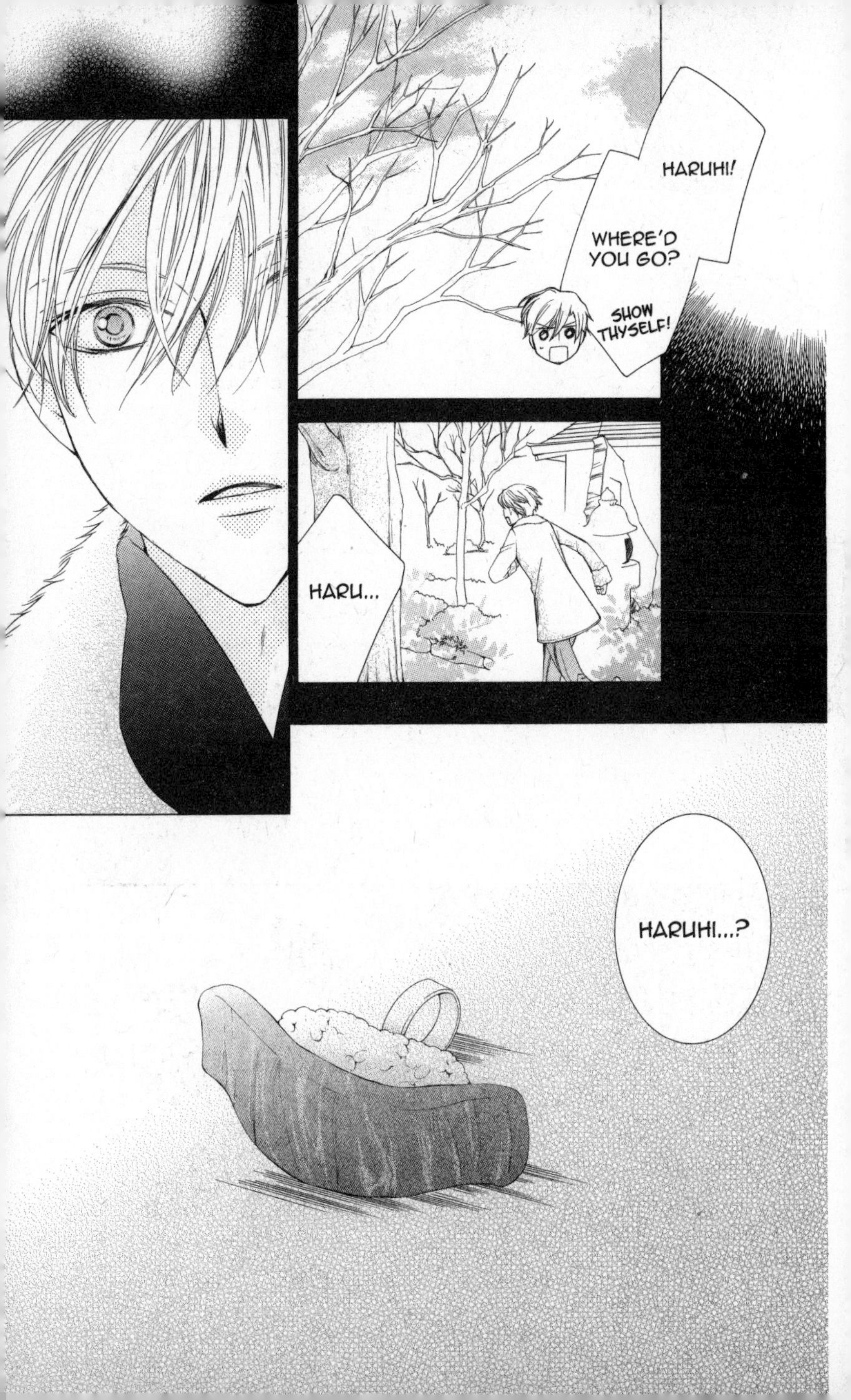
HARUHI!
WHERE'D YOU GO?
SHOW THYSELF!
HARU...
HARUHI...?

GUEST ROOM: FAXES ② SPECIAL THANKS TO HIRO FUJIWARA!!

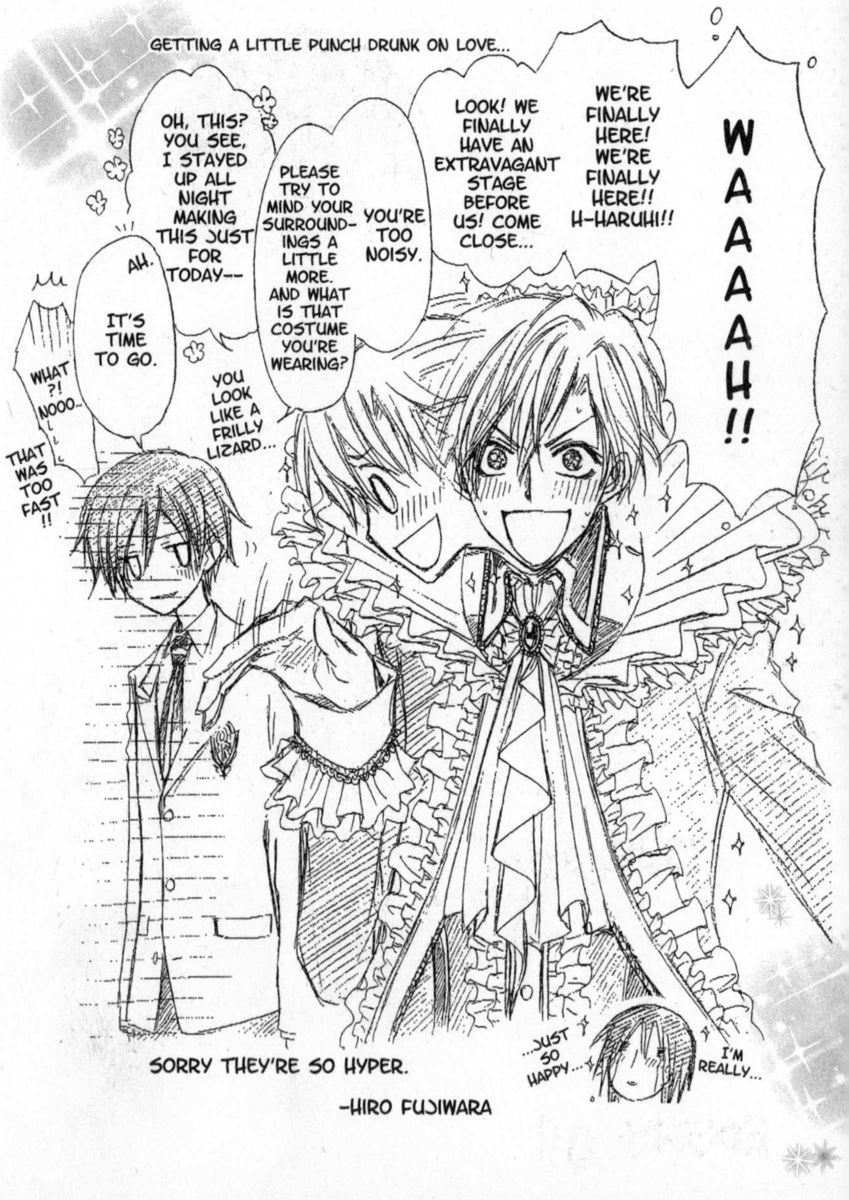
GETTING A LITTLE PUNCH DRUNK ON LOVE...
WAAAAAH!!
WE'RE FINALLY HERE! WE'RE FINALLY HERE!! H-HARUHI!!
LOOK! WE FINALLY HAVE AN EXTRAVAGANT STAGE BEFORE US! COME CLOSE...
YOU'RE TOO NOISY.
PLEASE TRY TO MIND YOUR SURROUNDINGS A LITTLE MORE. AND WHAT IS THAT COSTUME YOU'RE WEARING?
YOU LOOK LIKE A FRILLY LIZARD...
OH, THIS? YOU SEE, I STAYED UP ALL NIGHT MAKING THIS JUST FOR TODAY--
AH.
IT'S TIME TO GO.
WHAT?! NOOO~
THAT WAS TOO FAST!!
I'M REALLY...
...JUST SO HAPPY...
SORRY THEY'RE SO HYPER.
-HIRO FUJIWARA

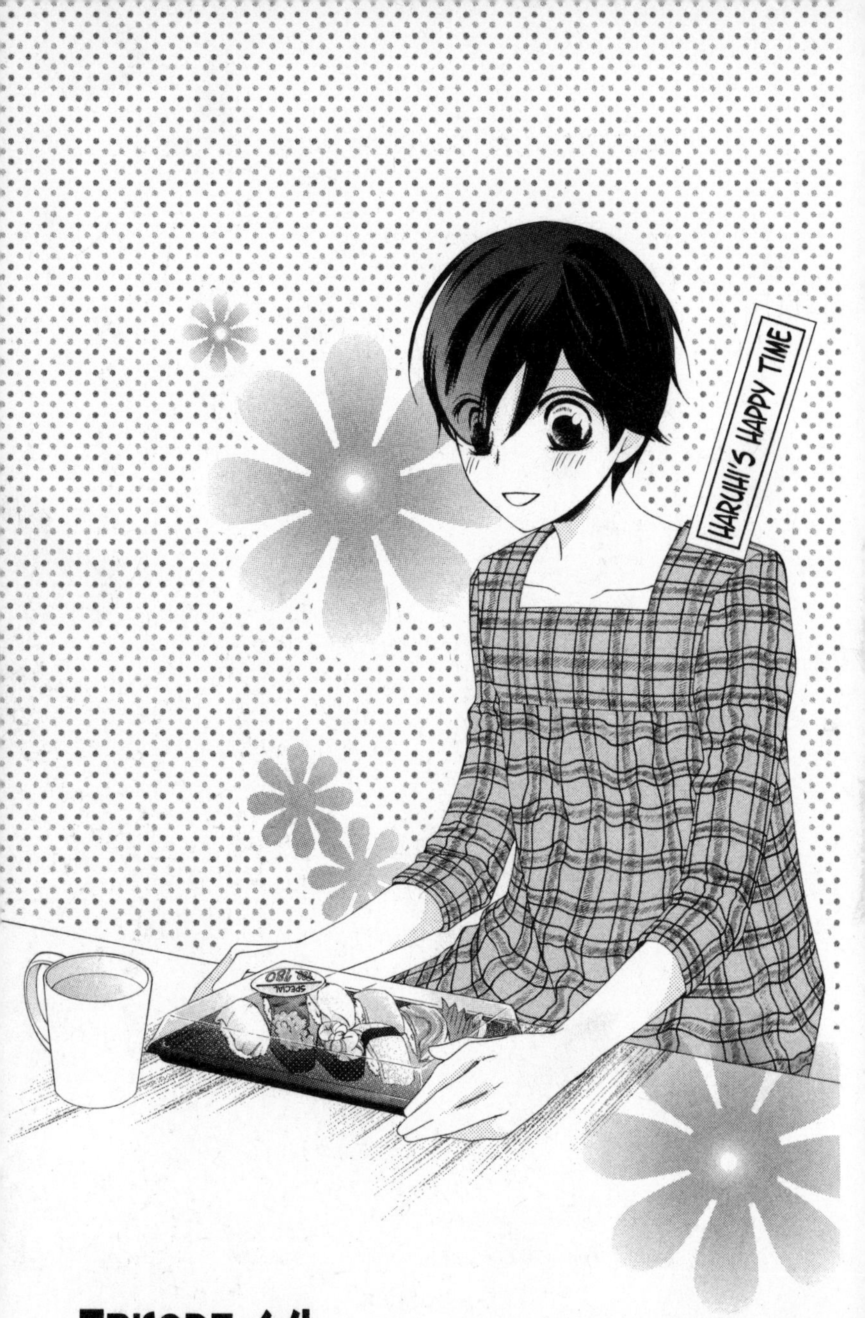
HARUHI'S HAPPY TIME

EPISODE 64

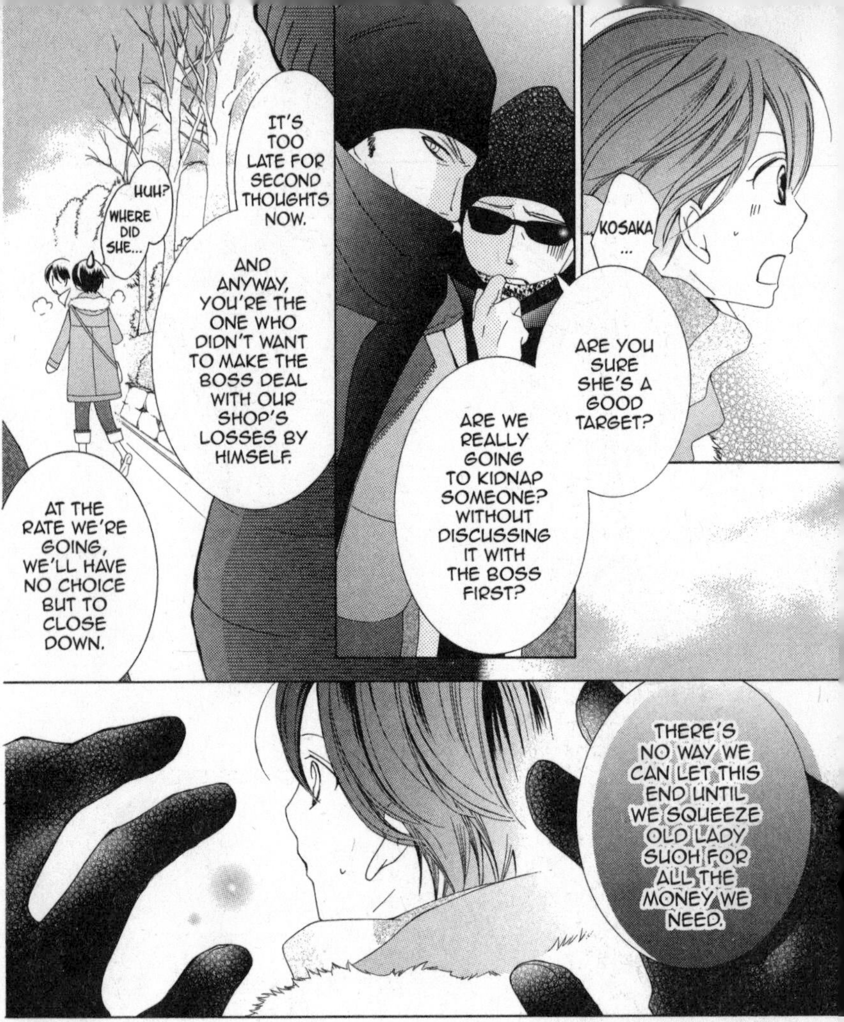
KOSAKA...
ARE YOU SURE SHE'S A GOOD TARGET?
ARE WE REALLY GOING TO KIDNAP SOMEONE? WITHOUT DISCUSSING IT WITH THE BOSS FIRST?
IT'S TOO LATE FOR SECOND THOUGHTS NOW.
AND ANYWAY, YOU'RE THE ONE WHO DIDN'T WANT TO MAKE THE BOSS DEAL WITH OUR SHOP'S LOSSES BY HIMSELF.
HUH? WHERE DID SHE...
AT THE RATE WE'RE GOING, WE'LL HAVE NO CHOICE BUT TO CLOSE DOWN.
THERE'S NO WAY WE CAN LET THIS END UNTIL WE SQUEEZE OLD LADY SUOH FOR ALL THE MONEY WE NEED.

SUPPORTING CHARACTERS INTRODUCTION

Mei Yasumura

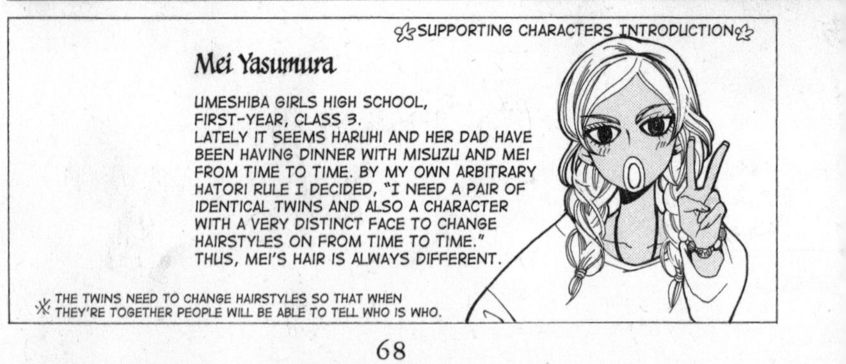

UMESHIBA GIRLS HIGH SCHOOL, FIRST-YEAR, CLASS 3.
LATELY IT SEEMS HARUHI AND HER DAD HAVE BEEN HAVING DINNER WITH MISUZU AND MEI FROM TIME TO TIME. BY MY OWN ARBITRARY HATORI RULE I DECIDED, "I NEED A PAIR OF IDENTICAL TWINS AND ALSO A CHARACTER WITH A VERY DISTINCT FACE TO CHANGE HAIRSTYLES ON FROM TIME TO TIME."
THUS, MEI'S HAIR IS ALWAYS DIFFERENT.

※ THE TWINS NEED TO CHANGE HAIRSTYLES SO THAT WHEN THEY'RE TOGETHER PEOPLE WILL BE ABLE TO TELL WHO IS WHO.

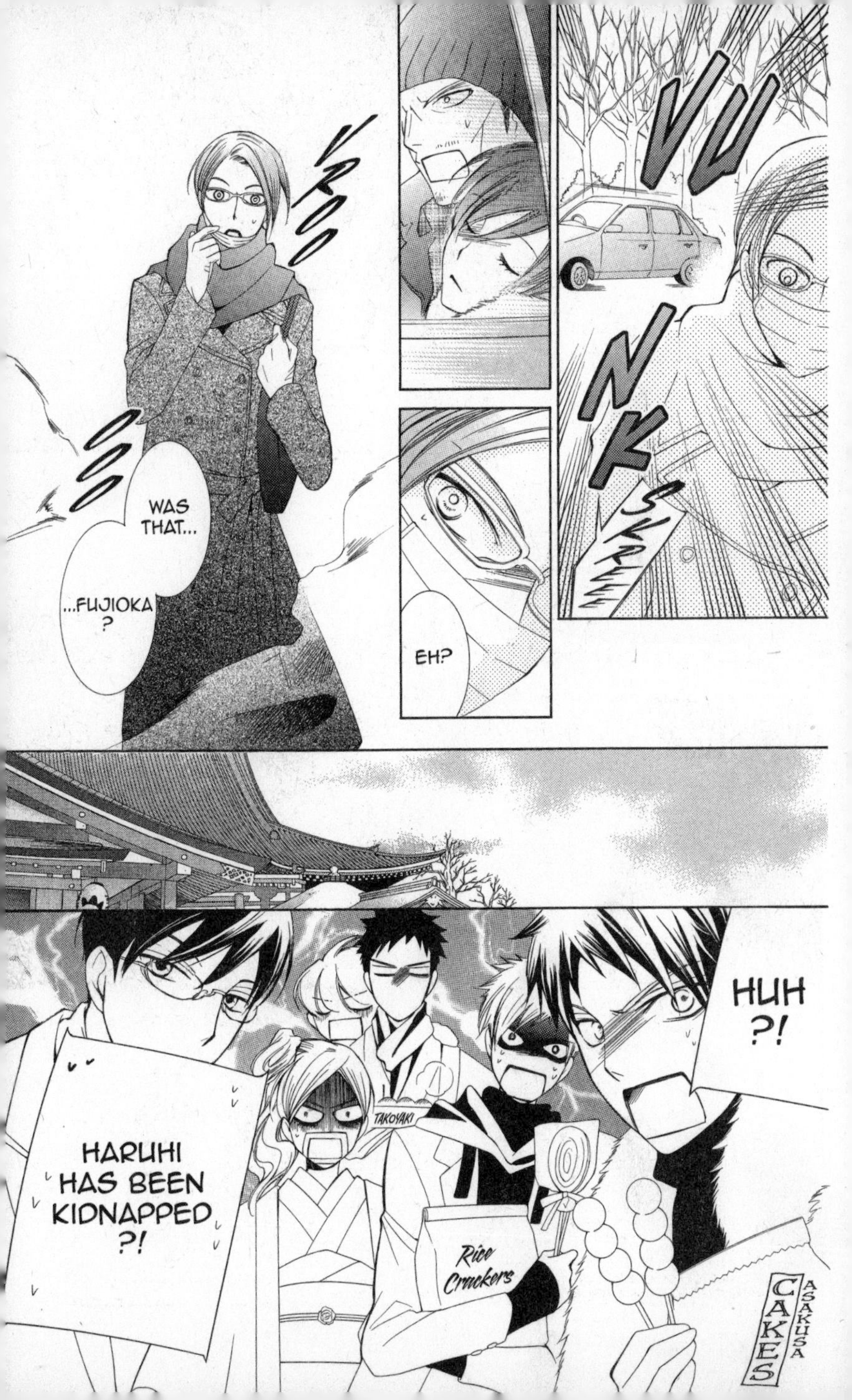
VUNNK
SKREE
EH?
VROOO
OOO
WAS THAT...
...FUJIOKA?
HUH?!
HARUHI HAS BEEN KIDNAPPED?!
TAKOYAKI
Rice Crackers
ASAKUSA CAKES

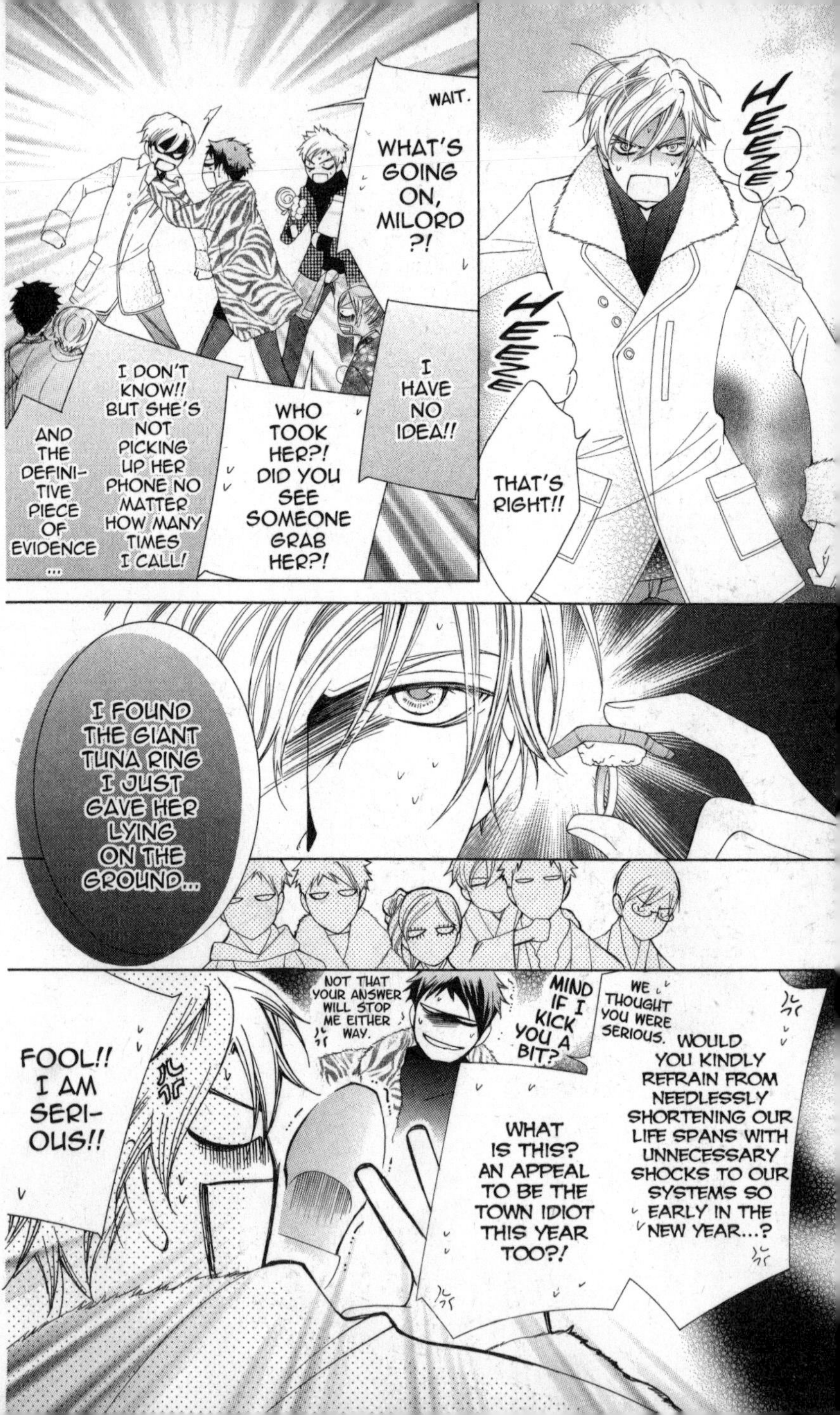
HEEZE
HEEZE
THAT'S RIGHT!!
WAIT.
WHAT'S GOING ON, MILORD?!
I HAVE NO IDEA!!
WHO TOOK HER?! DID YOU SEE SOMEONE GRAB HER?!
I DON'T KNOW!! BUT SHE'S NOT PICKING UP HER PHONE NO MATTER HOW MANY TIMES I CALL!
AND THE DEFINITIVE PIECE OF EVIDENCE...
I FOUND THE GIANT TUNA RING I JUST GAVE HER LYING ON THE GROUND...
WOULD YOU KINDLY REFRAIN FROM NEEDLESSLY SHORTENING OUR LIFE SPANS WITH UNNECESSARY SHOCKS TO OUR SYSTEMS SO EARLY IN THE NEW YEAR...?
WE THOUGHT YOU WERE SERIOUS.
WHAT IS THIS? AN APPEAL TO BE THE TOWN IDIOT THIS YEAR TOO?!
MIND IF I KICK YOU A BIT?
NOT THAT YOUR ANSWER WILL STOP ME EITHER WAY.
FOOL!! I AM SERIOUS!!

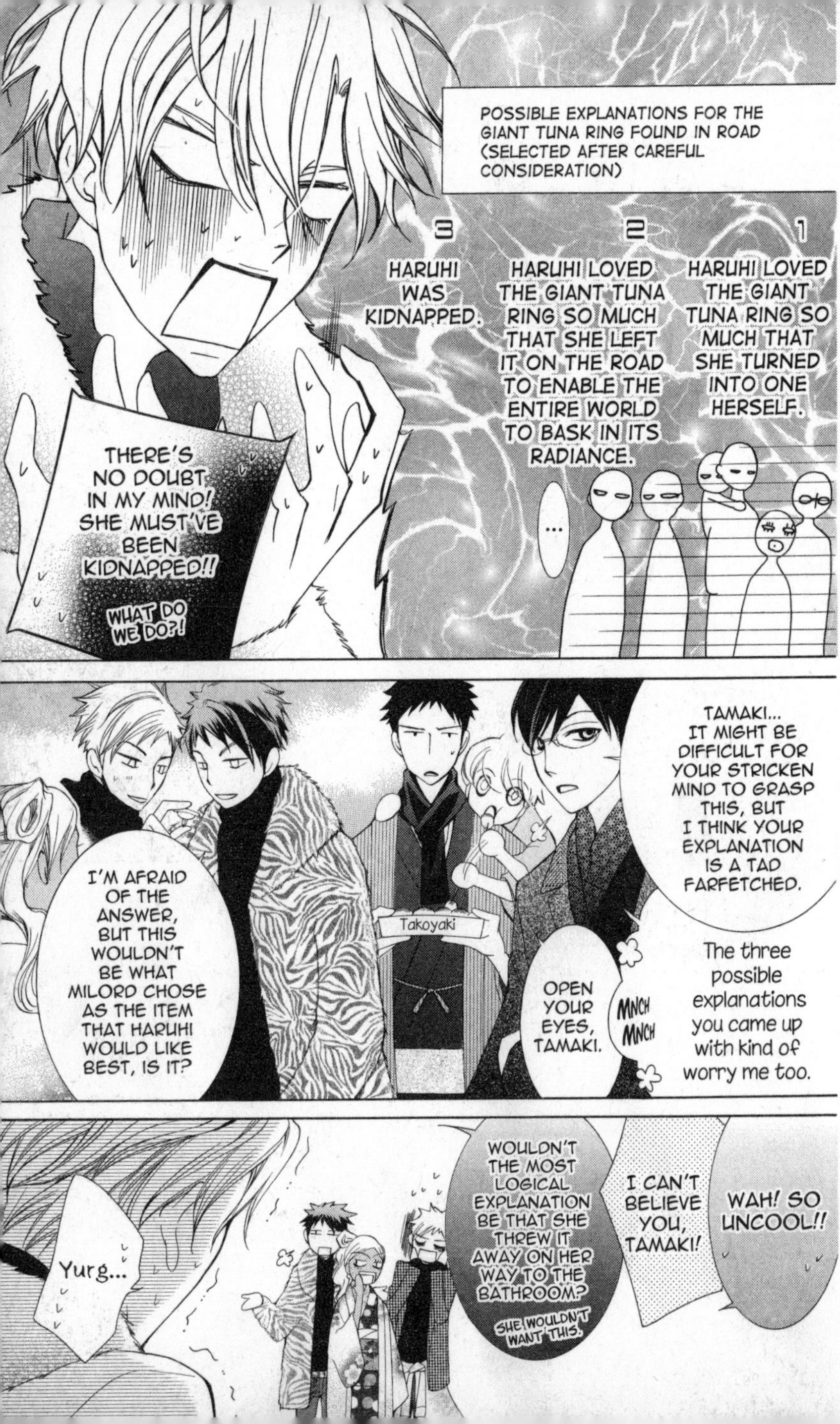
POSSIBLE EXPLANATIONS FOR THE GIANT TUNA RING FOUND IN ROAD (SELECTED AFTER CAREFUL CONSIDERATION)
1
HARUHI LOVED THE GIANT TUNA RING SO MUCH THAT SHE TURNED INTO ONE HERSELF.
2
HARUHI LOVED THE GIANT TUNA RING SO MUCH THAT SHE LEFT IT ON THE ROAD TO ENABLE THE ENTIRE WORLD TO BASK IN ITS RADIANCE.
3
HARUHI WAS KIDNAPPED.
...
THERE'S NO DOUBT IN MY MIND! SHE MUST'VE BEEN KIDNAPPED!!
WHAT DO WE DO?!
TAMAKI... IT MIGHT BE DIFFICULT FOR YOUR STRICKEN MIND TO GRASP THIS, BUT I THINK YOUR EXPLANATION IS A TAD FARFETCHED.
The three possible explanations you came up with kind of worry me too.
MNCH MNCH
OPEN YOUR EYES, TAMAKI.
Takoyaki
I'M AFRAID OF THE ANSWER, BUT THIS WOULDN'T BE WHAT MILORD CHOSE AS THE ITEM THAT HARUHI WOULD LIKE BEST, IS IT?
WAH! SO UNCOOL!!
I CAN'T BELIEVE YOU, TAMAKI!
WOULDN'T THE MOST LOGICAL EXPLANATION BE THAT SHE THREW IT AWAY ON HER WAY TO THE BATHROOM?
SHE WOULDN'T WANT THIS.
Yurg...

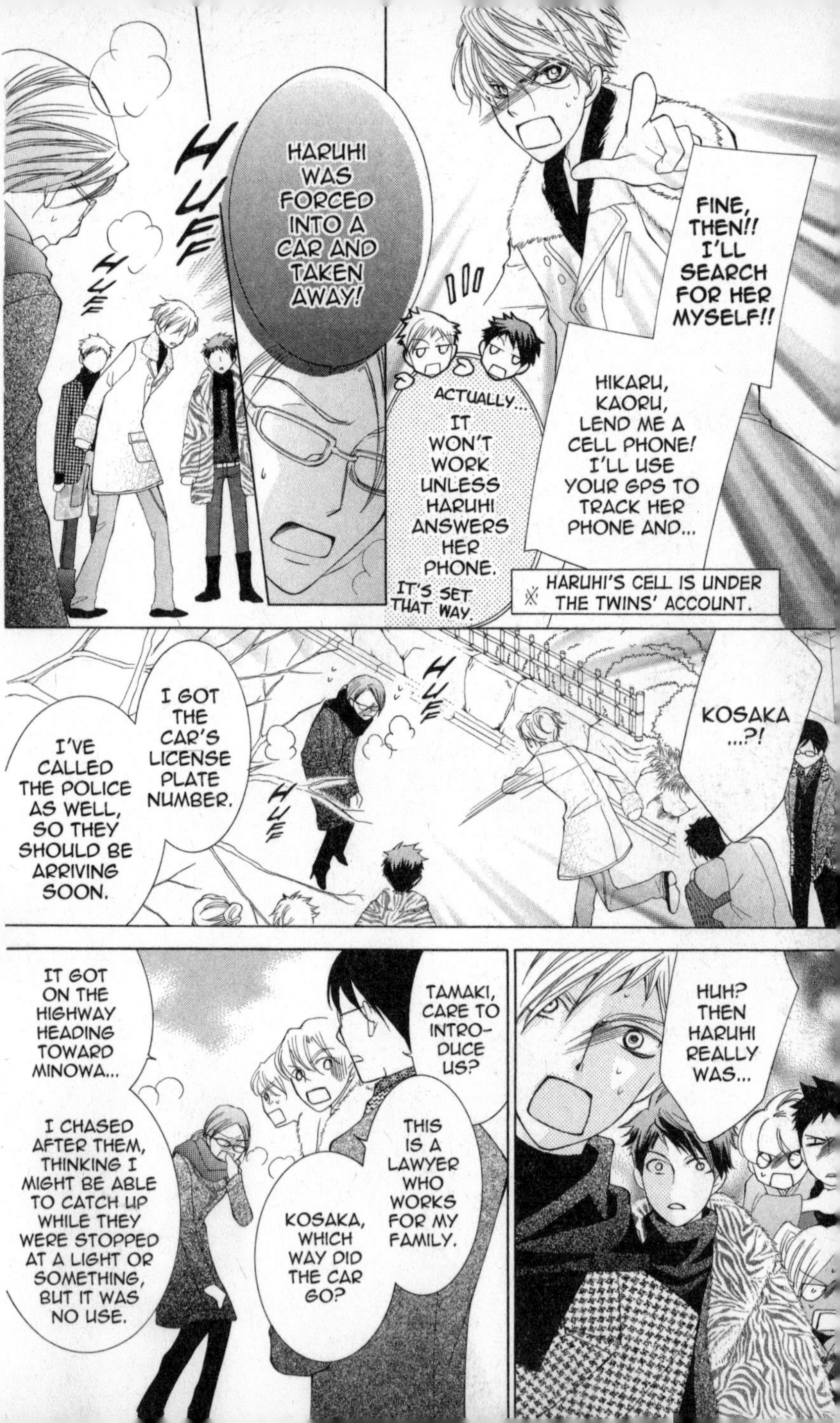
FINE, THEN!! I'LL SEARCH FOR HER MYSELF!!
HIKARU, KAORU, LEND ME A CELL PHONE! I'LL USE YOUR GPS TO TRACK HER PHONE AND...
※ HARUHI'S CELL IS UNDER THE TWINS' ACCOUNT.
ACTUALLY... IT WON'T WORK UNLESS HARUHI ANSWERS HER PHONE.
IT'S SET THAT WAY.
HUFF
HUE
HARUHI WAS FORCED INTO A CAR AND TAKEN AWAY!
KOSAKA ...?!
HUE
HUE
I GOT THE CAR'S LICENSE PLATE NUMBER.
I'VE CALLED THE POLICE AS WELL, SO THEY SHOULD BE ARRIVING SOON.
HUH? THEN HARUHI REALLY WAS...
TAMAKI, CARE TO INTRO-DUCE US?
THIS IS A LAWYER WHO WORKS FOR MY FAMILY.
KOSAKA, WHICH WAY DID THE CAR GO?
IT GOT ON THE HIGHWAY HEADING TOWARD MINOWA...
I CHASED AFTER THEM, THINKING I MIGHT BE ABLE TO CATCH UP WHILE THEY WERE STOPPED AT A LIGHT OR SOMETHING, BUT IT WAS NO USE.

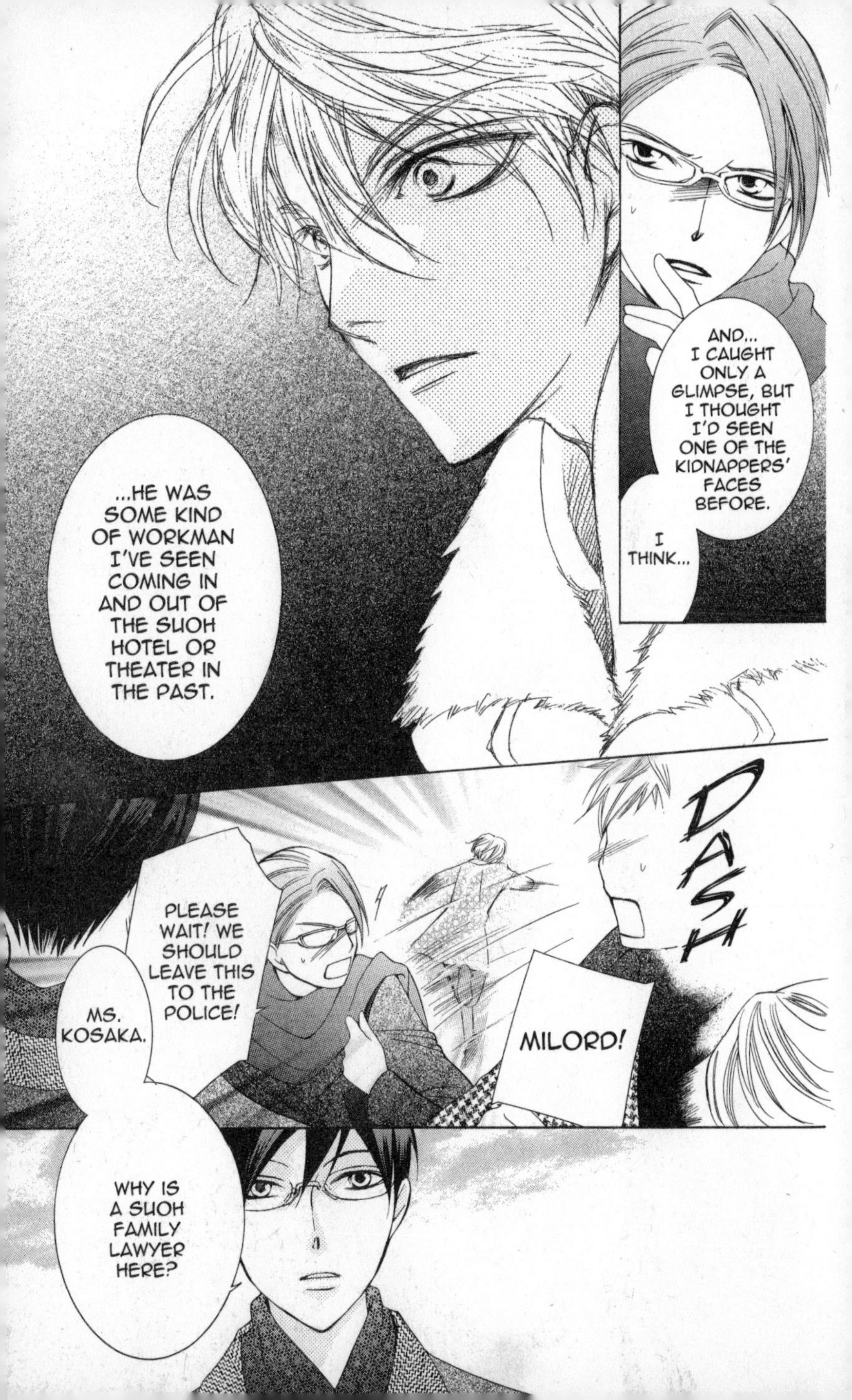
AND... I CAUGHT ONLY A GLIMPSE, BUT I THOUGHT I'D SEEN ONE OF THE KIDNAPPERS' FACES BEFORE.
I THINK...
...HE WAS SOME KIND OF WORKMAN I'VE SEEN COMING IN AND OUT OF THE SUOH HOTEL OR THEATER IN THE PAST.
DASH
MILORD!
PLEASE WAIT! WE SHOULD LEAVE THIS TO THE POLICE!
MS. KOSAKA.
WHY IS A SUOH FAMILY LAWYER HERE?

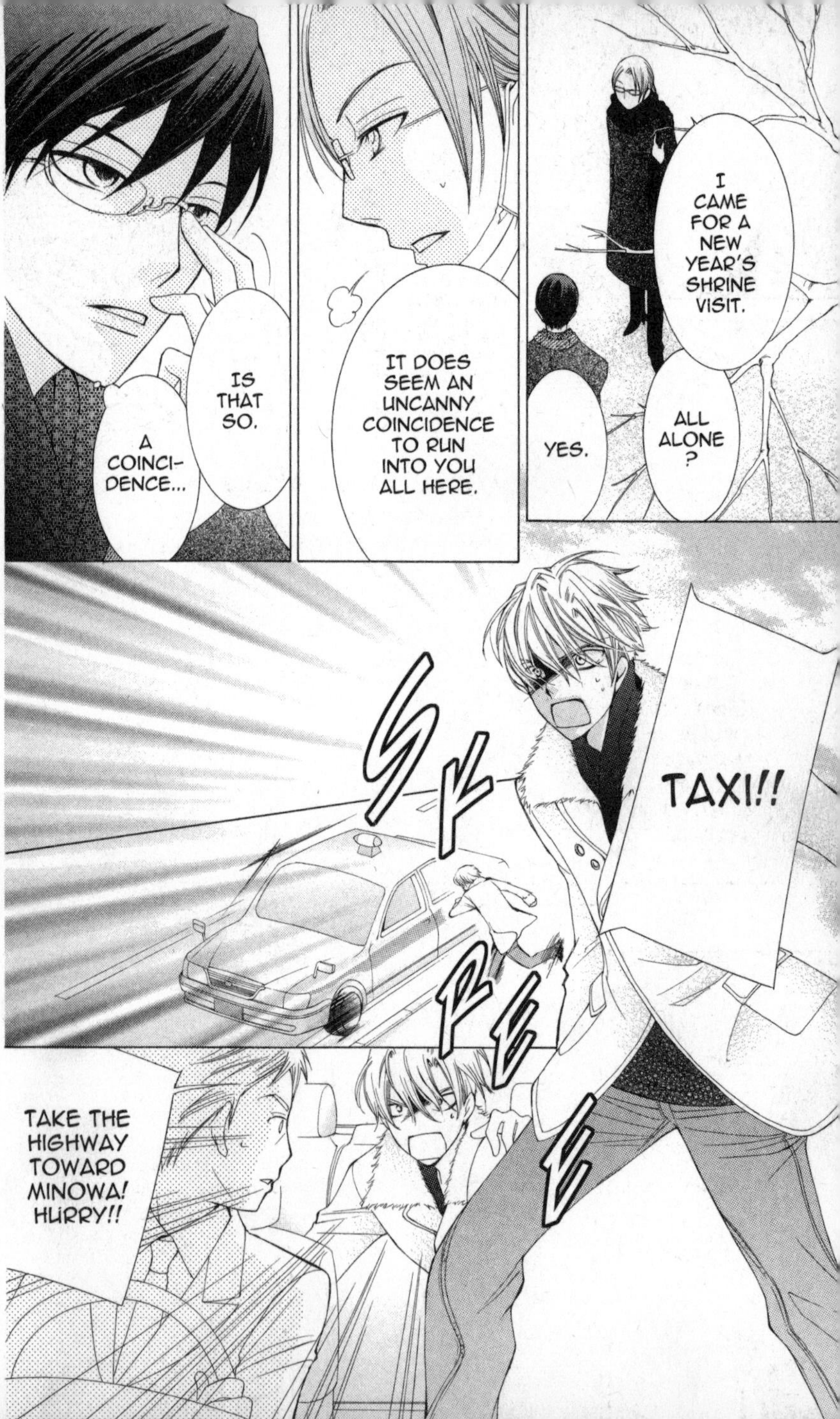
I CAME FOR A NEW YEAR'S SHRINE VISIT.
ALL ALONE?
YES.
IT DOES SEEM AN UNCANNY COINCIDENCE TO RUN INTO YOU ALL HERE.
IS THAT SO.
A COINCI-DENCE...
TAXI!!
SKREE
TAKE THE HIGHWAY TOWARD MINOWA! HURRY!!

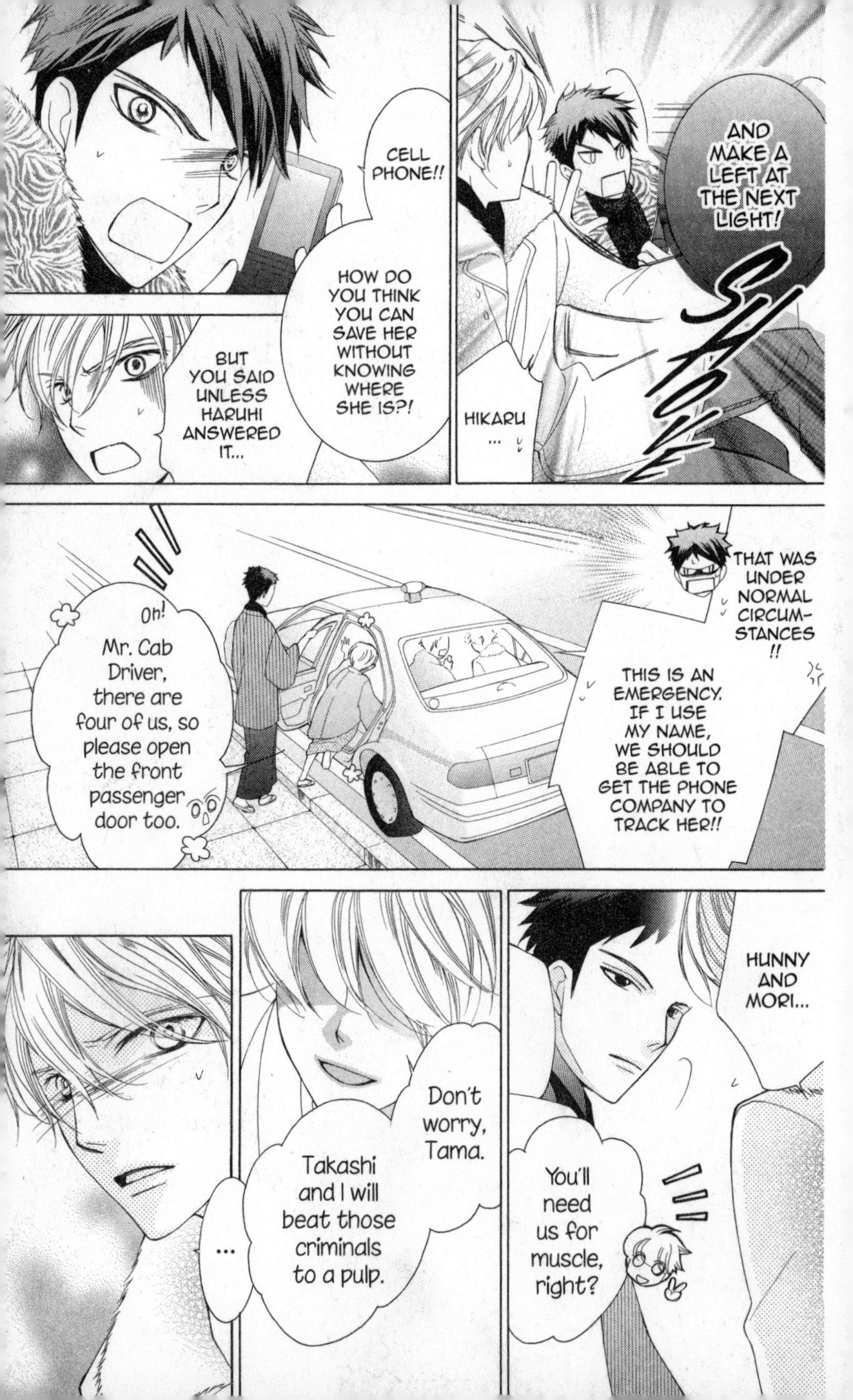
AND MAKE A LEFT AT THE NEXT LIGHT!
SHOOM
HIKARU...
CELL PHONE!!
HOW DO YOU THINK YOU CAN SAVE HER WITHOUT KNOWING WHERE SHE IS?!
BUT YOU SAID UNLESS HARUHI ANSWERED IT...
THAT WAS UNDER NORMAL CIRCUM-STANCES!!
THIS IS AN EMERGENCY. IF I USE MY NAME, WE SHOULD BE ABLE TO GET THE PHONE COMPANY TO TRACK HER!!
Oh!
Mr. Cab Driver, there are four of us, so please open the front passenger door too.
HUNNY AND MORI...
You'll need us for muscle, right?
Don't worry, Tama.
Takashi and I will beat those criminals to a pulp.
...

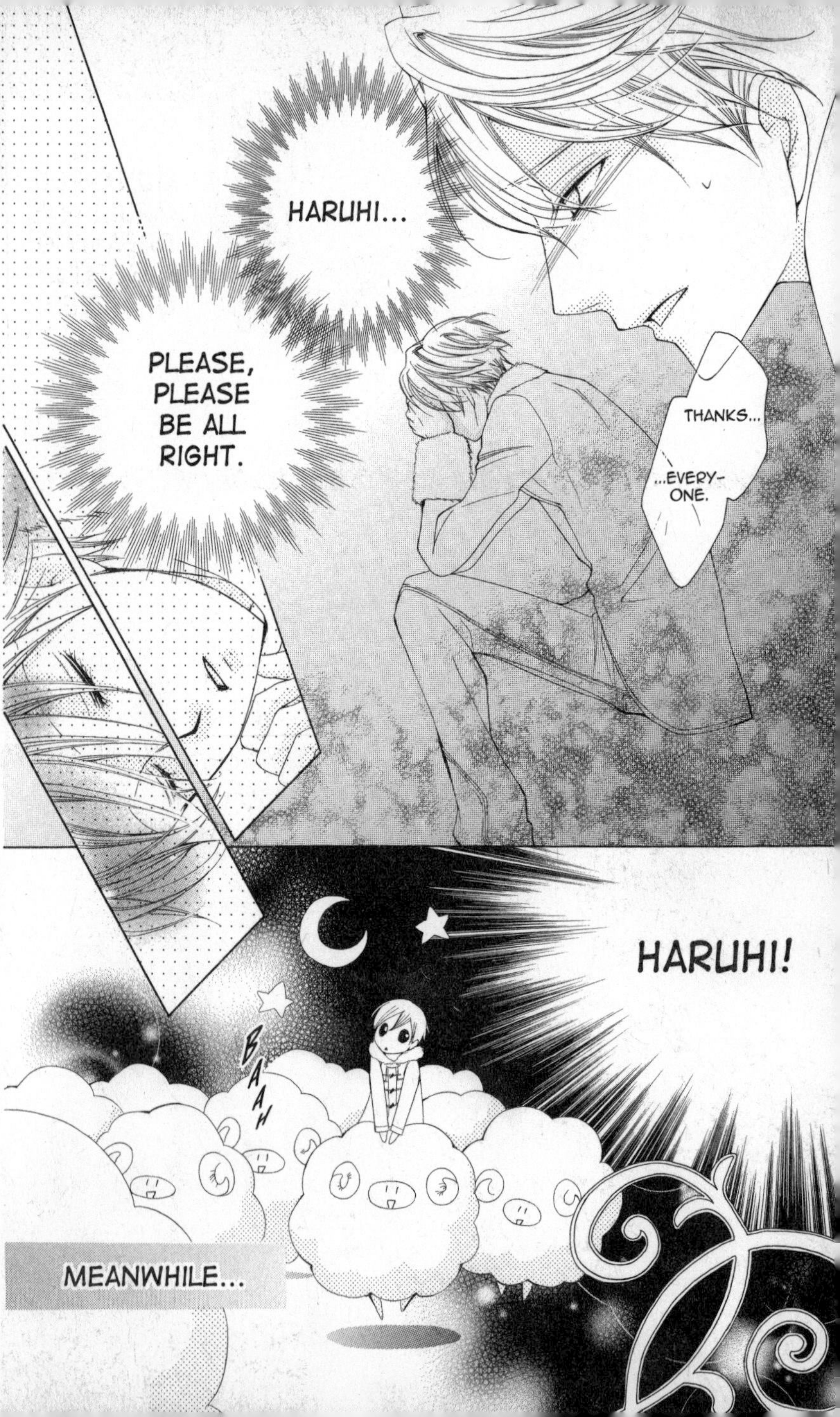
THANKS...
...EVERY-ONE.
HARUHI...
PLEASE, PLEASE BE ALL RIGHT.
HARUHI!
BAAH
MEANWHILE...

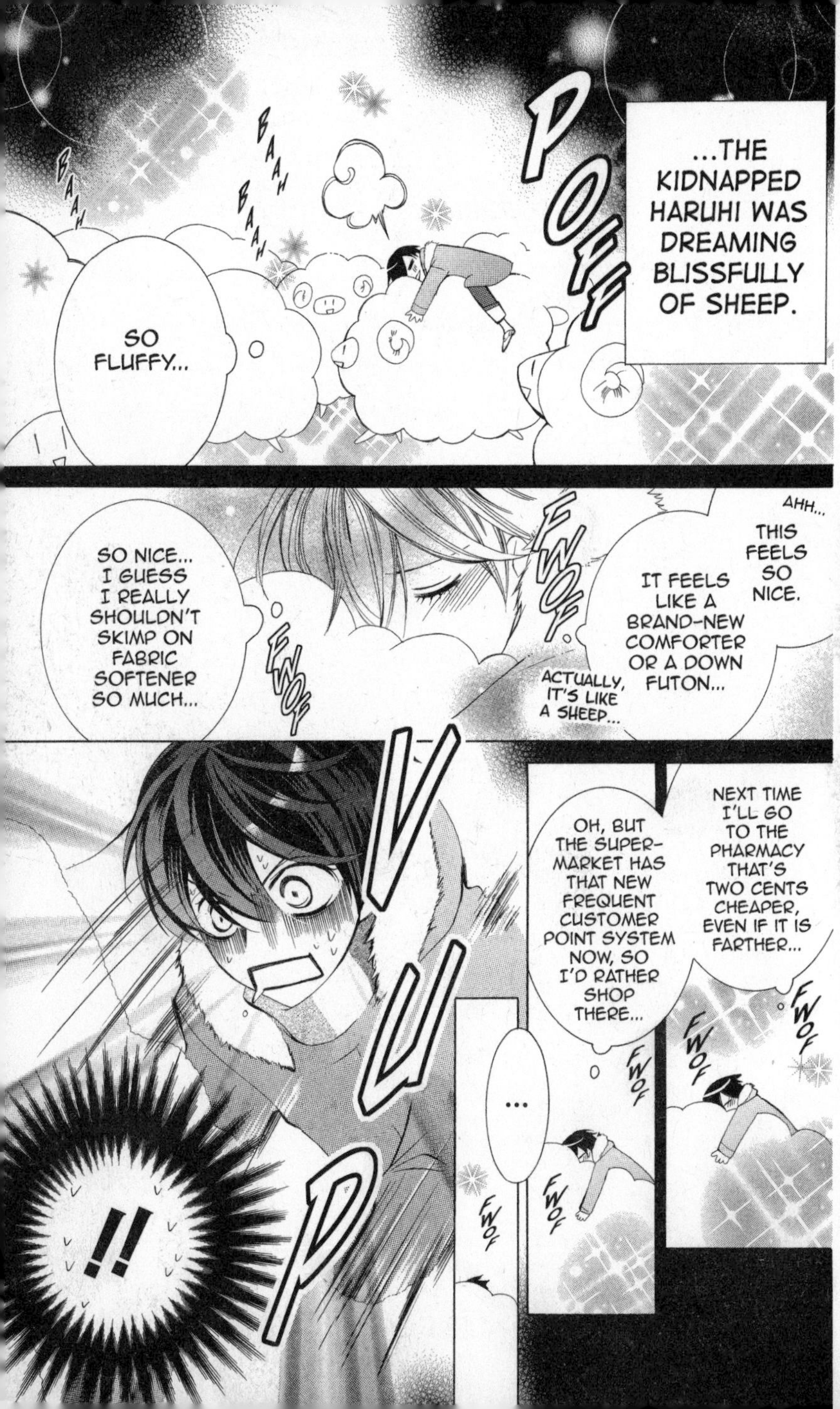
...THE KIDNAPPED HARUHI WAS DREAMING BLISSFULLY OF SHEEP.
POFF
BAAH
BAAH
BAAH
SO FLUFFY...
AHH...
THIS FEELS SO NICE.
IT FEELS LIKE A BRAND-NEW COMFORTER OR A DOWN FUTON...
ACTUALLY, IT'S LIKE A SHEEP...
FWOF
FWOF
SO NICE... I GUESS I REALLY SHOULDN'T SKIMP ON FABRIC SOFTENER SO MUCH...
NEXT TIME I'LL GO TO THE PHARMACY THAT'S TWO CENTS CHEAPER, EVEN IF IT IS FARTHER...
FWOF
FWOF
OH, BUT THE SUPER-MARKET HAS THAT NEW FREQUENT CUSTOMER POINT SYSTEM NOW, SO I'D RATHER SHOP THERE...
FWOF
FWOF
...
FWOF
VUUP
!!

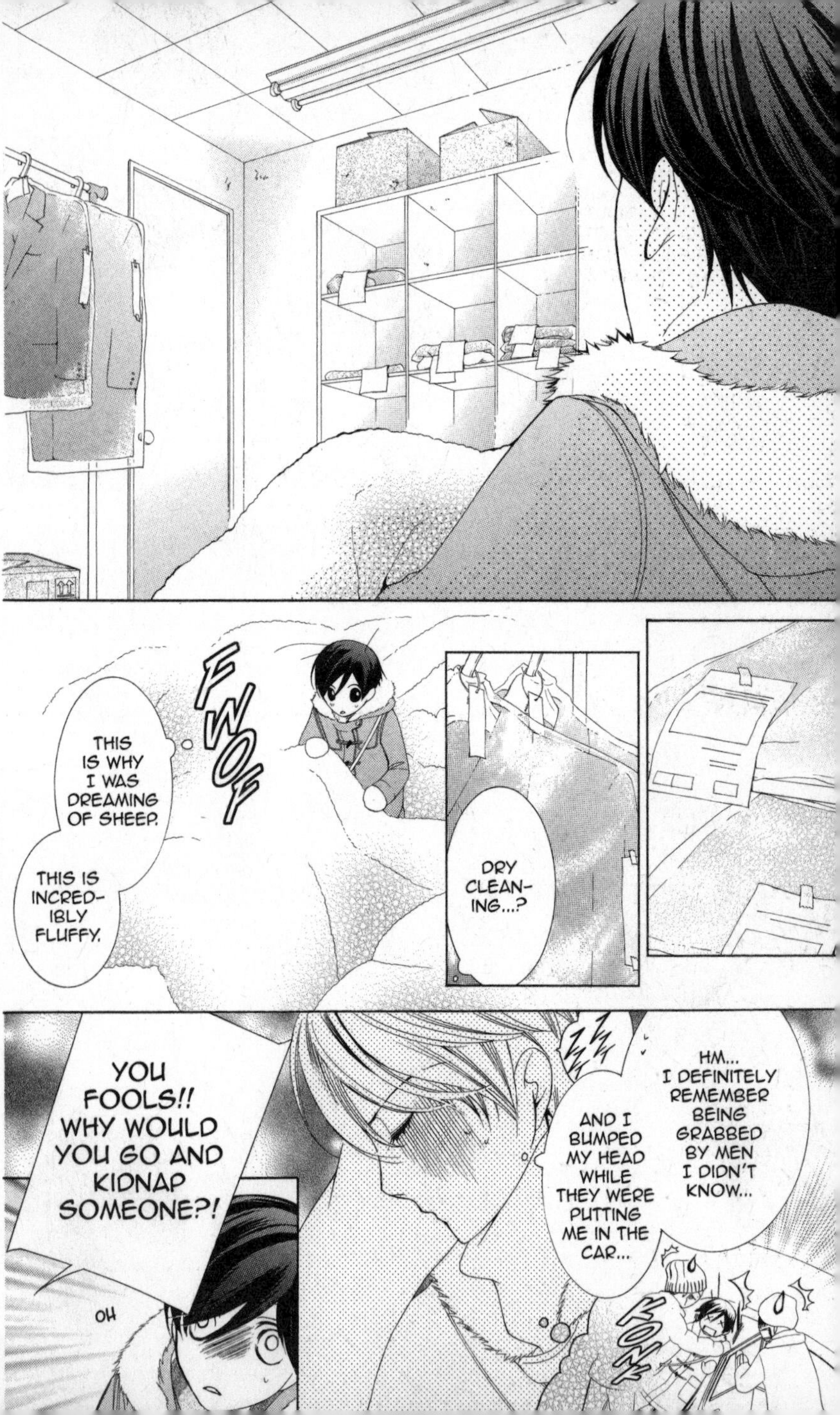
DRY CLEAN-ING...?
FWOF
THIS IS WHY I WAS DREAMING OF SHEEP.
THIS IS INCRED-IBLY FLUFFY.
HM... I DEFINITELY REMEMBER BEING GRABBED BY MEN I DIDN'T KNOW...
AND I BUMPED MY HEAD WHILE THEY WERE PUTTING ME IN THE CAR...
YOU FOOLS!! WHY WOULD YOU GO AND KIDNAP SOMEONE?!
OH

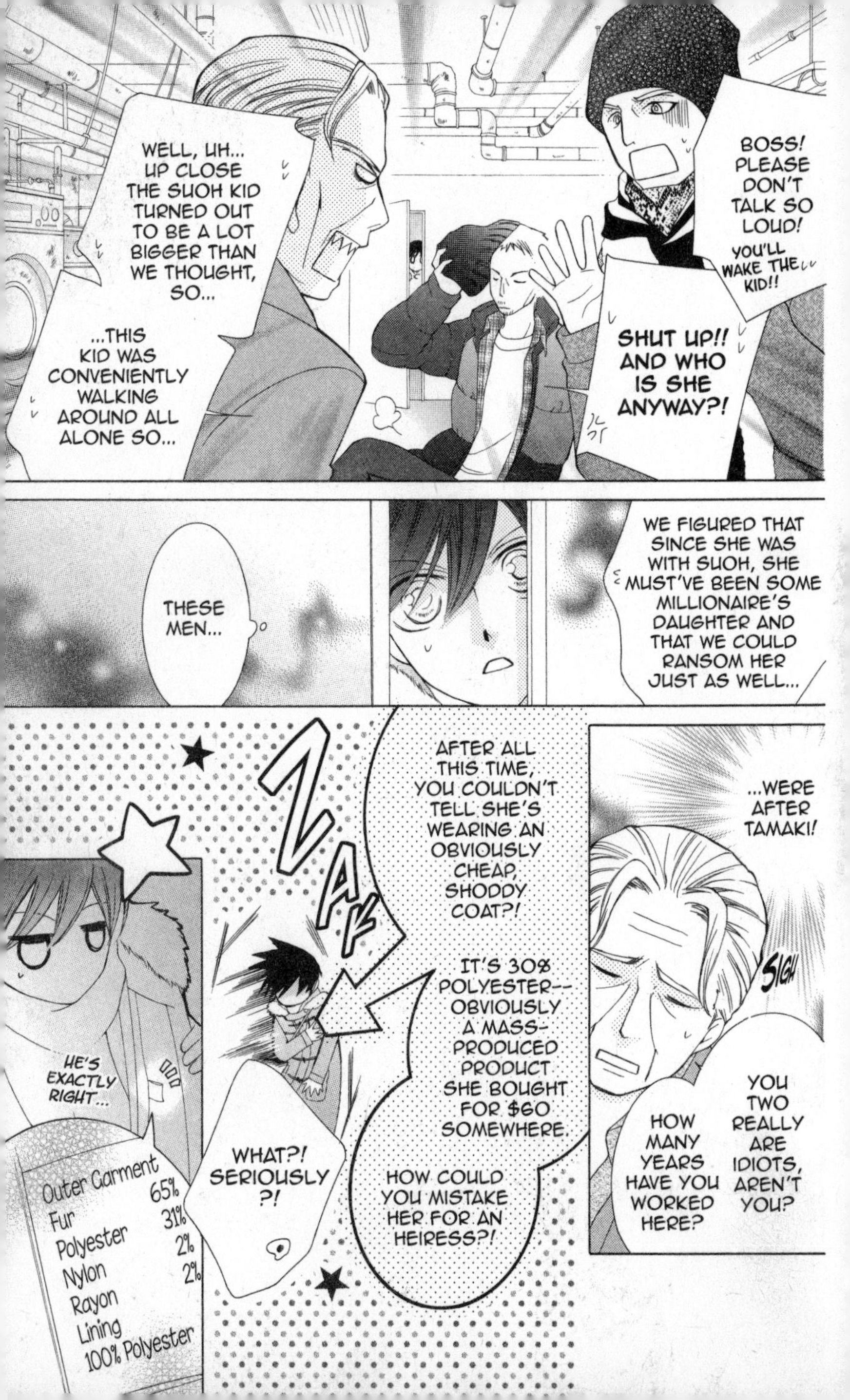
BOSS! PLEASE DON'T TALK SO LOUD!
YOU'LL WAKE THE KID!!
SHUT UP!! AND WHO IS SHE ANYWAY?!
WELL, UH... UP CLOSE THE SUOH KID TURNED OUT TO BE A LOT BIGGER THAN WE THOUGHT, SO...
...THIS KID WAS CONVENIENTLY WALKING AROUND ALL ALONE SO...
WE FIGURED THAT SINCE SHE WAS WITH SUOH, SHE MUST'VE BEEN SOME MILLIONAIRE'S DAUGHTER AND THAT WE COULD RANSOM HER JUST AS WELL...
THESE MEN...
...WERE AFTER TAMAKI!
SIGH
YOU TWO REALLY ARE IDIOTS, AREN'T YOU?
HOW MANY YEARS HAVE YOU WORKED HERE?
AFTER ALL THIS TIME, YOU COULDN'T TELL SHE'S WEARING AN OBVIOUSLY CHEAP, SHODDY COAT?!
IT'S 30% POLYESTER--OBVIOUSLY A MASS-PRODUCED PRODUCT SHE BOUGHT FOR $60 SOMEWHERE.
HOW COULD YOU MISTAKE HER FOR AN HEIRESS?!
ZAK
WHAT?! SERIOUSLY?!
HE'S EXACTLY RIGHT...
Outer Garment
Fur 65%
Polyester 31%
Nylon 2%
Rayon 2%
Lining
100% Polyester

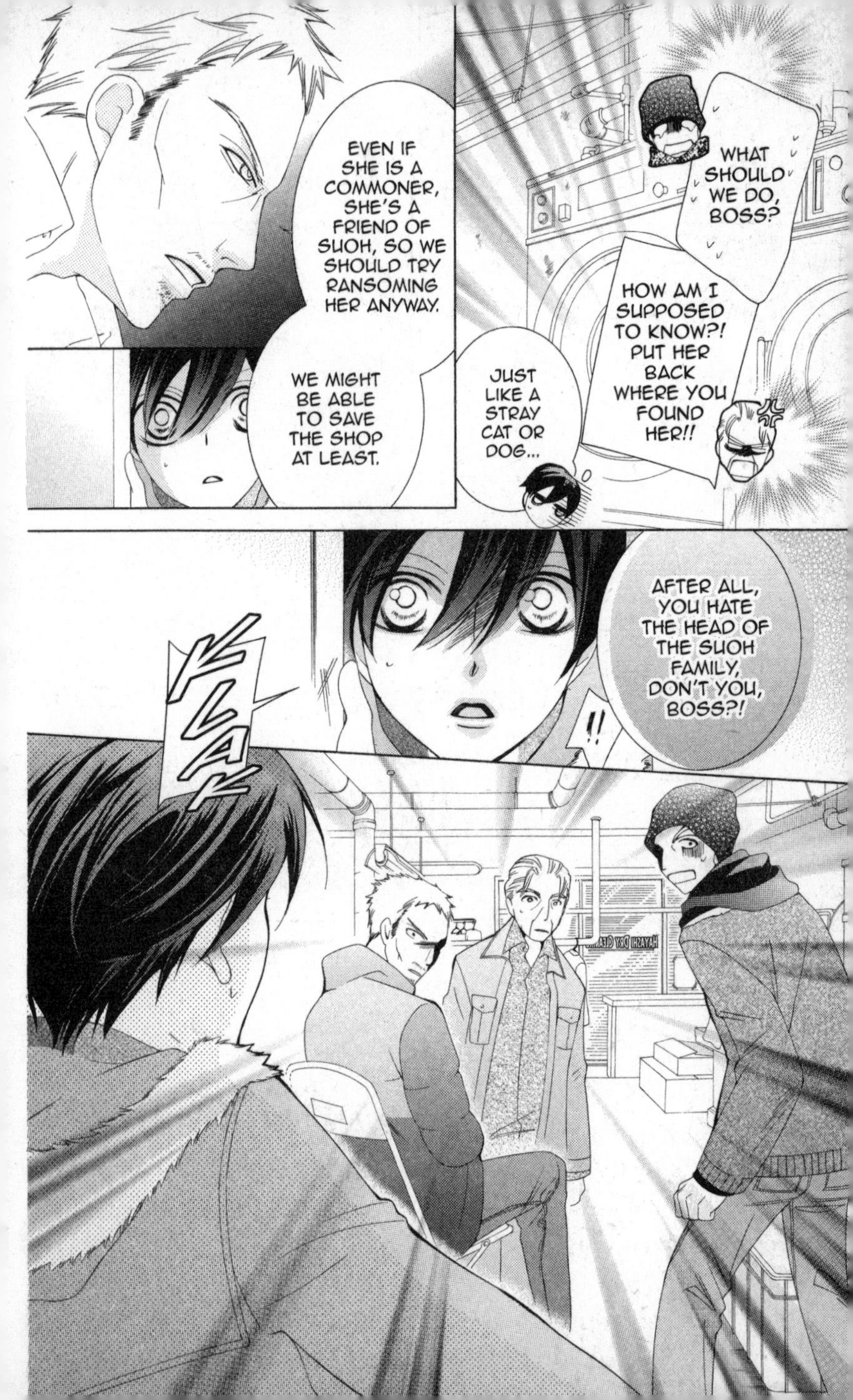
WHAT SHOULD WE DO, BOSS?
HOW AM I SUPPOSED TO KNOW?! PUT HER BACK WHERE YOU FOUND HER!!
JUST LIKE A STRAY CAT OR DOG...
EVEN IF SHE IS A COMMONER, SHE'S A FRIEND OF SUOH, SO WE SHOULD TRY RANSOMING HER ANYWAY.
WE MIGHT BE ABLE TO SAVE THE SHOP AT LEAST.
AFTER ALL, YOU HATE THE HEAD OF THE SUOH FAMILY, DON'T YOU, BOSS?!
!!
KLAK

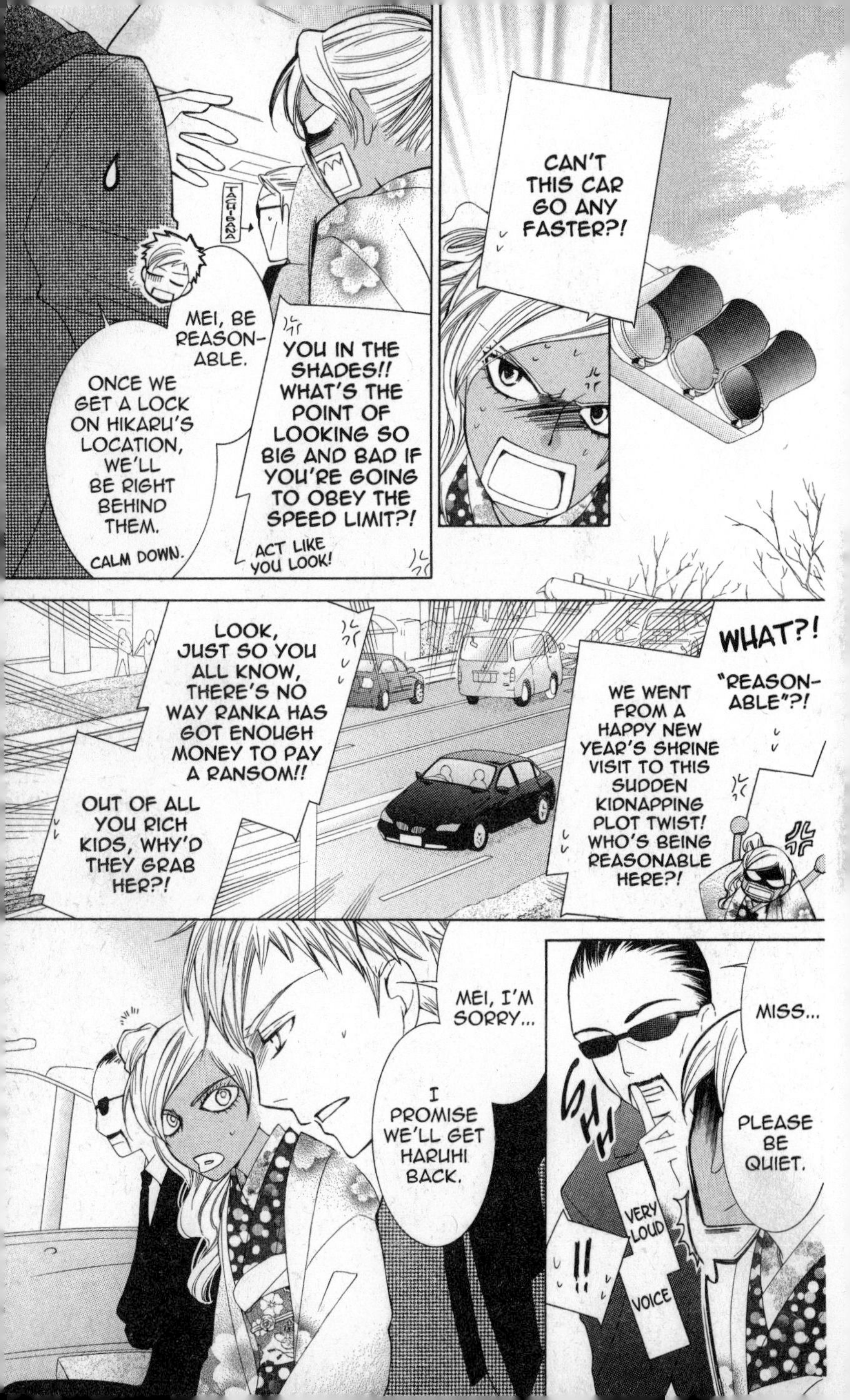
CAN'T THIS CAR GO ANY FASTER?!
YOU IN THE SHADES!! WHAT'S THE POINT OF LOOKING SO BIG AND BAD IF YOU'RE GOING TO OBEY THE SPEED LIMIT?!
ACT LIKE YOU LOOK!
TACHIBANA
MEI, BE REASONABLE.
ONCE WE GET A LOCK ON HIKARU'S LOCATION, WE'LL BE RIGHT BEHIND THEM.
CALM DOWN.
WHAT?!
"REASONABLE"?!
WE WENT FROM A HAPPY NEW YEAR'S SHRINE VISIT TO THIS SUDDEN KIDNAPPING PLOT TWIST! WHO'S BEING REASONABLE HERE?!
LOOK, JUST SO YOU ALL KNOW, THERE'S NO WAY RANKA HAS GOT ENOUGH MONEY TO PAY A RANSOM!!
OUT OF ALL YOU RICH KIDS, WHY'D THEY GRAB HER?!
MISS...
PLEASE BE QUIET.
VERY LOUD VOICE
!!
MEI, I'M SORRY...
I PROMISE WE'LL GET HARUHI BACK.

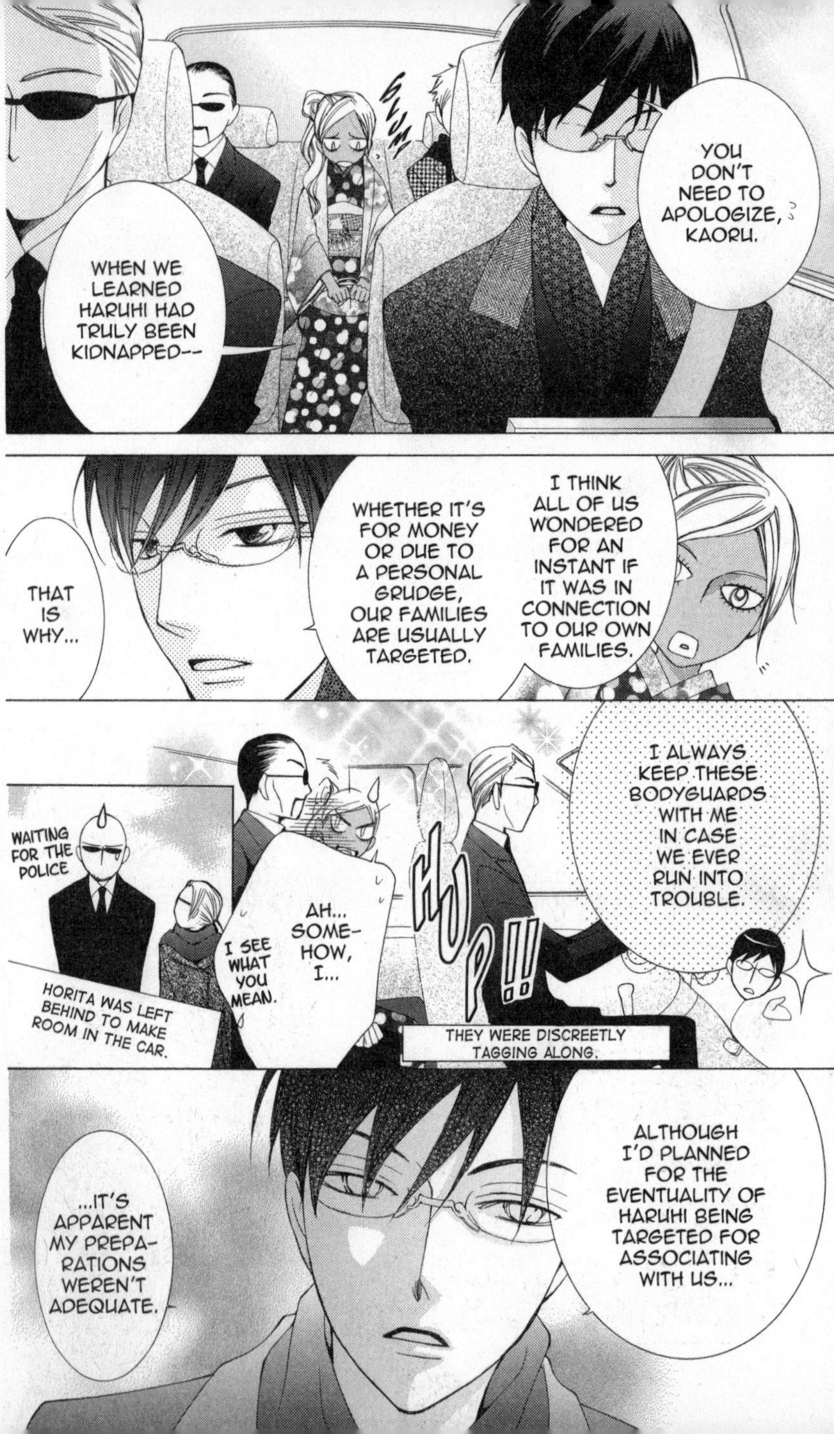
YOU DON'T NEED TO APOLOGIZE, KAORU.
WHEN WE LEARNED HARUHI HAD TRULY BEEN KIDNAPPED--
I THINK ALL OF US WONDERED FOR AN INSTANT IF IT WAS IN CONNECTION TO OUR OWN FAMILIES.
WHETHER IT'S FOR MONEY OR DUE TO A PERSONAL GRUDGE, OUR FAMILIES ARE USUALLY TARGETED.
THAT IS WHY...
I ALWAYS KEEP THESE BODYGUARDS WITH ME IN CASE WE EVER RUN INTO TROUBLE.
HUP!!
AH... SOMEHOW, I...
I SEE WHAT YOU MEAN.
WAITING FOR THE POLICE
HORITA WAS LEFT BEHIND TO MAKE ROOM IN THE CAR.
THEY WERE DISCREETLY TAGGING ALONG.
ALTHOUGH I'D PLANNED FOR THE EVENTUALITY OF HARUHI BEING TARGETED FOR ASSOCIATING WITH US...
...IT'S APPARENT MY PREPARATIONS WEREN'T ADEQUATE.

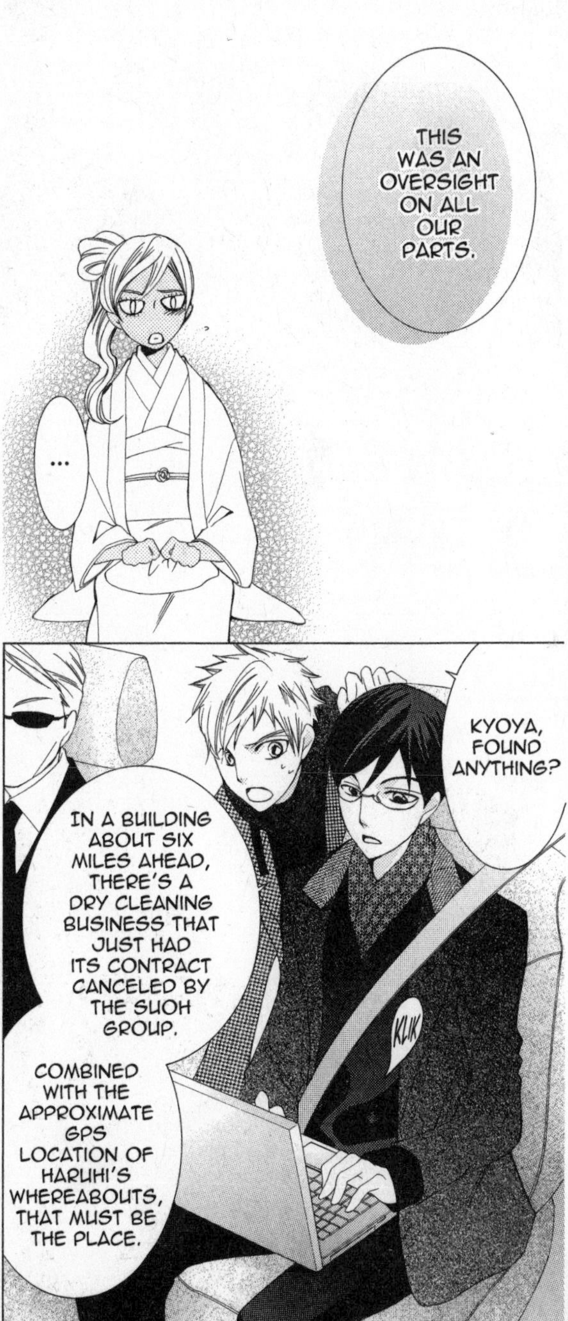
THIS WAS AN OVERSIGHT ON ALL OUR PARTS.
...
KYOYA, FOUND ANYTHING?
IN A BUILDING ABOUT SIX MILES AHEAD, THERE'S A DRY CLEANING BUSINESS THAT JUST HAD ITS CONTRACT CANCELED BY THE SUOH GROUP.
KLIK
COMBINED WITH THE APPROXIMATE GPS LOCATION OF HARUHI'S WHEREABOUTS, THAT MUST BE THE PLACE.

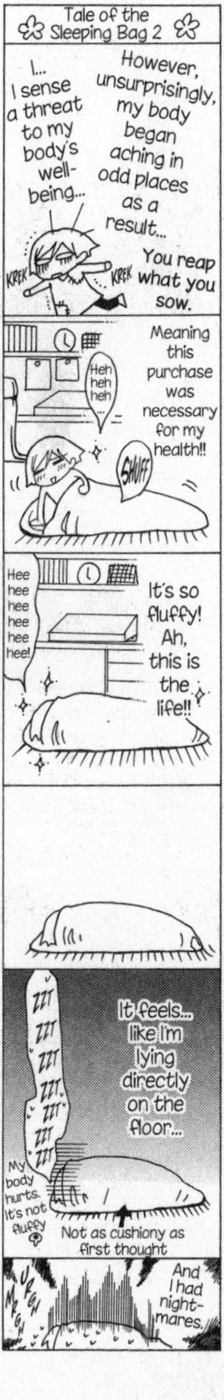
Tale of the Sleeping Bag 2
However, unsurprisingly, my body began aching in odd places as a result...
I... I sense a threat to my body's well-being...
KREK
KREK
You reap what you sow.
Meaning this purchase was necessary for my health!!
Heh heh heh
SHUFF
It's so fluffy! Ah, this is the life!!
Hee hee hee hee hee hee!
It feels... like I'm lying directly on the floor...
ZZT ZZT ZZT ZZT ZZT ZZT ZZT
My body hurts. It's not fluffy
Not as cushiony as first thought
And I had nightmares.

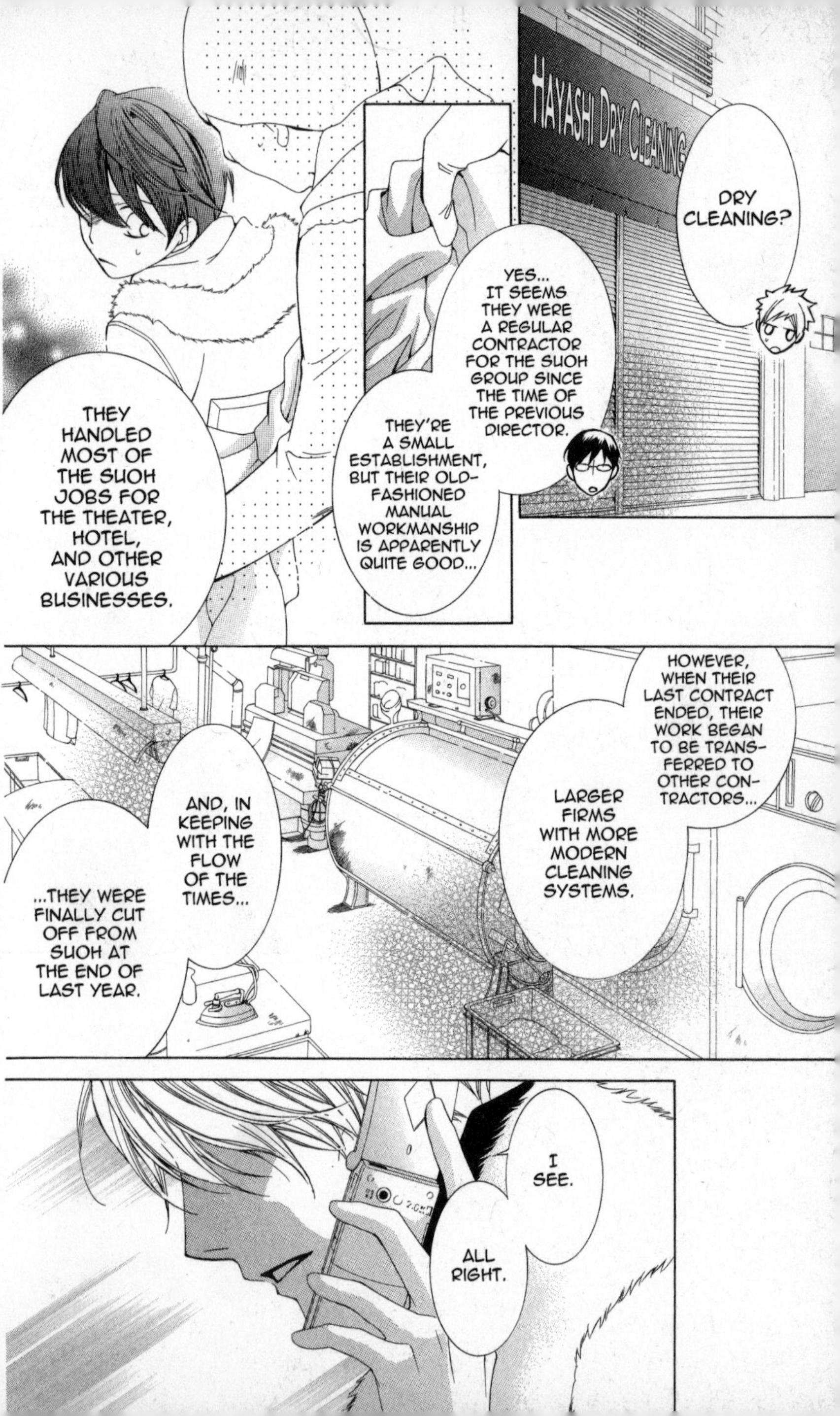
HAYASHI DRY CLEANING
DRY CLEANING?
YES... IT SEEMS THEY WERE A REGULAR CONTRACTOR FOR THE SUOH GROUP SINCE THE TIME OF THE PREVIOUS DIRECTOR.
THEY'RE A SMALL ESTABLISHMENT, BUT THEIR OLD-FASHIONED MANUAL WORKMANSHIP IS APPARENTLY QUITE GOOD...
THEY HANDLED MOST OF THE SUOH JOBS FOR THE THEATER, HOTEL, AND OTHER VARIOUS BUSINESSES.
HOWEVER, WHEN THEIR LAST CONTRACT ENDED, THEIR WORK BEGAN TO BE TRANS-FERRED TO OTHER CON-TRACTORS...
LARGER FIRMS WITH MORE MODERN CLEANING SYSTEMS.
AND, IN KEEPING WITH THE FLOW OF THE TIMES...
...THEY WERE FINALLY CUT OFF FROM SUOH AT THE END OF LAST YEAR.
I SEE.
ALL RIGHT.

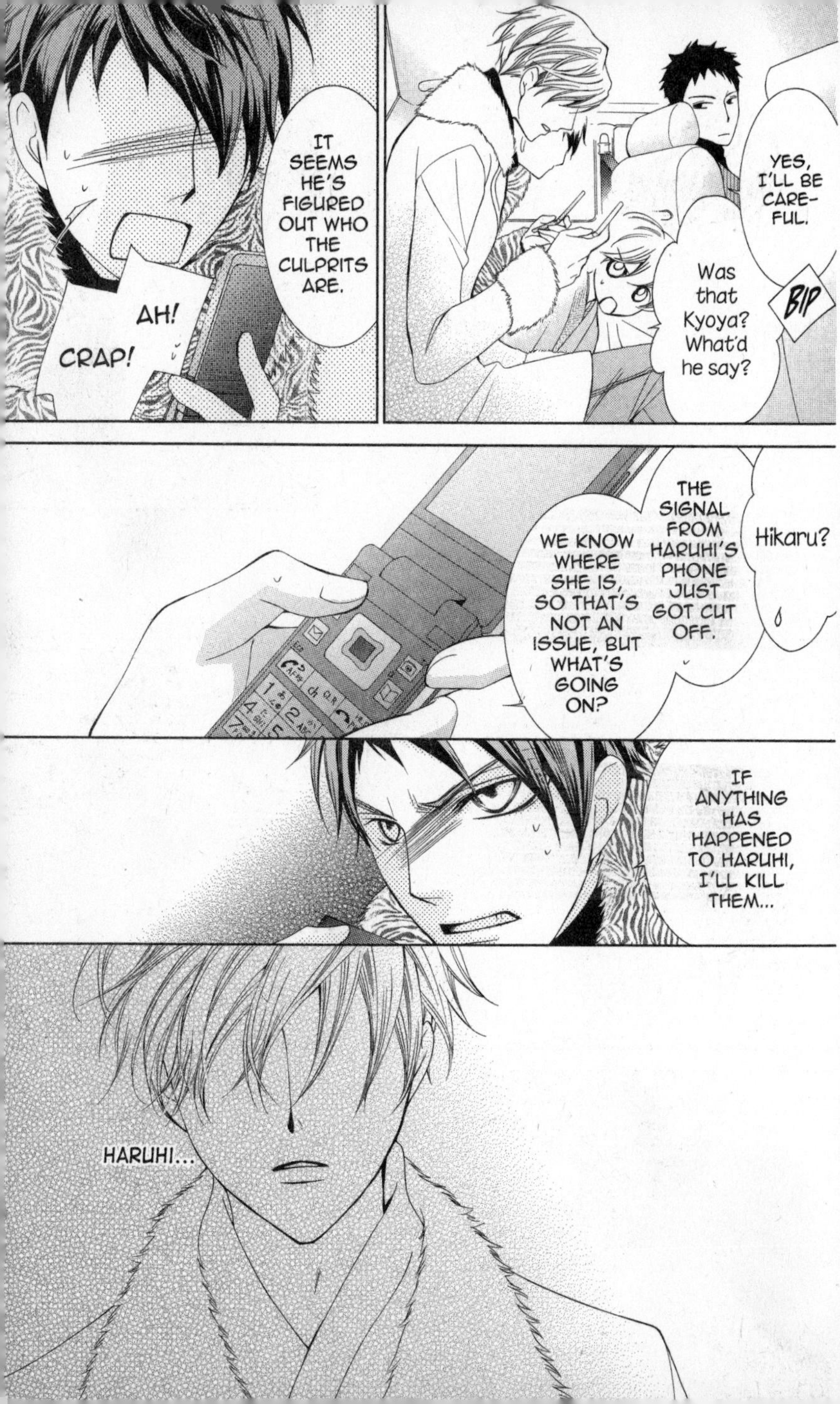
YES, I'LL BE CAREFUL.
BIP
Was that Kyoya? What'd he say?
IT SEEMS HE'S FIGURED OUT WHO THE CULPRITS ARE.
AH!
CRAP!
Hikaru?
THE SIGNAL FROM HARUHI'S PHONE JUST GOT CUT OFF.
WE KNOW WHERE SHE IS, SO THAT'S NOT AN ISSUE, BUT WHAT'S GOING ON?
IF ANYTHING HAS HAPPENED TO HARUHI, I'LL KILL THEM...
HARUHI...

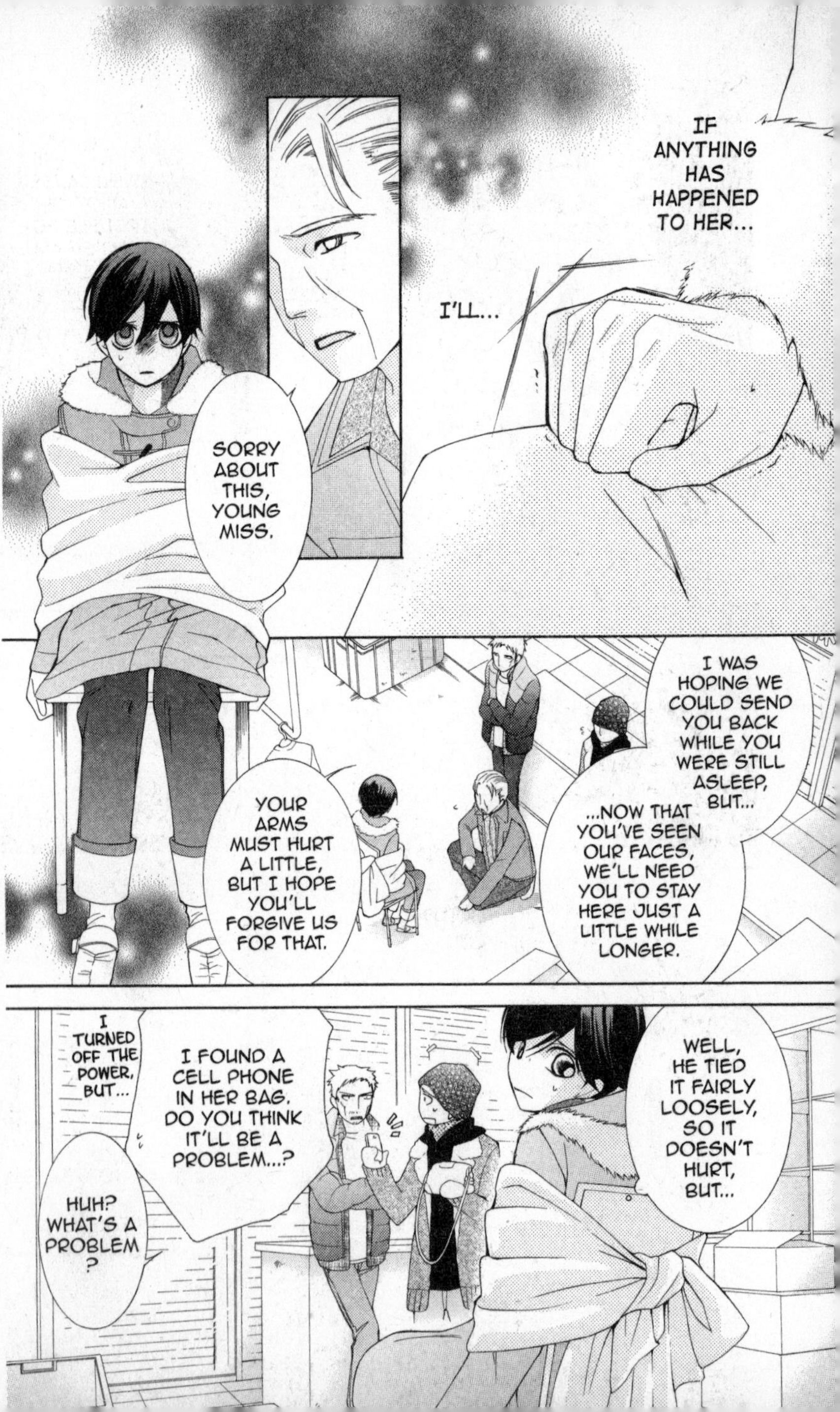
IF ANYTHING HAS HAPPENED TO HER...
I'LL...
SORRY ABOUT THIS, YOUNG MISS.
I WAS HOPING WE COULD SEND YOU BACK WHILE YOU WERE STILL ASLEEP, BUT...
...NOW THAT YOU'VE SEEN OUR FACES, WE'LL NEED YOU TO STAY HERE JUST A LITTLE WHILE LONGER.
YOUR ARMS MUST HURT A LITTLE, BUT I HOPE YOU'LL FORGIVE US FOR THAT.
WELL, HE TIED IT FAIRLY LOOSELY, SO IT DOESN'T HURT, BUT...
I FOUND A CELL PHONE IN HER BAG. DO YOU THINK IT'LL BE A PROBLEM...?
I TURNED OFF THE POWER, BUT...
HUH? WHAT'S A PROBLEM?

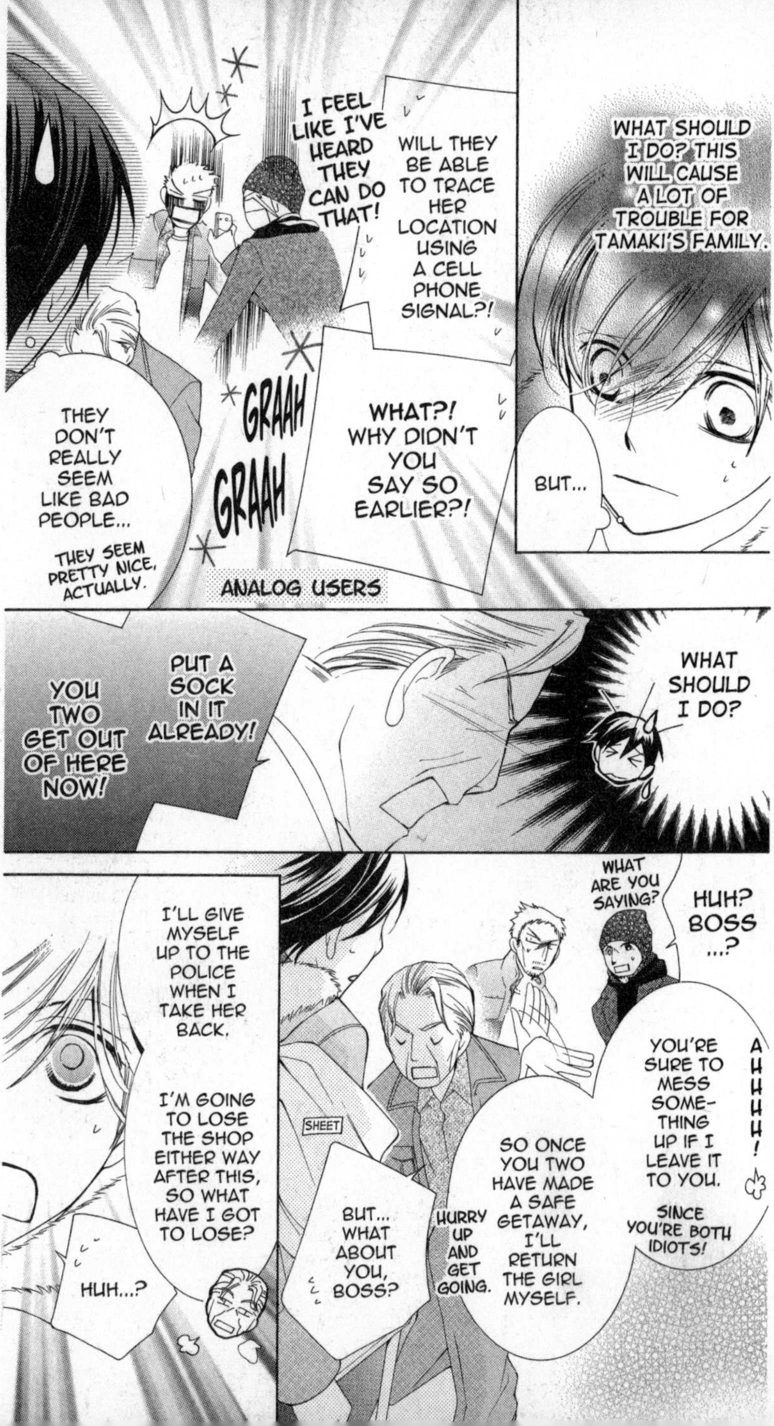
WHAT SHOULD I DO? THIS WILL CAUSE A LOT OF TROUBLE FOR TAMAKI'S FAMILY.
BUT...
WILL THEY BE ABLE TO TRACE HER LOCATION USING A CELL PHONE SIGNAL?!
I FEEL LIKE I'VE HEARD THEY CAN DO THAT!
WHAT?! WHY DIDN'T YOU SAY SO EARLIER?!
GRAAH
GRAAH
THEY DON'T REALLY SEEM LIKE BAD PEOPLE...
THEY SEEM PRETTY NICE, ACTUALLY.
ANALOG USERS
WHAT SHOULD I DO?
PUT A SOCK IN IT ALREADY!
YOU TWO GET OUT OF HERE NOW!
HUH? BOSS ...?
WHAT ARE YOU SAYING?
AHHHH!
YOU'RE SURE TO MESS SOMETHING UP IF I LEAVE IT TO YOU.
SINCE YOU'RE BOTH IDIOTS!
SO ONCE YOU TWO HAVE MADE A SAFE GETAWAY, I'LL RETURN THE GIRL MYSELF.
HURRY UP AND GET GOING.
BUT... WHAT ABOUT YOU, BOSS?
SHEET
I'LL GIVE MYSELF UP TO THE POLICE WHEN I TAKE HER BACK.
I'M GOING TO LOSE THE SHOP EITHER WAY AFTER THIS, SO WHAT HAVE I GOT TO LOSE?
HUH...?

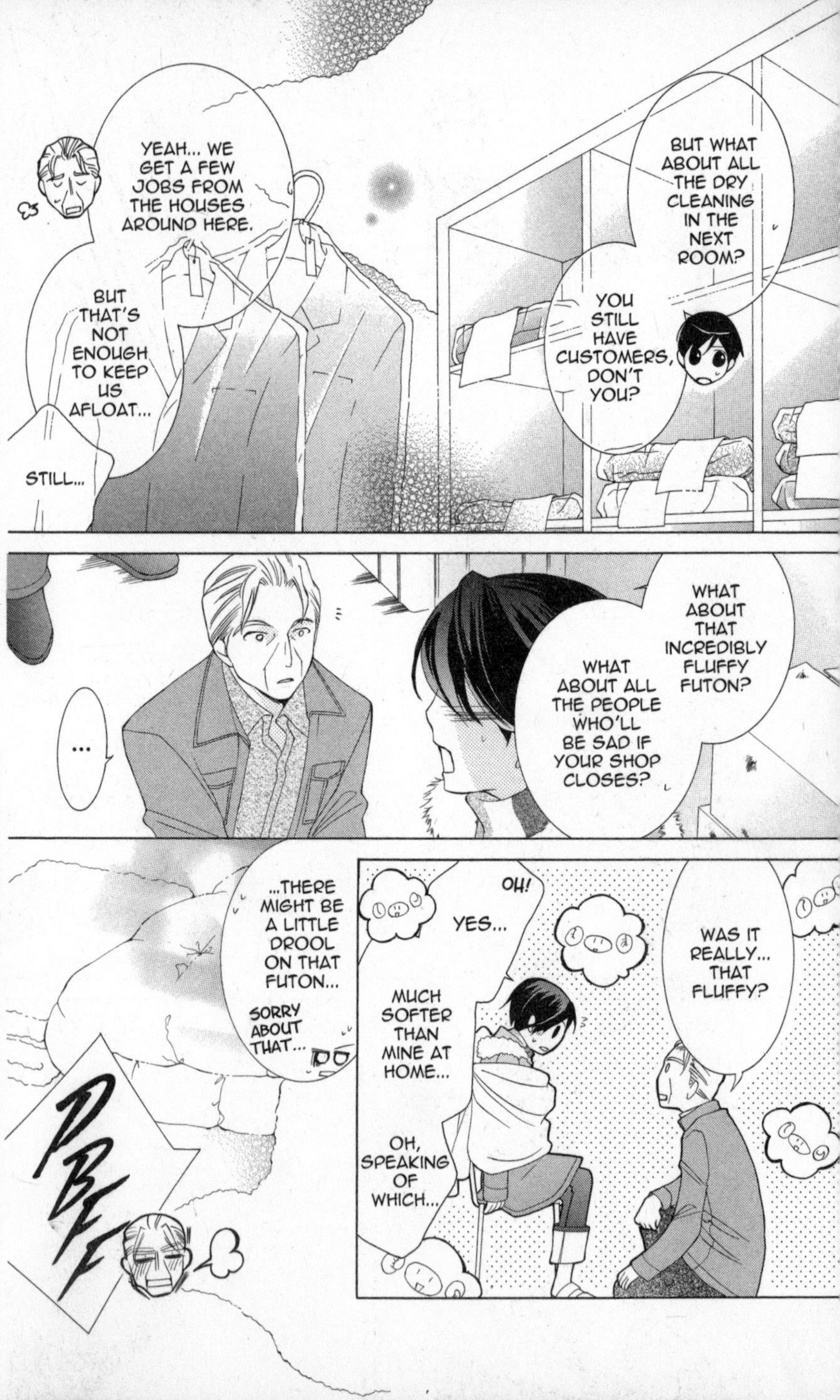
BUT WHAT ABOUT ALL THE DRY CLEANING IN THE NEXT ROOM?
YOU STILL HAVE CUSTOMERS, DON'T YOU?
YEAH... WE GET A FEW JOBS FROM THE HOUSES AROUND HERE.
BUT THAT'S NOT ENOUGH TO KEEP US AFLOAT...
STILL...
WHAT ABOUT THAT INCREDIBLY FLUFFY FUTON?
WHAT ABOUT ALL THE PEOPLE WHO'LL BE SAD IF YOUR SHOP CLOSES?
...
WAS IT REALLY... THAT FLUFFY?
OH!
YES...
MUCH SOFTER THAN MINE AT HOME...
OH, SPEAKING OF WHICH...
...THERE MIGHT BE A LITTLE DROOL ON THAT FUTON...
SORRY ABOUT THAT...

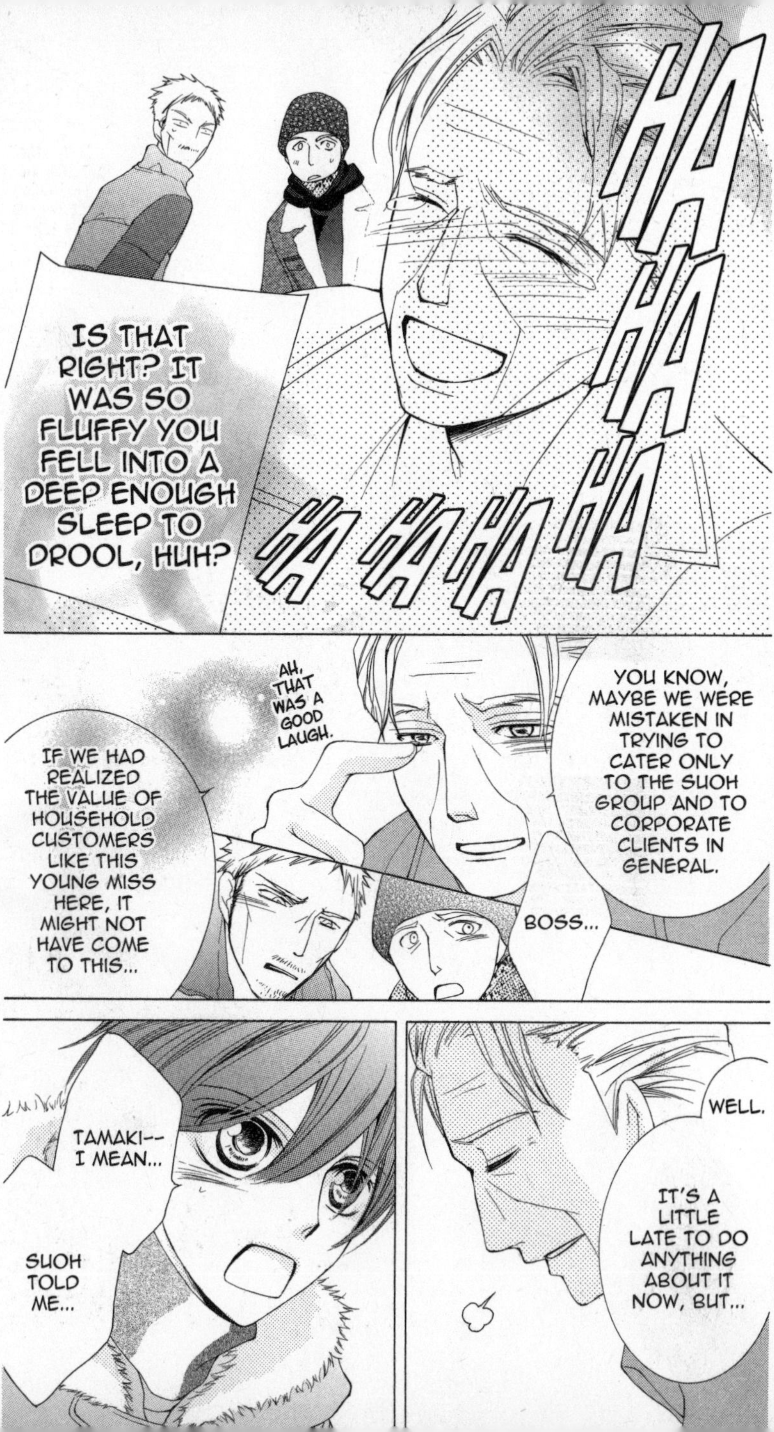
HA HA HA HA HA HA HA HA
IS THAT RIGHT? IT WAS SO FLUFFY YOU FELL INTO A DEEP ENOUGH SLEEP TO DROOL, HUH?
YOU KNOW, MAYBE WE WERE MISTAKEN IN TRYING TO CATER ONLY TO THE SUOH GROUP AND TO CORPORATE CLIENTS IN GENERAL.
AH, THAT WAS A GOOD LAUGH.
BOSS...
IF WE HAD REALIZED THE VALUE OF HOUSEHOLD CUSTOMERS LIKE THIS YOUNG MISS HERE, IT MIGHT NOT HAVE COME TO THIS...
WELL.
IT'S A LITTLE LATE TO DO ANYTHING ABOUT IT NOW, BUT...
TAMAKI-- I MEAN...
SUOH TOLD ME...

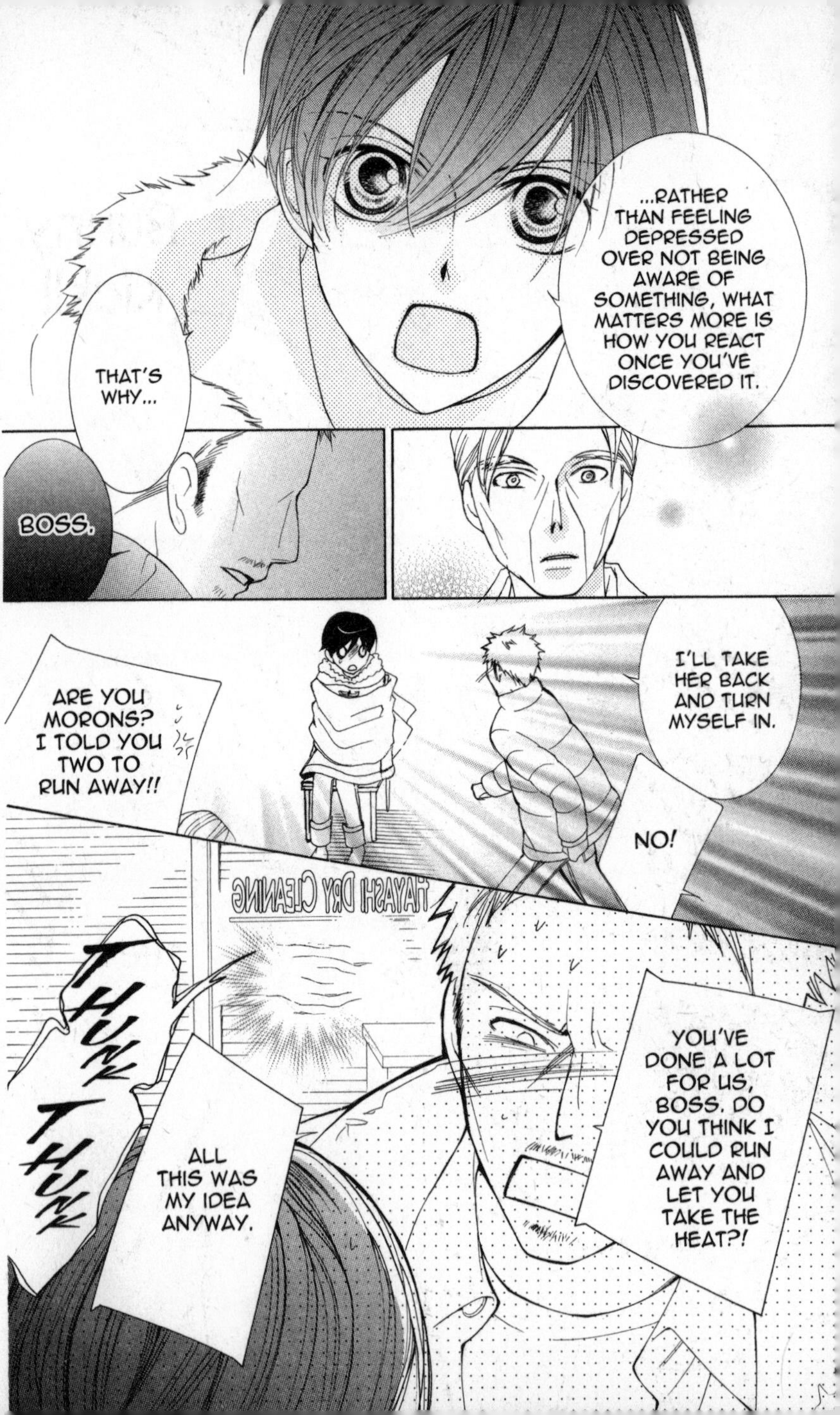
...RATHER THAN FEELING DEPRESSED OVER NOT BEING AWARE OF SOMETHING, WHAT MATTERS MORE IS HOW YOU REACT ONCE YOU'VE DISCOVERED IT.
THAT'S WHY...
BOSS.
I'LL TAKE HER BACK AND TURN MYSELF IN.
ARE YOU MORONS? I TOLD YOU TWO TO RUN AWAY!!
NO!
HAYASHI DRY CLEANING
YOU'VE DONE A LOT FOR US, BOSS. DO YOU THINK I COULD RUN AWAY AND LET YOU TAKE THE HEAT?!
ALL THIS WAS MY IDEA ANYWAY.
THUNK
THUNK

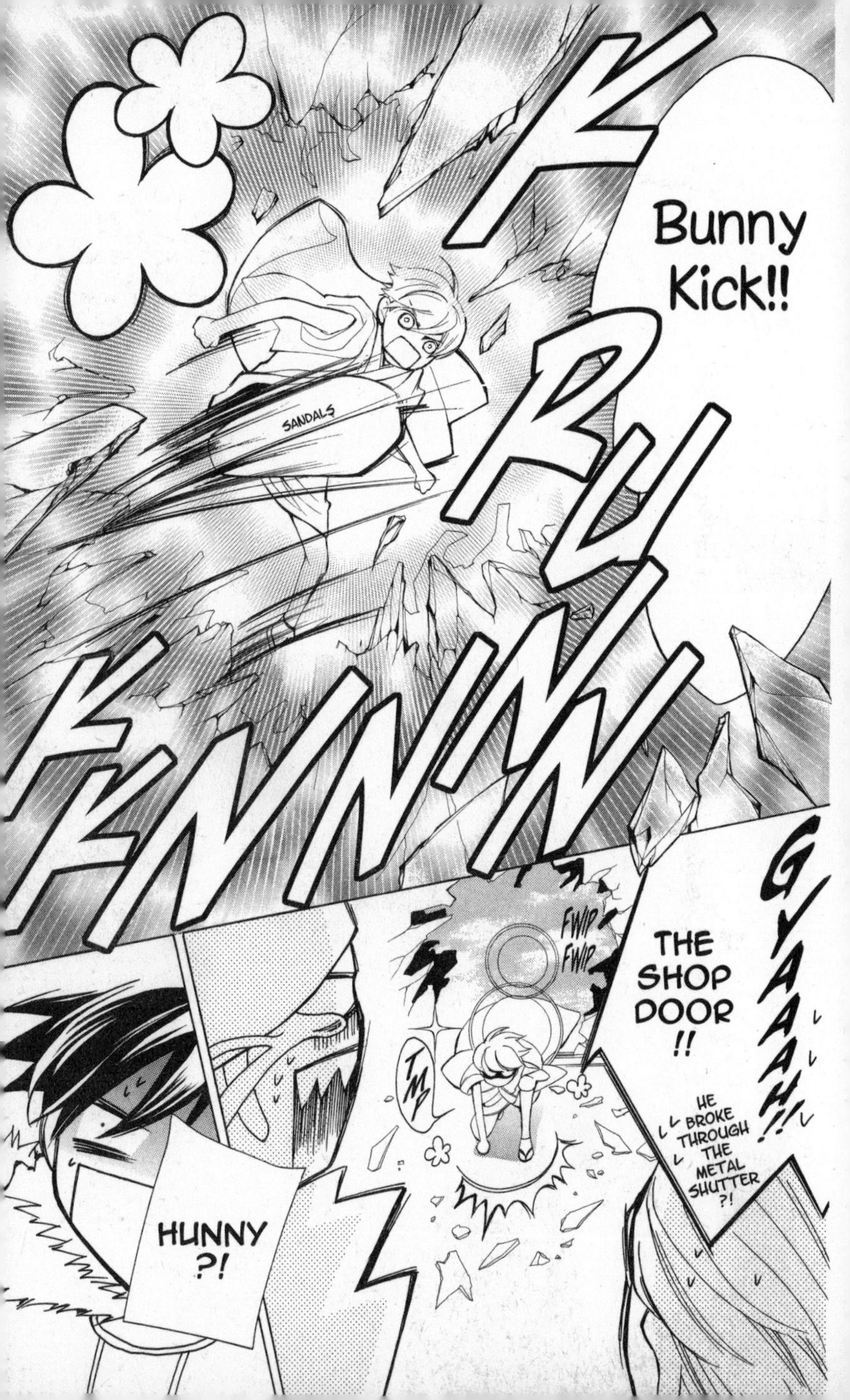
Bunny Kick!!
SANDALS
KRUNNN
GYAAAH!!
THE SHOP DOOR !!
HE BROKE THROUGH THE METAL SHUTTER ?!
FWIP FWIP
TMP
HUNNY ?!

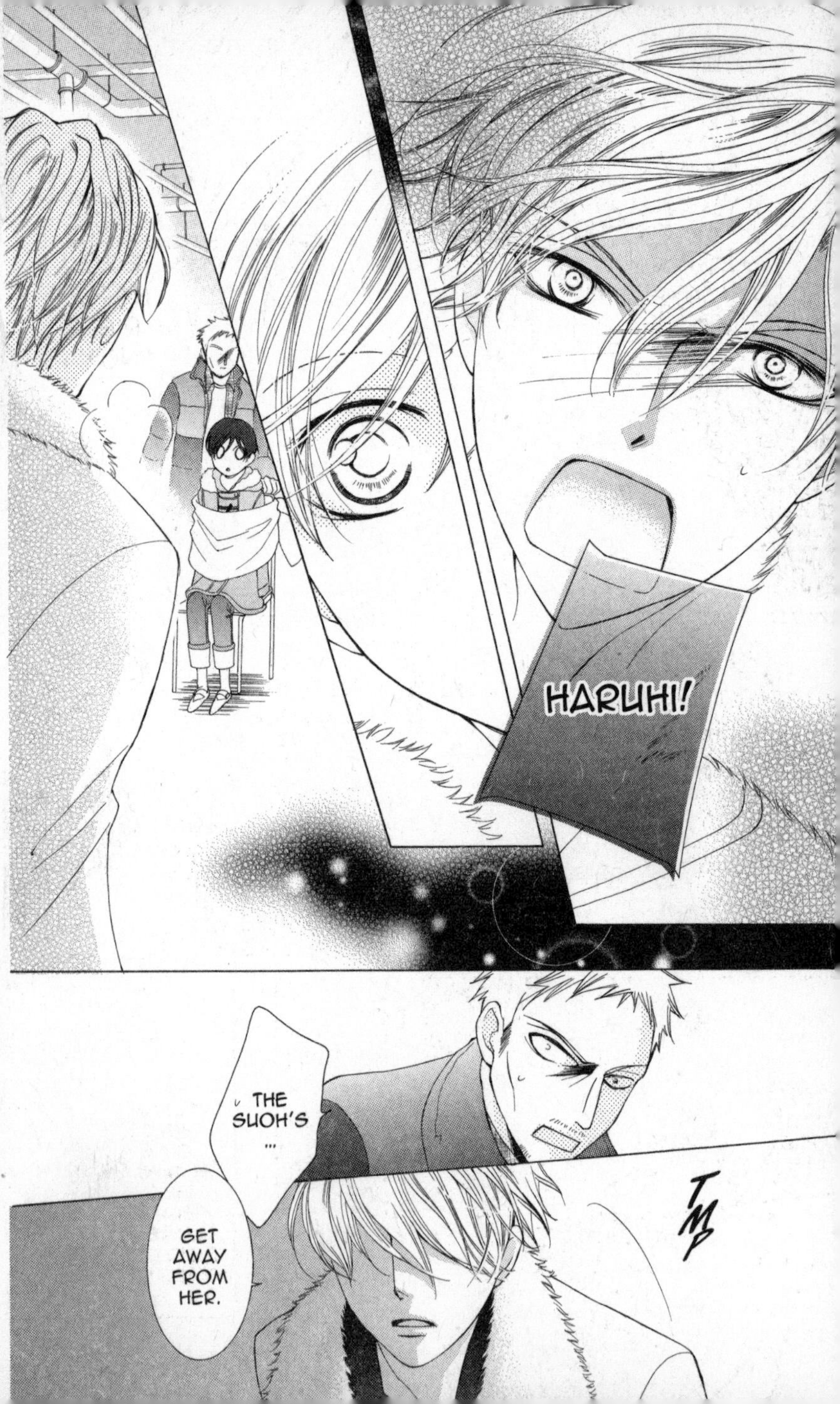
HARUHI!
THE SUOH'S ...
TMP
GET AWAY FROM HER.

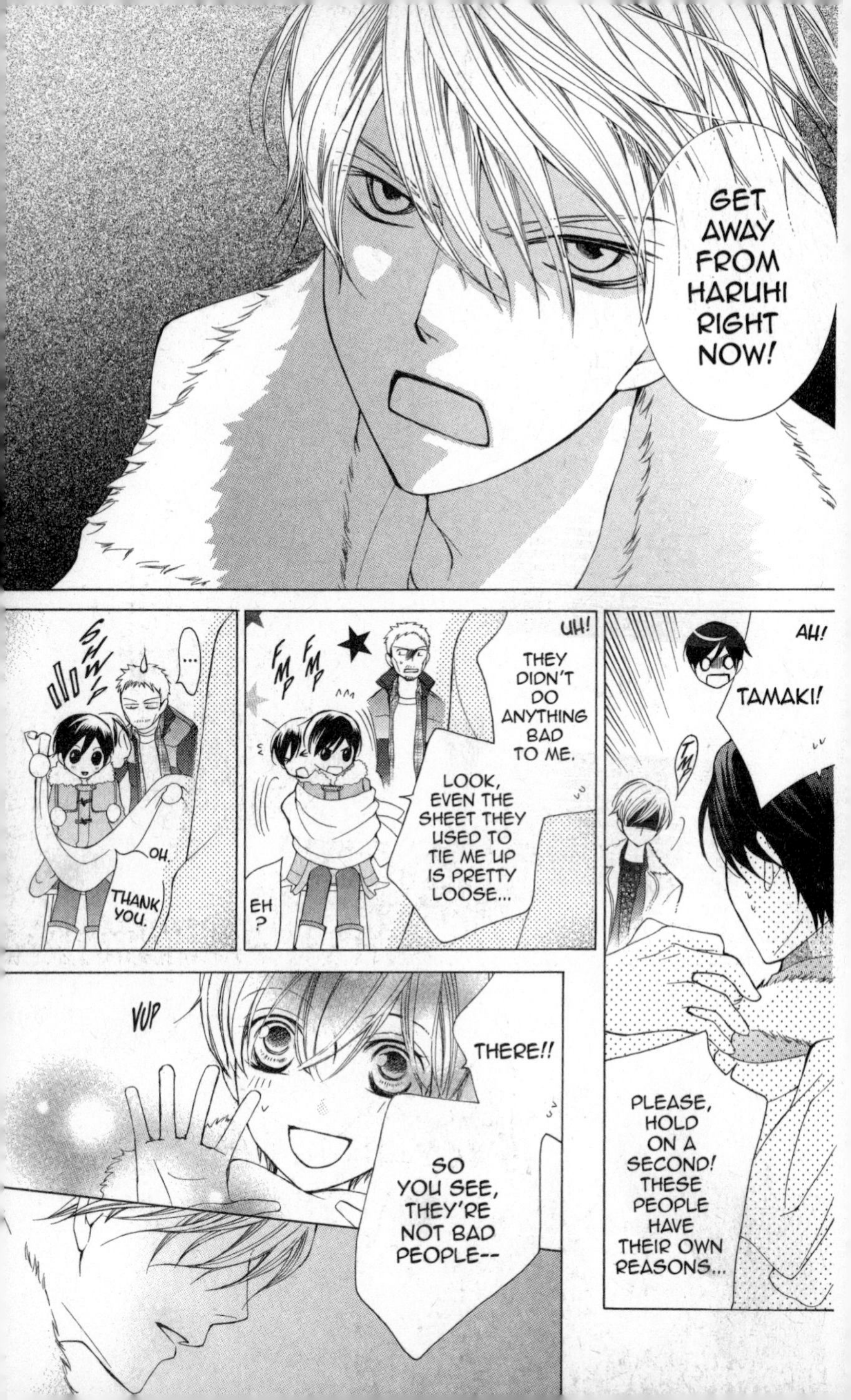
GET AWAY FROM HARUHI RIGHT NOW!
AH!
TAMAKI!
TM
PLEASE, HOLD ON A SECOND! THESE PEOPLE HAVE THEIR OWN REASONS...
UH!
THEY DIDN'T DO ANYTHING BAD TO ME.
FMP FMP
LOOK, EVEN THE SHEET THEY USED TO TIE ME UP IS PRETTY LOOSE...
EH?
...
SHWIP
OH.
THANK YOU.
VUP
THERE!!
SO YOU SEE, THEY'RE NOT BAD PEOPLE--

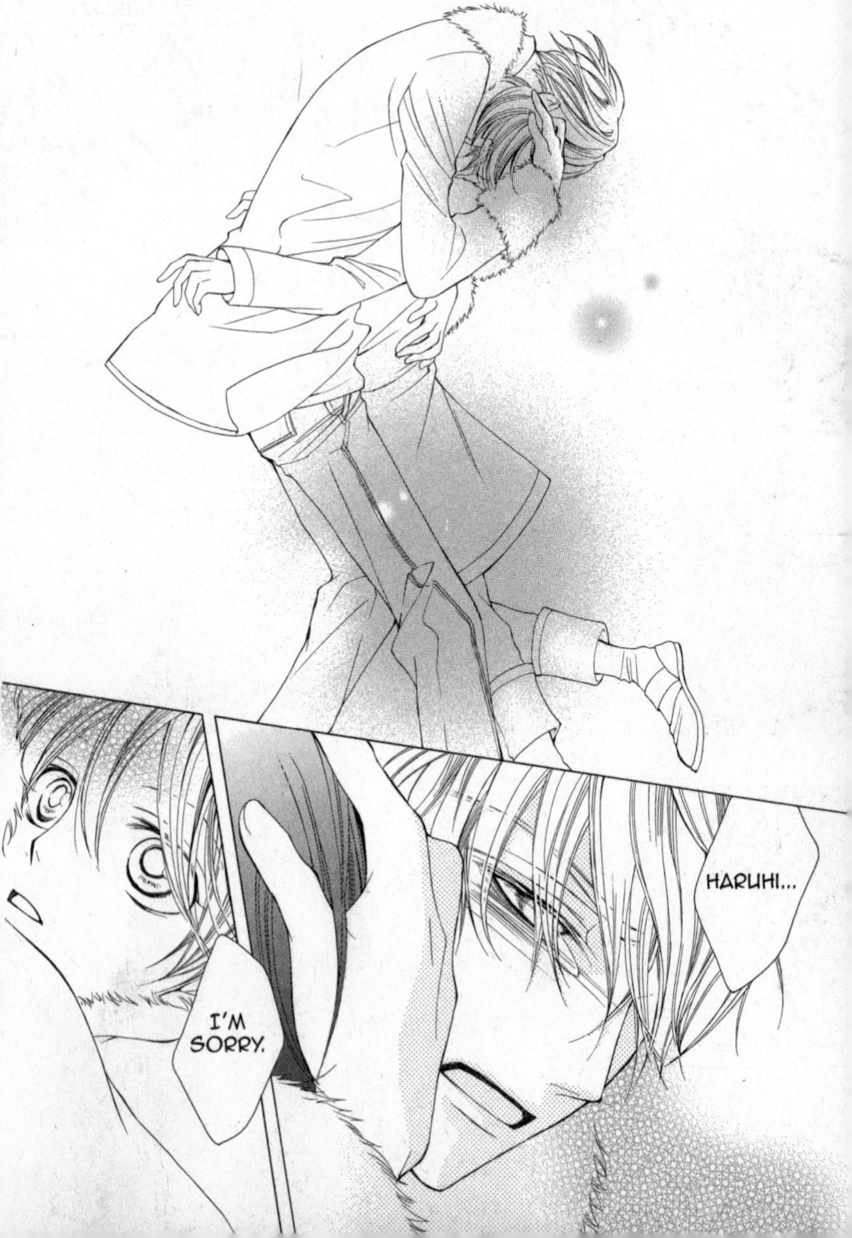
HARUHI...
I'M SORRY.

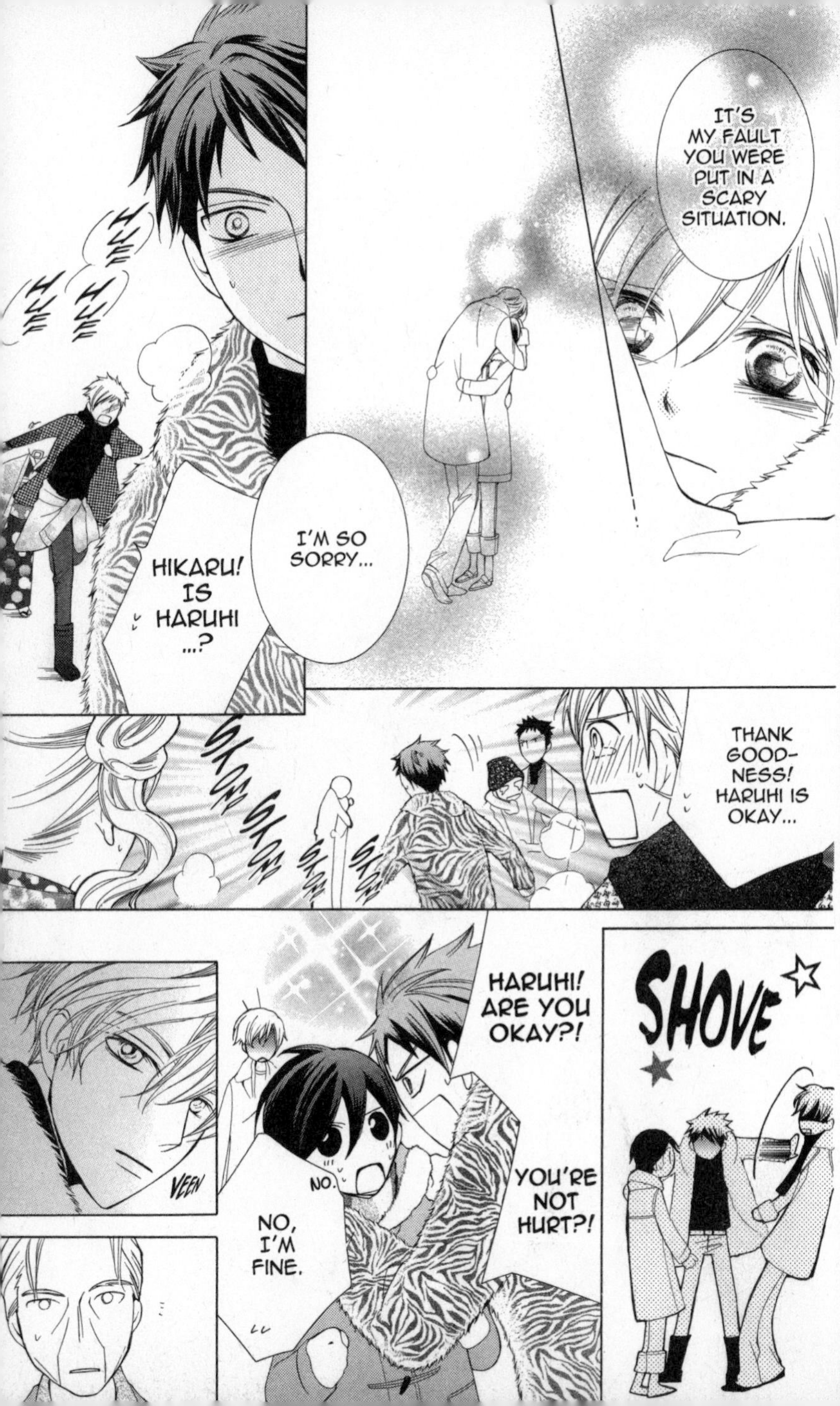
IT'S MY FAULT YOU WERE PUT IN A SCARY SITUATION.
I'M SO SORRY...
HUFF HUFF
HUFF
HIKARU! IS HARUHI ...?
THANK GOODNESS! HARUHI IS OKAY...
SHOVE
HARUHI! ARE YOU OKAY?!
YOU'RE NOT HURT?!
NO.
NO, I'M FINE.
VEEN

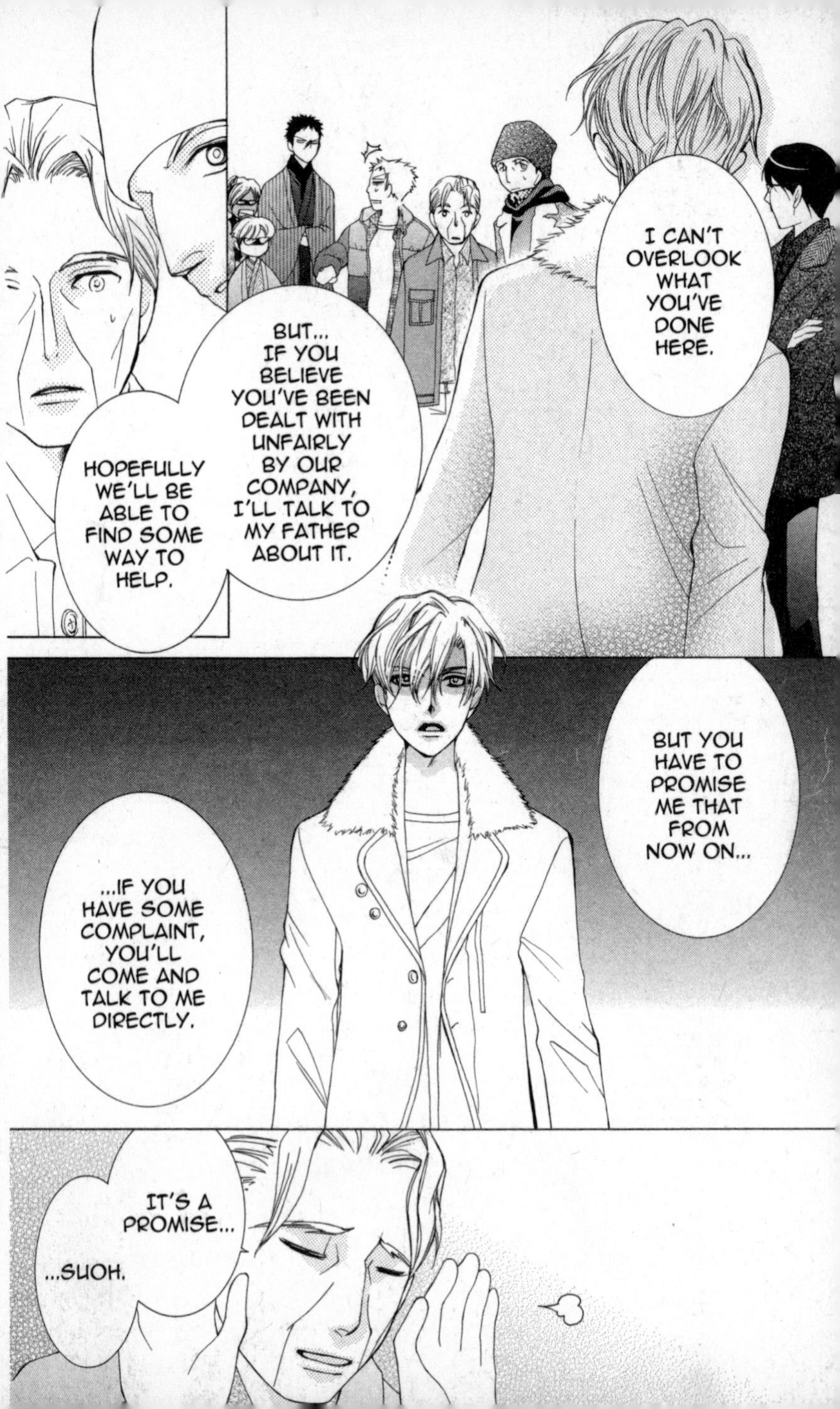
I CAN'T OVERLOOK WHAT YOU'VE DONE HERE.
BUT... IF YOU BELIEVE YOU'VE BEEN DEALT WITH UNFAIRLY BY OUR COMPANY, I'LL TALK TO MY FATHER ABOUT IT.
HOPEFULLY WE'LL BE ABLE TO FIND SOME WAY TO HELP.
BUT YOU HAVE TO PROMISE ME THAT FROM NOW ON...
...IF YOU HAVE SOME COMPLAINT, YOU'LL COME AND TALK TO ME DIRECTLY.
IT'S A PROMISE...
...SUOH.

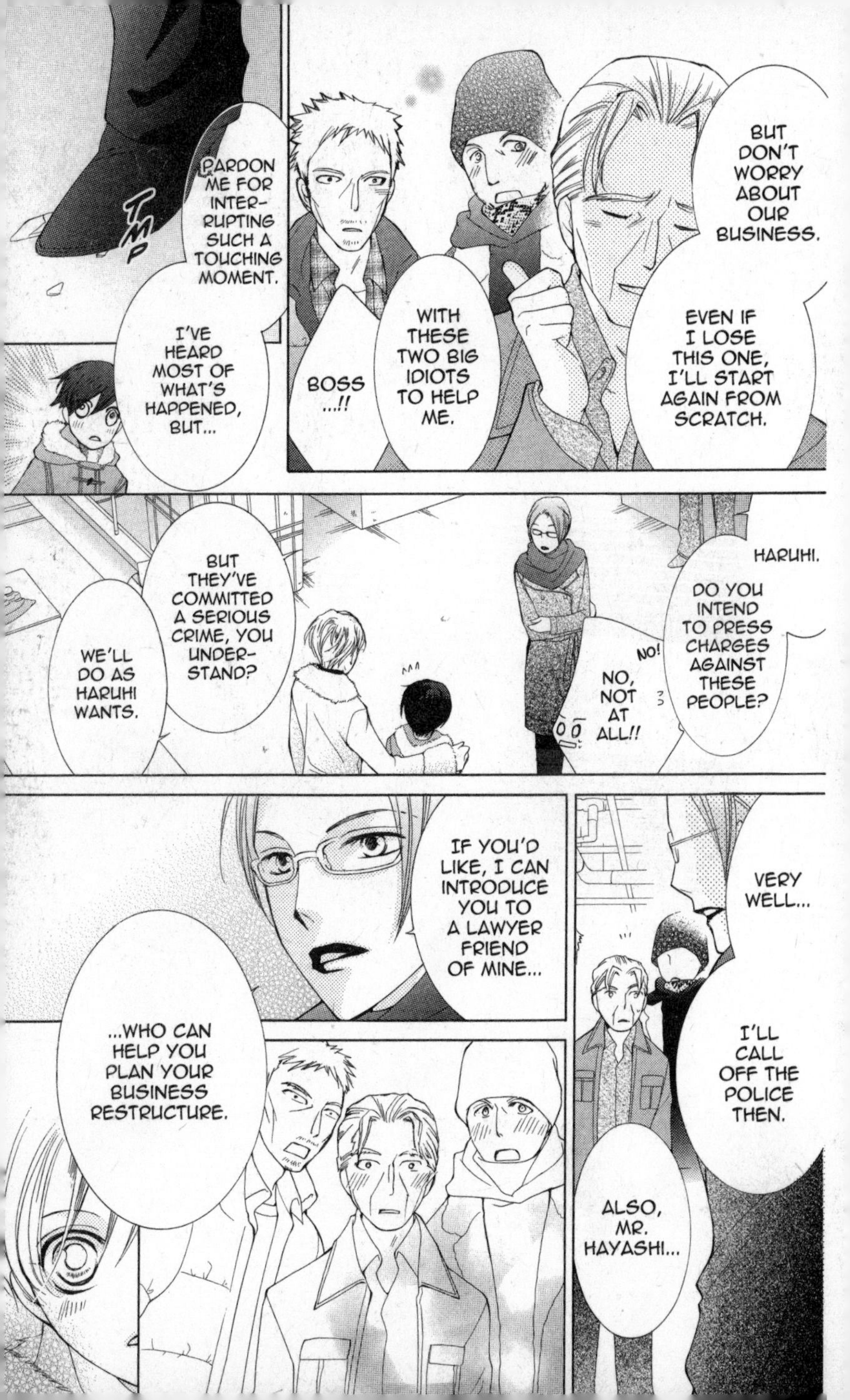
BUT DON'T WORRY ABOUT OUR BUSINESS.
EVEN IF I LOSE THIS ONE, I'LL START AGAIN FROM SCRATCH.
WITH THESE TWO BIG IDIOTS TO HELP ME.
BOSS ...!!
TMP
PARDON ME FOR INTERRUPTING SUCH A TOUCHING MOMENT.
I'VE HEARD MOST OF WHAT'S HAPPENED, BUT...
HARUHI.
DO YOU INTEND TO PRESS CHARGES AGAINST THESE PEOPLE?
NO!
NO, NOT AT ALL!!
BUT THEY'VE COMMITTED A SERIOUS CRIME, YOU UNDERSTAND?
WE'LL DO AS HARUHI WANTS.
VERY WELL...
I'LL CALL OFF THE POLICE THEN.
ALSO, MR. HAYASHI...
IF YOU'D LIKE, I CAN INTRODUCE YOU TO A LAWYER FRIEND OF MINE...
...WHO CAN HELP YOU PLAN YOUR BUSINESS RESTRUCTURE.

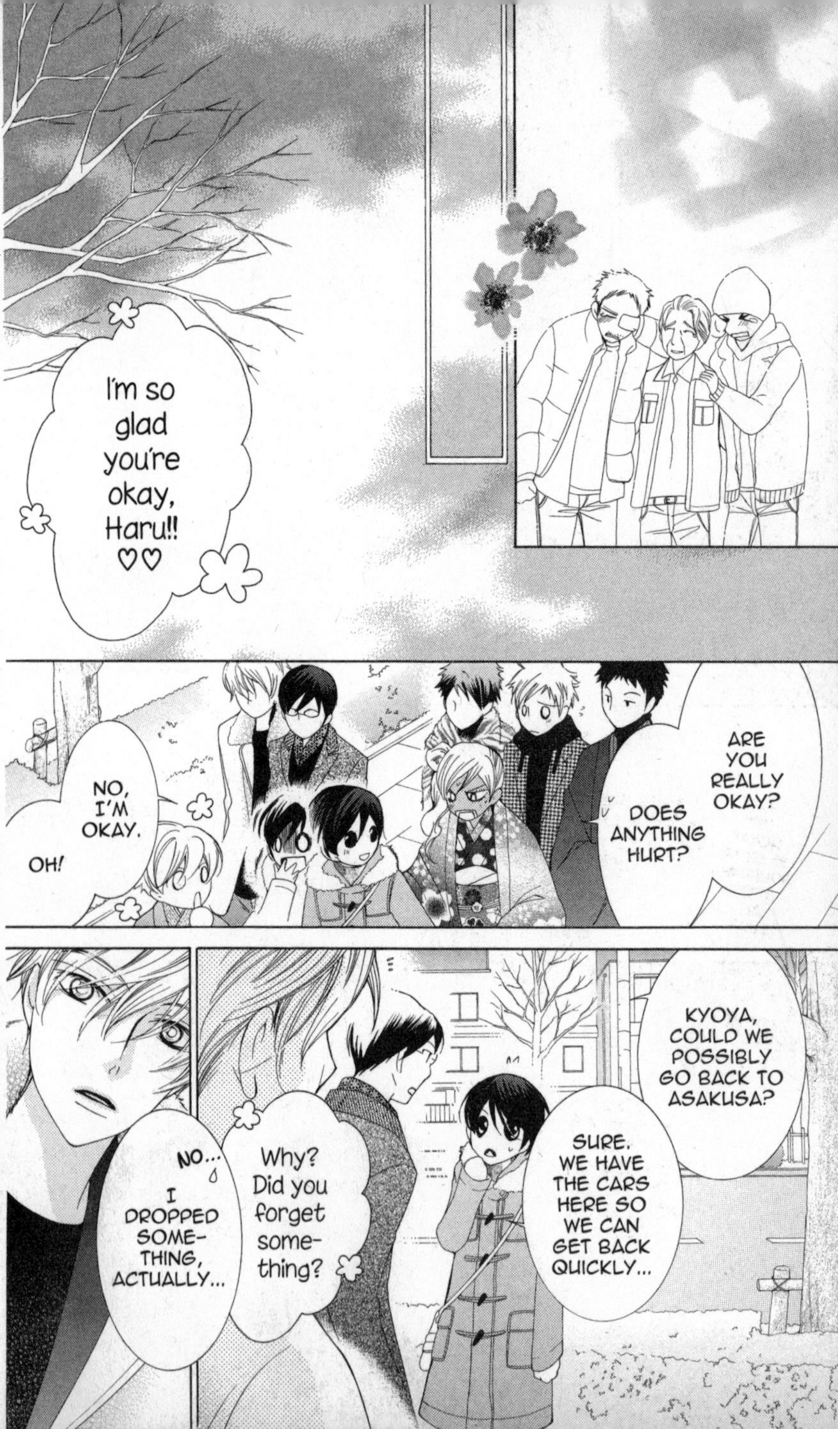
I'm so glad you're okay, Haru!! ♡♡
ARE YOU REALLY OKAY?
DOES ANYTHING HURT?
NO, I'M OKAY.
OH!
KYOYA, COULD WE POSSIBLY GO BACK TO ASAKUSA?
SURE. WE HAVE THE CARS HERE SO WE CAN GET BACK QUICKLY...
Why? Did you forget some-thing?
NO...
I DROPPED SOME-THING, ACTUALLY...

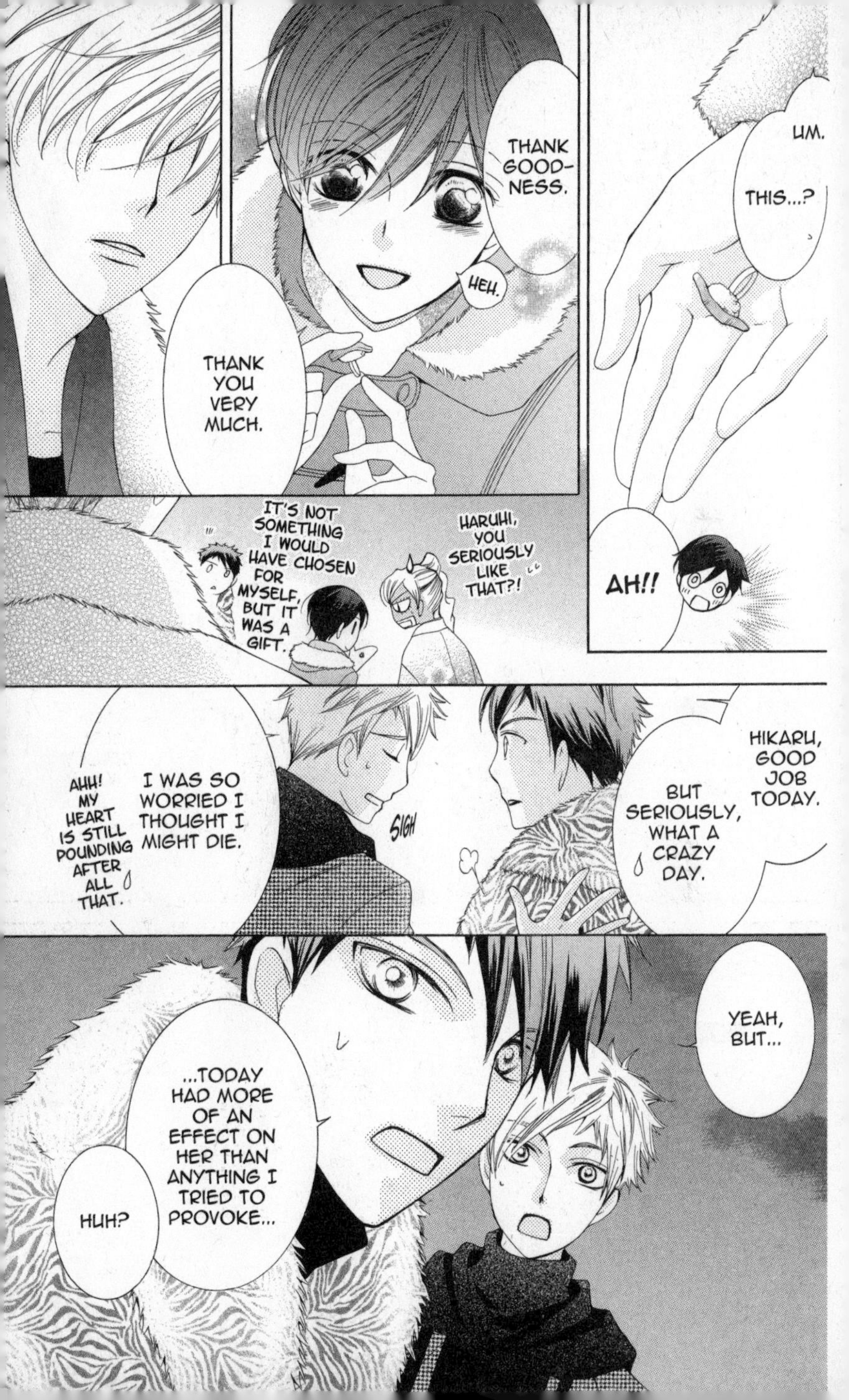
UM.
THIS...?
AH!!
THANK GOODNESS.
HEH.
THANK YOU VERY MUCH.
HARUHI, YOU SERIOUSLY LIKE THAT?!
IT'S NOT SOMETHING I WOULD HAVE CHOSEN FOR MYSELF, BUT IT WAS A GIFT.
HIKARU, GOOD JOB TODAY.
BUT SERIOUSLY, WHAT A CRAZY DAY.
SIGH
I WAS SO WORRIED I THOUGHT I MIGHT DIE.
AHH! MY HEART IS STILL POUNDING AFTER ALL THAT.
YEAH, BUT...
...TODAY HAD MORE OF AN EFFECT ON HER THAN ANYTHING I TRIED TO PROVOKE...
HUH?

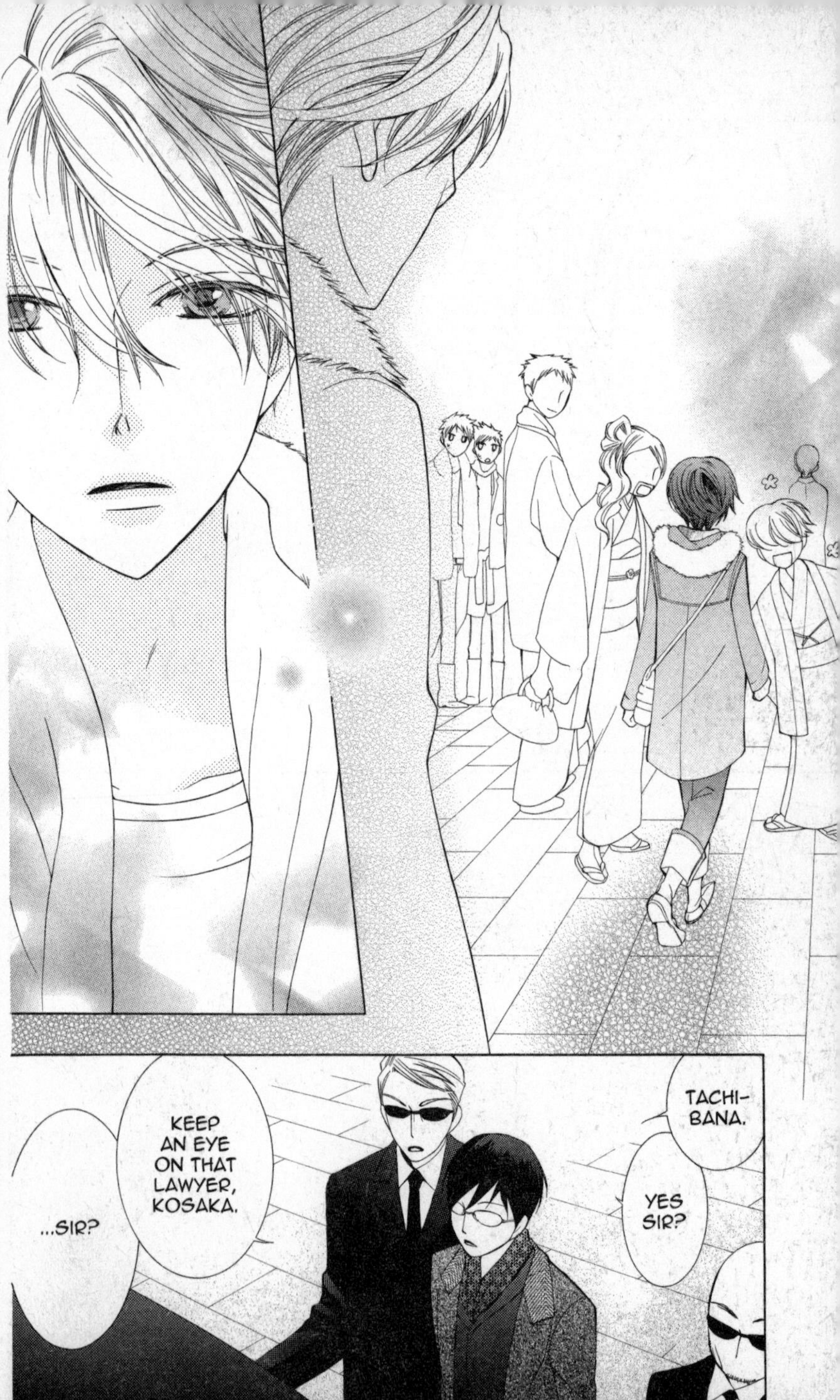
TACHI-BANA.
YES SIR?
KEEP AN EYE ON THAT LAWYER, KOSAKA.
...SIR?

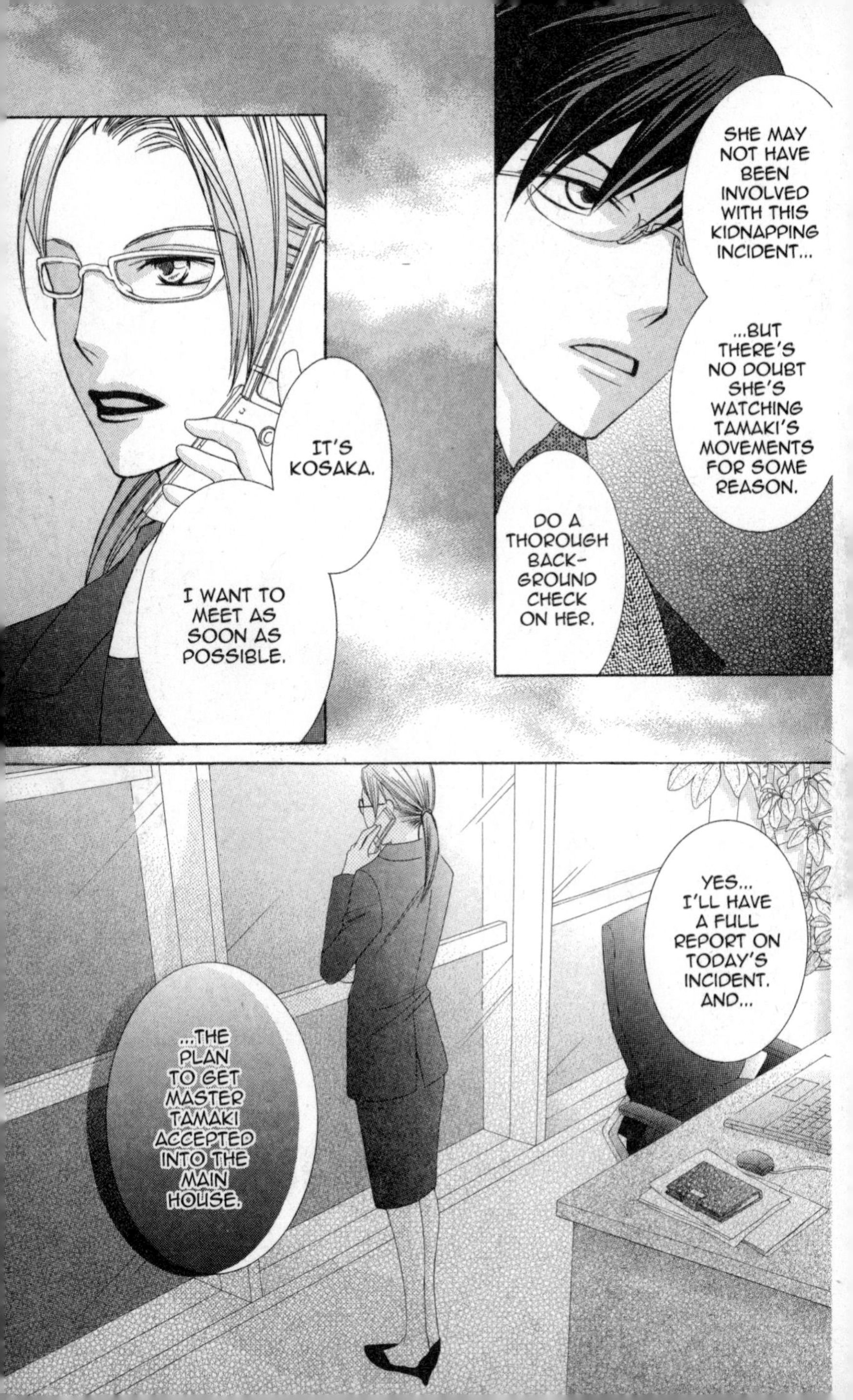
SHE MAY NOT HAVE BEEN INVOLVED WITH THIS KIDNAPPING INCIDENT...
...BUT THERE'S NO DOUBT SHE'S WATCHING TAMAKI'S MOVEMENTS FOR SOME REASON.
DO A THOROUGH BACK-GROUND CHECK ON HER.
IT'S KOSAKA.
I WANT TO MEET AS SOON AS POSSIBLE.
YES... I'LL HAVE A FULL REPORT ON TODAY'S INCIDENT. AND...
...THE PLAN TO GET MASTER TAMAKI ACCEPTED INTO THE MAIN HOUSE.

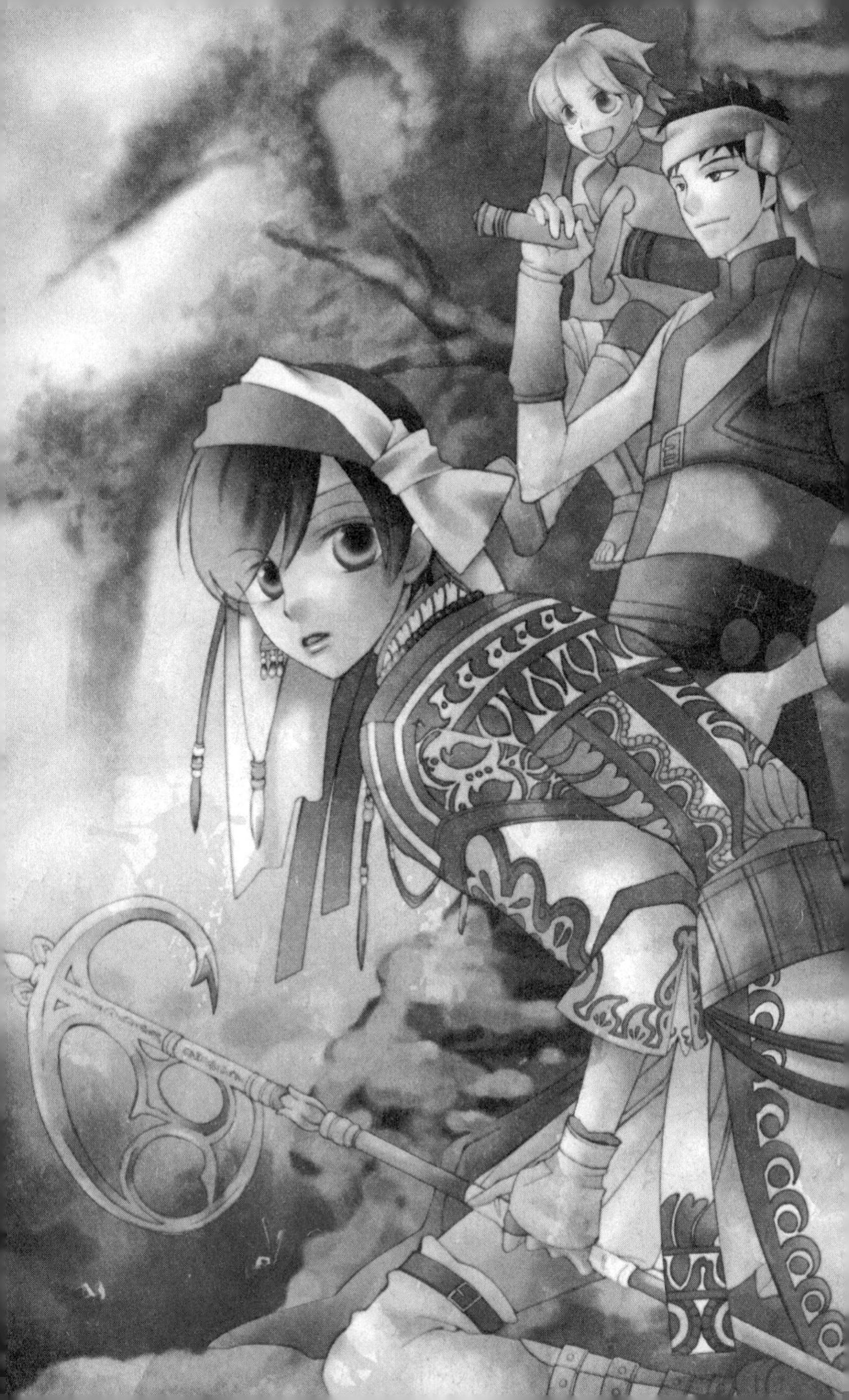

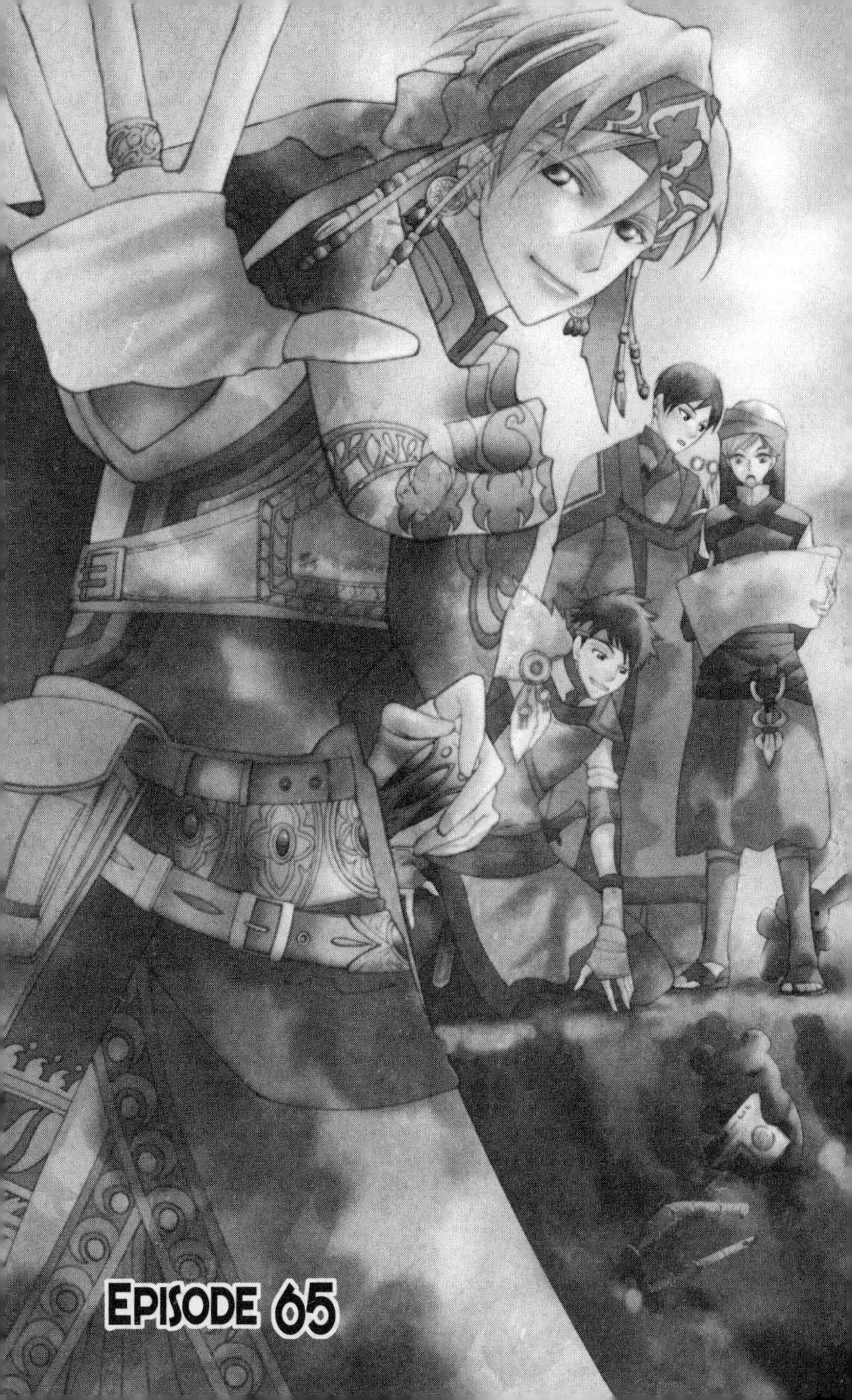
EPISODE 65

TEAM☆HATORI'S ROOM

RIKU

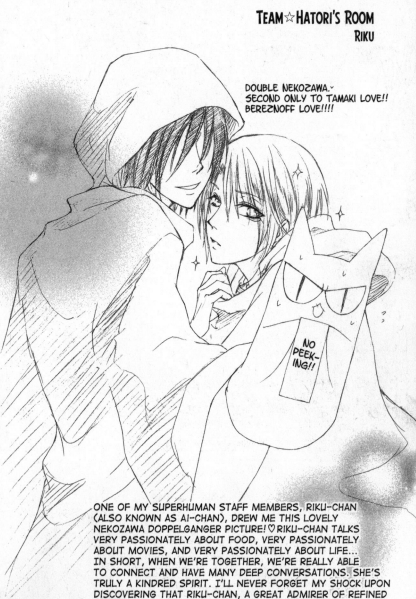

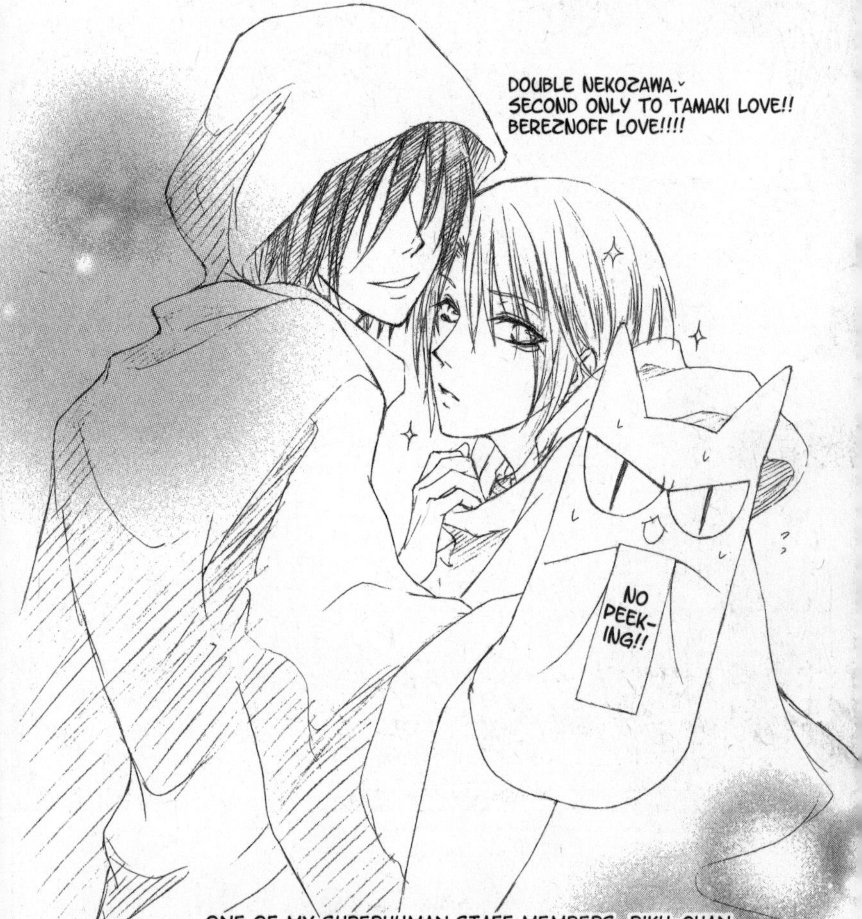
DOUBLE NEKOZAWA.
SECOND ONLY TO TAMAKI LOVE!!
BEREZNOFF LOVE!!!!
NO PEEK-ING!!

ONE OF MY SUPERHUMAN STAFF MEMBERS, RIKU-CHAN (ALSO KNOWN AS AI-CHAN), DREW ME THIS LOVELY NEKOZAWA DOPPELGANGER PICTURE! ♡ RIKU-CHAN TALKS VERY PASSIONATELY ABOUT FOOD, VERY PASSIONATELY ABOUT MOVIES, AND VERY PASSIONATELY ABOUT LIFE... IN SHORT, WHEN WE'RE TOGETHER, WE'RE REALLY ABLE TO CONNECT AND HAVE MANY DEEP CONVERSATIONS. SHE'S TRULY A KINDRED SPIRIT. I'LL NEVER FORGET MY SHOCK UPON DISCOVERING THAT RIKU-CHAN, A GREAT ADMIRER OF REFINED AESTHETICS, COLLECTS RILAKKUMA CHARACTER GOODS!

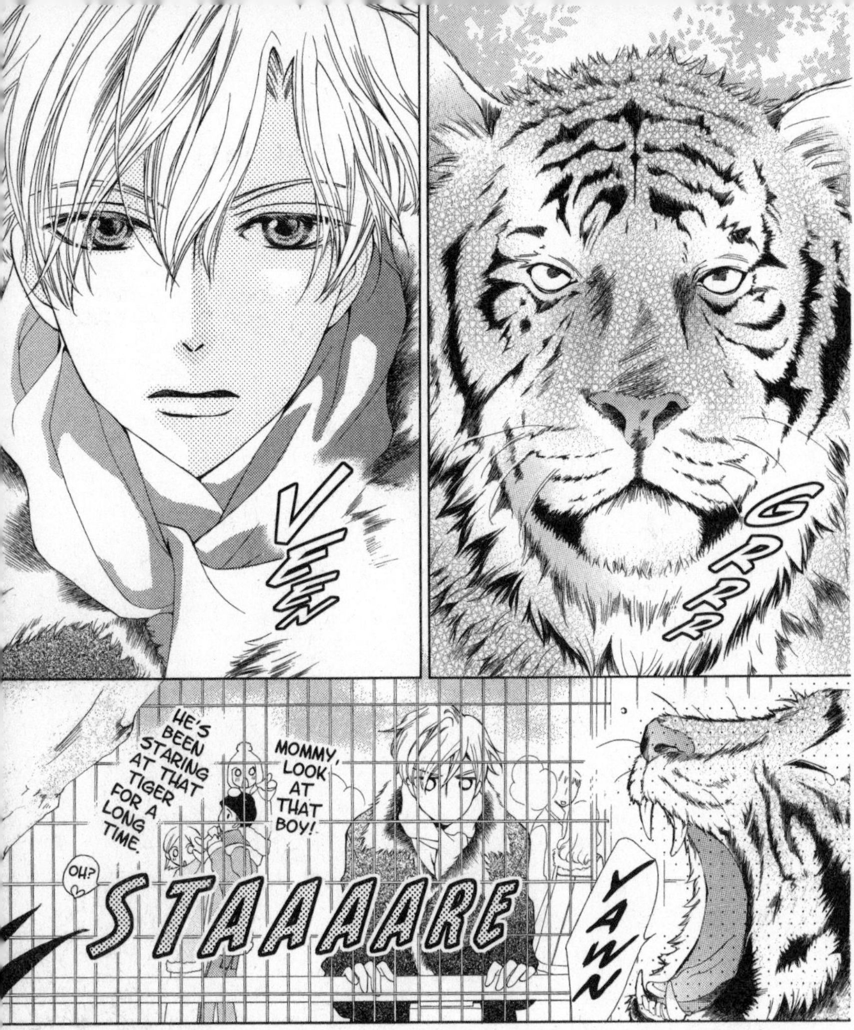
GRRRR
YAWN
STAAAARE
MOMMY, LOOK AT THAT BOY!
HE'S BEEN STARING AT THAT TIGER FOR A LONG TIME.
OH?

SUPPORTING CHARACTERS INTRODUCTION

Kazukiyo Souga

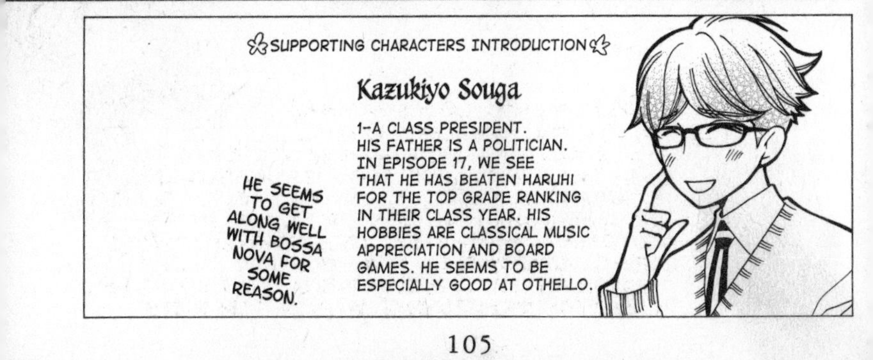

1-A CLASS PRESIDENT. HIS FATHER IS A POLITICIAN. IN EPISODE 17, WE SEE THAT HE HAS BEATEN HARUHI FOR THE TOP GRADE RANKING IN THEIR CLASS YEAR. HIS HOBBIES ARE CLASSICAL MUSIC APPRECIATION AND BOARD GAMES. HE SEEMS TO BE ESPECIALLY GOOD AT OTHELLO.

HE SEEMS TO GET ALONG WELL WITH BOSSA NOVA FOR SOME REASON.

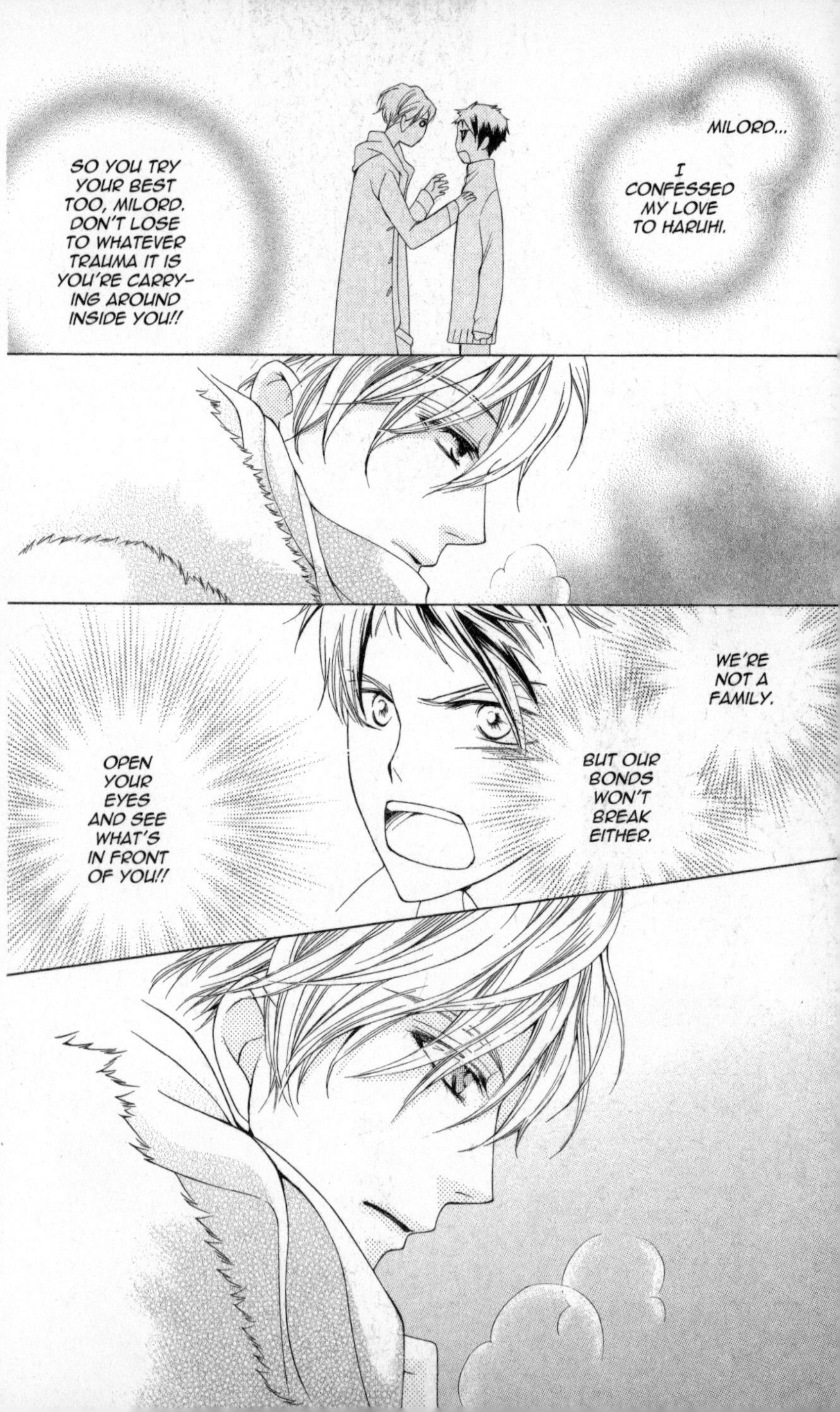
MILORD...
I CONFESSED MY LOVE TO HARUHI.
SO YOU TRY YOUR BEST TOO, MILORD. DON'T LOSE TO WHATEVER TRAUMA IT IS YOU'RE CARRYING AROUND INSIDE YOU!!
WE'RE NOT A FAMILY.
BUT OUR BONDS WON'T BREAK EITHER.
OPEN YOUR EYES AND SEE WHAT'S IN FRONT OF YOU!!

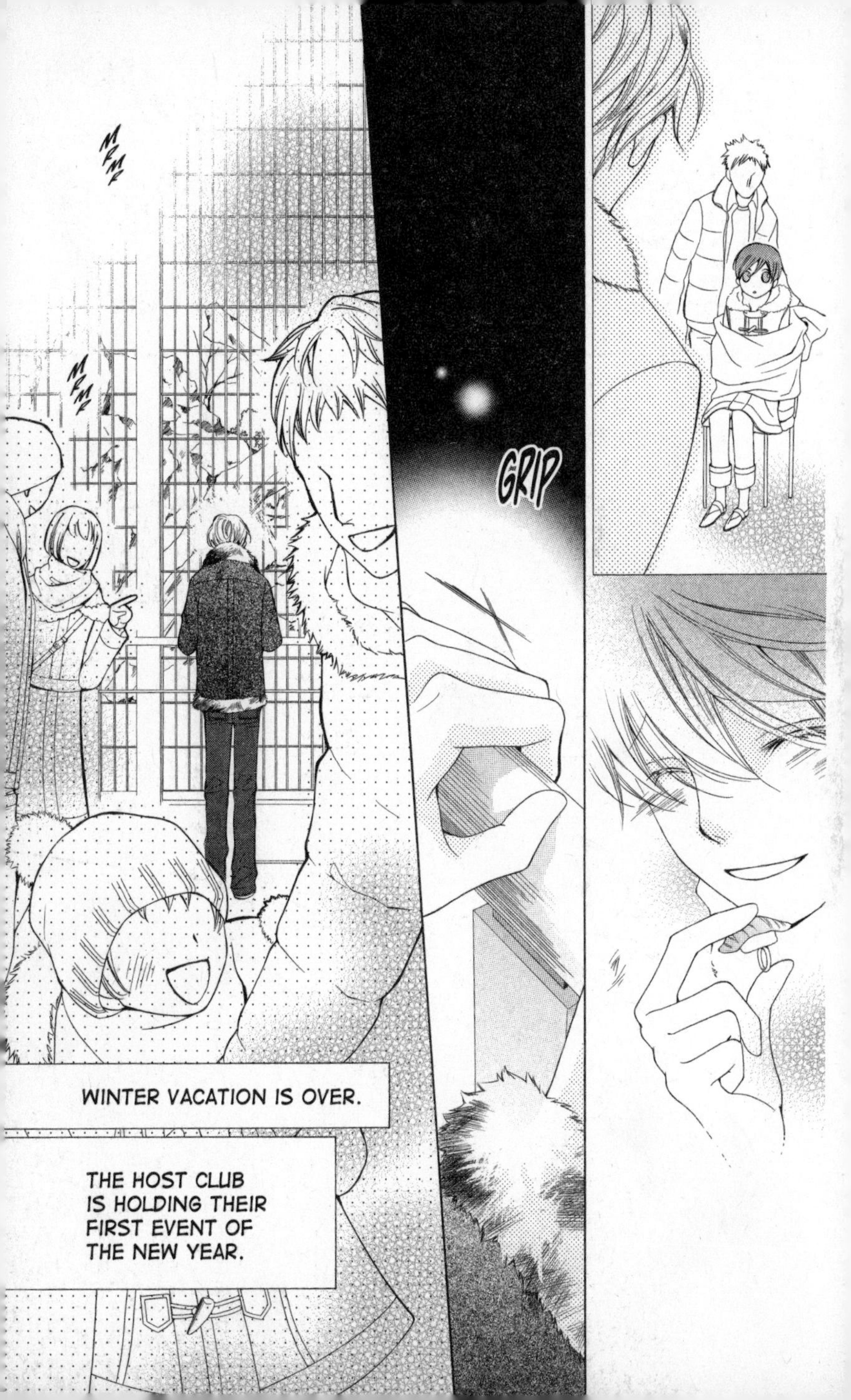
GRIP
MRMR
MRMR
WINTER VACATION IS OVER.
THE HOST CLUB IS HOLDING THEIR FIRST EVENT OF THE NEW YEAR.

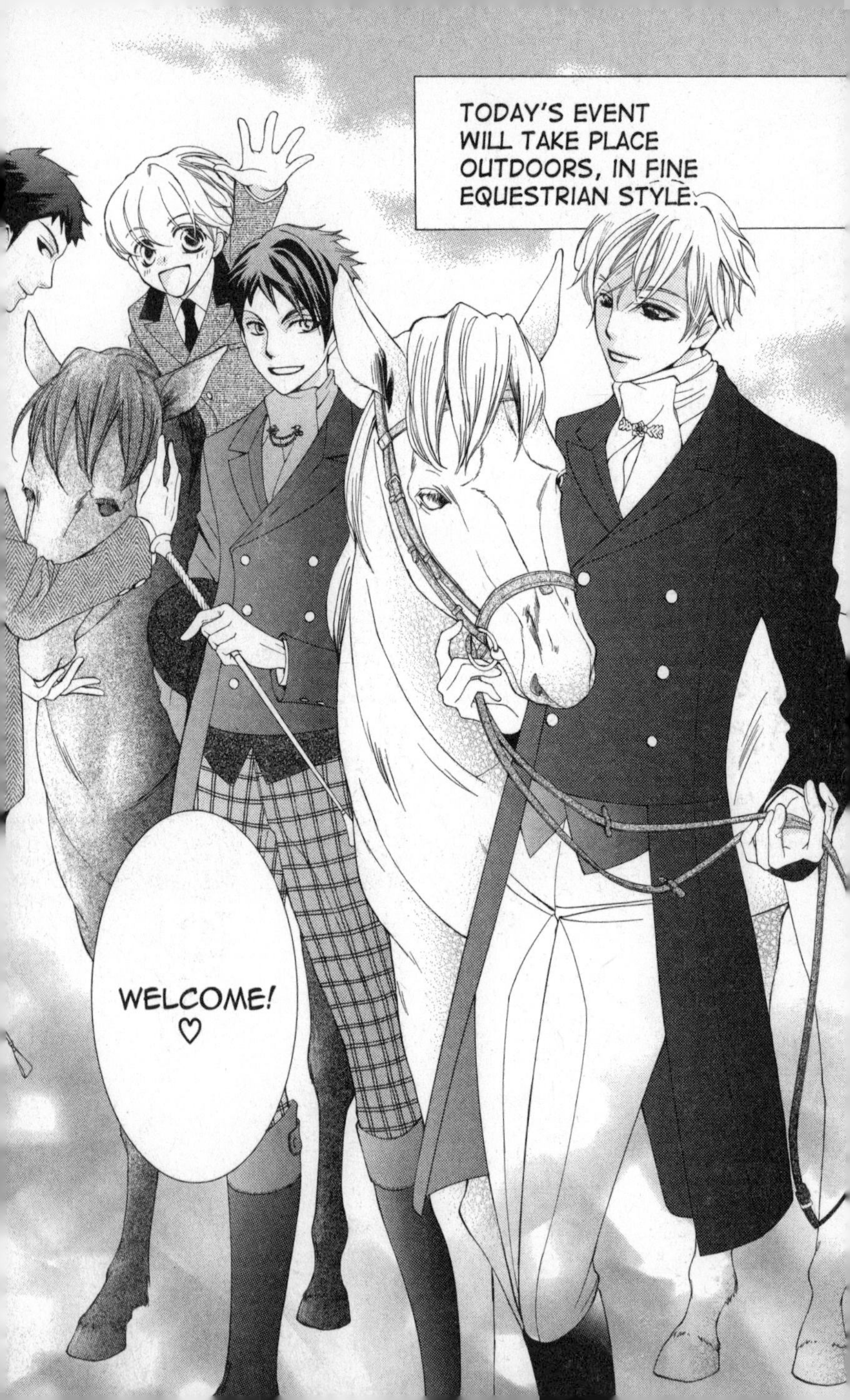
TODAY'S EVENT WILL TAKE PLACE OUTDOORS, IN FINE EQUESTRIAN STYLE.
WELCOME! ♡

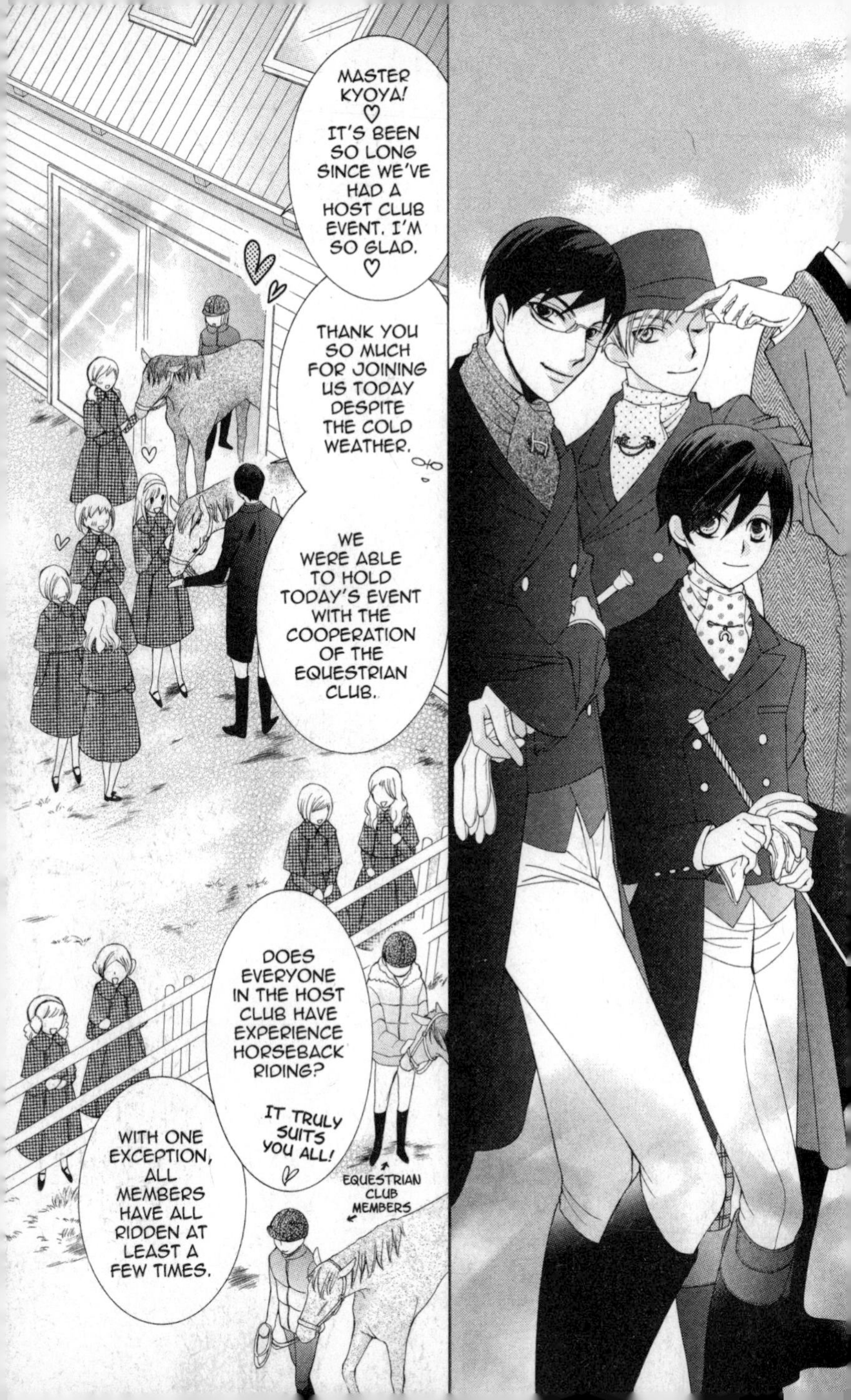
MASTER KYOYA! ♡ IT'S BEEN SO LONG SINCE WE'VE HAD A HOST CLUB EVENT. I'M SO GLAD. ♡
THANK YOU SO MUCH FOR JOINING US TODAY DESPITE THE COLD WEATHER.
WE WERE ABLE TO HOLD TODAY'S EVENT WITH THE COOPERATION OF THE EQUESTRIAN CLUB.
DOES EVERYONE IN THE HOST CLUB HAVE EXPERIENCE HORSEBACK RIDING?
IT TRULY SUITS YOU ALL! ♡
EQUESTRIAN CLUB MEMBERS
WITH ONE EXCEPTION, ALL MEMBERS HAVE ALL RIDDEN AT LEAST A FEW TIMES.

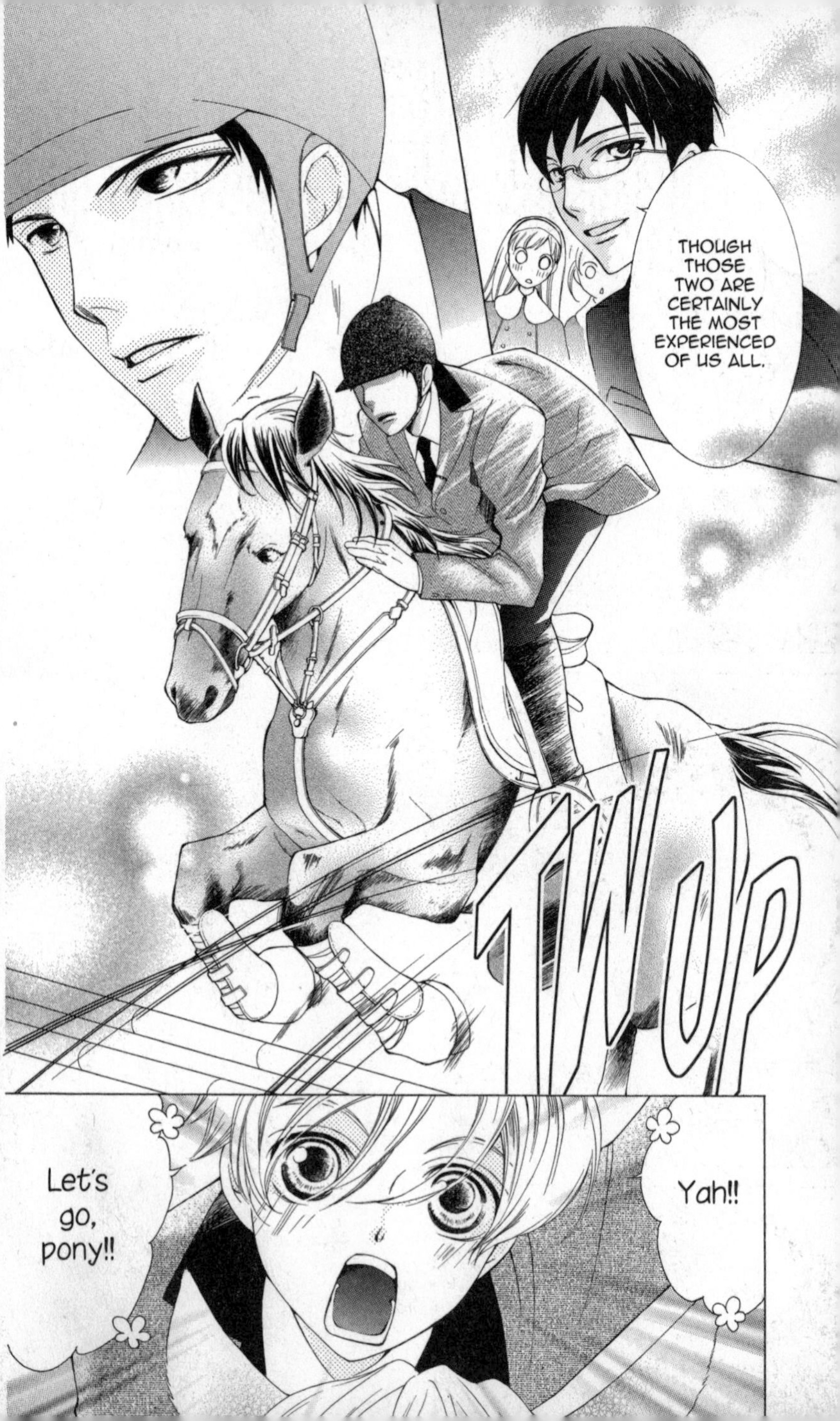
THOUGH THOSE TWO ARE CERTAINLY THE MOST EXPERIENCED OF US ALL.
TWUP
Yah!!
Let's go, pony!!

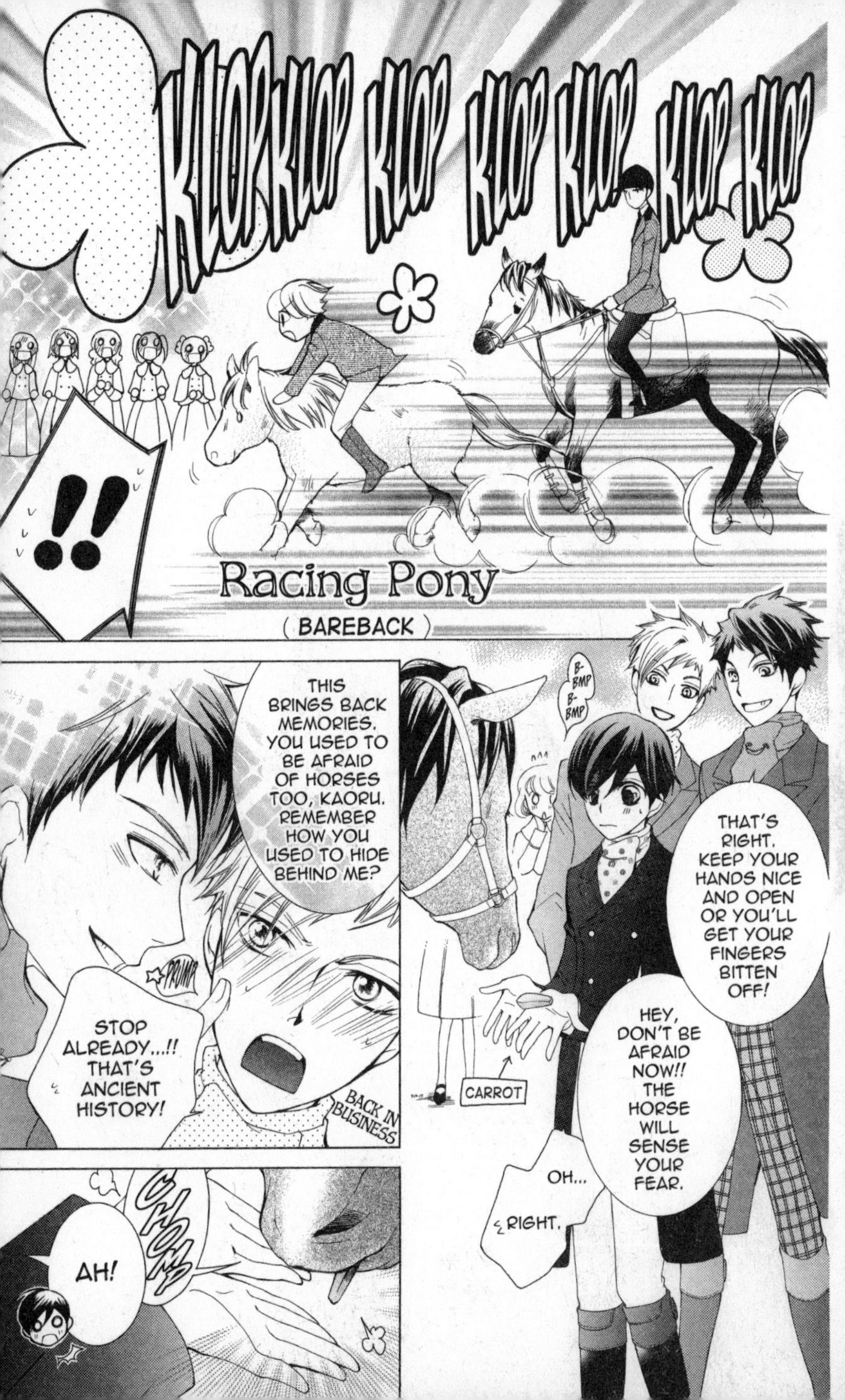

KLOP KLOP KLOP KLOP KLOP KLOP KLOP
!!
Racing Pony
(BAREBACK)
B-BMP B-BMP
THAT'S RIGHT. KEEP YOUR HANDS NICE AND OPEN OR YOU'LL GET YOUR FINGERS BITTEN OFF!
HEY, DON'T BE AFRAID NOW!! THE HORSE WILL SENSE YOUR FEAR.
CARROT
OH...
RIGHT.
THIS BRINGS BACK MEMORIES. YOU USED TO BE AFRAID OF HORSES TOO, KAORU. REMEMBER HOW YOU USED TO HIDE BEHIND ME?
PROMP
STOP ALREADY...!! THAT'S ANCIENT HISTORY!
BACK IN BUSINESS
CHOMP
AH!

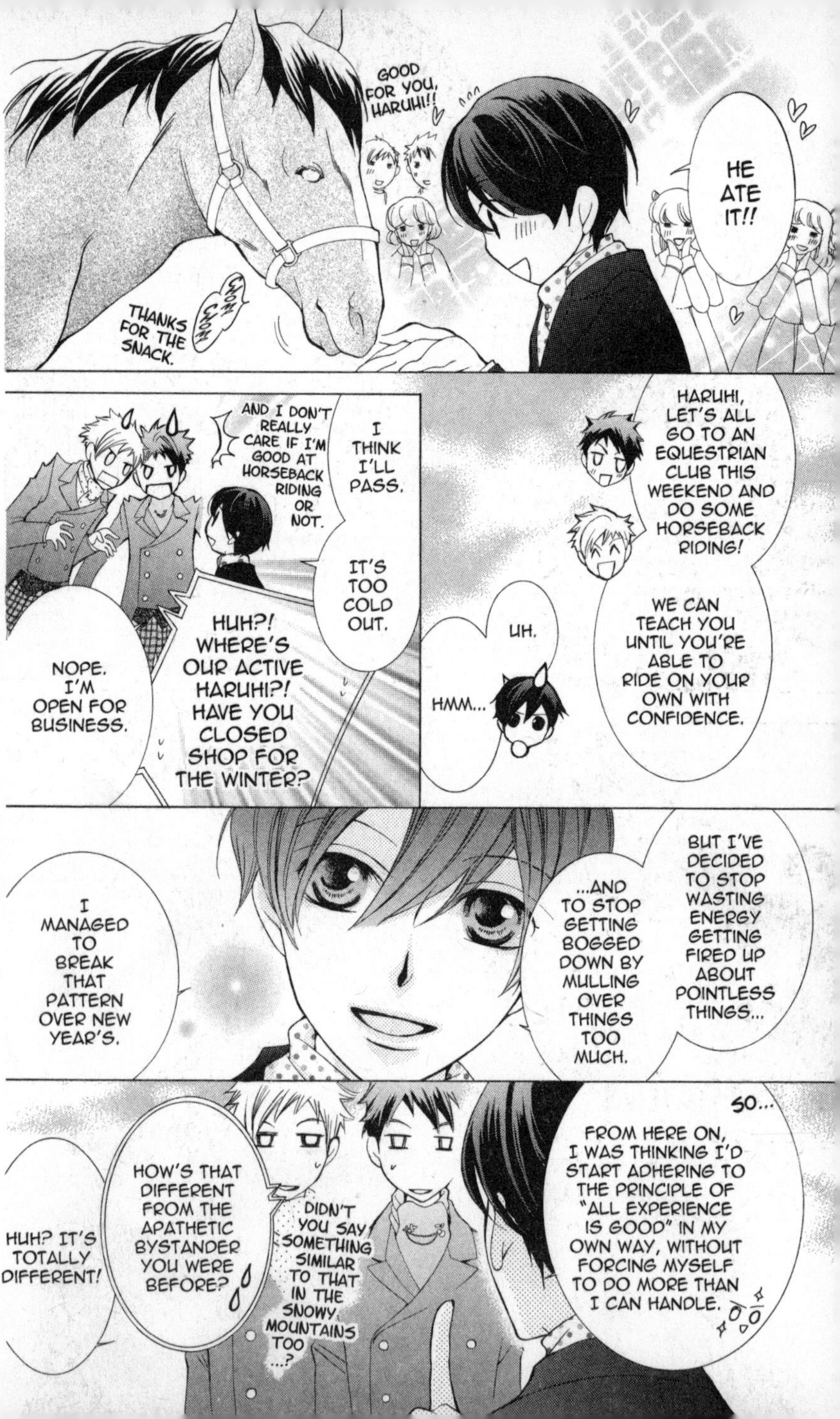
HE ATE IT!!
GOOD FOR YOU, HARUHI!!
CHOM! CHOM!
THANKS FOR THE SNACK.
HARUHI, LET'S ALL GO TO AN EQUESTRIAN CLUB THIS WEEKEND AND DO SOME HORSEBACK RIDING!
WE CAN TEACH YOU UNTIL YOU'RE ABLE TO RIDE ON YOUR OWN WITH CONFIDENCE.
UH.
HMM...
I THINK I'LL PASS.
AND I DON'T REALLY CARE IF I'M GOOD AT HORSEBACK RIDING OR NOT.
IT'S TOO COLD OUT.
HUH?! WHERE'S OUR ACTIVE HARUHI?! HAVE YOU CLOSED SHOP FOR THE WINTER?
NOPE. I'M OPEN FOR BUSINESS.
BUT I'VE DECIDED TO STOP WASTING ENERGY GETTING FIRED UP ABOUT POINTLESS THINGS...
...AND TO STOP GETTING BOGGED DOWN BY MULLING OVER THINGS TOO MUCH.
I MANAGED TO BREAK THAT PATTERN OVER NEW YEAR'S.
SO...
FROM HERE ON, I WAS THINKING I'D START ADHERING TO THE PRINCIPLE OF "ALL EXPERIENCE IS GOOD" IN MY OWN WAY, WITHOUT FORCING MYSELF TO DO MORE THAN I CAN HANDLE.
DIDN'T YOU SAY SOMETHING SIMILAR TO THAT IN THE SNOWY MOUNTAINS TOO...?
HOW'S THAT DIFFERENT FROM THE APATHETIC BYSTANDER YOU WERE BEFORE?
HUH? IT'S TOTALLY DIFFERENT!

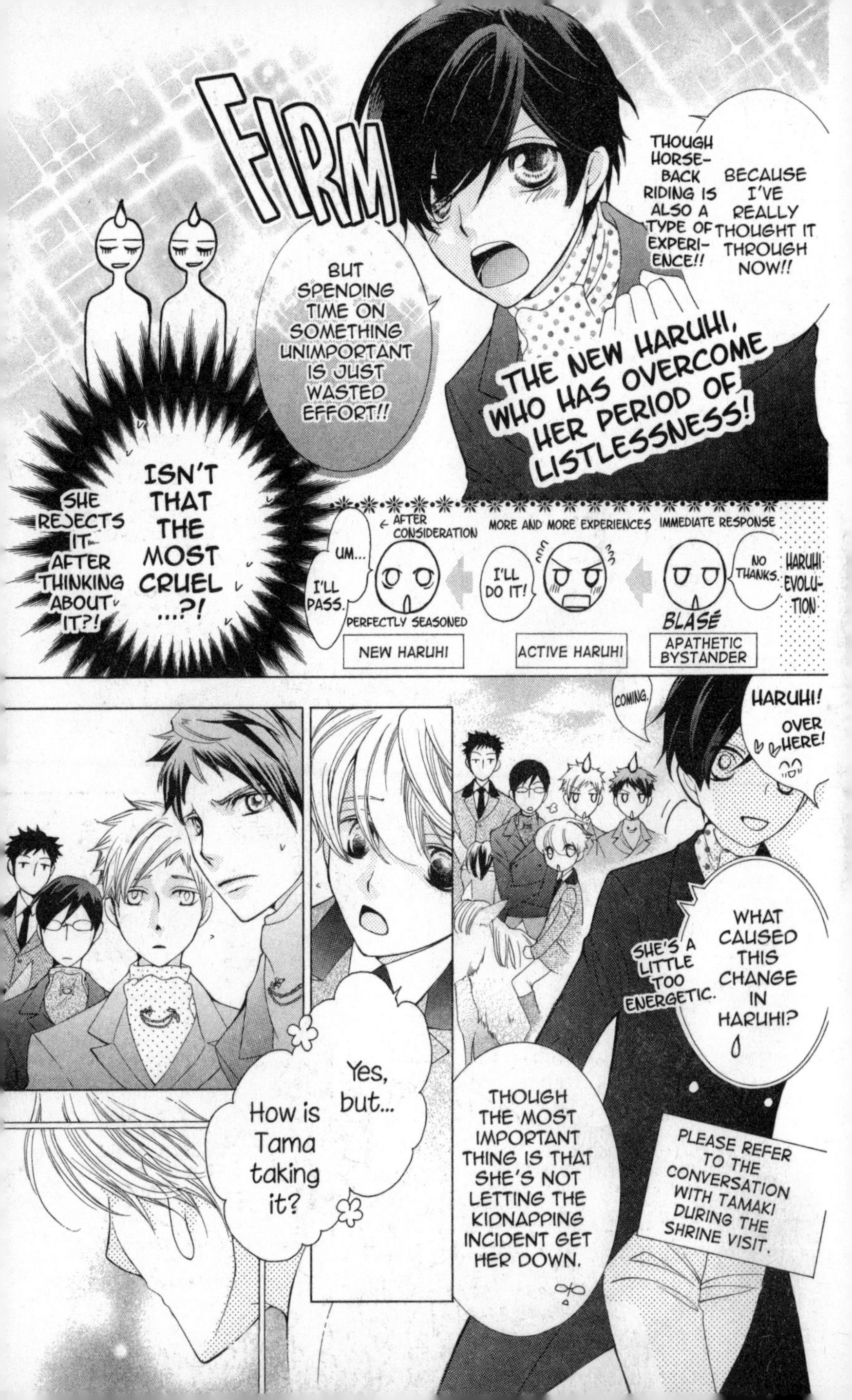
BECAUSE I'VE REALLY THOUGHT IT THROUGH NOW!!
THOUGH HORSE-BACK RIDING IS ALSO A TYPE OF EXPERI-ENCE!!
FIRM
BUT SPENDING TIME ON SOMETHING UNIMPORTANT IS JUST WASTED EFFORT!!
THE NEW HARUHI, WHO HAS OVERCOME HER PERIOD OF LISTLESSNESS!
ISN'T THAT THE MOST CRUEL ...?!
SHE REJECTS IT AFTER THINKING ABOUT IT?!
HARUHI EVOLU-TION
IMMEDIATE RESPONSE
NO THANKS.
BLASÉ
APATHETIC BYSTANDER
MORE AND MORE EXPERIENCES
I'LL DO IT!
ACTIVE HARUHI
← AFTER CONSIDERATION
UM... I'LL PASS.
PERFECTLY SEASONED
NEW HARUHI
HARUHI! OVER HERE!
COMING.
WHAT CAUSED THIS CHANGE IN HARUHI?
SHE'S A LITTLE TOO ENERGETIC.
THOUGH THE MOST IMPORTANT THING IS THAT SHE'S NOT LETTING THE KIDNAPPING INCIDENT GET HER DOWN.
PLEASE REFER TO THE CONVERSATION WITH TAMAKI DURING THE SHRINE VISIT.
Yes, but...
How is Tama taking it?

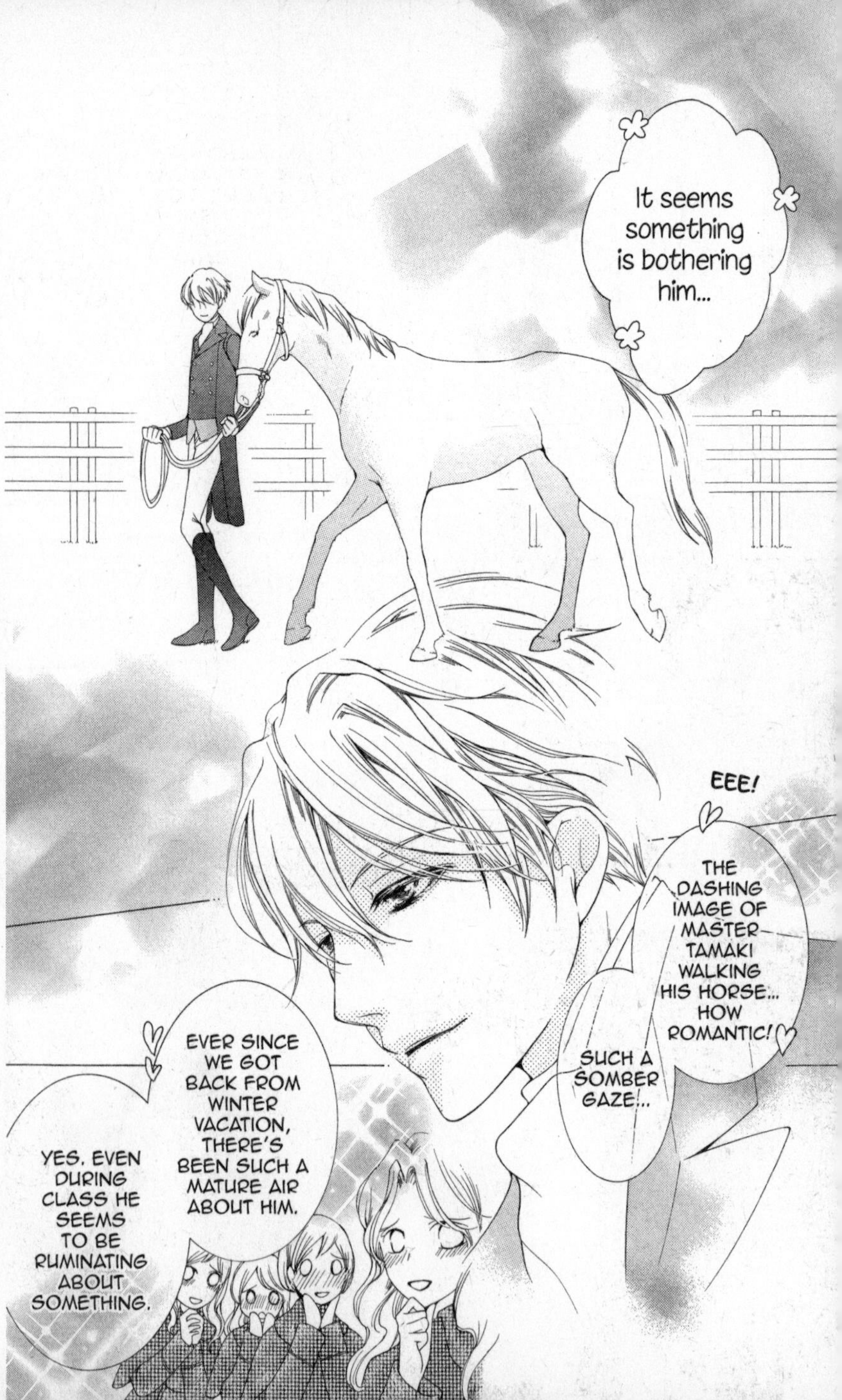
It seems something is bothering him...
EEE!
THE DASHING IMAGE OF MASTER TAMAKI WALKING HIS HORSE... HOW ROMANTIC!
SUCH A SOMBER GAZE...
EVER SINCE WE GOT BACK FROM WINTER VACATION, THERE'S BEEN SUCH A MATURE AIR ABOUT HIM.
YES. EVEN DURING CLASS HE SEEMS TO BE RUMINATING ABOUT SOMETHING.

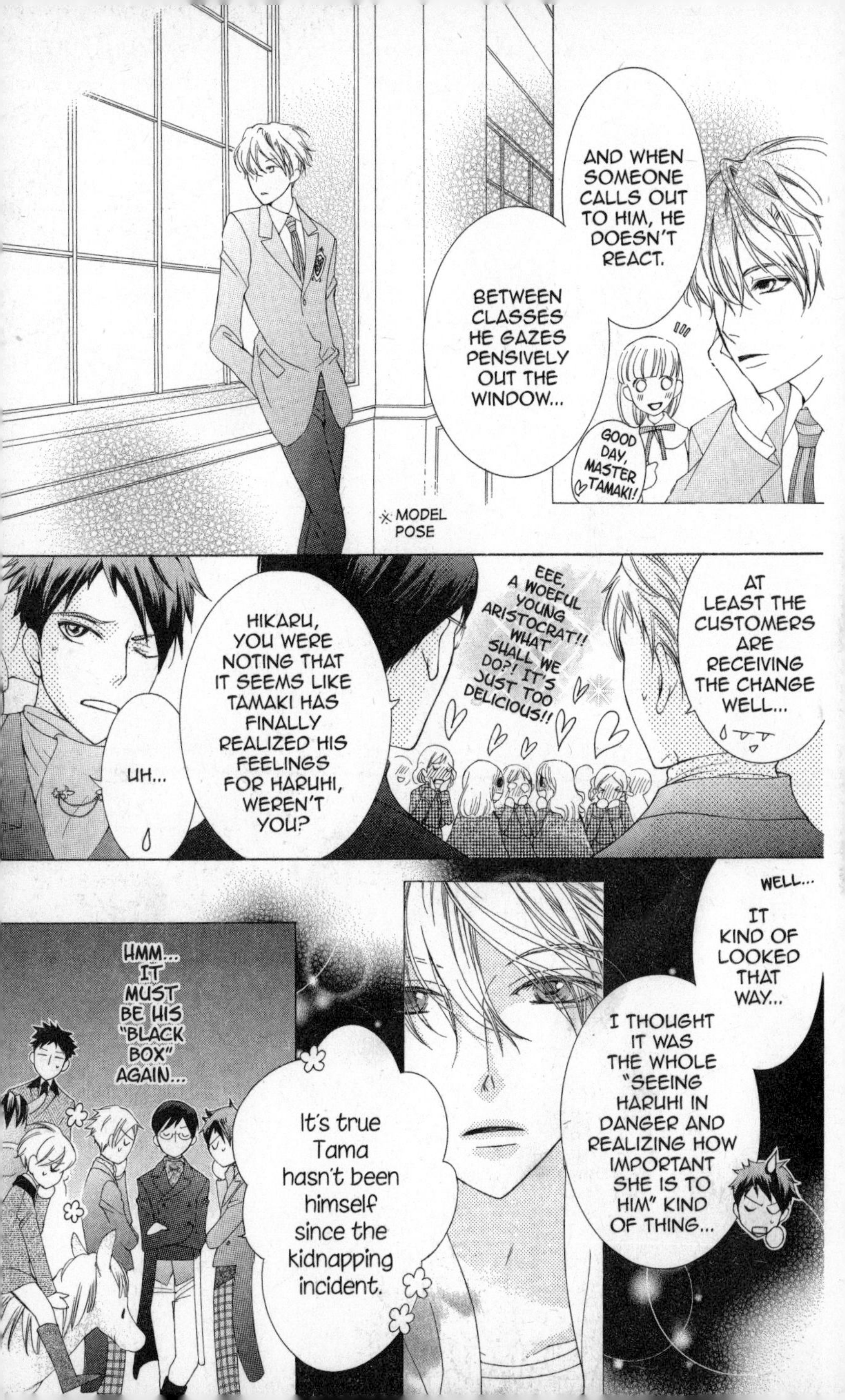
AND WHEN SOMEONE CALLS OUT TO HIM, HE DOESN'T REACT.
BETWEEN CLASSES HE GAZES PENSIVELY OUT THE WINDOW...
GOOD DAY, MASTER TAMAKI!
※MODEL POSE
AT LEAST THE CUSTOMERS ARE RECEIVING THE CHANGE WELL...
EEE, A WOEFUL YOUNG ARISTOCRAT!! WHAT SHALL WE DO?! IT'S JUST TOO DELICIOUS!!
HIKARU, YOU WERE NOTING THAT IT SEEMS LIKE TAMAKI HAS FINALLY REALIZED HIS FEELINGS FOR HARUHI, WEREN'T YOU?
UH...
WELL... IT KIND OF LOOKED THAT WAY...
I THOUGHT IT WAS THE WHOLE "SEEING HARUHI IN DANGER AND REALIZING HOW IMPORTANT SHE IS TO HIM" KIND OF THING...
It's true Tama hasn't been himself since the kidnapping incident.
HMM... IT MUST BE HIS "BLACK BOX" AGAIN...

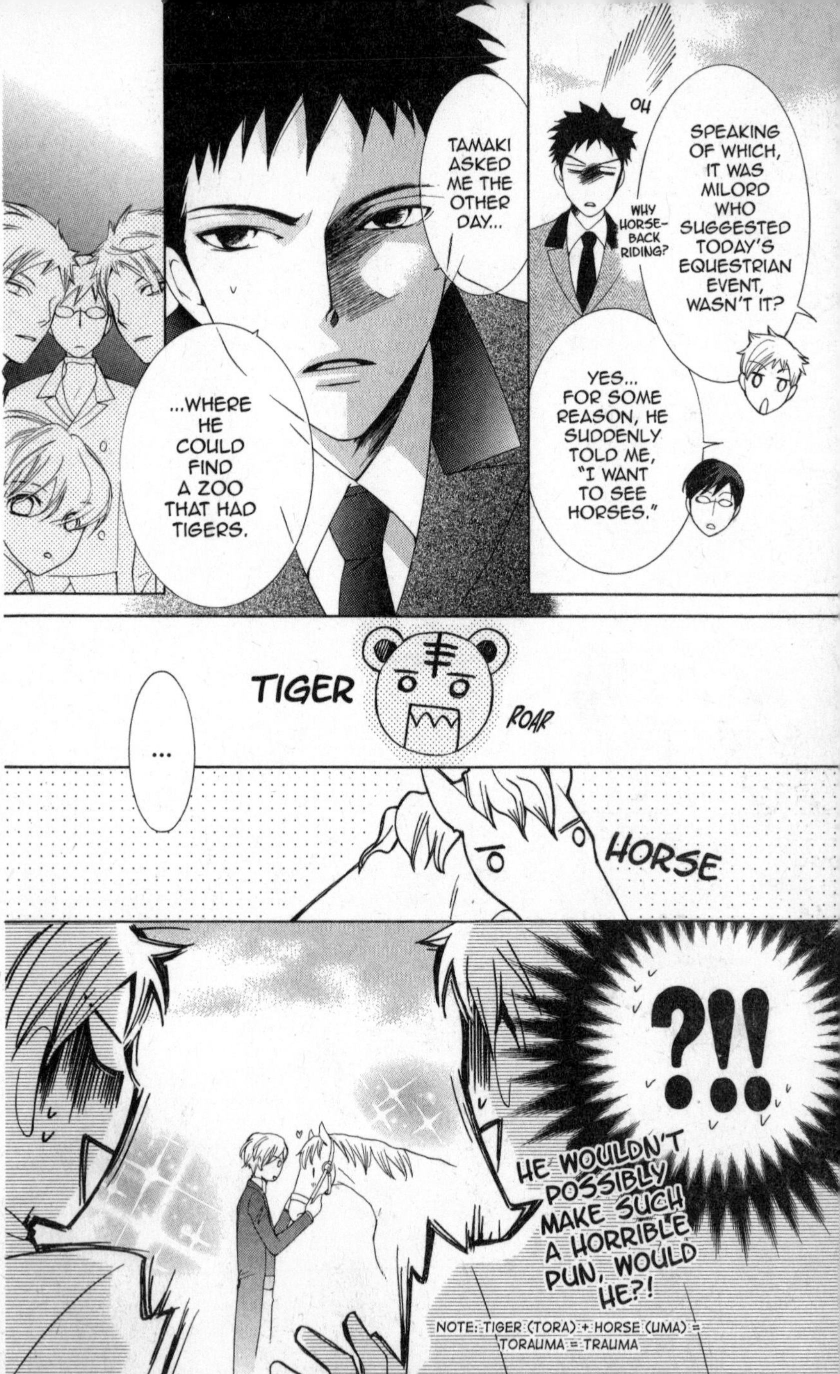
OH
SPEAKING OF WHICH, IT WAS MILORD WHO SUGGESTED TODAY'S EQUESTRIAN EVENT, WASN'T IT?
WHY HORSE-BACK RIDING?
YES... FOR SOME REASON, HE SUDDENLY TOLD ME, "I WANT TO SEE HORSES."
TAMAKI ASKED ME THE OTHER DAY...
...WHERE HE COULD FIND A ZOO THAT HAD TIGERS.
TIGER
ROAR
...
HORSE
?!!
HE WOULDN'T POSSIBLY MAKE SUCH A HORRIBLE PUN, WOULD HE?!
NOTE: TIGER (TORA) + HORSE (UMA) = TORAUMA = TRAUMA

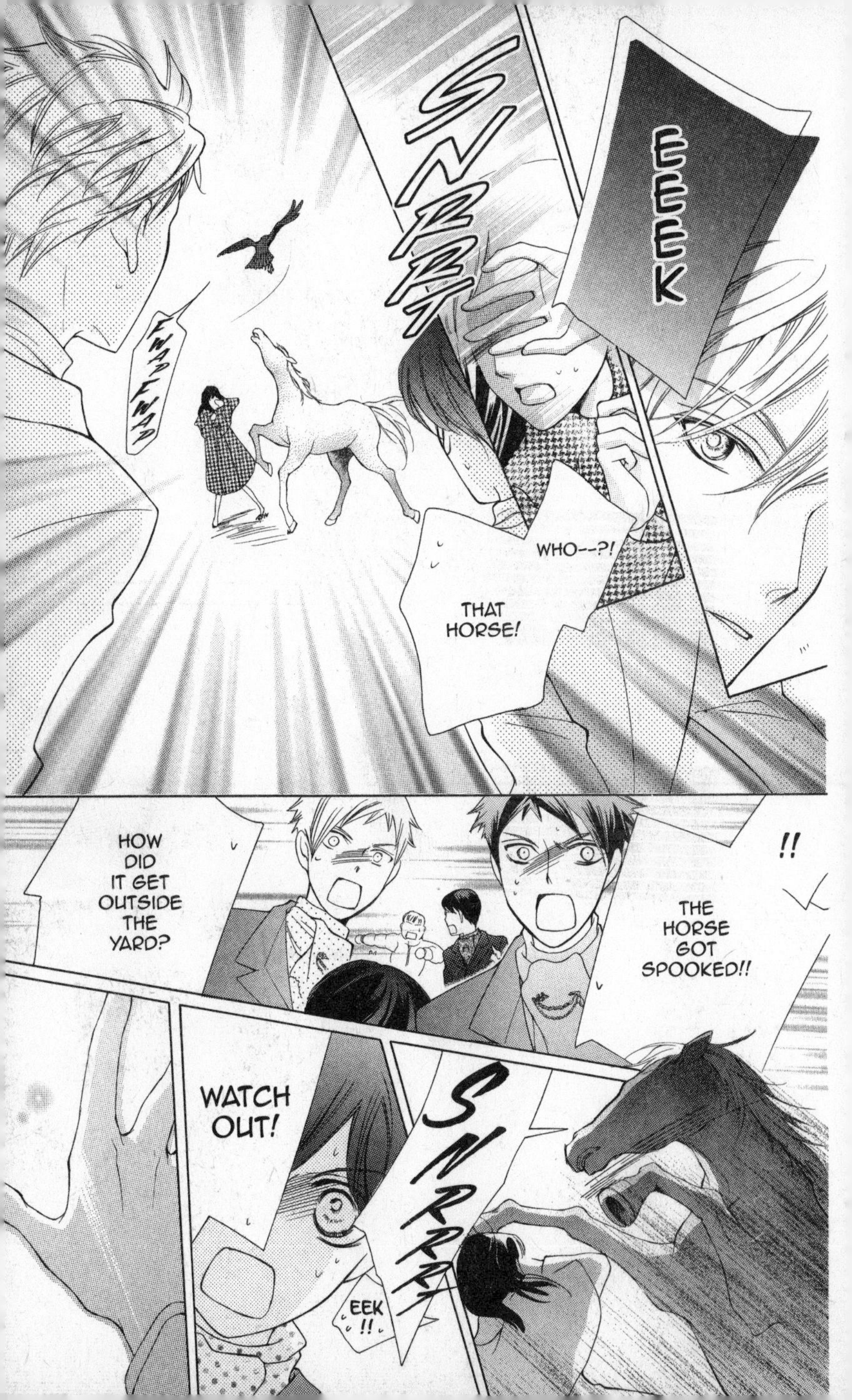
EEEK
SNRRR
WHO--?!
THAT HORSE!
FWAP FWAP
!!
THE HORSE GOT SPOOKED!!
HOW DID IT GET OUTSIDE THE YARD?
SNRRR
WATCH OUT!
EEK !!

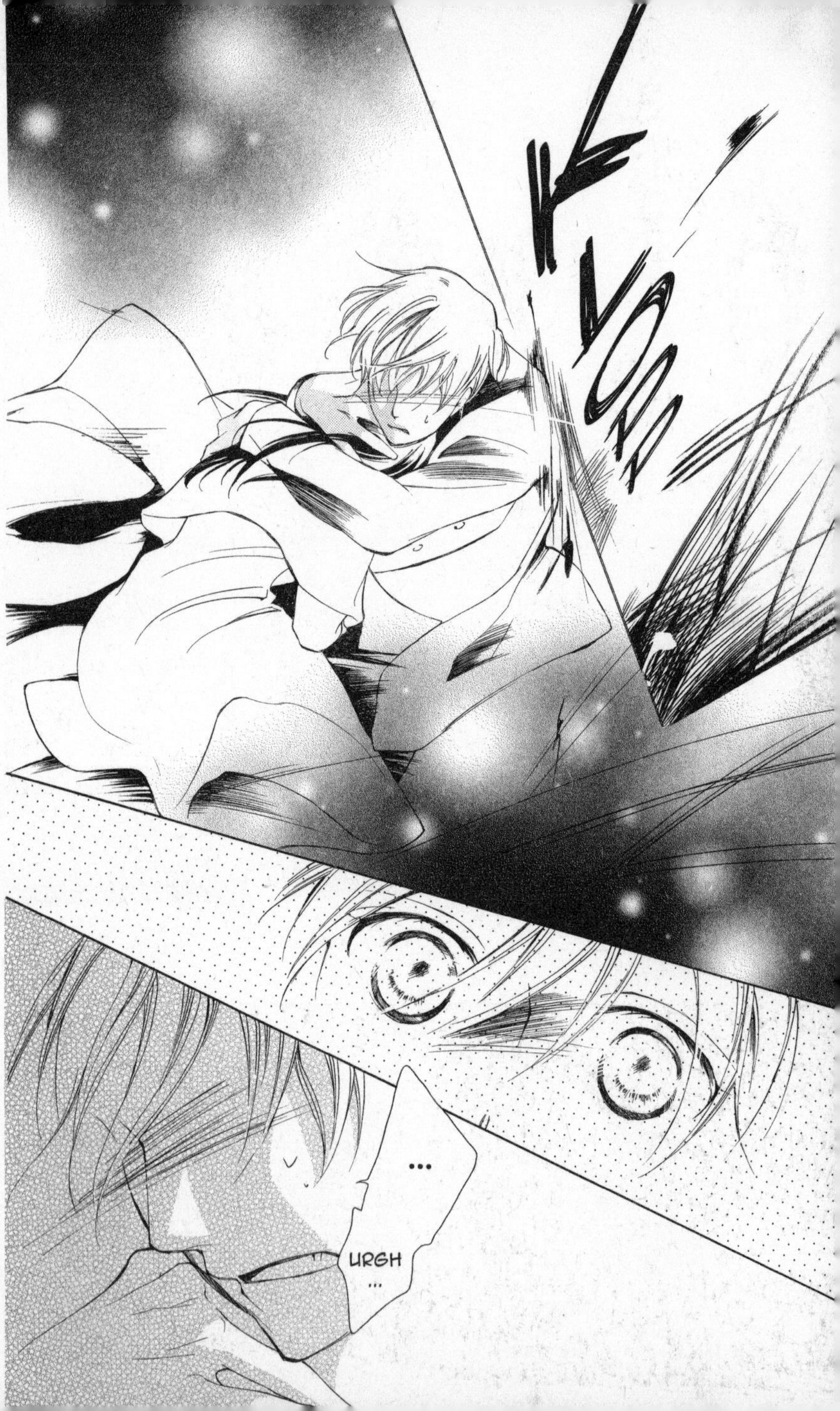
...
URGH ...

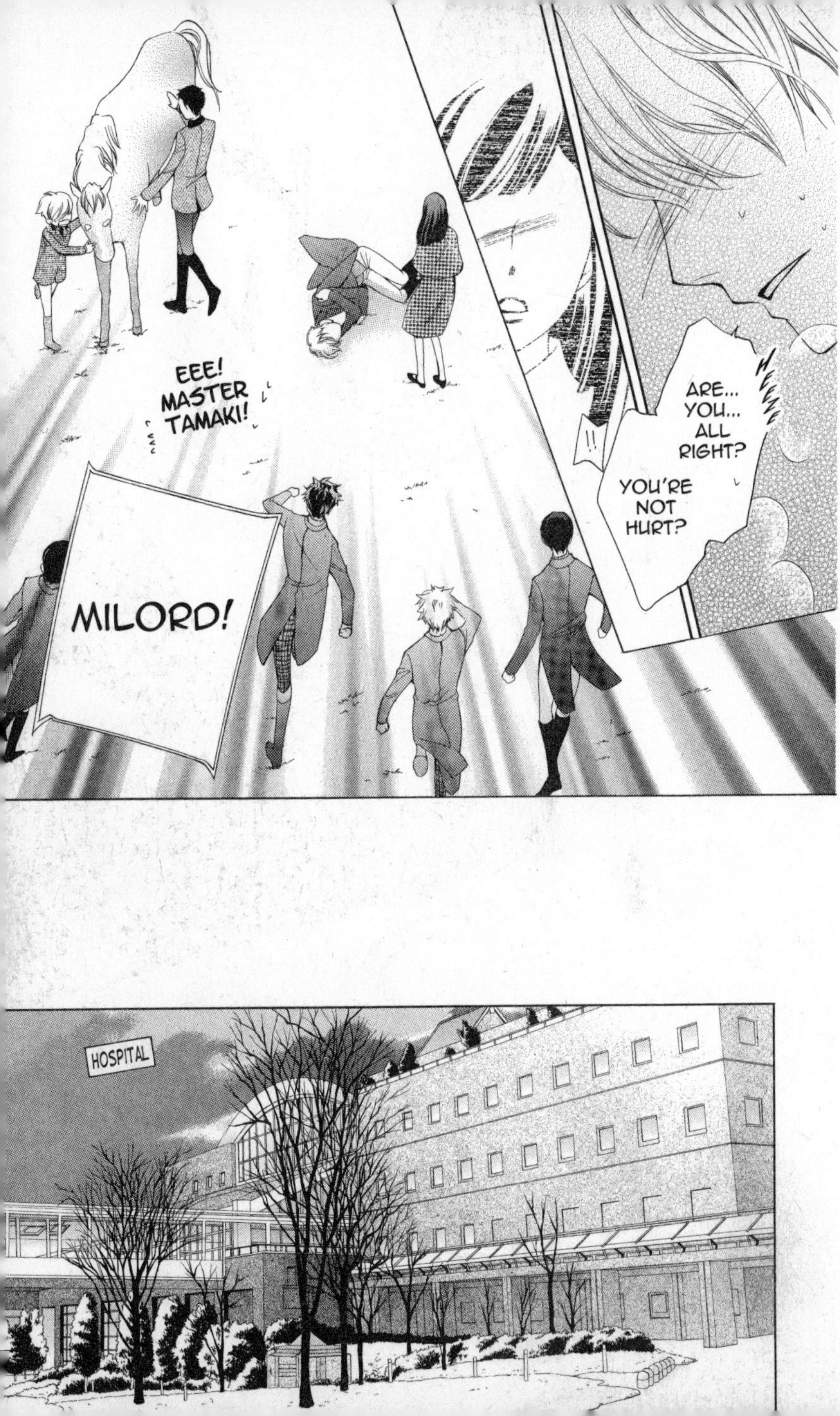
ARE... YOU... ALL RIGHT?
YOU'RE NOT HURT?
!!
EEE! MASTER TAMAKI!
MILORD!
HOSPITAL

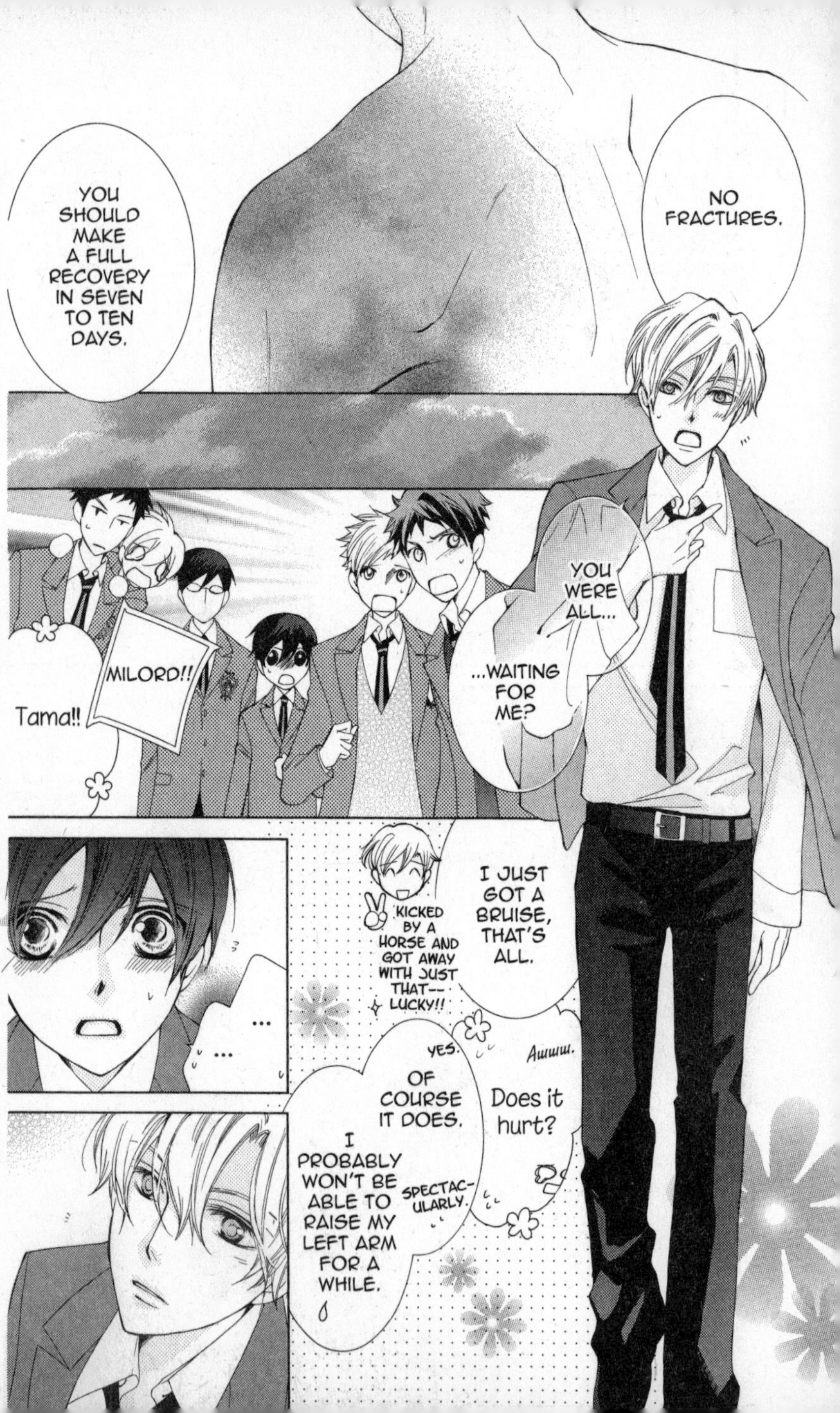
NO FRACTURES.
YOU SHOULD MAKE A FULL RECOVERY IN SEVEN TO TEN DAYS.
YOU WERE ALL...
...WAITING FOR ME?
MILORD!!
Tama!!
I JUST GOT A BRUISE, THAT'S ALL.
KICKED BY A HORSE AND GOT AWAY WITH JUST THAT-- LUCKY!!
...
...
Awww.
Does it hurt?
YES.
OF COURSE IT DOES.
SPECTACULARLY.
I PROBABLY WON'T BE ABLE TO RAISE MY LEFT ARM FOR A WHILE.

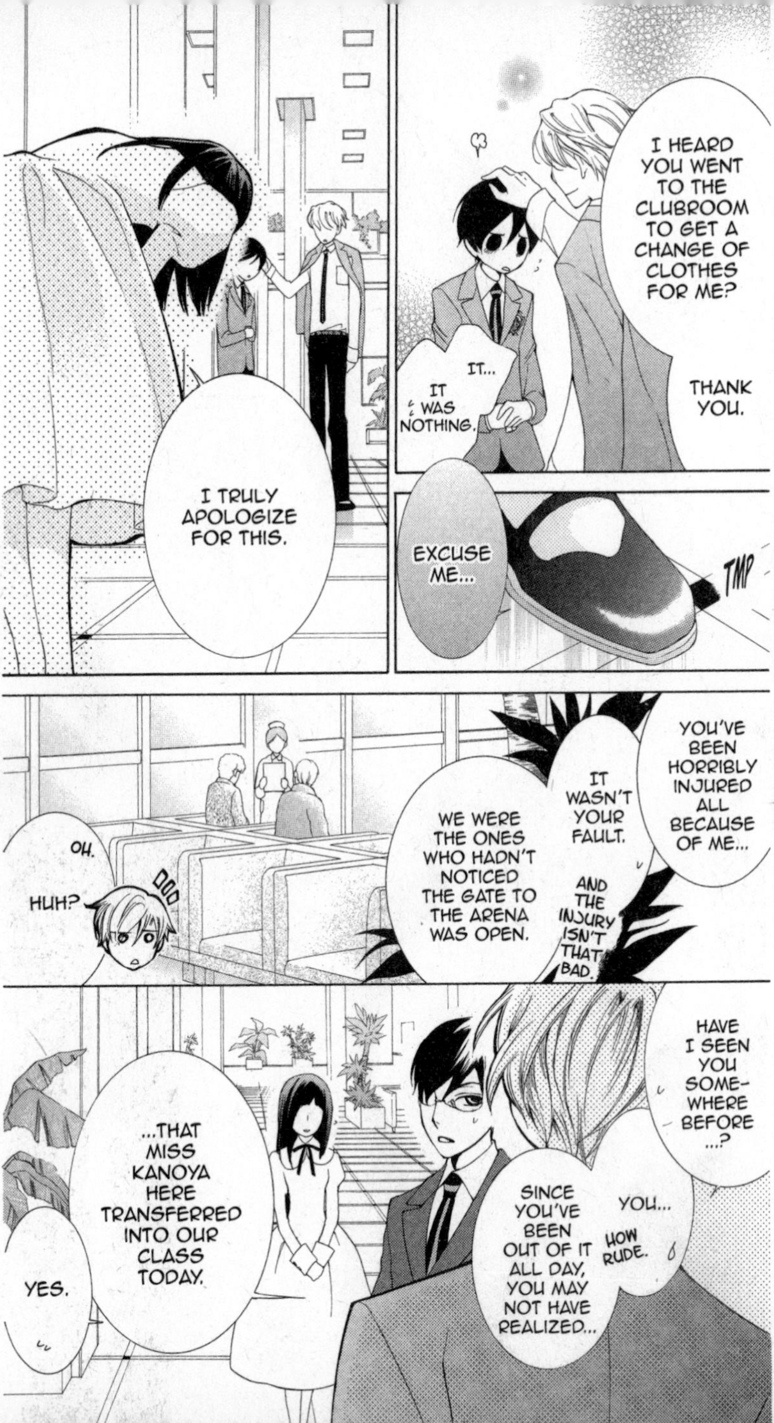

I HEARD YOU WENT TO THE CLUBROOM TO GET A CHANGE OF CLOTHES FOR ME?
THANK YOU.
IT...
IT WAS NOTHING.
EXCUSE ME...
TMP
I TRULY APOLOGIZE FOR THIS.
YOU'VE BEEN HORRIBLY INJURED ALL BECAUSE OF ME...
IT WASN'T YOUR FAULT.
AND THE INJURY ISN'T THAT BAD.
WE WERE THE ONES WHO HADN'T NOTICED THE GATE TO THE ARENA WAS OPEN.
OH.
DOO
HUH?
HAVE I SEEN YOU SOME-WHERE BEFORE ...?
YOU...
HOW RUDE.
SINCE YOU'VE BEEN OUT OF IT ALL DAY, YOU MAY NOT HAVE REALIZED...
...THAT MISS KANOYA HERE TRANSFERRED INTO OUR CLASS TODAY.
YES.

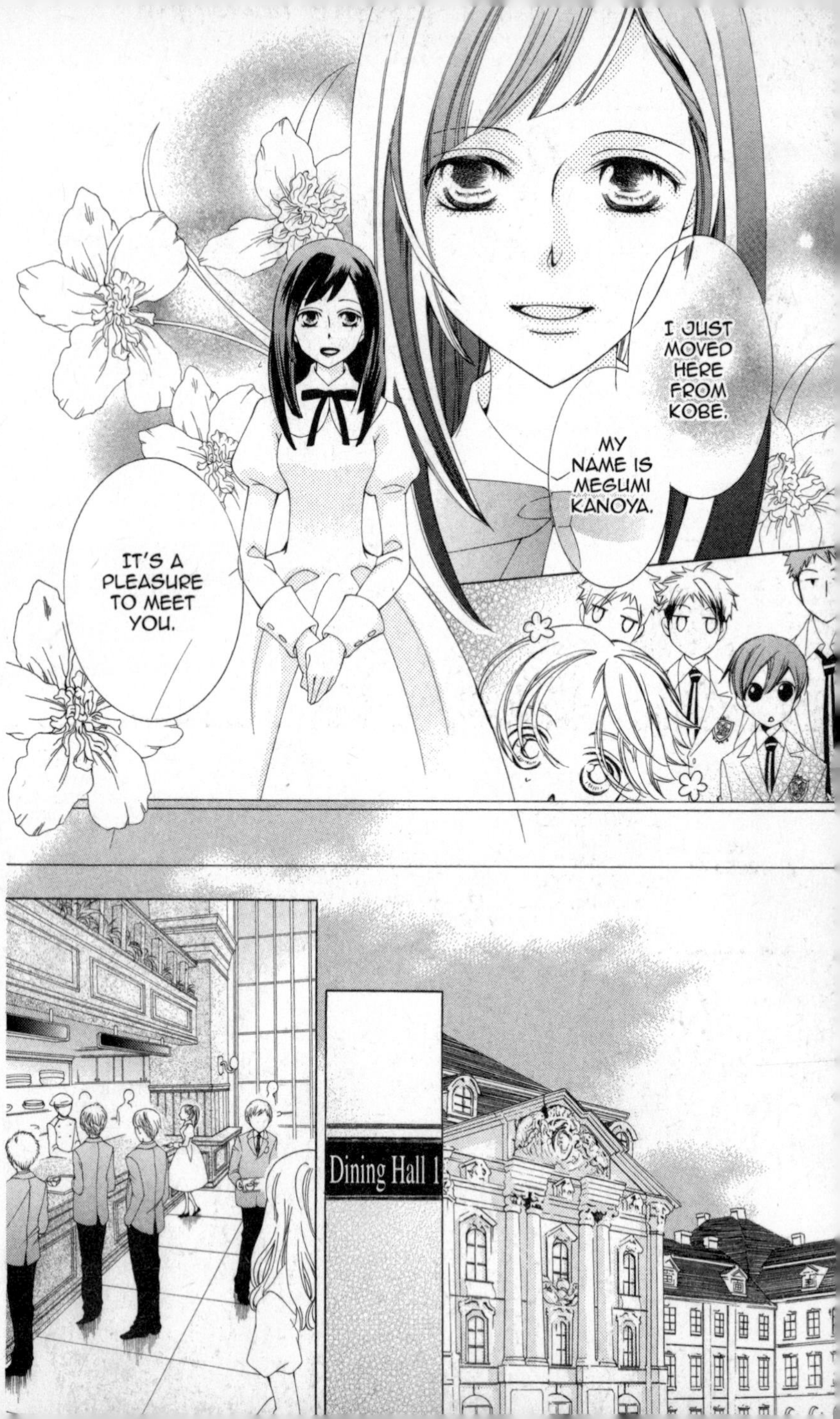
I JUST MOVED HERE FROM KOBE.
MY NAME IS MEGUMI KANOYA.
IT'S A PLEASURE TO MEET YOU.
Dining Hall 1

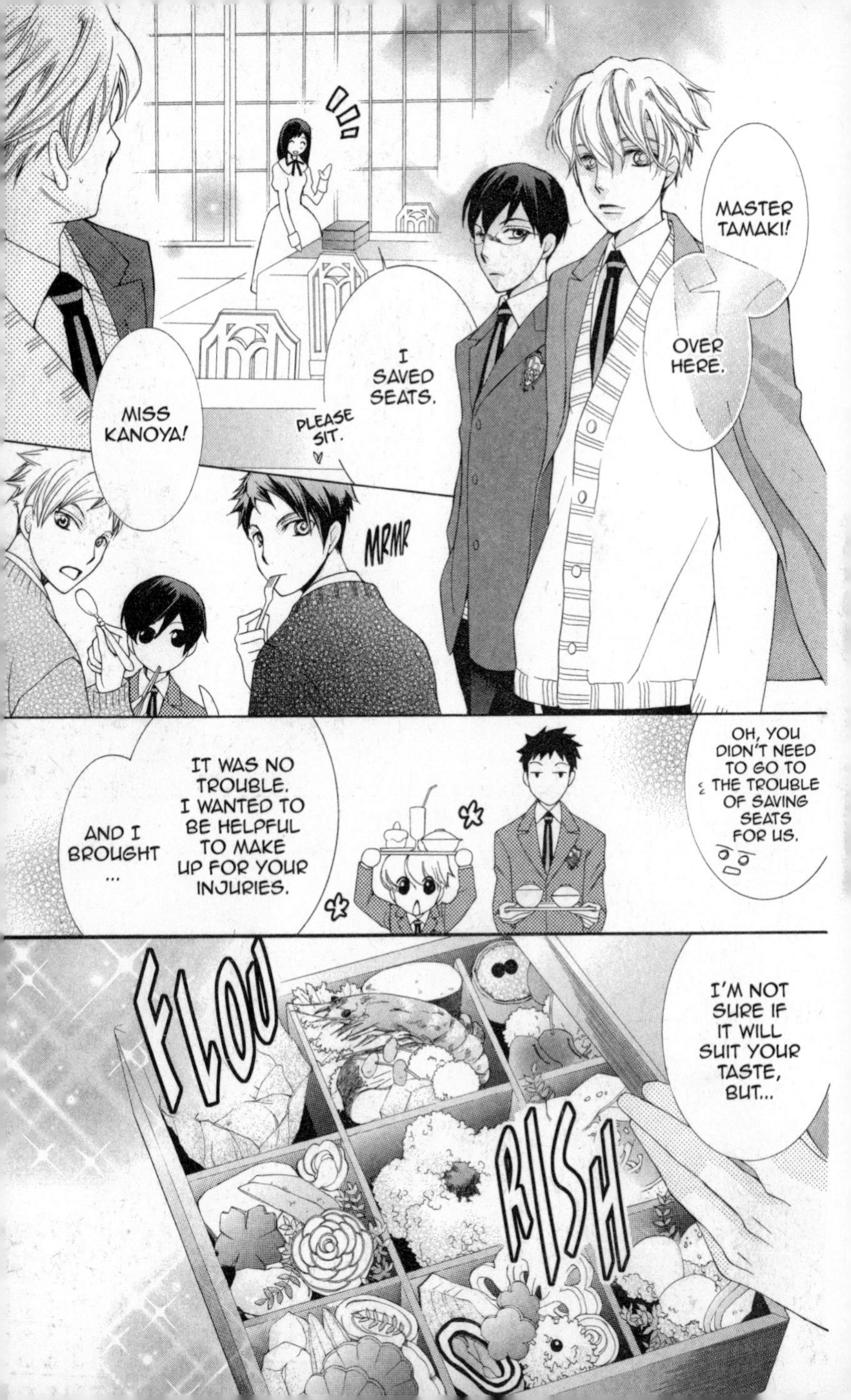
MASTER TAMAKI!
OVER HERE.
I SAVED SEATS.
PLEASE SIT.
MISS KANOYA!
MRMR
OH, YOU DIDN'T NEED TO GO TO THE TROUBLE OF SAVING SEATS FOR US.
IT WAS NO TROUBLE. I WANTED TO BE HELPFUL TO MAKE UP FOR YOUR INJURIES.
AND I BROUGHT ...
I'M NOT SURE IF IT WILL SUIT YOUR TASTE, BUT...
FLOURISH

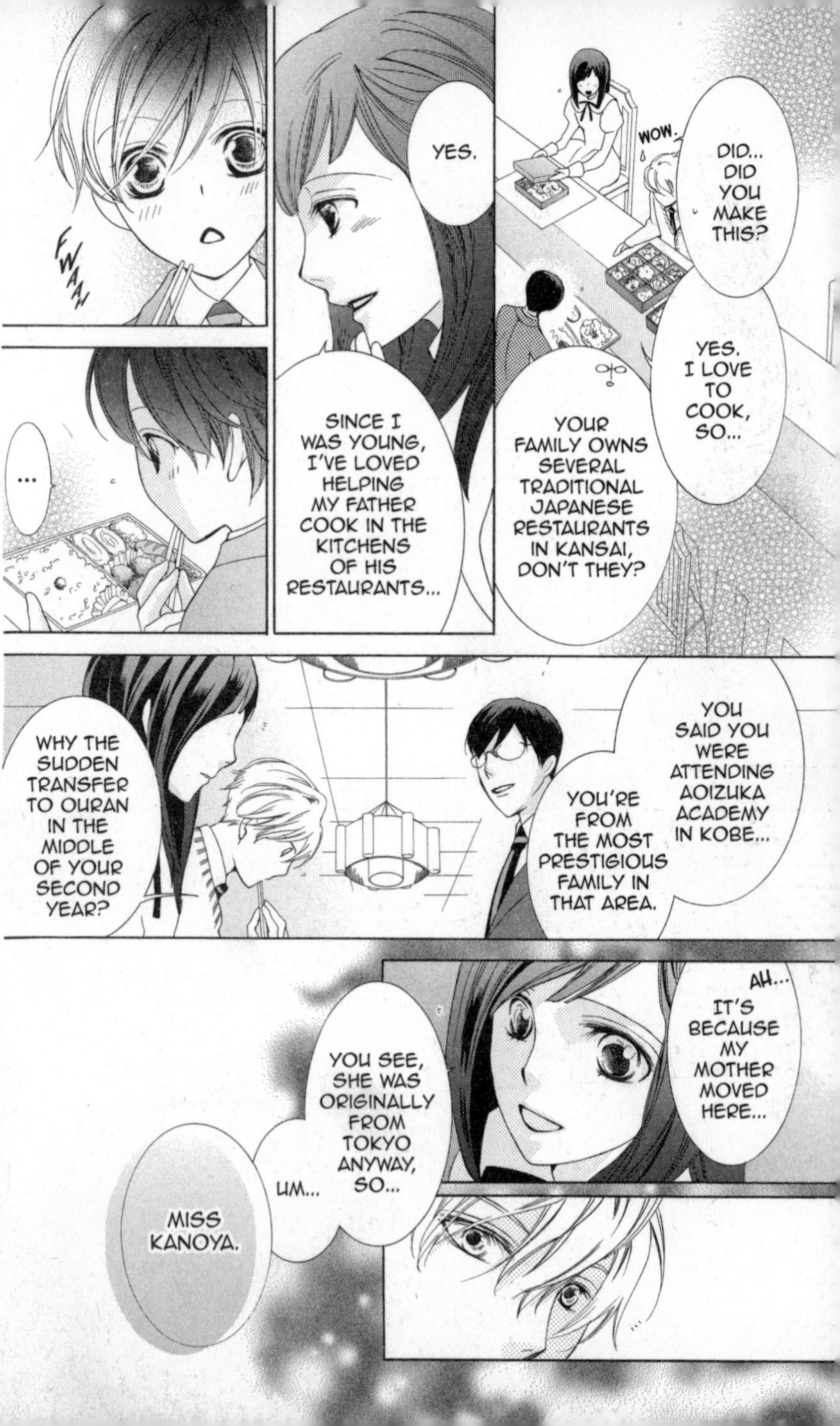
WOW.
DID... DID YOU MAKE THIS?
YES. I LOVE TO COOK, SO...
YOUR FAMILY OWNS SEVERAL TRADITIONAL JAPANESE RESTAURANTS IN KANSAI, DON'T THEY?
YES.
SINCE I WAS YOUNG, I'VE LOVED HELPING MY FATHER COOK IN THE KITCHENS OF HIS RESTAURANTS...
FWAAH
...
YOU SAID YOU WERE ATTENDING AOIZUKA ACADEMY IN KOBE...
YOU'RE FROM THE MOST PRESTIGIOUS FAMILY IN THAT AREA.
WHY THE SUDDEN TRANSFER TO OURAN IN THE MIDDLE OF YOUR SECOND YEAR?
AH... IT'S BECAUSE MY MOTHER MOVED HERE...
YOU SEE, SHE WAS ORIGINALLY FROM TOKYO ANYWAY, SO...
UM...
MISS KANOYA.

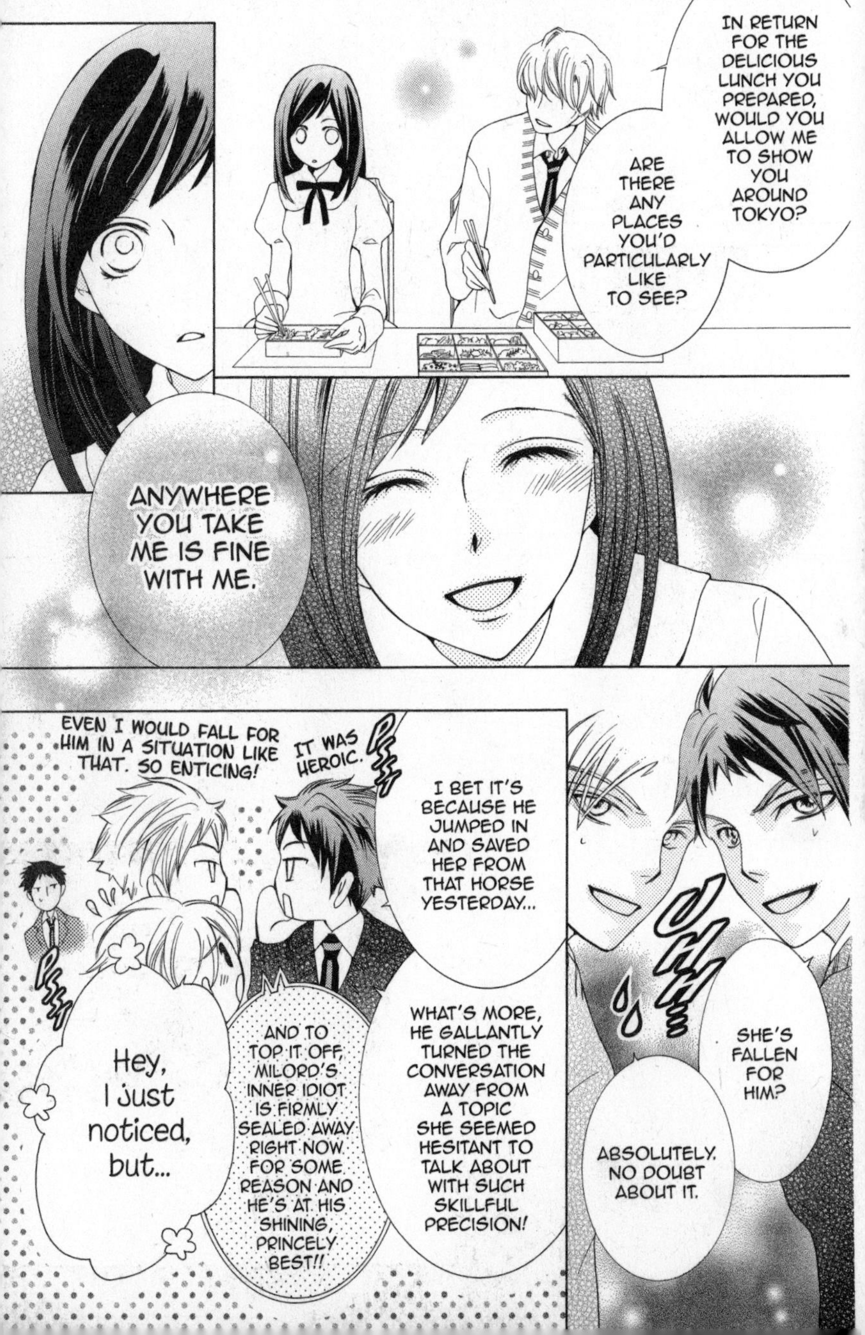
IN RETURN FOR THE DELICIOUS LUNCH YOU PREPARED, WOULD YOU ALLOW ME TO SHOW YOU AROUND TOKYO?
ARE THERE ANY PLACES YOU'D PARTICULARLY LIKE TO SEE?
ANYWHERE YOU TAKE ME IS FINE WITH ME.
SHE'S FALLEN FOR HIM?
ABSOLUTELY. NO DOUBT ABOUT IT.
I BET IT'S BECAUSE HE JUMPED IN AND SAVED HER FROM THAT HORSE YESTERDAY...
IT WAS HEROIC.
EVEN I WOULD FALL FOR HIM IN A SITUATION LIKE THAT. SO ENTICING!
WHAT'S MORE, HE GALLANTLY TURNED THE CONVERSATION AWAY FROM A TOPIC SHE SEEMED HESITANT TO TALK ABOUT WITH SUCH SKILLFUL PRECISION!
AND TO TOP IT OFF, MILORD'S INNER IDIOT IS FIRMLY SEALED AWAY RIGHT NOW FOR SOME REASON AND HE'S AT HIS SHINING, PRINCELY BEST!!
Hey, I just noticed, but...

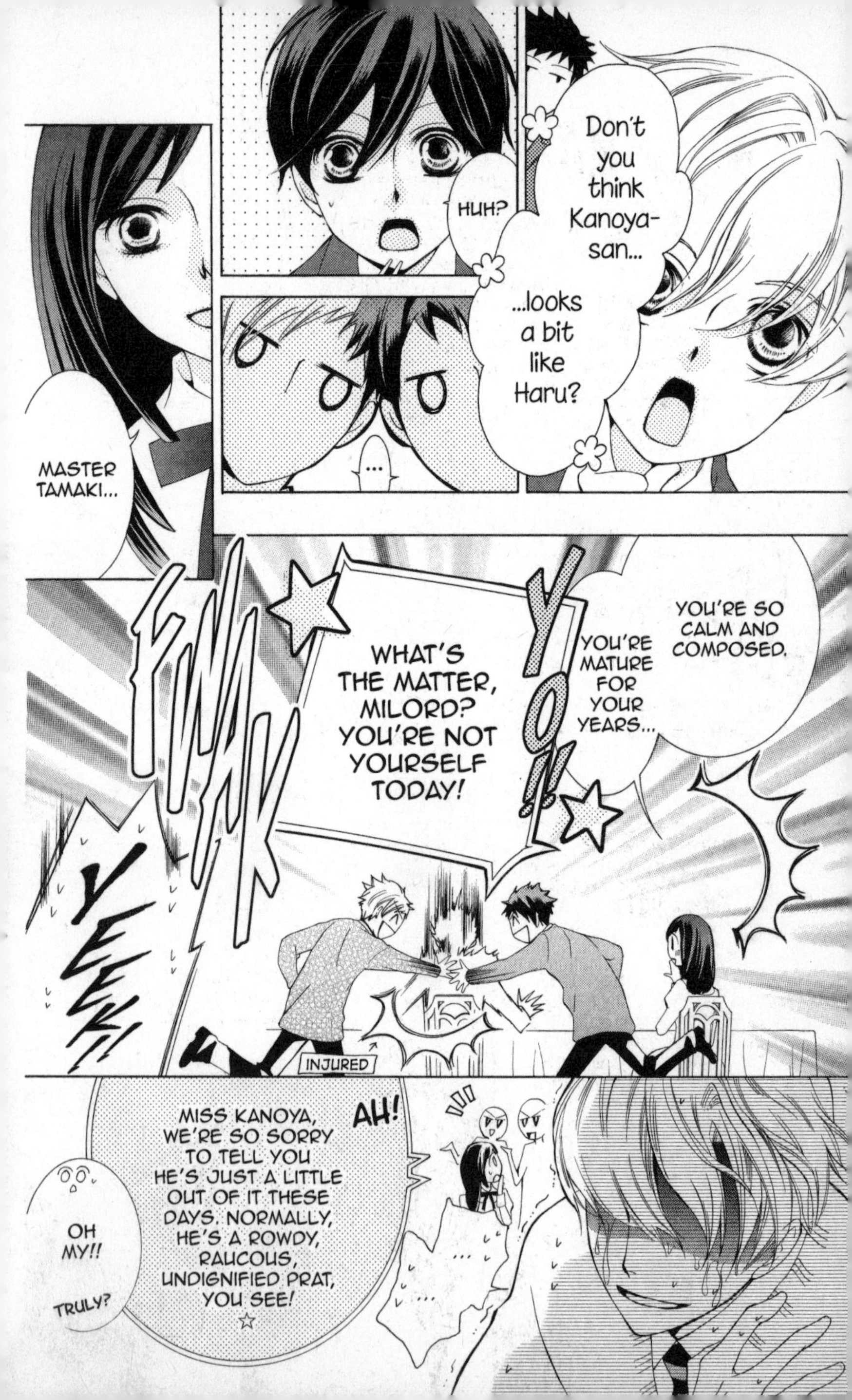

Don't you think Kanoya-san...
...looks a bit like Haru?
HUH?
...
MASTER TAMAKI...
YOU'RE SO CALM AND COMPOSED.
YOU'RE MATURE FOR YOUR YEARS...
YOON!!
WHAT'S THE MATTER, MILORD? YOU'RE NOT YOURSELF TODAY!
FWAK
YEEEK!
INJURED
...
...
AH!
MISS KANOYA, WE'RE SO SORRY TO TELL YOU HE'S JUST A LITTLE OUT OF IT THESE DAYS. NORMALLY, HE'S A ROWDY, RAUCOUS, UNDIGNIFIED PRAT, YOU SEE! ☆
OH MY!!
TRULY?

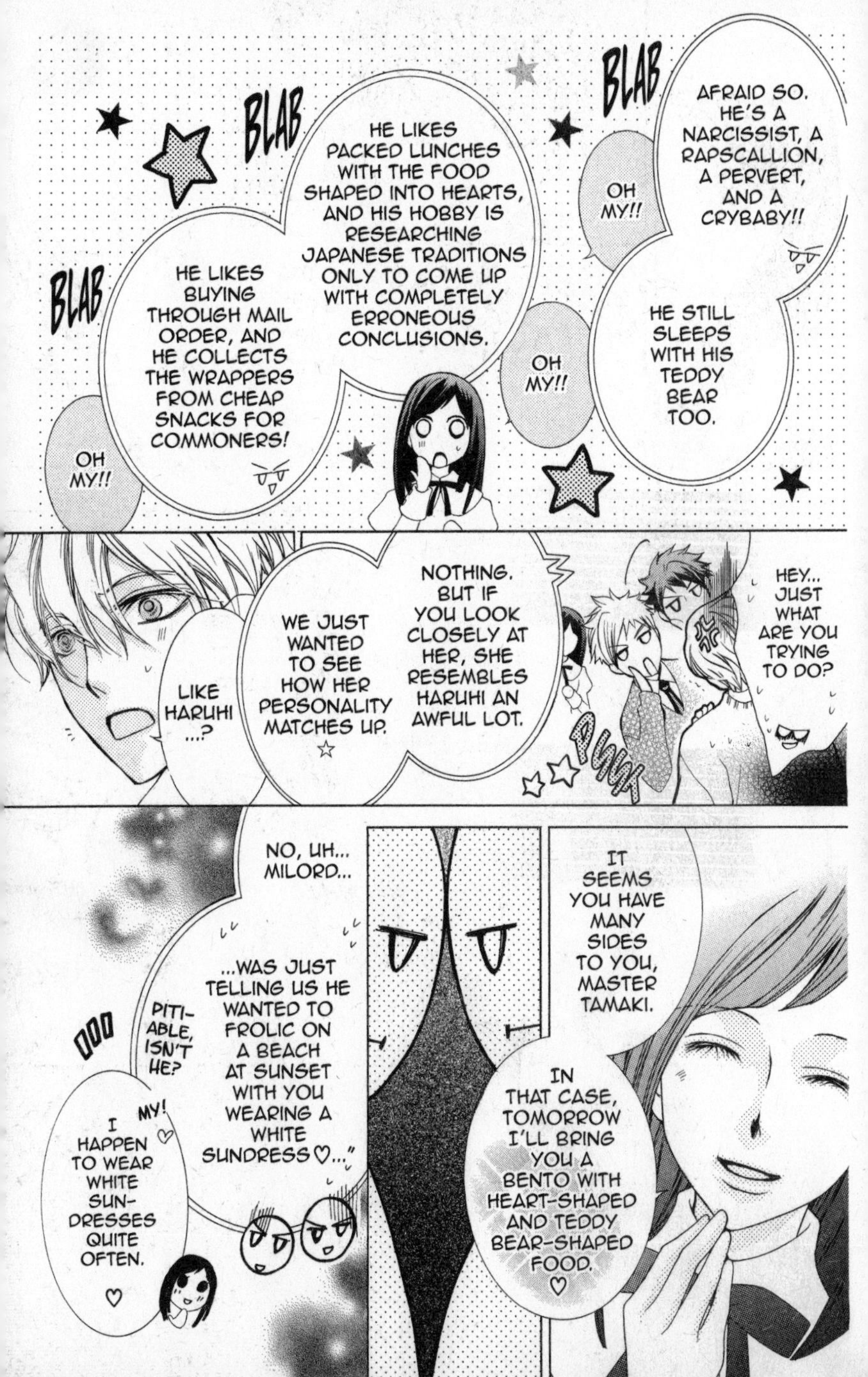
BLAB
AFRAID SO. HE'S A NARCISSIST, A RAPSCALLION, A PERVERT, AND A CRYBABY!!
OH MY!!
HE STILL SLEEPS WITH HIS TEDDY BEAR TOO.
BLAB
HE LIKES PACKED LUNCHES WITH THE FOOD SHAPED INTO HEARTS, AND HIS HOBBY IS RESEARCHING JAPANESE TRADITIONS ONLY TO COME UP WITH COMPLETELY ERRONEOUS CONCLUSIONS.
OH MY!!
BLAB
HE LIKES BUYING THROUGH MAIL ORDER, AND HE COLLECTS THE WRAPPERS FROM CHEAP SNACKS FOR COMMONERS!
OH MY!!
HEY... JUST WHAT ARE YOU TRYING TO DO?
PWNK
NOTHING. BUT IF YOU LOOK CLOSELY AT HER, SHE RESEMBLES HARUHI AN AWFUL LOT.
WE JUST WANTED TO SEE HOW HER PERSONALITY MATCHES UP. ☆
LIKE HARUHI ...?
IT SEEMS YOU HAVE MANY SIDES TO YOU, MASTER TAMAKI.
IN THAT CASE, TOMORROW I'LL BRING YOU A BENTO WITH HEART-SHAPED AND TEDDY BEAR-SHAPED FOOD. ♡
NO, UH... MILORD...
...WAS JUST TELLING US HE WANTED TO FROLIC ON A BEACH AT SUNSET WITH YOU WEARING A WHITE SUNDRESS ♡..."
PITI-ABLE, ISN'T HE?
MY! ♡
I HAPPEN TO WEAR WHITE SUN-DRESSES QUITE OFTEN. ♡

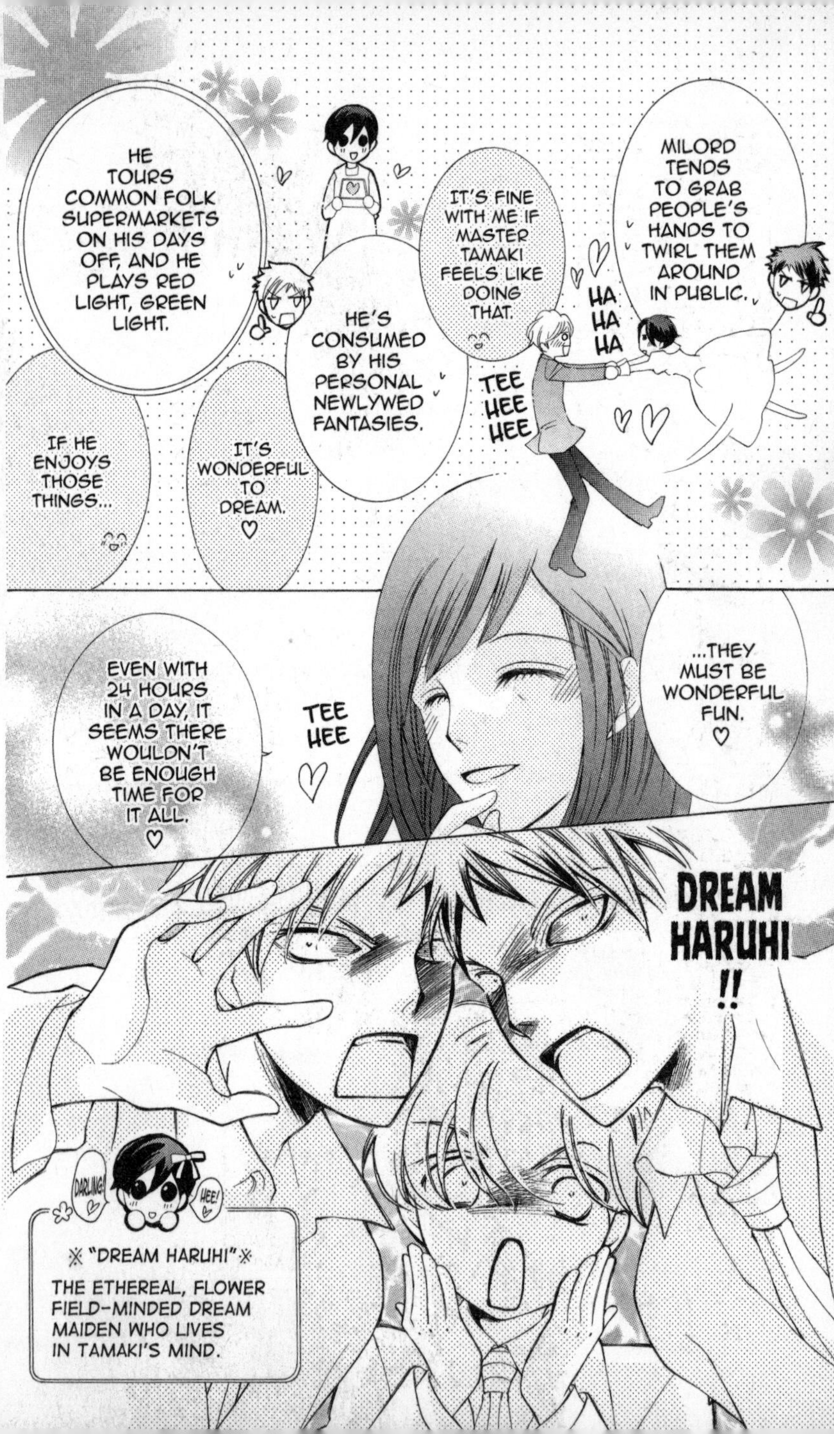
MILORD TENDS TO GRAB PEOPLE'S HANDS TO TWIRL THEM AROUND IN PUBLIC.
HA HA HA
IT'S FINE WITH ME IF MASTER TAMAKI FEELS LIKE DOING THAT.
TEE HEE HEE
HE'S CONSUMED BY HIS PERSONAL NEWLYWED FANTASIES.
HE TOURS COMMON FOLK SUPERMARKETS ON HIS DAYS OFF, AND HE PLAYS RED LIGHT, GREEN LIGHT.
IT'S WONDERFUL TO DREAM. ♡
IF HE ENJOYS THOSE THINGS...
...THEY MUST BE WONDERFUL FUN. ♡
TEE HEE
EVEN WITH 24 HOURS IN A DAY, IT SEEMS THERE WOULDN'T BE ENOUGH TIME FOR IT ALL. ♡
DREAM HARUHI!!
DARLING!
HEE!
※"DREAM HARUHI"※
THE ETHEREAL, FLOWER FIELD-MINDED DREAM MAIDEN WHO LIVES IN TAMAKI'S MIND.

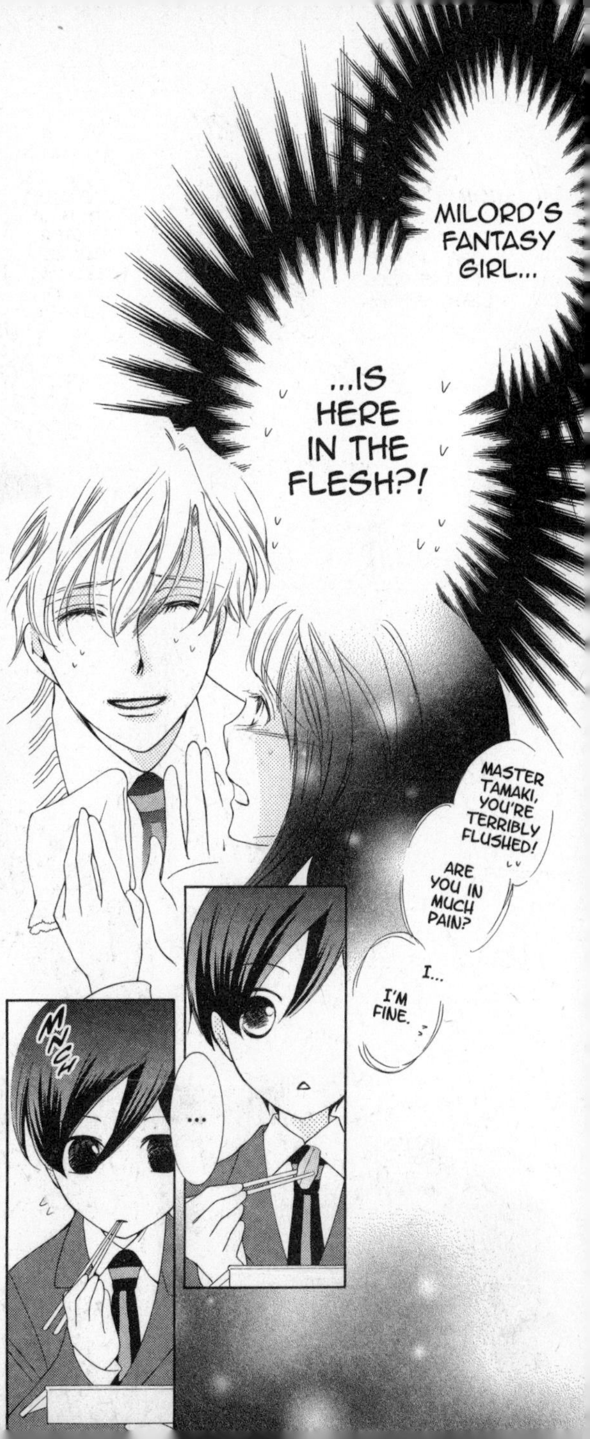
MILORD'S FANTASY GIRL...
...IS HERE IN THE FLESH?!
MASTER TAMAKI, YOU'RE TERRIBLY FLUSHED!
ARE YOU IN MUCH PAIN?
I...
I'M FINE.
...

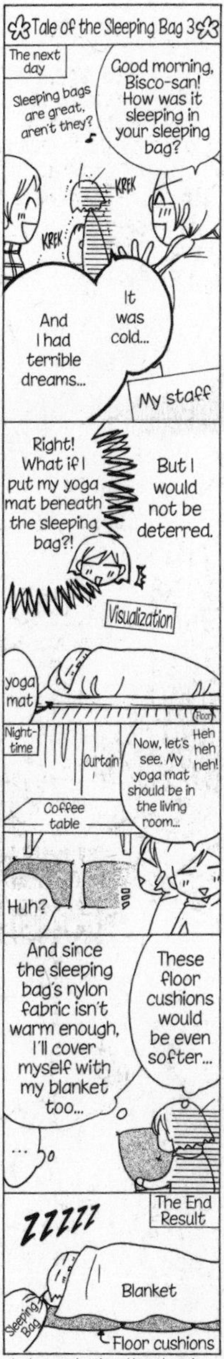
Tale of the Sleeping Bag 3
The next day
Good morning, Bisco-san! How was it sleeping in your sleeping bag?
Sleeping bags are great, aren't they?
KREK
KREK
It was cold...
And I had terrible dreams...
My staff
But I would not be deterred.
Right! What if I put my yoga mat beneath the sleeping bag?!
Visualization
yoga mat
Floor
Night-time
Curtain
Heh heh heh!
Now, let's see. My yoga mat should be in the living room...
Coffee table
Huh?
These floor cushions would be even softer...
And since the sleeping bag's nylon fabric isn't warm enough, I'll cover myself with my blanket too...
...
The End Result
ZZZZZ
Blanket
Sleeping Bag
Floor cushions
I stopped using the sleeping bag after that.

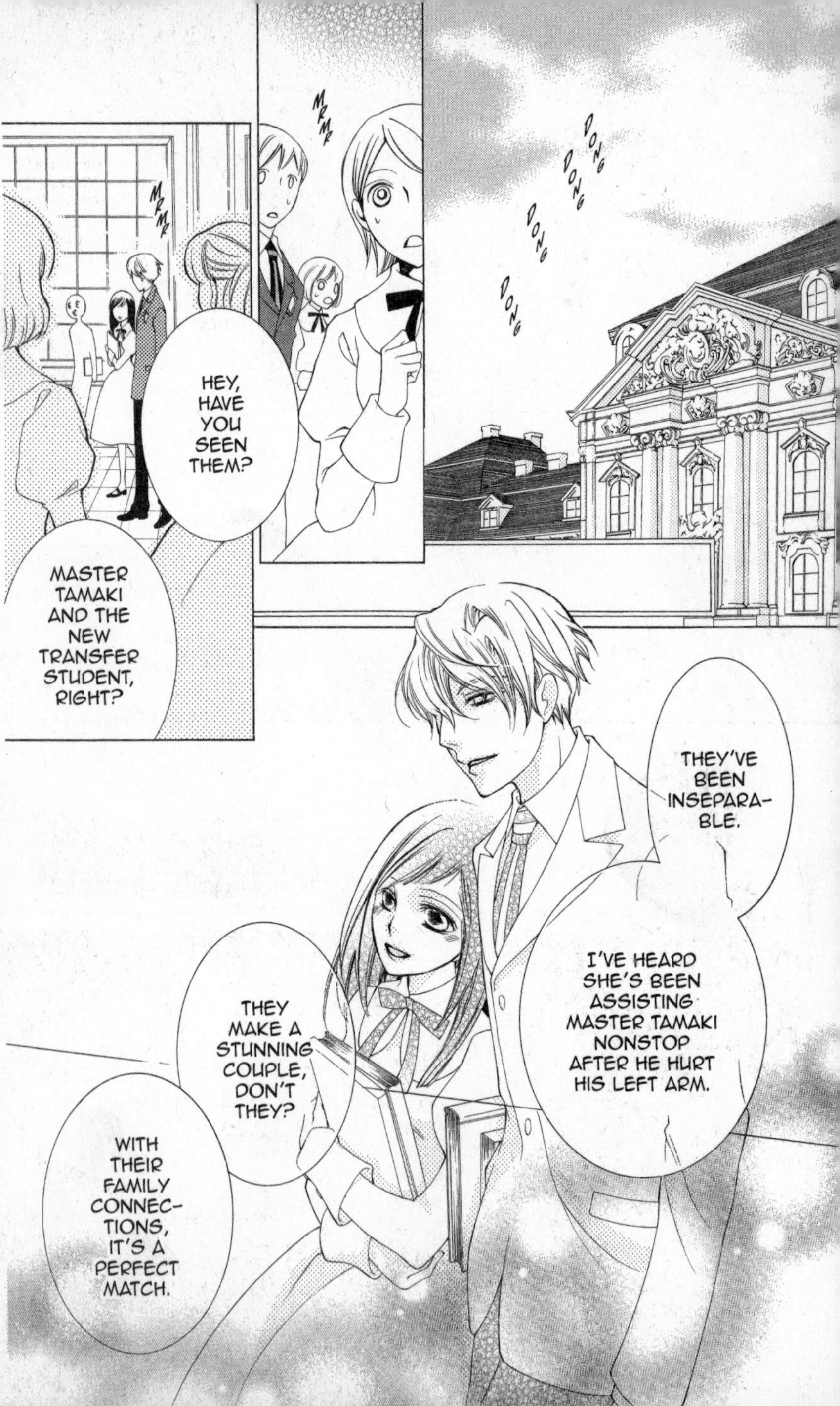
DONG DONG DONG DONG
MRMR
MRMR
HEY, HAVE YOU SEEN THEM?
MASTER TAMAKI AND THE NEW TRANSFER STUDENT, RIGHT?
THEY'VE BEEN INSEPARABLE.
I'VE HEARD SHE'S BEEN ASSISTING MASTER TAMAKI NONSTOP AFTER HE HURT HIS LEFT ARM.
THEY MAKE A STUNNING COUPLE, DON'T THEY?
WITH THEIR FAMILY CONNECTIONS, IT'S A PERFECT MATCH.

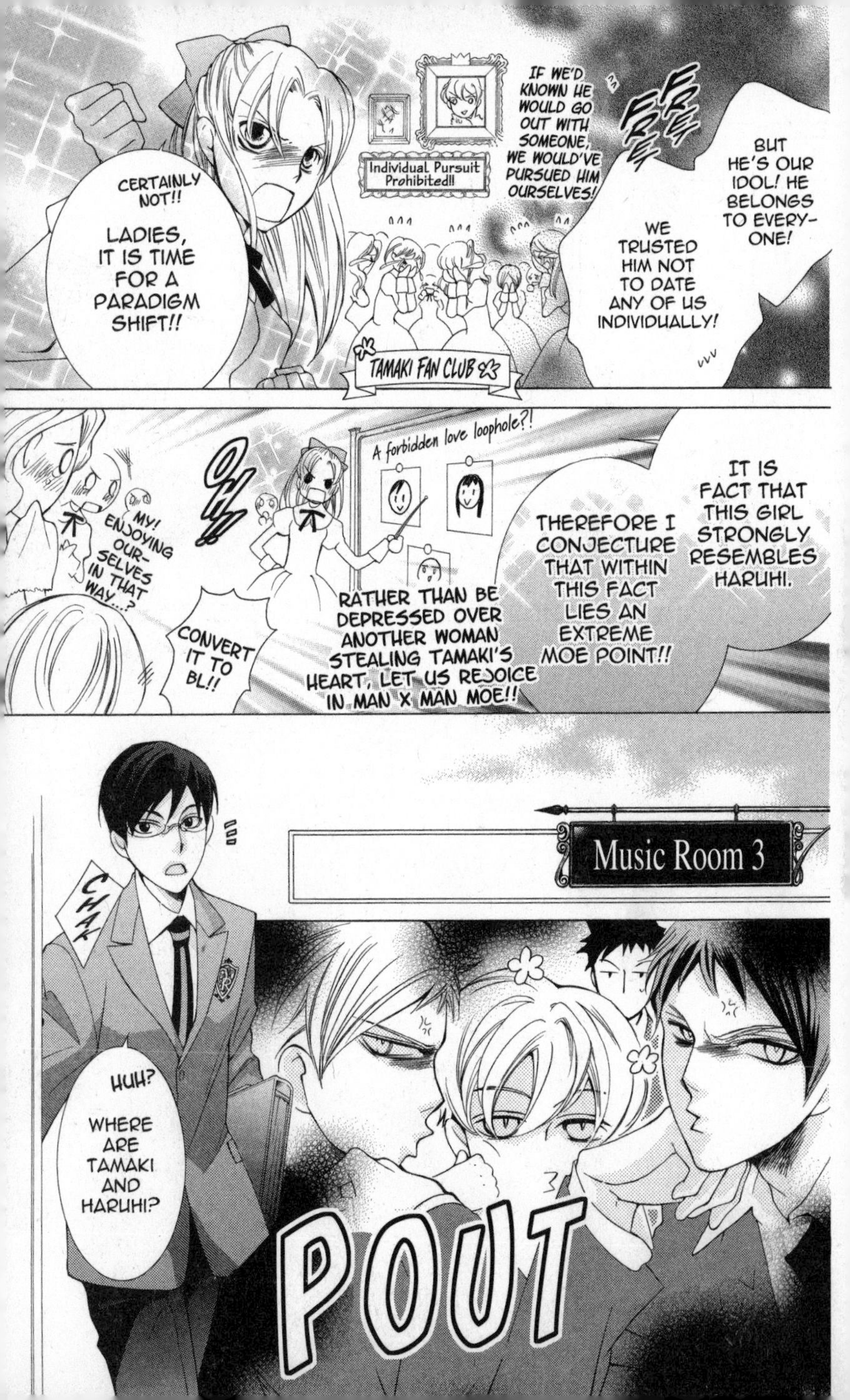
BUT HE'S OUR IDOL! HE BELONGS TO EVERY-ONE!
WE TRUSTED HIM NOT TO DATE ANY OF US INDIVIDUALLY!
IF WE'D KNOWN HE WOULD GO OUT WITH SOMEONE, WE WOULD'VE PURSUED HIM OURSELVES!
Individual Pursuit Prohibited!!
CERTAINLY NOT!!
LADIES, IT IS TIME FOR A PARADIGM SHIFT!!
TAMAKI FAN CLUB
IT IS FACT THAT THIS GIRL STRONGLY RESEMBLES HARUHI.
THEREFORE I CONJECTURE THAT WITHIN THIS FACT LIES AN EXTREME MOE POINT!!
A forbidden love loophole?!
RATHER THAN BE DEPRESSED OVER ANOTHER WOMAN STEALING TAMAKI'S HEART, LET US REJOICE IN MAN X MAN MOE!!
OH
CONVERT IT TO BL!!
MY! ENJOYING OUR-SELVES IN THAT WAY...?
Music Room 3
POUT
CHAK
HUH?
WHERE ARE TAMAKI AND HARUHI?

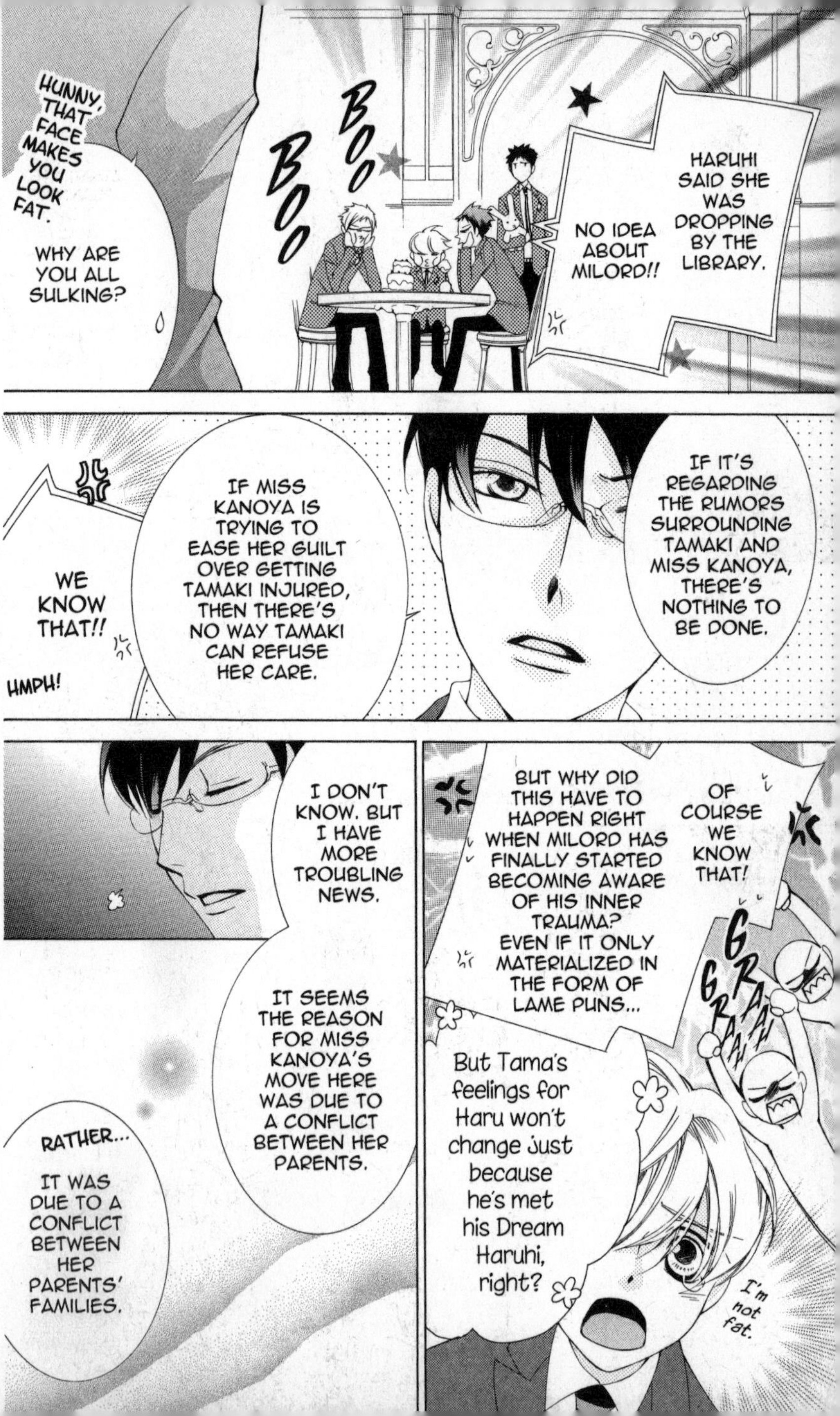
HARUHI SAID SHE WAS DROPPING BY THE LIBRARY.
NO IDEA ABOUT MILORD!!
BOO BOO
HUNNY, THAT FACE MAKES YOU LOOK FAT.
WHY ARE YOU ALL SULKING?
IF IT'S REGARDING THE RUMORS SURROUNDING TAMAKI AND MISS KANOYA, THERE'S NOTHING TO BE DONE.
IF MISS KANOYA IS TRYING TO EASE HER GUILT OVER GETTING TAMAKI INJURED, THEN THERE'S NO WAY TAMAKI CAN REFUSE HER CARE.
WE KNOW THAT!!
HMPH!
OF COURSE WE KNOW THAT!
BUT WHY DID THIS HAVE TO HAPPEN RIGHT WHEN MILORD HAS FINALLY STARTED BECOMING AWARE OF HIS INNER TRAUMA? EVEN IF IT ONLY MATERIALIZED IN THE FORM OF LAME PUNS...
GRAAAH GRAAAH
But Tama's feelings for Haru won't change just because he's met his Dream Haruhi, right?
I'm not fat.
I DON'T KNOW. BUT I HAVE MORE TROUBLING NEWS.
IT SEEMS THE REASON FOR MISS KANOYA'S MOVE HERE WAS DUE TO A CONFLICT BETWEEN HER PARENTS.
RATHER...
IT WAS DUE TO A CONFLICT BETWEEN HER PARENTS' FAMILIES.

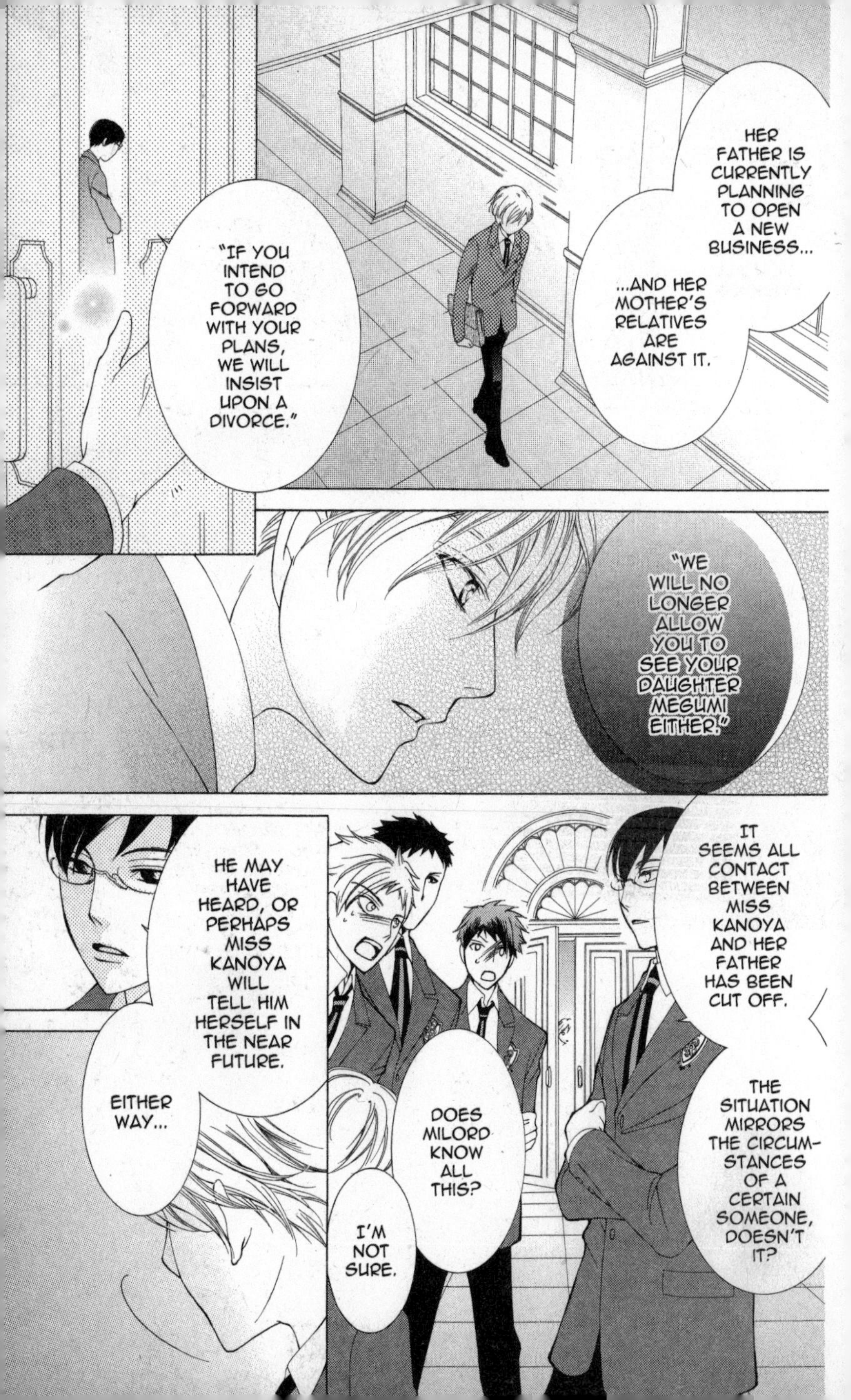
HER FATHER IS CURRENTLY PLANNING TO OPEN A NEW BUSINESS...
...AND HER MOTHER'S RELATIVES ARE AGAINST IT.
"IF YOU INTEND TO GO FORWARD WITH YOUR PLANS, WE WILL INSIST UPON A DIVORCE."
"WE WILL NO LONGER ALLOW YOU TO SEE YOUR DAUGHTER MEGUMI EITHER."
IT SEEMS ALL CONTACT BETWEEN MISS KANOYA AND HER FATHER HAS BEEN CUT OFF.
THE SITUATION MIRRORS THE CIRCUM-STANCES OF A CERTAIN SOMEONE, DOESN'T IT?
DOES MILORD KNOW ALL THIS?
I'M NOT SURE.
HE MAY HAVE HEARD, OR PERHAPS MISS KANOYA WILL TELL HIM HERSELF IN THE NEAR FUTURE.
EITHER WAY...

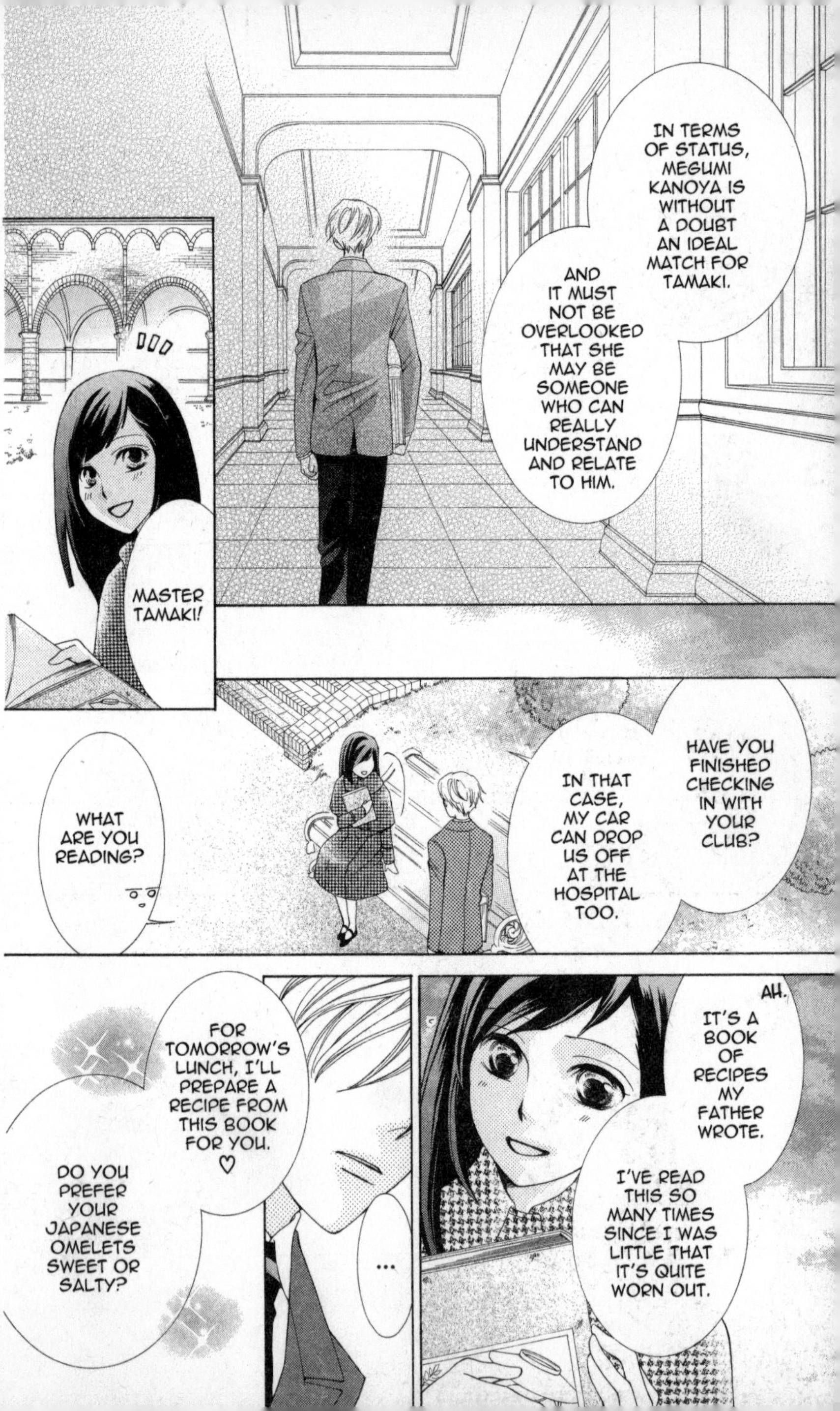
IN TERMS OF STATUS, MEGUMI KANOYA IS WITHOUT A DOUBT AN IDEAL MATCH FOR TAMAKI.
AND IT MUST NOT BE OVERLOOKED THAT SHE MAY BE SOMEONE WHO CAN REALLY UNDERSTAND AND RELATE TO HIM.
MASTER TAMAKI!
HAVE YOU FINISHED CHECKING IN WITH YOUR CLUB?
IN THAT CASE, MY CAR CAN DROP US OFF AT THE HOSPITAL TOO.
WHAT ARE YOU READING?
AH.
IT'S A BOOK OF RECIPES MY FATHER WROTE.
I'VE READ THIS SO MANY TIMES SINCE I WAS LITTLE THAT IT'S QUITE WORN OUT.
FOR TOMORROW'S LUNCH, I'LL PREPARE A RECIPE FROM THIS BOOK FOR YOU. ♡
...
DO YOU PREFER YOUR JAPANESE OMELETS SWEET OR SALTY?

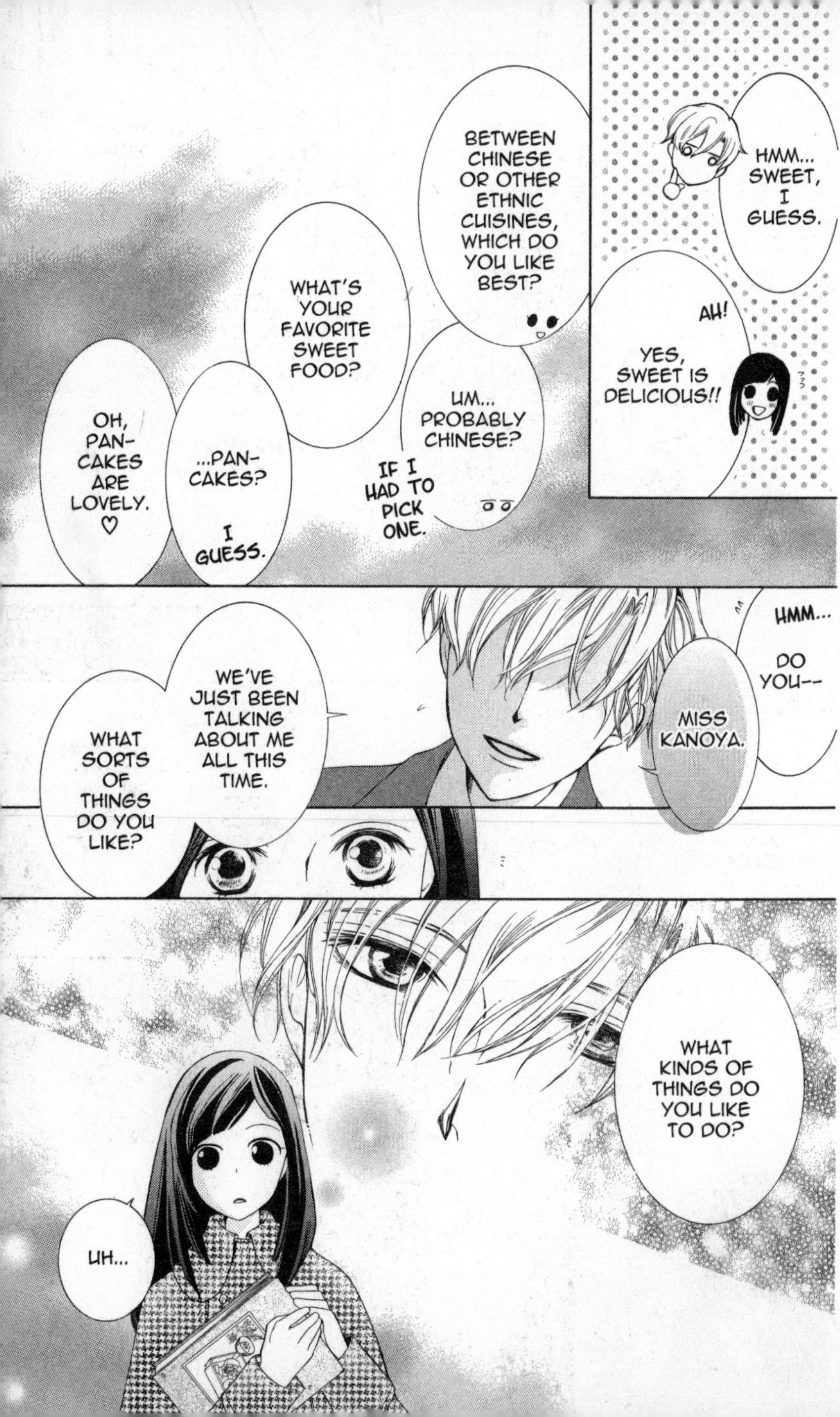
HMM... SWEET, I GUESS.
AH!
YES, SWEET IS DELICIOUS!!
BETWEEN CHINESE OR OTHER ETHNIC CUISINES, WHICH DO YOU LIKE BEST?
UM... PROBABLY CHINESE?
IF I HAD TO PICK ONE.
WHAT'S YOUR FAVORITE SWEET FOOD?
...PAN-CAKES?
I GUESS.
OH, PAN-CAKES ARE LOVELY. ♡
HMM...
DO YOU--
MISS KANOYA.
WE'VE JUST BEEN TALKING ABOUT ME ALL THIS TIME.
WHAT SORTS OF THINGS DO YOU LIKE?
WHAT KINDS OF THINGS DO YOU LIKE TO DO?
UH...

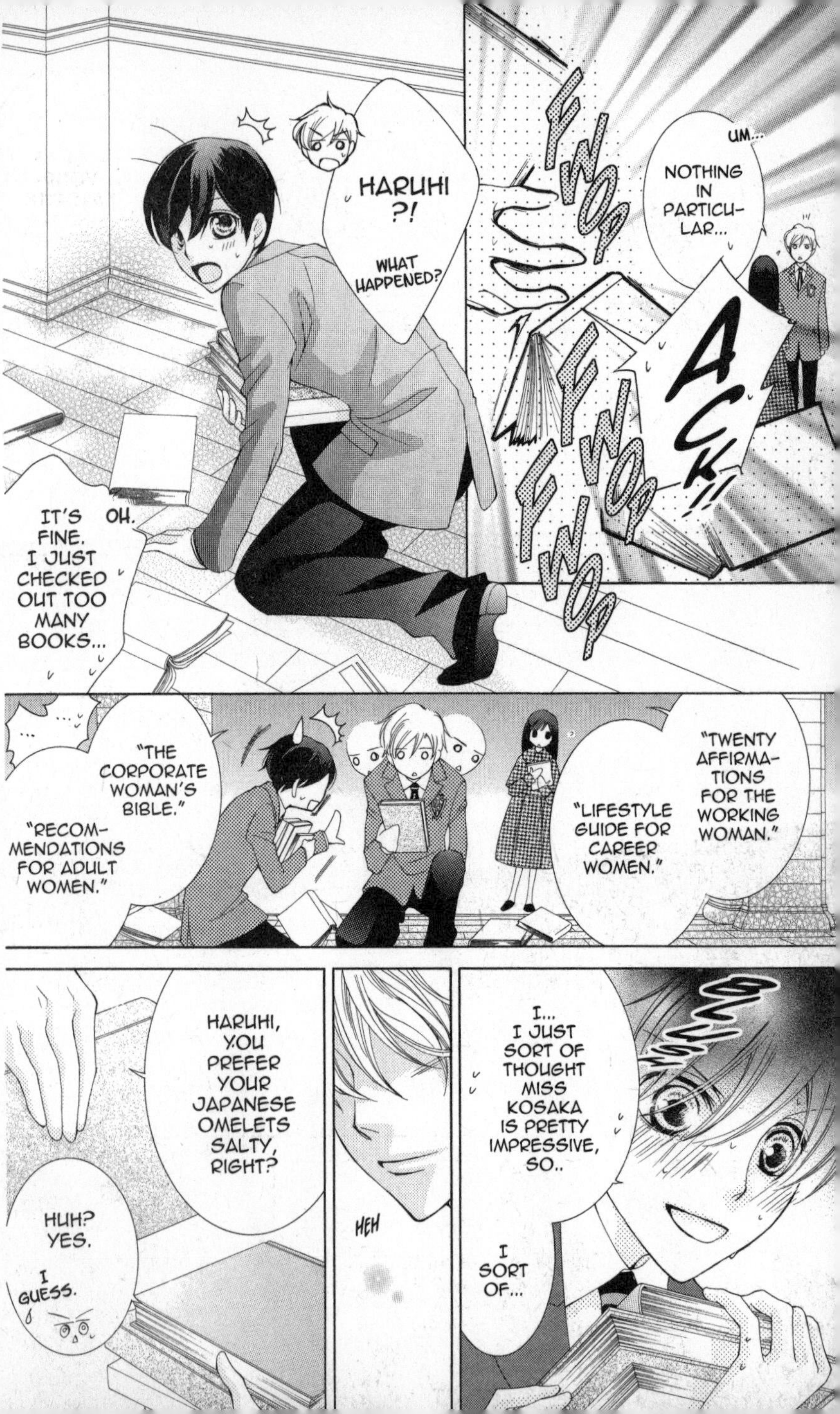
UM... NOTHING IN PARTICULAR...
ACK!!
FWOP FWOP FWOP FWOP
HARUHI?!
WHAT HAPPENED?
OH.
IT'S FINE. I JUST CHECKED OUT TOO MANY BOOKS...
"TWENTY AFFIRMATIONS FOR THE WORKING WOMAN."
"LIFESTYLE GUIDE FOR CAREER WOMEN."
"THE CORPORATE WOMAN'S BIBLE."
"RECOMMENDATIONS FOR ADULT WOMEN."
......
I... I JUST SORT OF THOUGHT MISS KOSAKA IS PRETTY IMPRESSIVE, SO..
I SORT OF...
HEH
HARUHI, YOU PREFER YOUR JAPANESE OMELETS SALTY, RIGHT?
HUH? YES.
I GUESS.

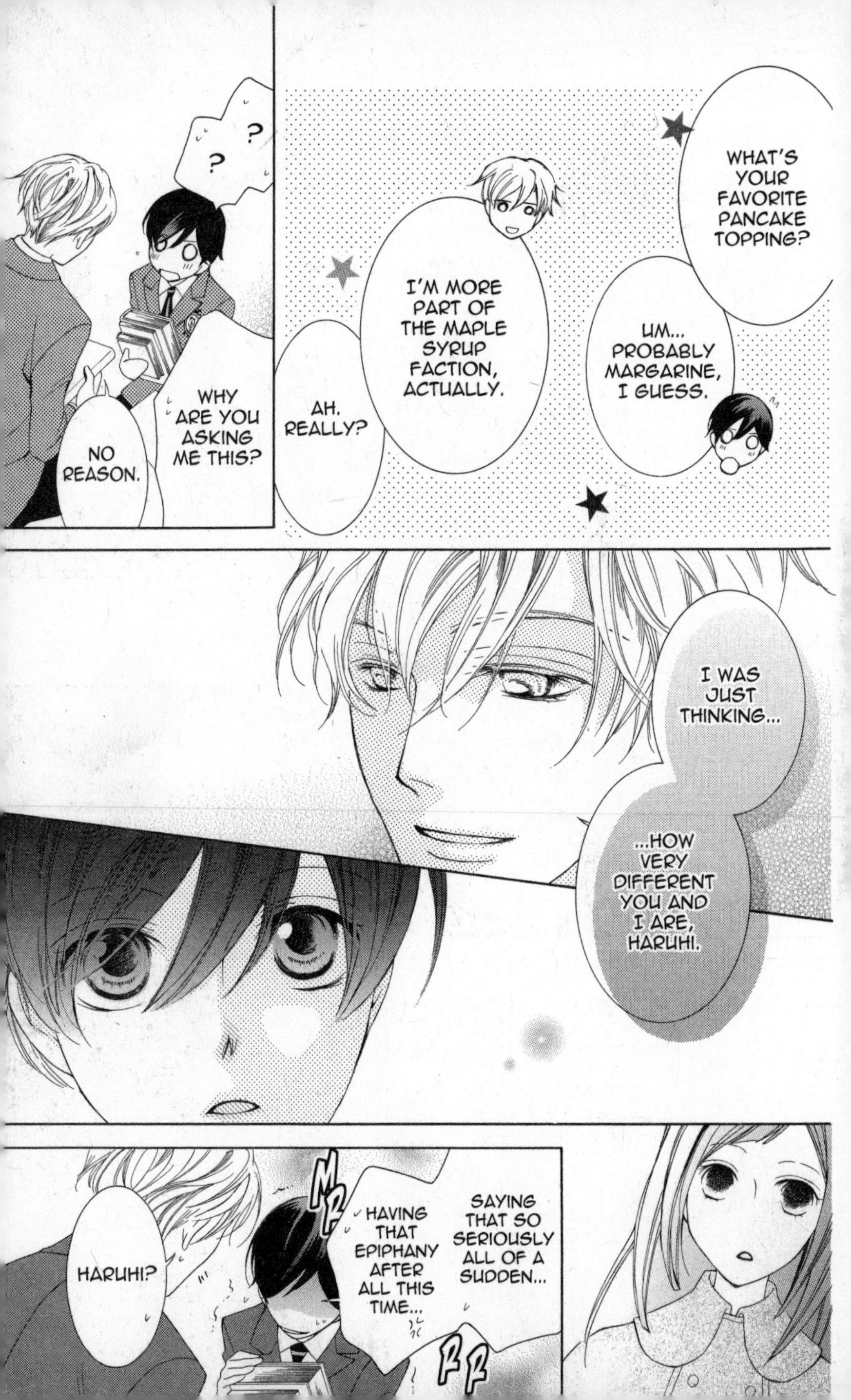
WHAT'S YOUR FAVORITE PANCAKE TOPPING?
UM... PROBABLY MARGARINE, I GUESS.
I'M MORE PART OF THE MAPLE SYRUP FACTION, ACTUALLY.
AH. REALLY?
?
?
WHY ARE YOU ASKING ME THIS?
NO REASON.
I WAS JUST THINKING...
...HOW VERY DIFFERENT YOU AND I ARE, HARUHI.
SAYING THAT SO SERIOUSLY ALL OF A SUDDEN...
HAVING THAT EPIPHANY AFTER ALL THIS TIME...
HARUHI?

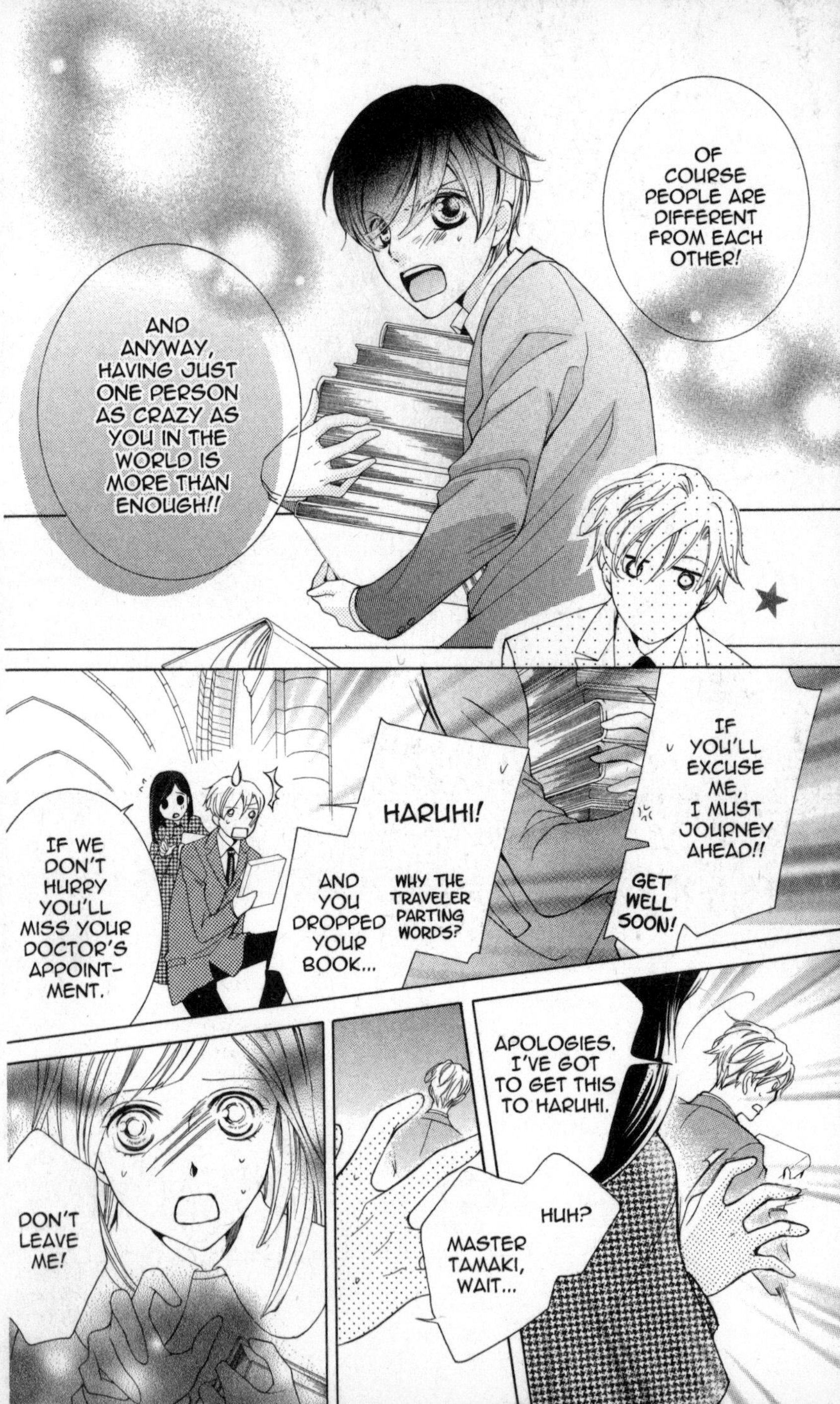
OF COURSE PEOPLE ARE DIFFERENT FROM EACH OTHER!
AND ANYWAY, HAVING JUST ONE PERSON AS CRAZY AS YOU IN THE WORLD IS MORE THAN ENOUGH!!
IF YOU'LL EXCUSE ME, I MUST JOURNEY AHEAD!!
GET WELL SOON!
HARUHI!
WHY THE TRAVELER PARTING WORDS?
AND YOU DROPPED YOUR BOOK...
IF WE DON'T HURRY YOU'LL MISS YOUR DOCTOR'S APPOINT-MENT.
APOLOGIES. I'VE GOT TO GET THIS TO HARUHI.
HUH?
MASTER TAMAKI, WAIT...
DON'T LEAVE ME!

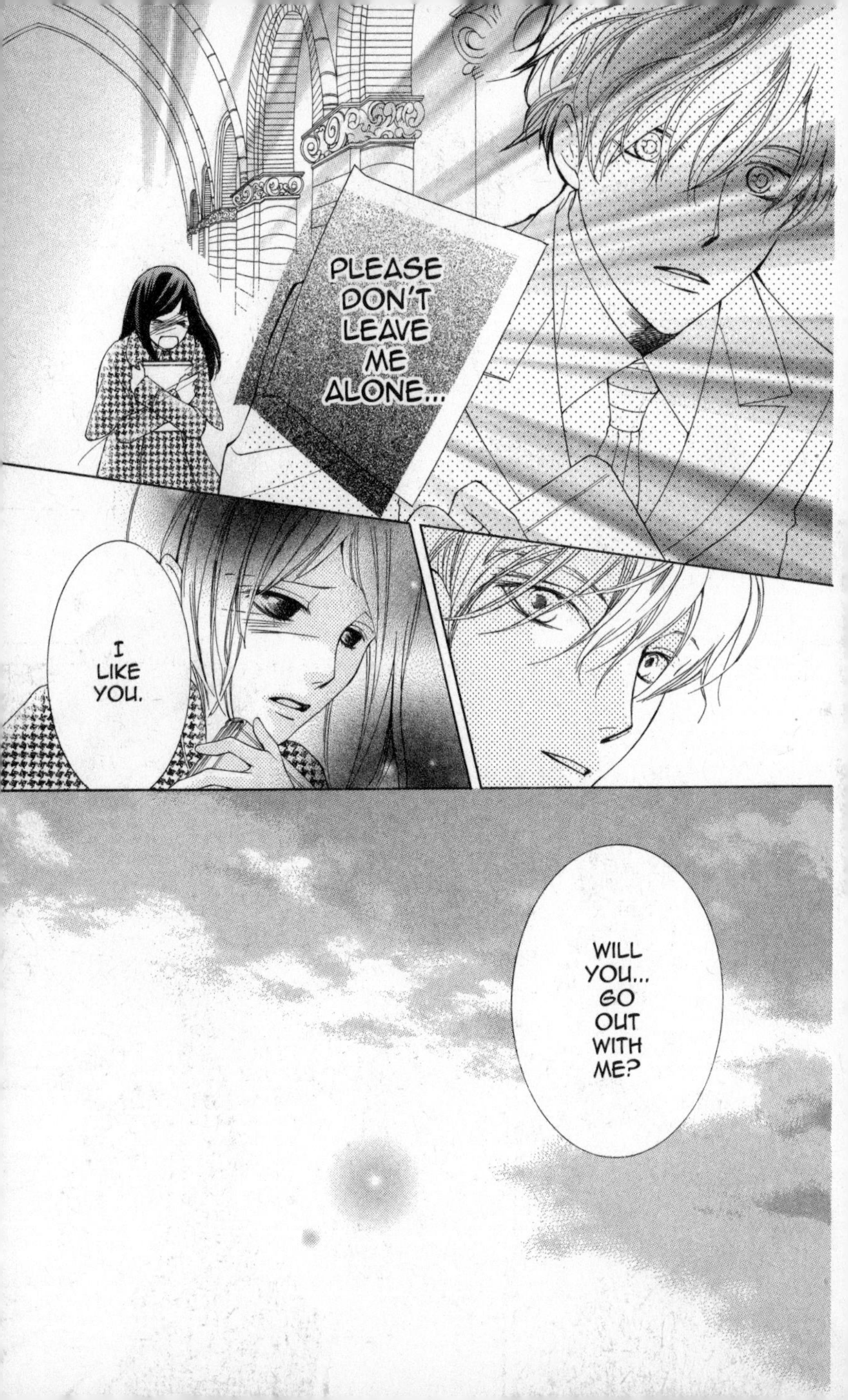
PLEASE DON'T LEAVE ME ALONE...
I LIKE YOU.
WILL YOU... GO OUT WITH ME?

TEAM ☆ HATORI'S ROOM
AYA AOMURA

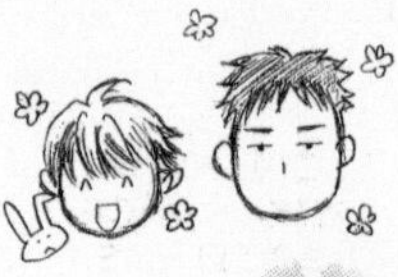

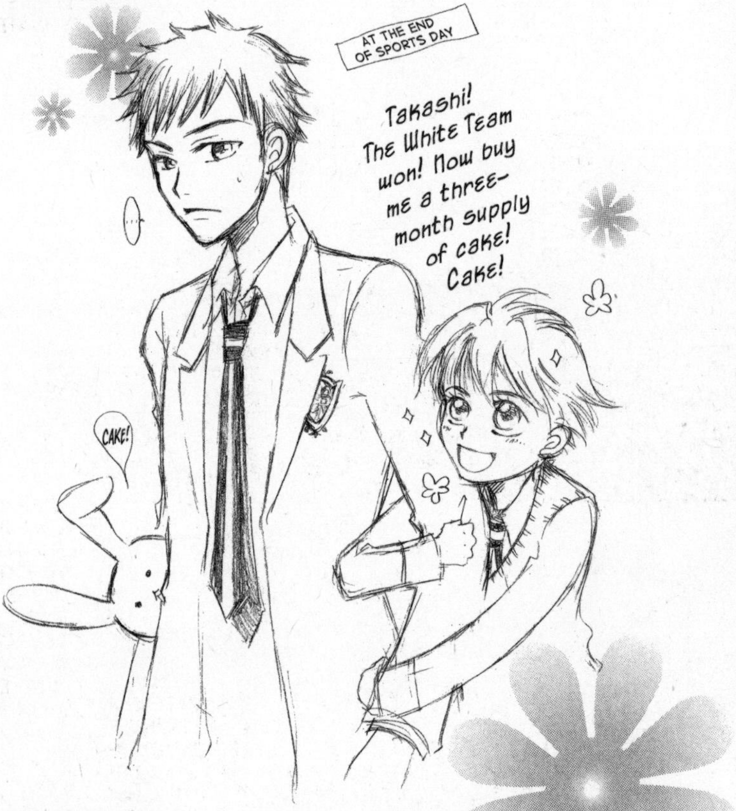
AT THE END OF SPORTS DAY
Takashi! The White Team won! Now buy me a three-month supply of cake! Cake!
...
CAKE!

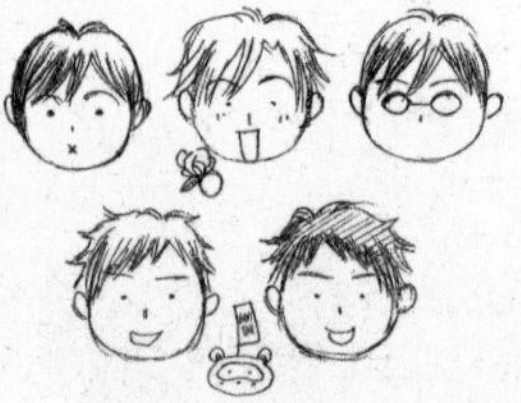

TEAM☆HATORI VETERAN (FROM THE DAYS OF *MILLENNIUM SNOW* AND RESIDENT "BUBBLEHEAD CHARACTER") AYA-CHAN DREW THIS LOVELY PICTURE OF MORI X HUNNY AND FRIENDS AFTER SPORTS DAY.♡AYA-CHAN, IT WAS ONLY AFTER I MET YOU THAT I CAME TO UNDERSTAND THE TRUE MEANING OF "AIRHEAD"... YOU ARE AN OASIS FOR MY HEART. THANK YOU SO MUCH FOR ALL THE COMFORT AND SOLACE YOU PROVIDE ME!!

OURAN HIGH SCHOOL HOST CLUB

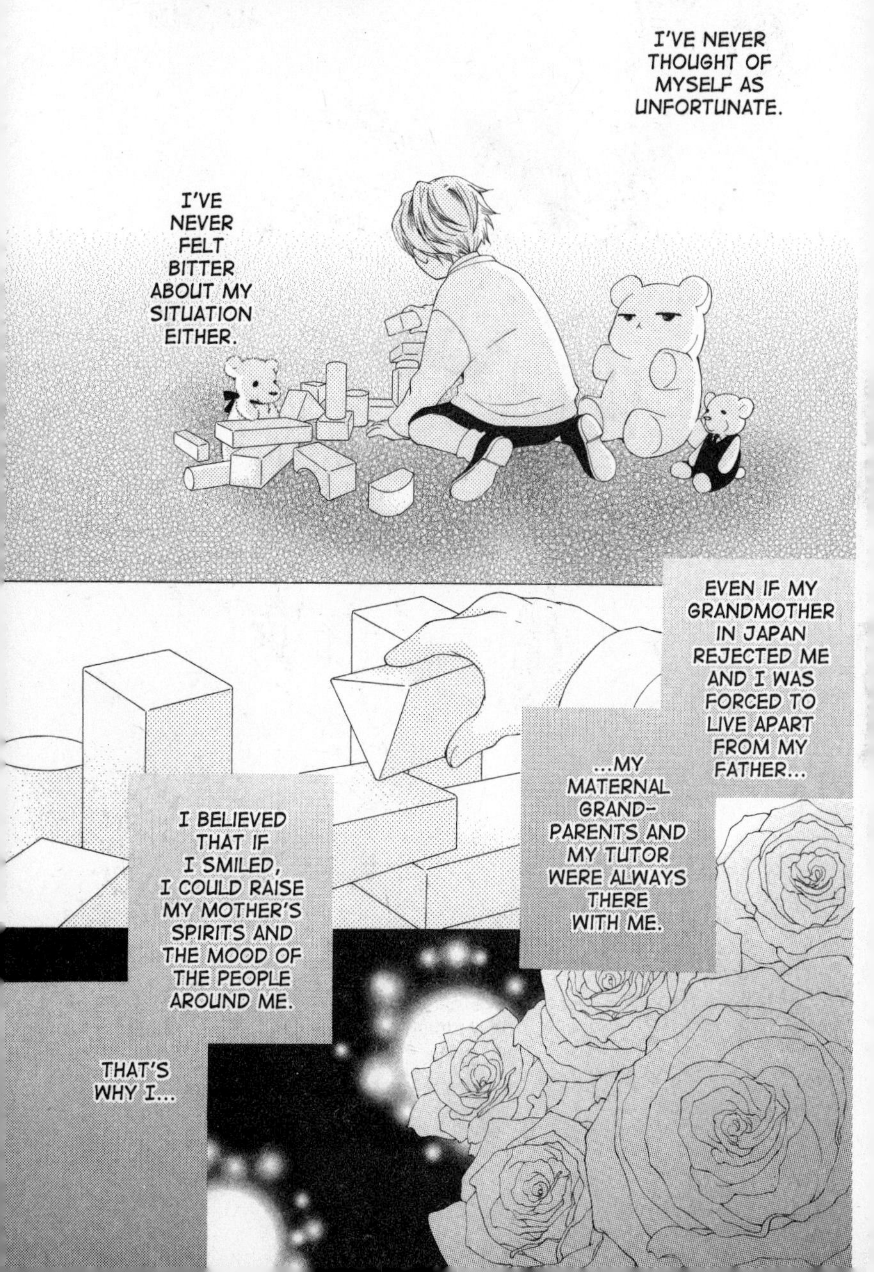
I'VE NEVER THOUGHT OF MYSELF AS UNFORTUNATE.
I'VE NEVER FELT BITTER ABOUT MY SITUATION EITHER.
EVEN IF MY GRANDMOTHER IN JAPAN REJECTED ME AND I WAS FORCED TO LIVE APART FROM MY FATHER...
...MY MATERNAL GRAND-PARENTS AND MY TUTOR WERE ALWAYS THERE WITH ME.
I BELIEVED THAT IF I SMILED, I COULD RAISE MY MOTHER'S SPIRITS AND THE MOOD OF THE PEOPLE AROUND ME.
THAT'S WHY I...

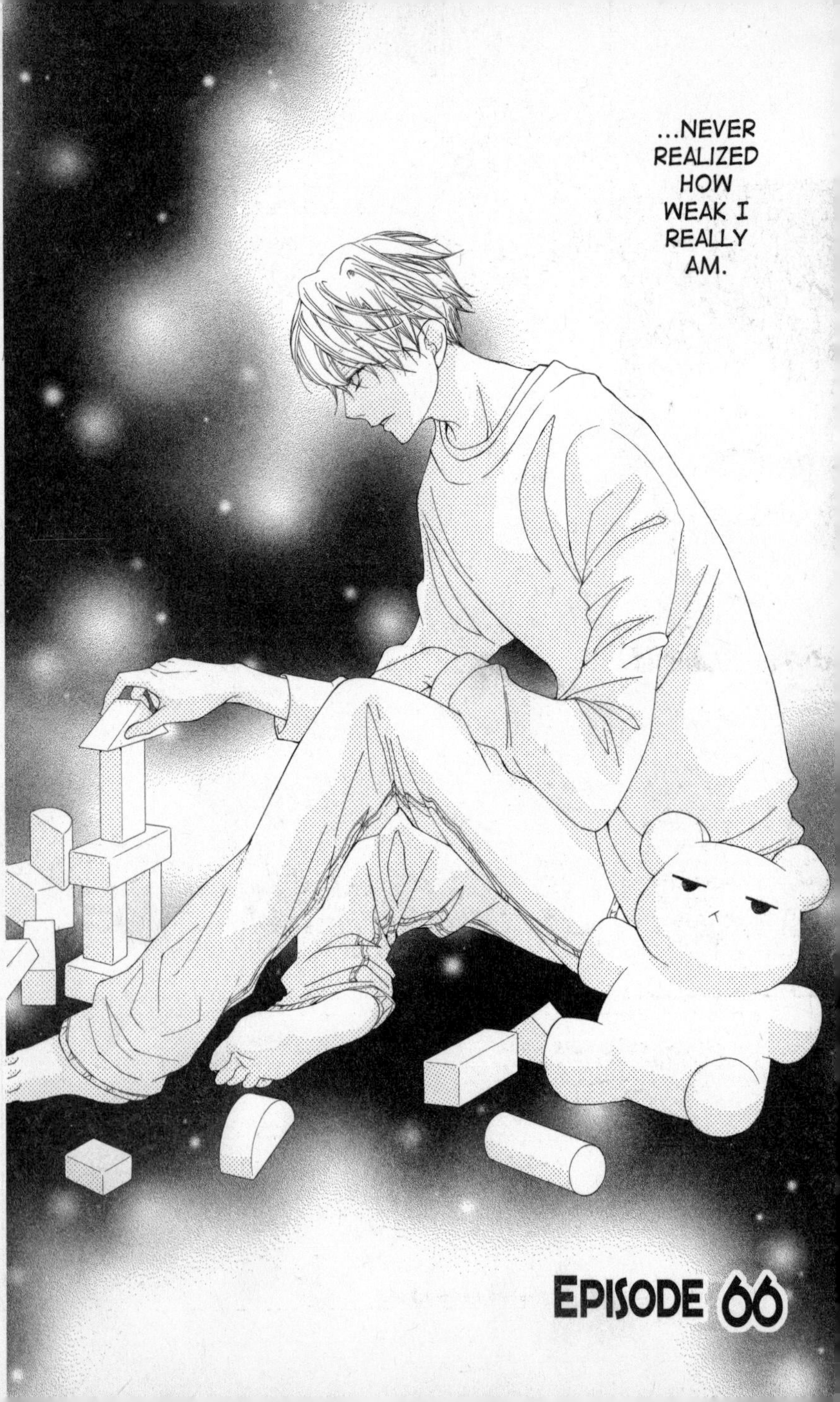
...NEVER REALIZED HOW WEAK I REALLY AM.
EPISODE 66

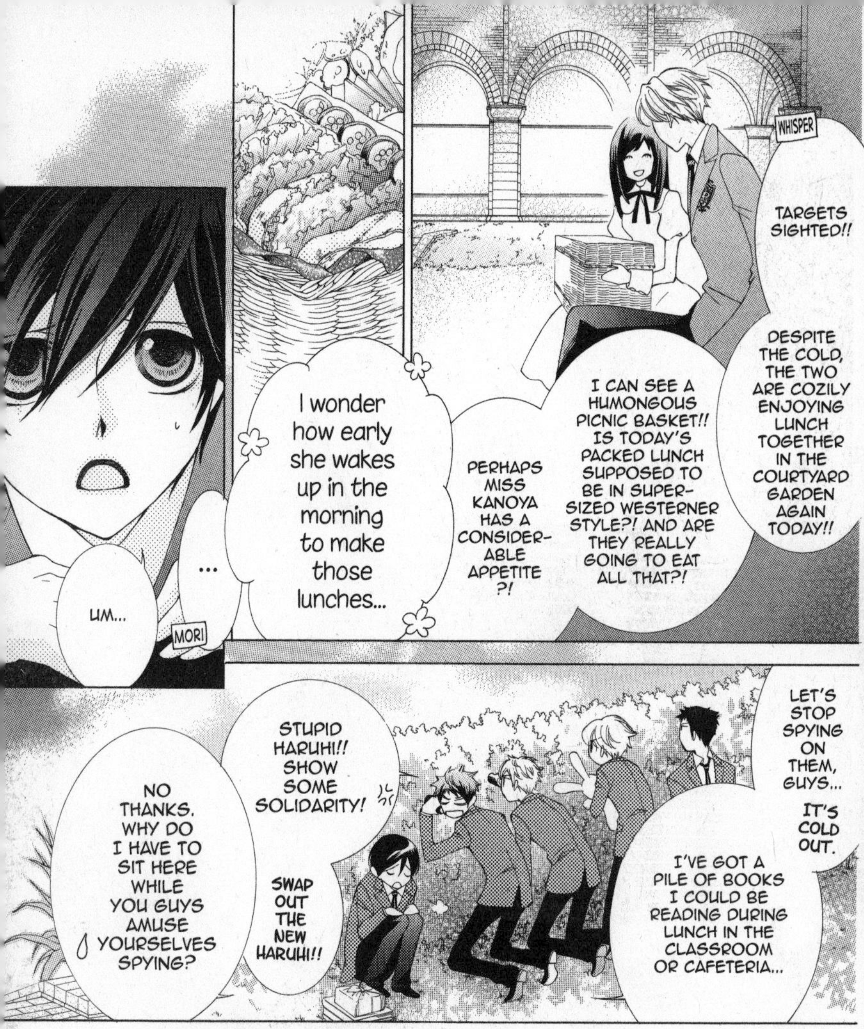
WHISPER
TARGETS SIGHTED!!
DESPITE THE COLD, THE TWO ARE COZILY ENJOYING LUNCH TOGETHER IN THE COURTYARD GARDEN AGAIN TODAY!!
I CAN SEE A HUMONGOUS PICNIC BASKET!! IS TODAY'S PACKED LUNCH SUPPOSED TO BE IN SUPER-SIZED WESTERNER STYLE?! AND ARE THEY REALLY GOING TO EAT ALL THAT?!
PERHAPS MISS KANOYA HAS A CONSIDER-ABLE APPETITE ?!
I wonder how early she wakes up in the morning to make those lunches...
MORI
...
UM...
LET'S STOP SPYING ON THEM, GUYS...
IT'S COLD OUT.
I'VE GOT A PILE OF BOOKS I COULD BE READING DURING LUNCH IN THE CLASSROOM OR CAFETERIA...
STUPID HARUHI!! SHOW SOME SOLIDARITY!
SWAP OUT THE NEW HARUHI!!
NO THANKS. WHY DO I HAVE TO SIT HERE WHILE YOU GUYS AMUSE YOURSELVES SPYING?

THANK YOU SO MUCH FOR ALWAYS BEING THERE FOR ME!! PLEASE SEND IN YOUR THOUGHTS TO THE ADDRESS BELOW.

NANCY THISTLETHWAITE, EDITOR
VIZ MEDIA, LLC
P.O. BOX 77010
SAN FRANCISCO, CA 94107

DREADLOCK TWINS

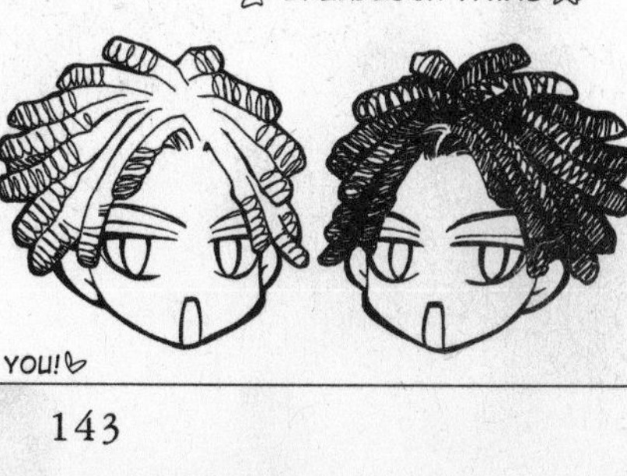

LOOKING FORWARD TO HEARING FROM YOU!

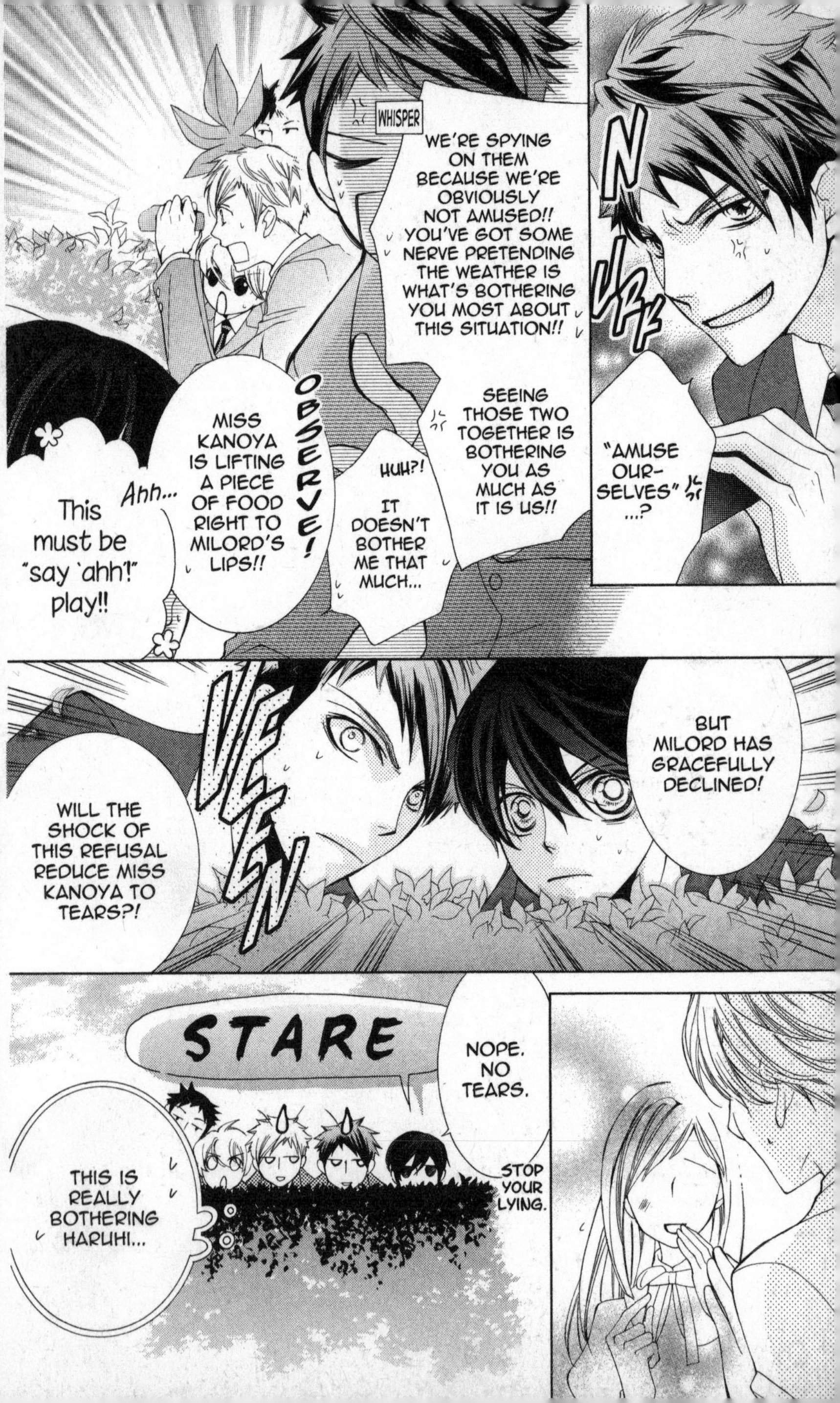
"AMUSE OURSELVES" ...?
WHISPER
WE'RE SPYING ON THEM BECAUSE WE'RE OBVIOUSLY NOT AMUSED!! YOU'VE GOT SOME NERVE PRETENDING THE WEATHER IS WHAT'S BOTHERING YOU MOST ABOUT THIS SITUATION!!
SEEING THOSE TWO TOGETHER IS BOTHERING YOU AS MUCH AS IT IS US!!
HUH?!
IT DOESN'T BOTHER ME THAT MUCH...
OBSERVE!
MISS KANOYA IS LIFTING A PIECE OF FOOD RIGHT TO MILORD'S LIPS!!
Ahh...
This must be "say 'ahh'!" play!!
BUT MILORD HAS GRACEFULLY DECLINED!
WILL THE SHOCK OF THIS REFUSAL REDUCE MISS KANOYA TO TEARS?!
NOPE. NO TEARS.
STOP YOUR LYING.
STARE
THIS IS REALLY BOTHERING HARUHI...

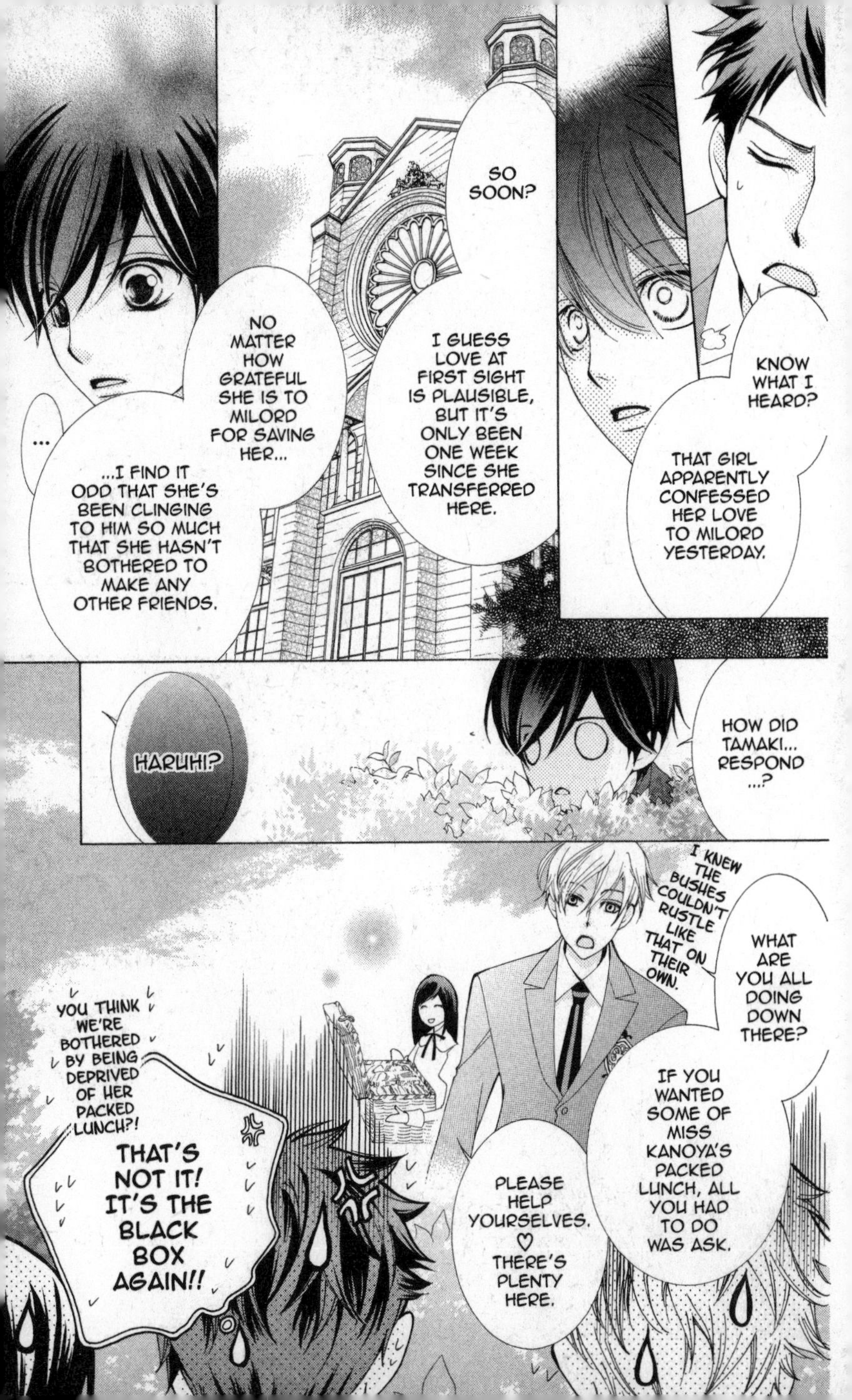
KNOW WHAT I HEARD?
THAT GIRL APPARENTLY CONFESSED HER LOVE TO MILORD YESTERDAY.
SO SOON?
I GUESS LOVE AT FIRST SIGHT IS PLAUSIBLE, BUT IT'S ONLY BEEN ONE WEEK SINCE SHE TRANSFERRED HERE.
NO MATTER HOW GRATEFUL SHE IS TO MILORD FOR SAVING HER...
...I FIND IT ODD THAT SHE'S BEEN CLINGING TO HIM SO MUCH THAT SHE HASN'T BOTHERED TO MAKE ANY OTHER FRIENDS.
...
HOW DID TAMAKI... RESPOND ...?
HARUHI?
I KNEW THE BUSHES COULDN'T RUSTLE LIKE THAT ON THEIR OWN.
WHAT ARE YOU ALL DOING DOWN THERE?
IF YOU WANTED SOME OF MISS KANOYA'S PACKED LUNCH, ALL YOU HAD TO DO WAS ASK.
PLEASE HELP YOURSELVES. ♡ THERE'S PLENTY HERE.
YOU THINK WE'RE BOTHERED BY BEING DEPRIVED OF HER PACKED LUNCH?!
THAT'S NOT IT! IT'S THE BLACK BOX AGAIN!!

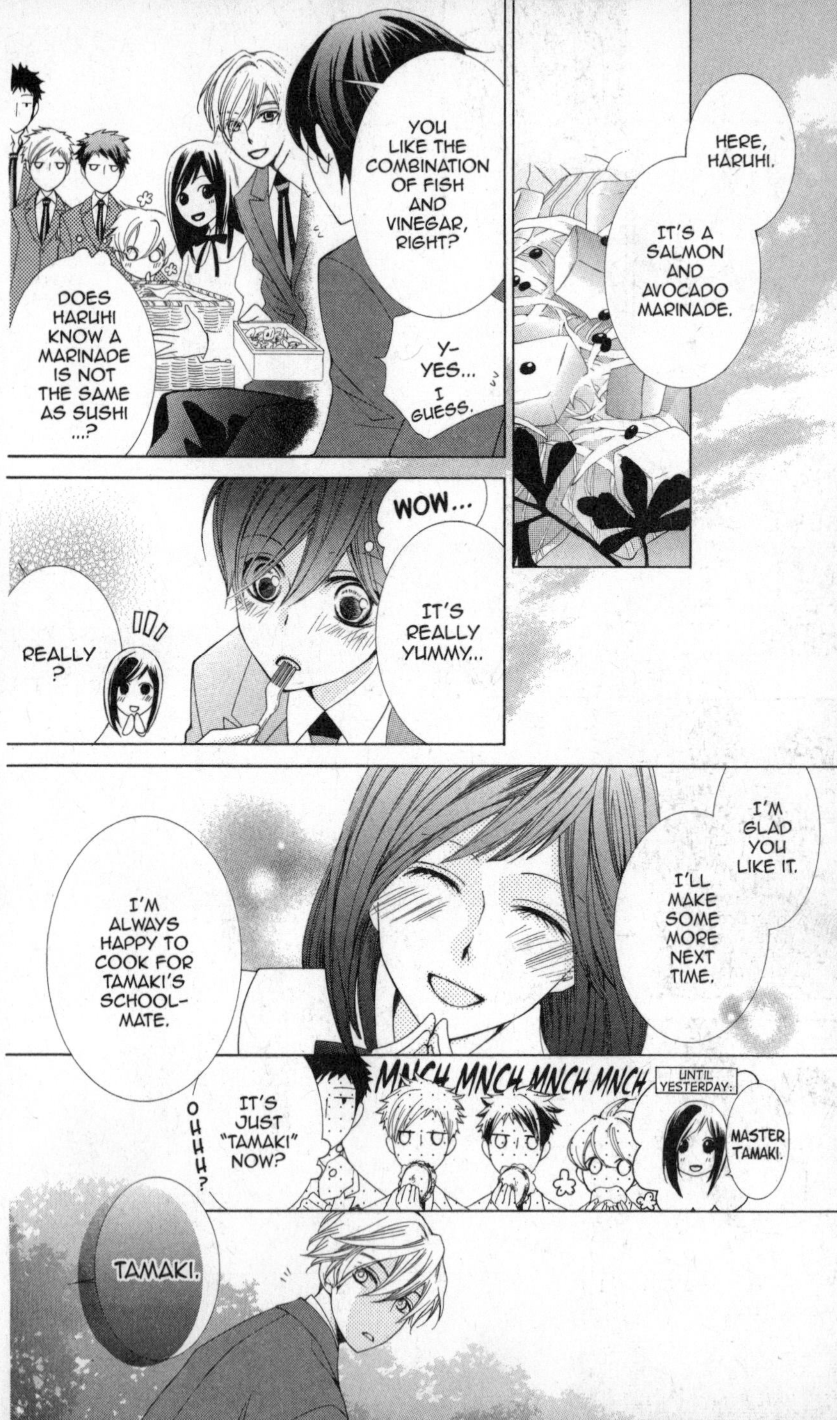
HERE, HARUHI.
IT'S A SALMON AND AVOCADO MARINADE.
YOU LIKE THE COMBINATION OF FISH AND VINEGAR, RIGHT?
Y- YES... I GUESS.
DOES HARUHI KNOW A MARINADE IS NOT THE SAME AS SUSHI ...?
WOW...
IT'S REALLY YUMMY...
REALLY ?
I'M GLAD YOU LIKE IT.
I'LL MAKE SOME MORE NEXT TIME.
I'M ALWAYS HAPPY TO COOK FOR TAMAKI'S SCHOOL-MATE.
UNTIL YESTERDAY:
MASTER TAMAKI.
MNCH MNCH MNCH MNCH
IT'S JUST "TAMAKI" NOW?
OHHH?
TAMAKI.

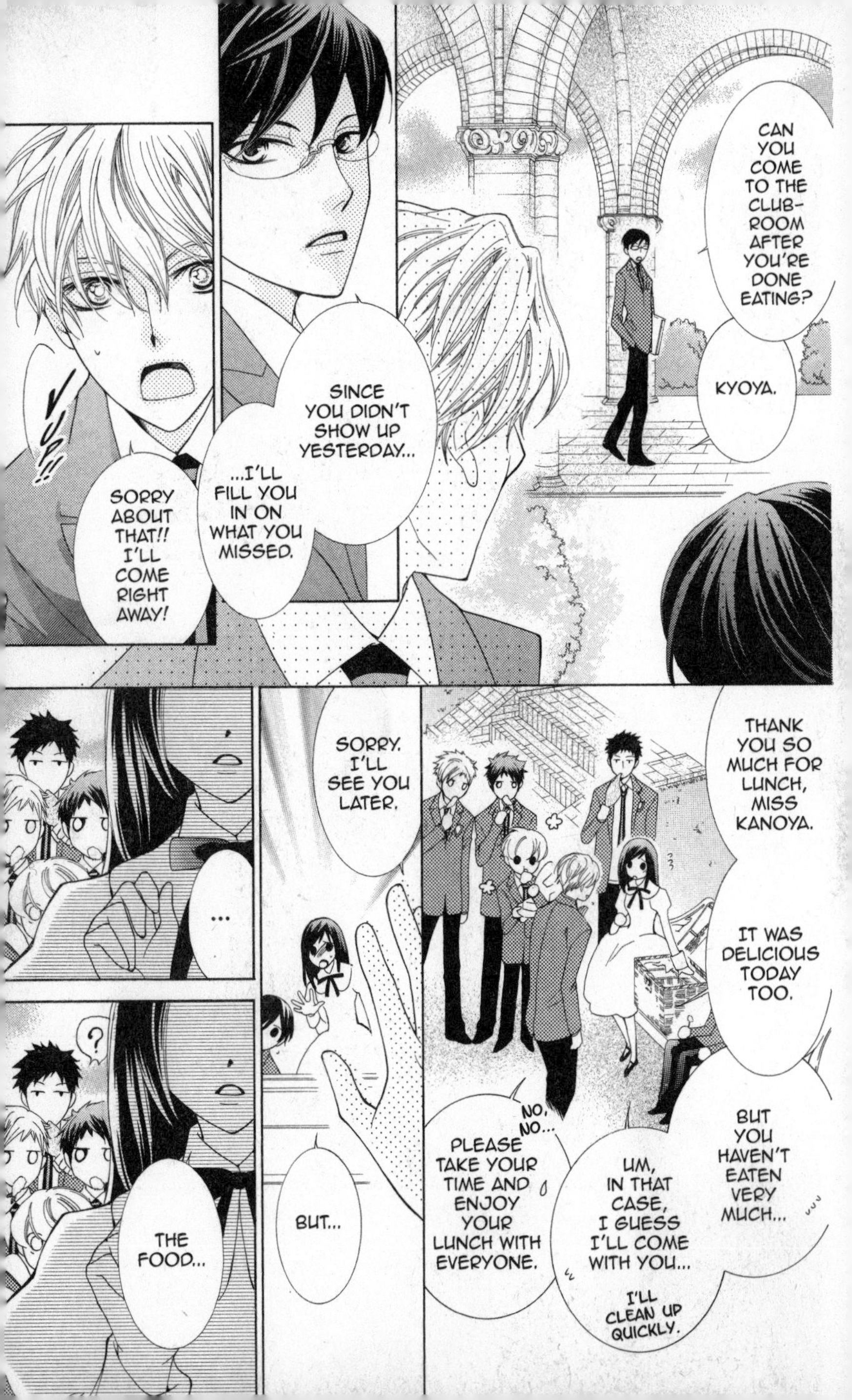
CAN YOU COME TO THE CLUB-ROOM AFTER YOU'RE DONE EATING?
KYOYA.
SINCE YOU DIDN'T SHOW UP YESTERDAY...
...I'LL FILL YOU IN ON WHAT YOU MISSED.
VUP!!
SORRY ABOUT THAT!! I'LL COME RIGHT AWAY!
THANK YOU SO MUCH FOR LUNCH, MISS KANOYA.
IT WAS DELICIOUS TODAY TOO.
BUT YOU HAVEN'T EATEN VERY MUCH...
UM, IN THAT CASE, I GUESS I'LL COME WITH YOU...
I'LL CLEAN UP QUICKLY.
NO, NO...
PLEASE TAKE YOUR TIME AND ENJOY YOUR LUNCH WITH EVERYONE.
SORRY. I'LL SEE YOU LATER.
BUT...
...
?
THE FOOD...

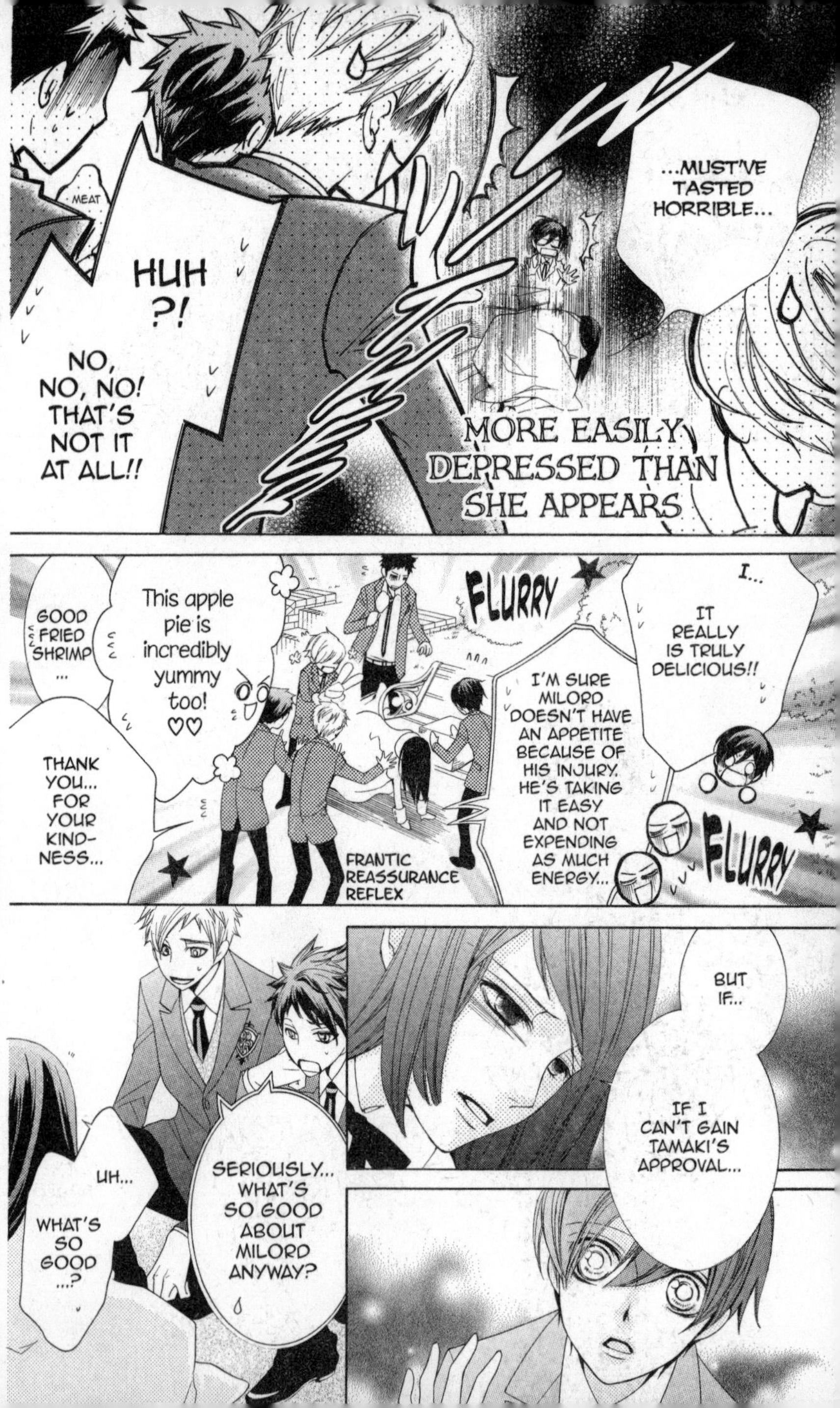
...MUST'VE TASTED HORRIBLE...
MORE EASILY DEPRESSED THAN SHE APPEARS
HUH ?!
NO, NO, NO! THAT'S NOT IT AT ALL!!
MEAT
I...
IT REALLY IS TRULY DELICIOUS!!
FLURRY
I'M SURE MILORD DOESN'T HAVE AN APPETITE BECAUSE OF HIS INJURY. HE'S TAKING IT EASY AND NOT EXPENDING AS MUCH ENERGY...
FLURRY
FRANTIC REASSURANCE REFLEX
This apple pie is incredibly yummy too! ♡♡
GOOD FRIED SHRIMP...
THANK YOU... FOR YOUR KINDNESS...
BUT IF...
IF I CAN'T GAIN TAMAKI'S APPROVAL...
SERIOUSLY... WHAT'S SO GOOD ABOUT MILORD ANYWAY?
UH...
WHAT'S SO GOOD ...?

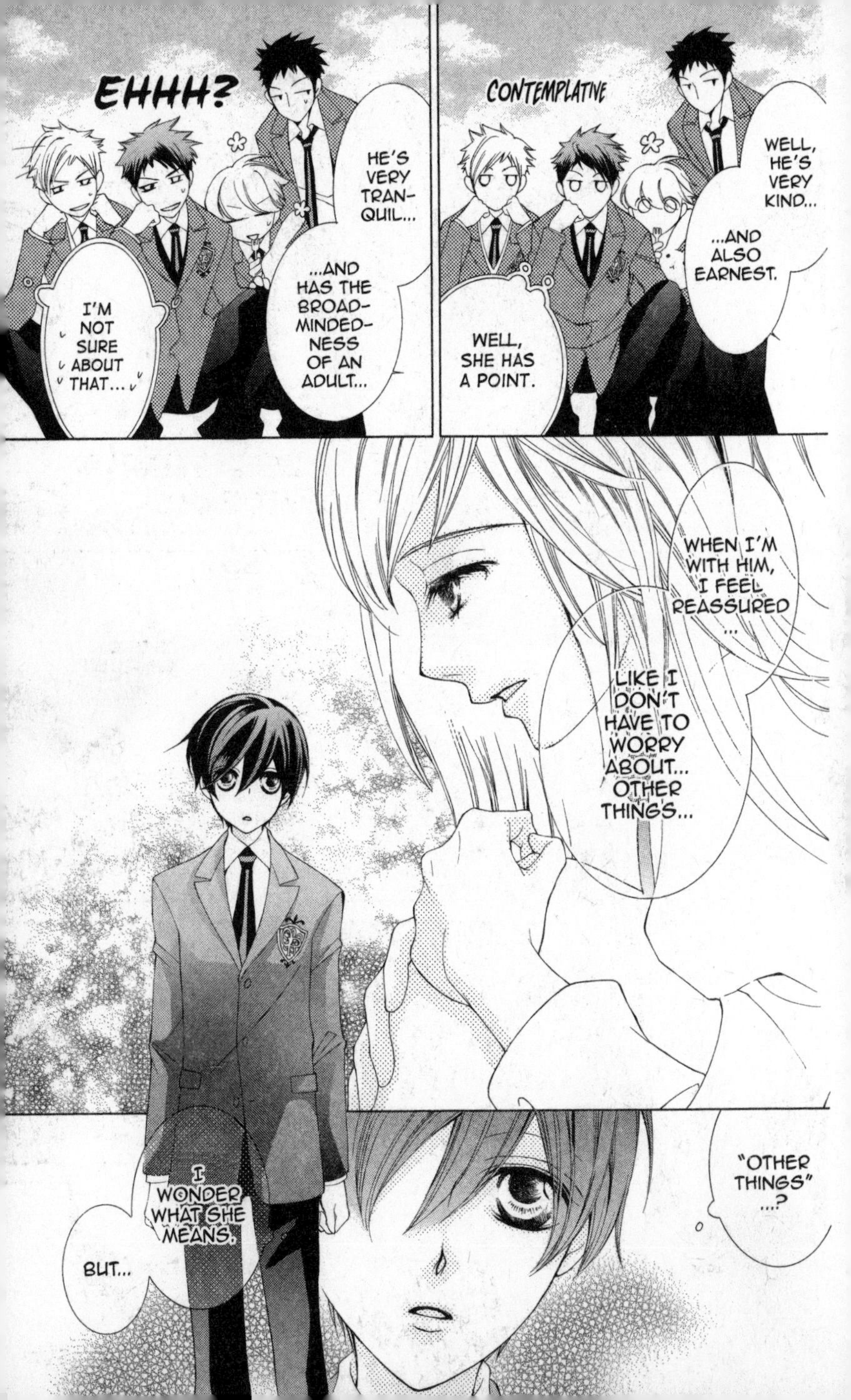
CONTEMPLATIVE
WELL, HE'S VERY KIND...
...AND ALSO EARNEST.
WELL, SHE HAS A POINT.
HE'S VERY TRAN-QUIL...
...AND HAS THE BROAD-MINDED-NESS OF AN ADULT...
EHHH?
I'M NOT SURE ABOUT THAT...
WHEN I'M WITH HIM, I FEEL REASSURED...
LIKE I DON'T HAVE TO WORRY ABOUT... OTHER THINGS...
"OTHER THINGS" ...?
I WONDER WHAT SHE MEANS.
BUT...

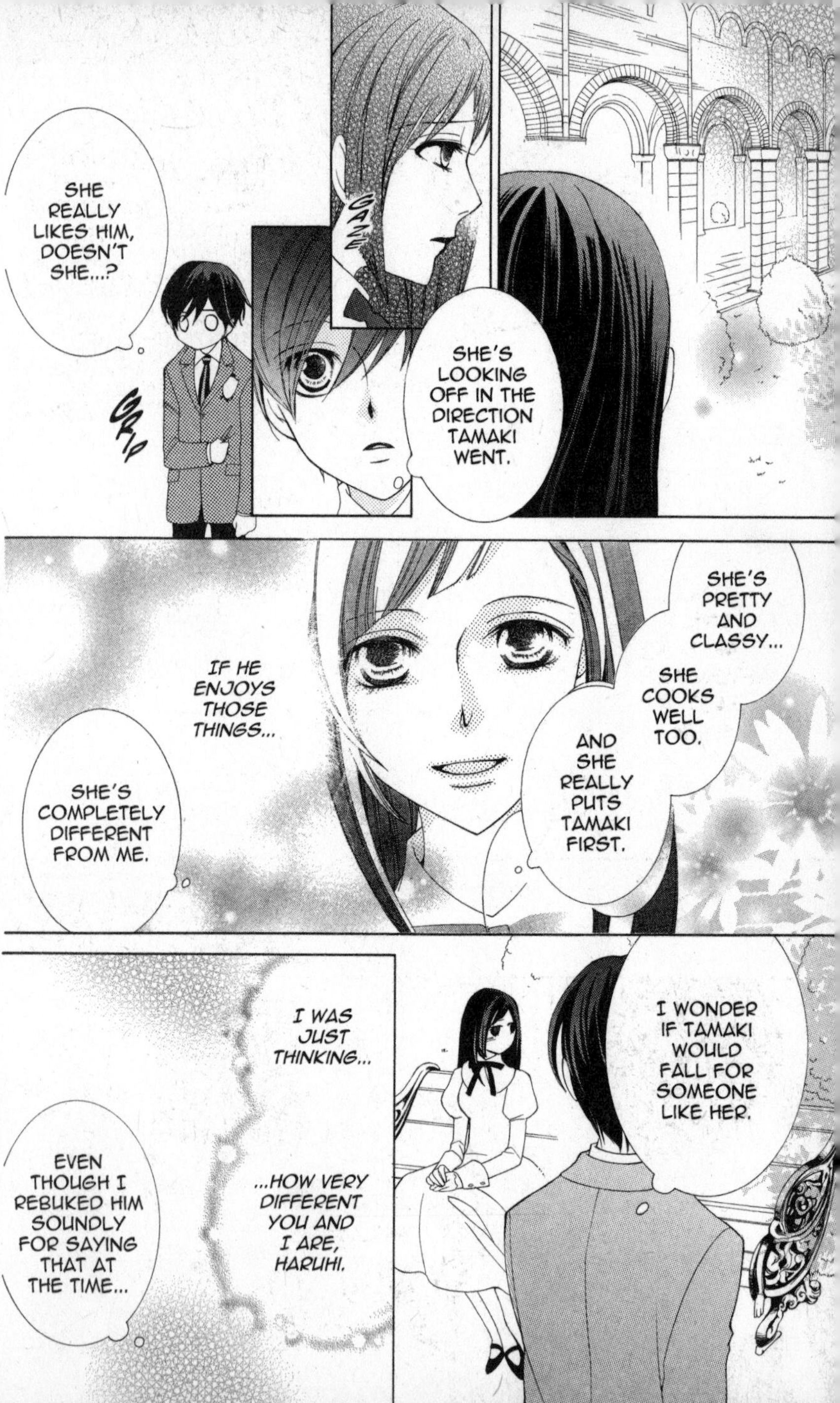

SHE'S LOOKING OFF IN THE DIRECTION TAMAKI WENT.
GAZE
SHE REALLY LIKES HIM, DOESN'T SHE...?
GRIP
SHE'S PRETTY AND CLASSY...
SHE COOKS WELL TOO.
AND SHE REALLY PUTS TAMAKI FIRST.
IF HE ENJOYS THOSE THINGS...
SHE'S COMPLETELY DIFFERENT FROM ME.
I WONDER IF TAMAKI WOULD FALL FOR SOMEONE LIKE HER.
I WAS JUST THINKING...
...HOW VERY DIFFERENT YOU AND I ARE, HARUHI.
EVEN THOUGH I REBUKED HIM SOUNDLY FOR SAYING THAT AT THE TIME...

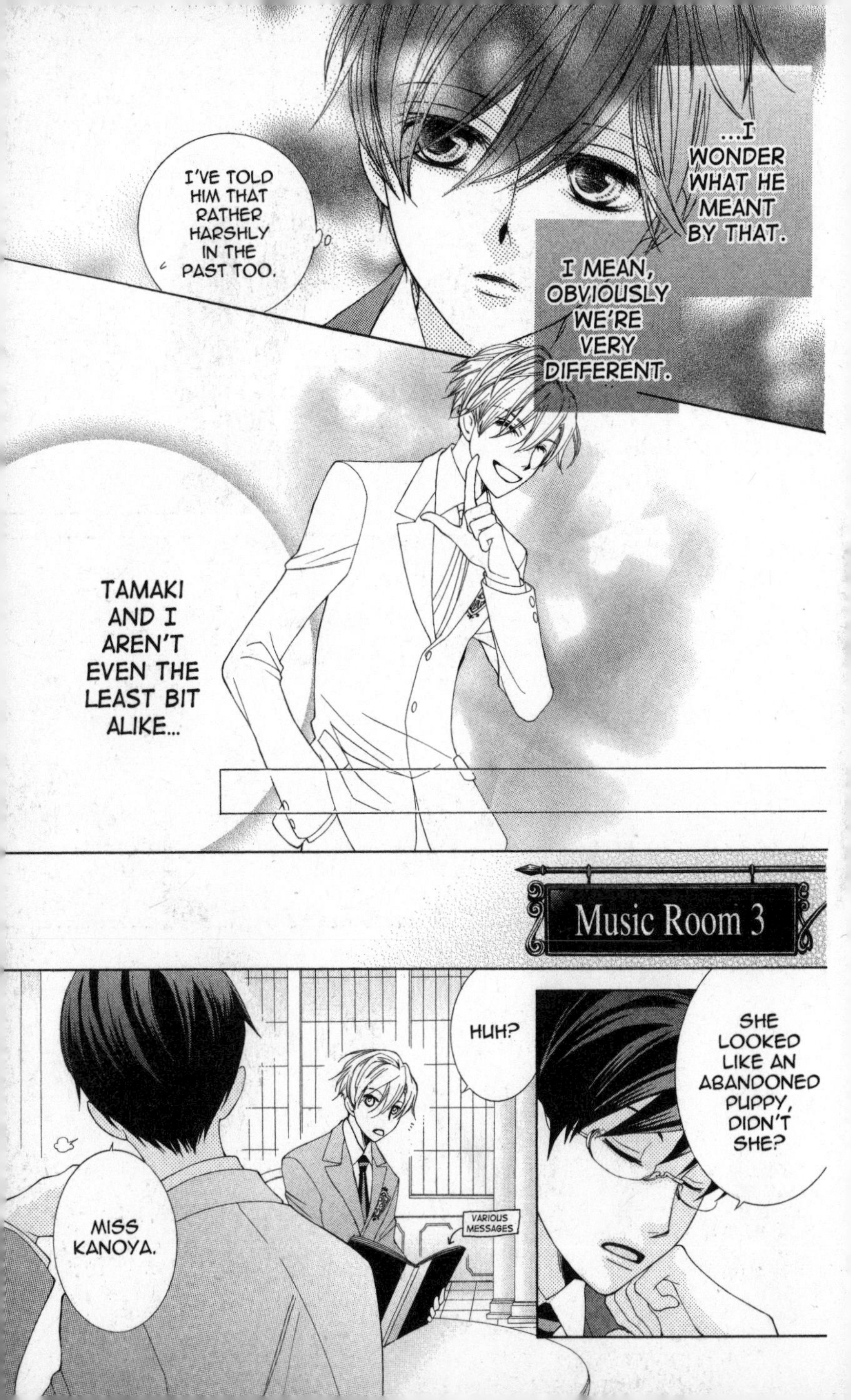
...I WONDER WHAT HE MEANT BY THAT.
I MEAN, OBVIOUSLY WE'RE VERY DIFFERENT.
I'VE TOLD HIM THAT RATHER HARSHLY IN THE PAST TOO.
TAMAKI AND I AREN'T EVEN THE LEAST BIT ALIKE...
Music Room 3
SHE LOOKED LIKE AN ABANDONED PUPPY, DIDN'T SHE?
HUH?
MISS KANOYA.
VARIOUS MESSAGES

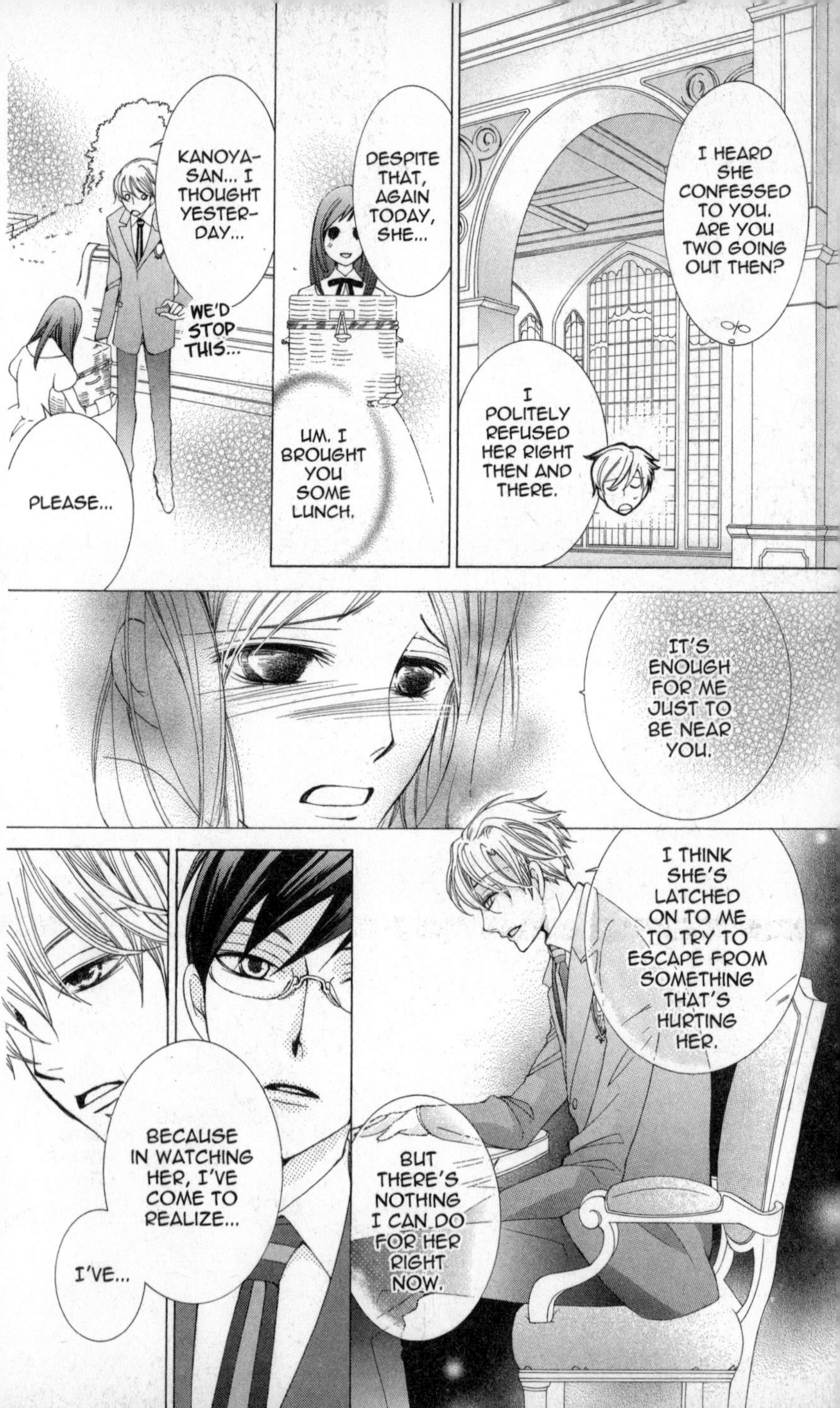
I HEARD SHE CONFESSED TO YOU. ARE YOU TWO GOING OUT THEN?
I POLITELY REFUSED HER RIGHT THEN AND THERE.
DESPITE THAT, AGAIN TODAY, SHE...
UM. I BROUGHT YOU SOME LUNCH.
KANOYA-SAN... I THOUGHT YESTER-DAY...
WE'D STOP THIS...
PLEASE...
IT'S ENOUGH FOR ME JUST TO BE NEAR YOU.
I THINK SHE'S LATCHED ON TO ME TO TRY TO ESCAPE FROM SOMETHING THAT'S HURTING HER.
BUT THERE'S NOTHING I CAN DO FOR HER RIGHT NOW.
BECAUSE IN WATCHING HER, I'VE COME TO REALIZE...
I'VE...

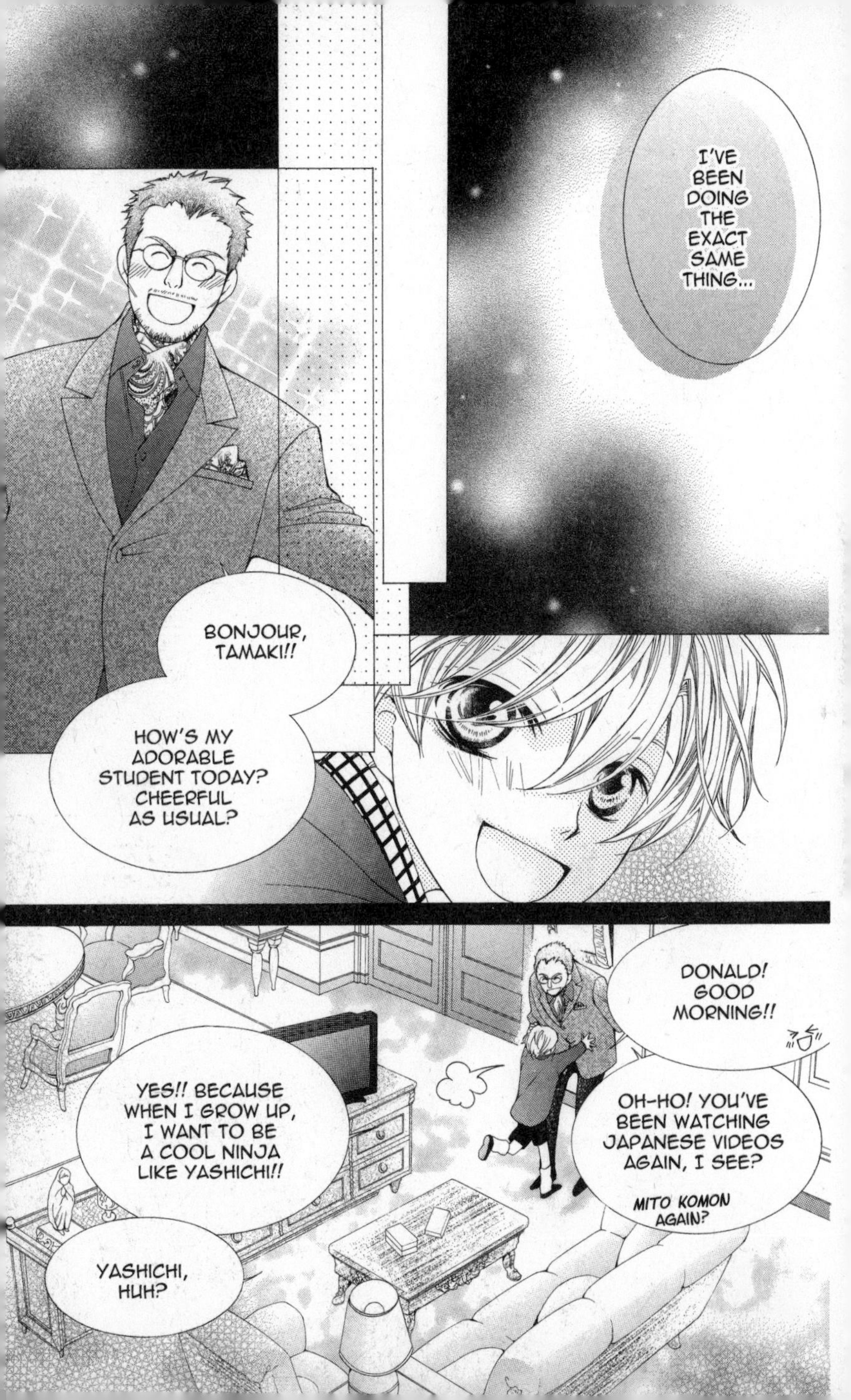

I'VE BEEN DOING THE EXACT SAME THING...
BONJOUR, TAMAKI!!
HOW'S MY ADORABLE STUDENT TODAY? CHEERFUL AS USUAL?
DONALD! GOOD MORNING!!
OH-HO! YOU'VE BEEN WATCHING JAPANESE VIDEOS AGAIN, I SEE?
MITO KOMON AGAIN?
YES!! BECAUSE WHEN I GROW UP, I WANT TO BE A COOL NINJA LIKE YASHICHI!!
YASHICHI, HUH?

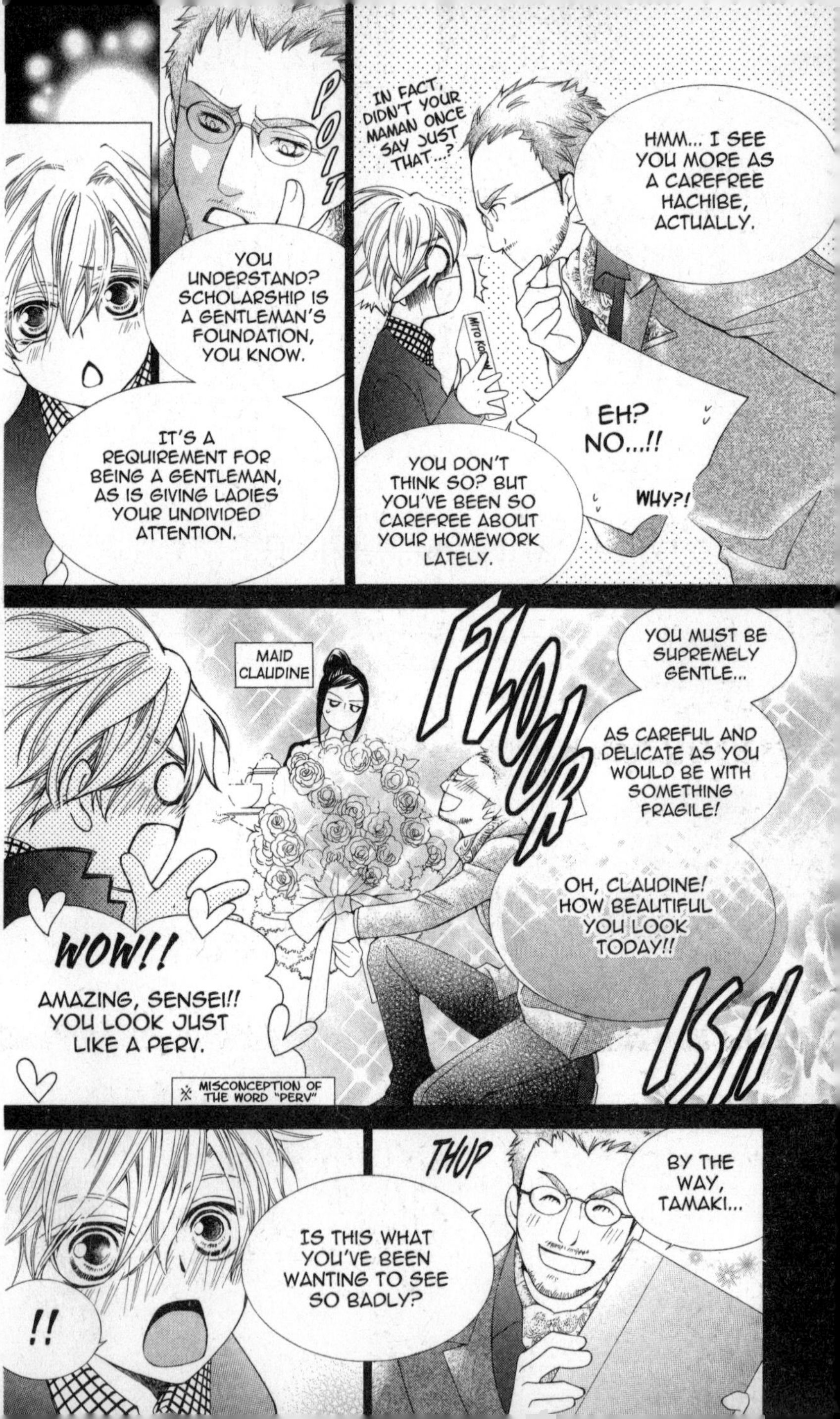
HMM... I SEE YOU MORE AS A CAREFREE HACHIBE, ACTUALLY.
IN FACT, DIDN'T YOUR MAMAN ONCE SAY JUST THAT...?
MITO KOMON
EH? NO...!!
WHY?!
YOU DON'T THINK SO? BUT YOU'VE BEEN SO CAREFREE ABOUT YOUR HOMEWORK LATELY.
POIT
YOU UNDERSTAND? SCHOLARSHIP IS A GENTLEMAN'S FOUNDATION, YOU KNOW.
IT'S A REQUIREMENT FOR BEING A GENTLEMAN, AS IS GIVING LADIES YOUR UNDIVIDED ATTENTION.
YOU MUST BE SUPREMELY GENTLE...
AS CAREFUL AND DELICATE AS YOU WOULD BE WITH SOMETHING FRAGILE!
FLOURISH
OH, CLAUDINE! HOW BEAUTIFUL YOU LOOK TODAY!!
MAID CLAUDINE
WOW!!
AMAZING, SENSEI!! YOU LOOK JUST LIKE A PERV.
※ MISCONCEPTION OF THE WORD "PERV"
THUP
BY THE WAY, TAMAKI...
IS THIS WHAT YOU'VE BEEN WANTING TO SEE SO BADLY?
!!

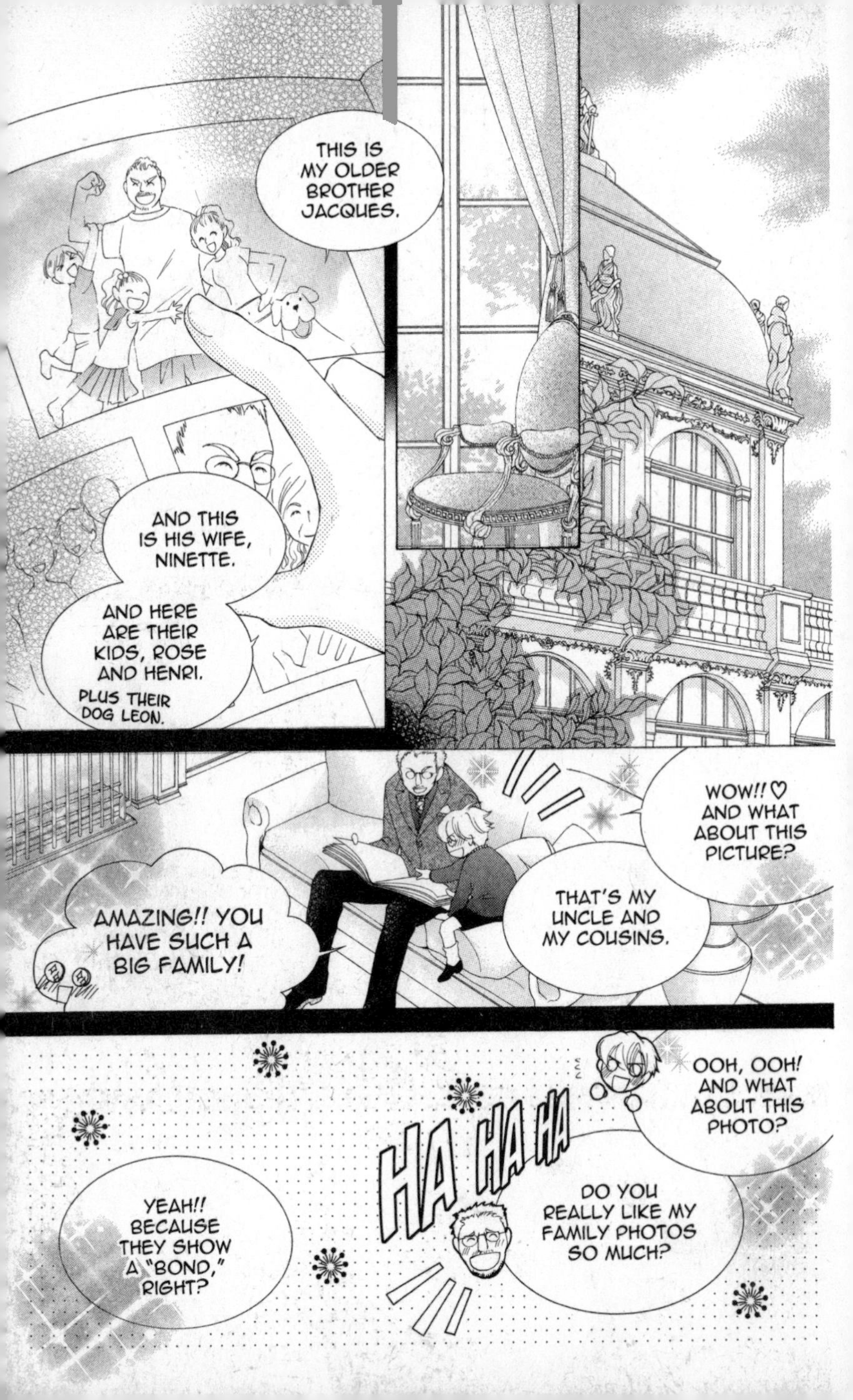
THIS IS MY OLDER BROTHER JACQUES.
AND THIS IS HIS WIFE, NINETTE.
AND HERE ARE THEIR KIDS, ROSE AND HENRI.
PLUS THEIR DOG LEON.
WOW!! ♡ AND WHAT ABOUT THIS PICTURE?
THAT'S MY UNCLE AND MY COUSINS.
AMAZING!! YOU HAVE SUCH A BIG FAMILY!
OOH, OOH! AND WHAT ABOUT THIS PHOTO?
HA HA HA
DO YOU REALLY LIKE MY FAMILY PHOTOS SO MUCH?
YEAH!! BECAUSE THEY SHOW A "BOND," RIGHT?

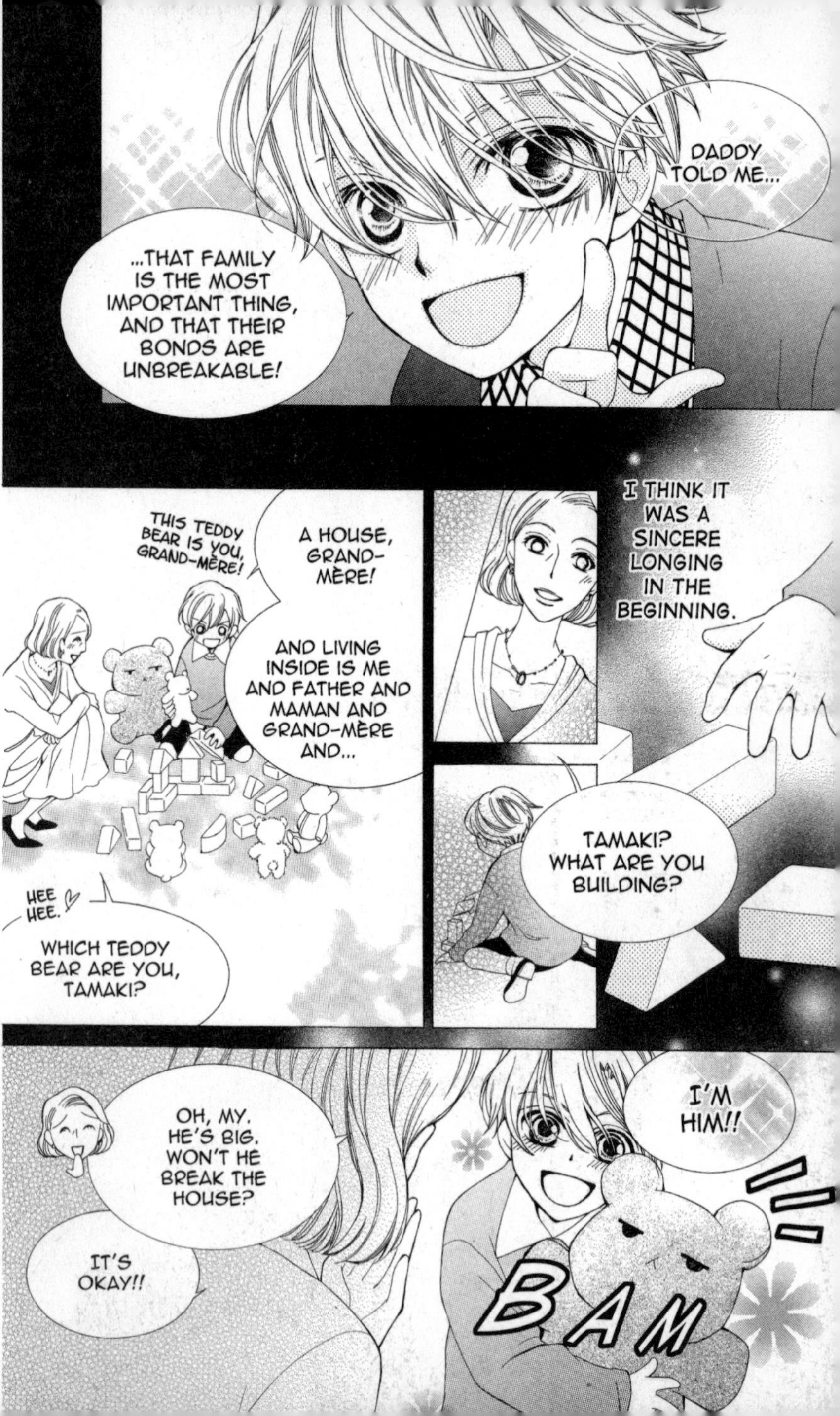
DADDY TOLD ME...
...THAT FAMILY IS THE MOST IMPORTANT THING, AND THAT THEIR BONDS ARE UNBREAKABLE!
I THINK IT WAS A SINCERE LONGING IN THE BEGINNING.
TAMAKI? WHAT ARE YOU BUILDING?
A HOUSE, GRAND-MÈRE!
THIS TEDDY BEAR IS YOU, GRAND-MÈRE!
AND LIVING INSIDE IS ME AND FATHER AND MAMAN AND GRAND-MÈRE AND...
HEE HEE. ♡
WHICH TEDDY BEAR ARE YOU, TAMAKI?
I'M HIM!!
BAM
OH, MY. HE'S BIG. WON'T HE BREAK THE HOUSE?
IT'S OKAY!!

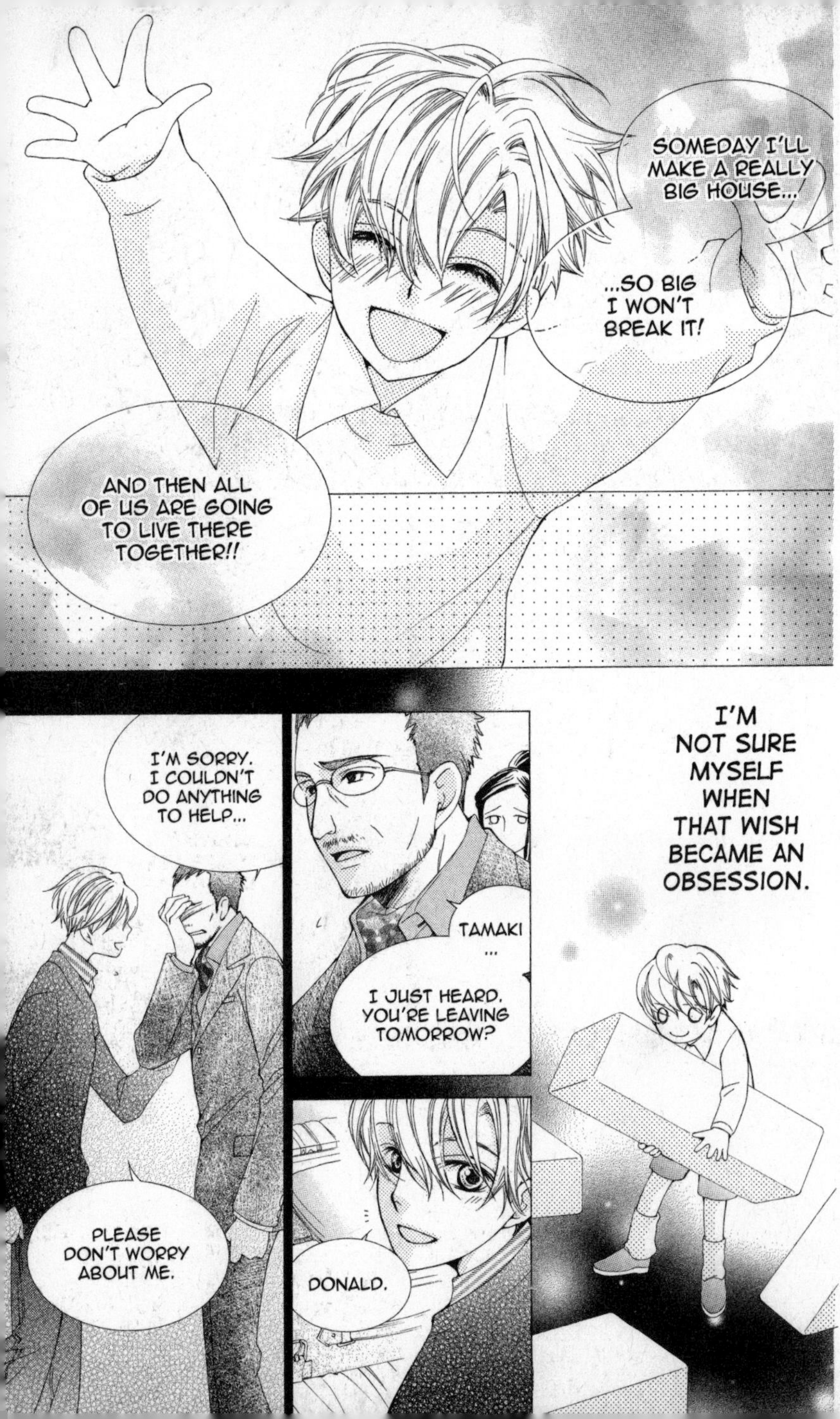
SOMEDAY I'LL MAKE A REALLY BIG HOUSE...
...SO BIG I WON'T BREAK IT!
AND THEN ALL OF US ARE GOING TO LIVE THERE TOGETHER!!
I'M NOT SURE MYSELF WHEN THAT WISH BECAME AN OBSESSION.
TAMAKI ...
I JUST HEARD. YOU'RE LEAVING TOMORROW?
DONALD.
I'M SORRY. I COULDN'T DO ANYTHING TO HELP...
PLEASE DON'T WORRY ABOUT ME.

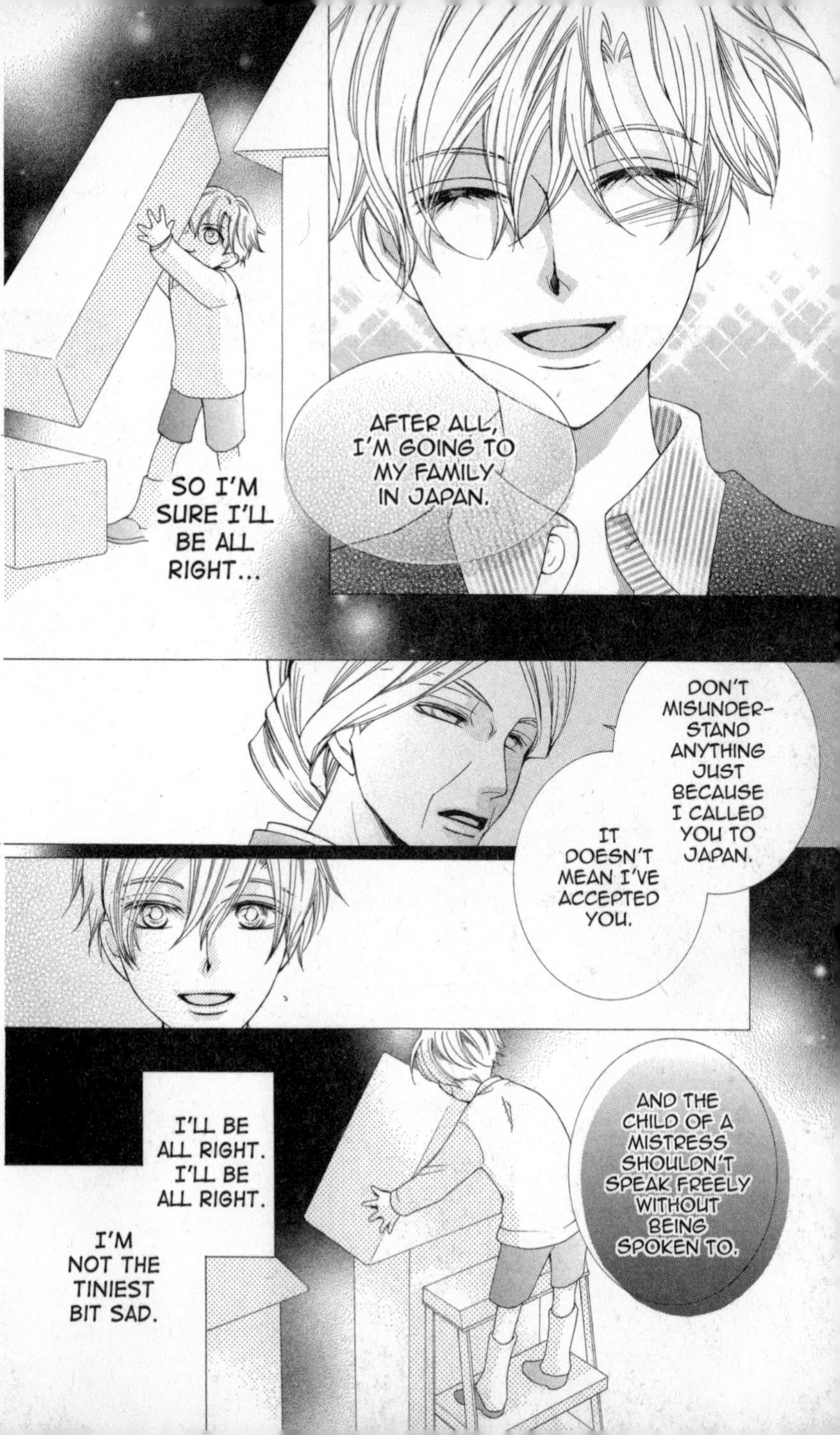
AFTER ALL, I'M GOING TO MY FAMILY IN JAPAN.
SO I'M SURE I'LL BE ALL RIGHT...
DON'T MISUNDER-STAND ANYTHING JUST BECAUSE I CALLED YOU TO JAPAN.
IT DOESN'T MEAN I'VE ACCEPTED YOU.
AND THE CHILD OF A MISTRESS SHOULDN'T SPEAK FREELY WITHOUT BEING SPOKEN TO.
I'LL BE ALL RIGHT. I'LL BE ALL RIGHT.
I'M NOT THE TINIEST BIT SAD.

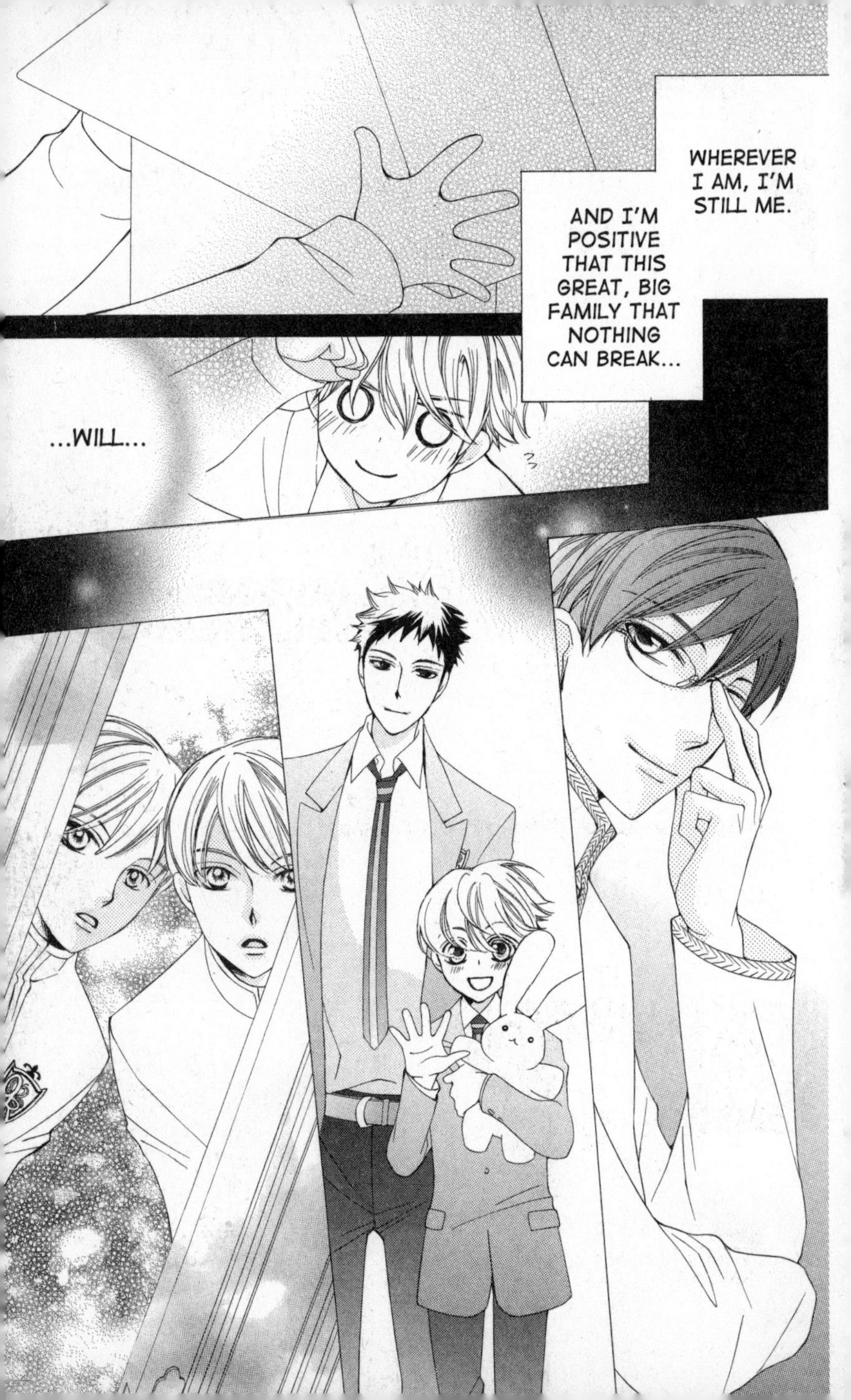
WHEREVER I AM, I'M STILL ME.
AND I'M POSITIVE THAT THIS GREAT, BIG FAMILY THAT NOTHING CAN BREAK...
...WILL...

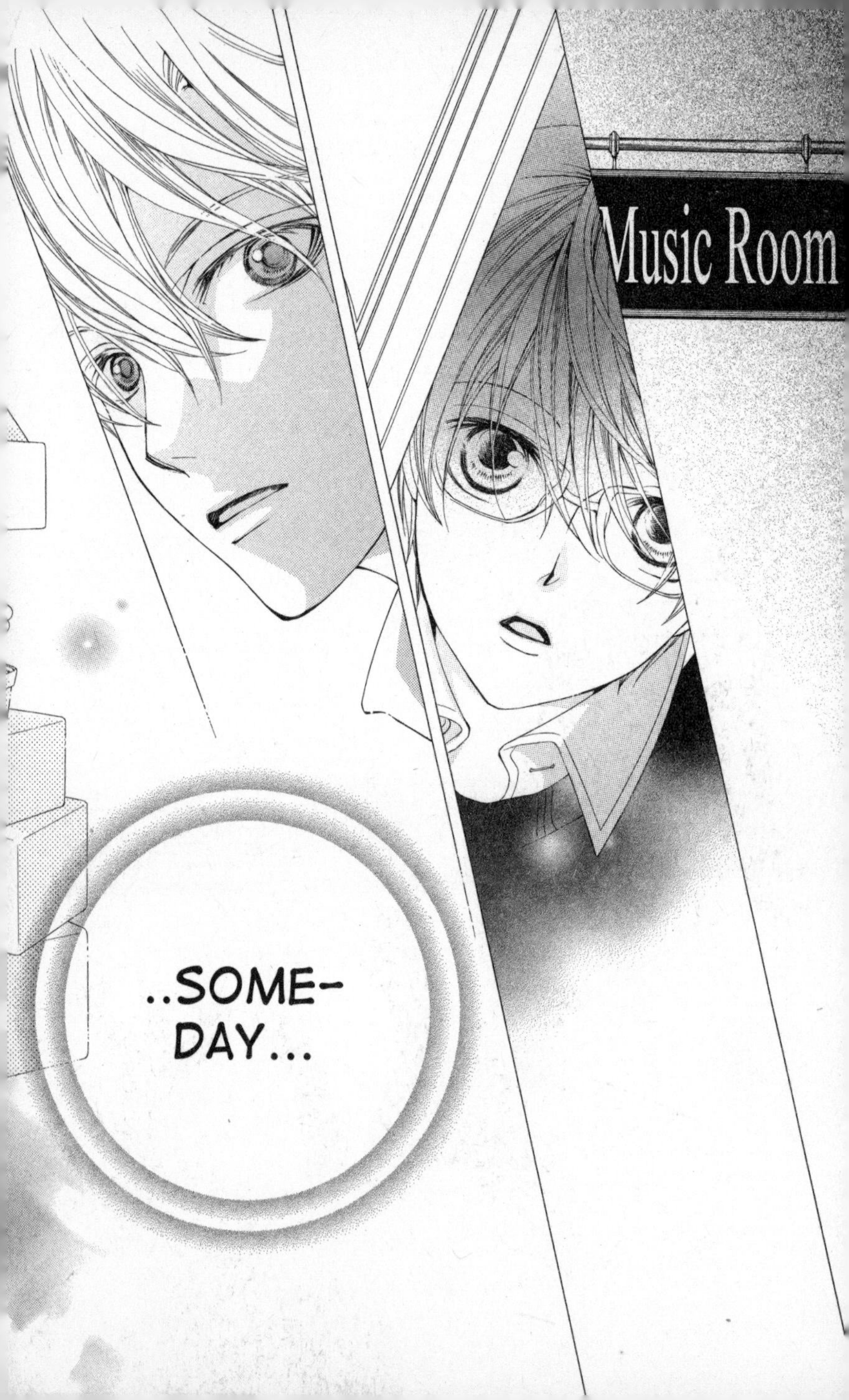
Music Room
..SOME-
DAY...

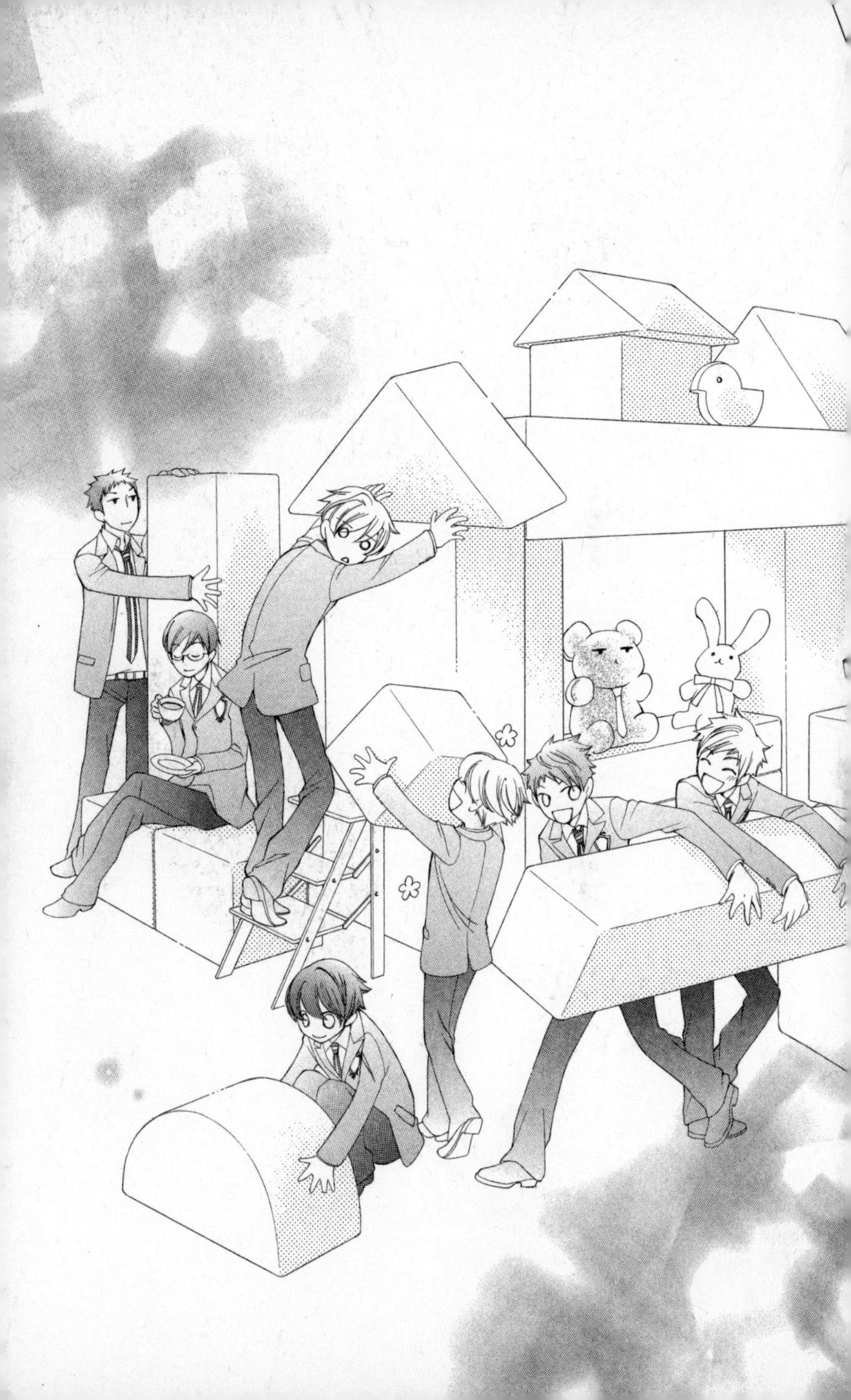

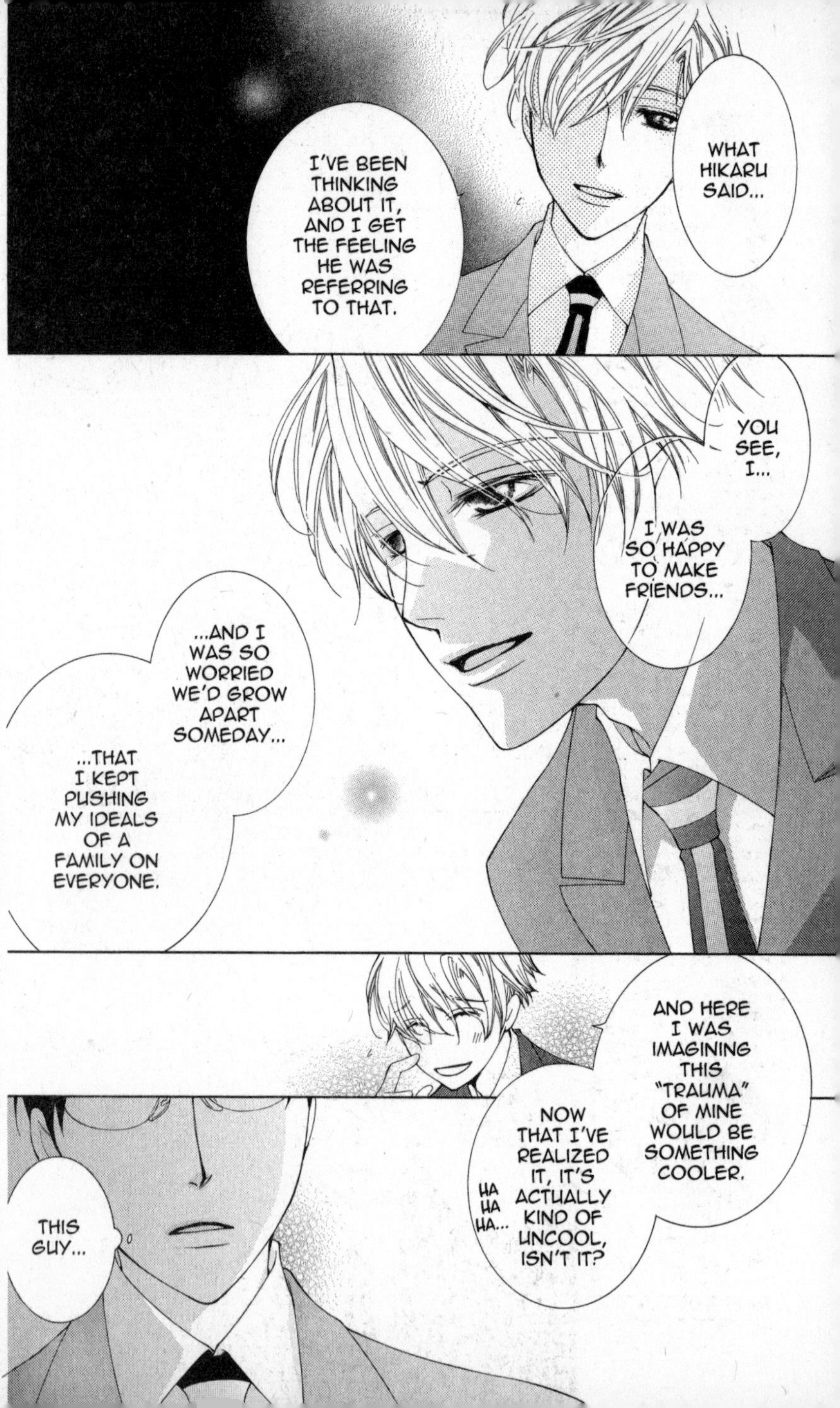
WHAT HIKARU SAID...
I'VE BEEN THINKING ABOUT IT, AND I GET THE FEELING HE WAS REFERRING TO THAT.
YOU SEE, I...
I WAS SO HAPPY TO MAKE FRIENDS...
...AND I WAS SO WORRIED WE'D GROW APART SOMEDAY...
...THAT I KEPT PUSHING MY IDEALS OF A FAMILY ON EVERYONE.
AND HERE I WAS IMAGINING THIS "TRAUMA" OF MINE WOULD BE SOMETHING COOLER.
NOW THAT I'VE REALIZED IT, IT'S ACTUALLY KIND OF UNCOOL, ISN'T IT?
HA HA HA...
THIS GUY...

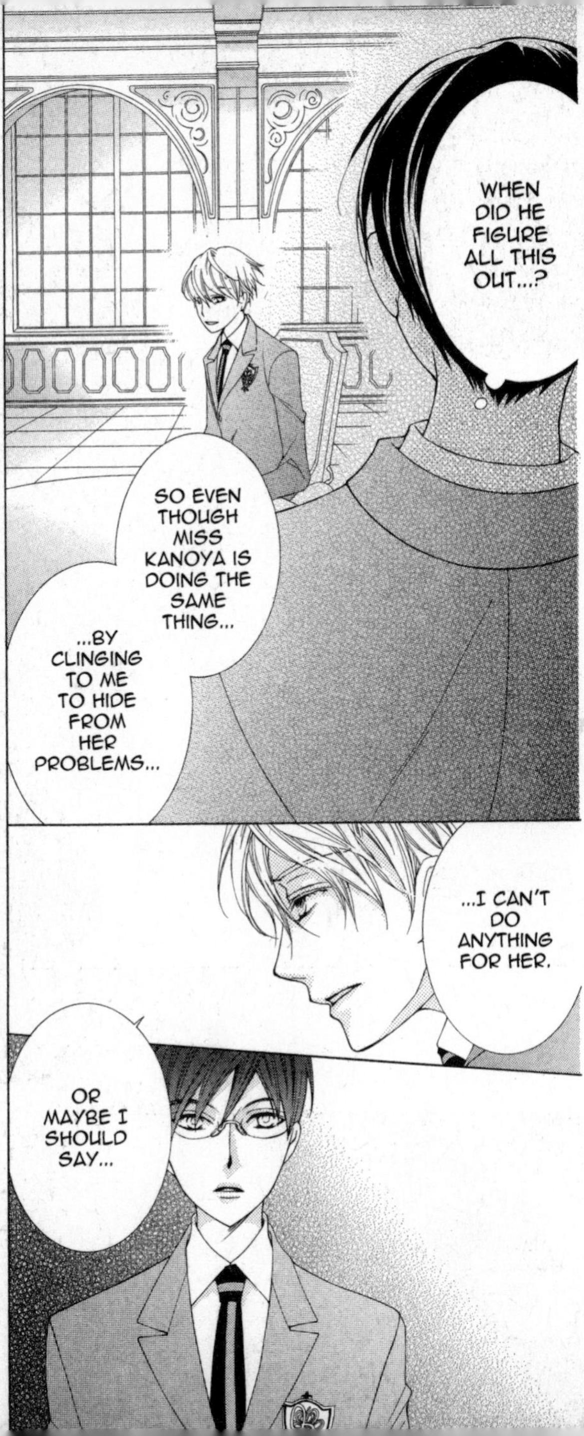
WHEN DID HE FIGURE ALL THIS OUT...?
SO EVEN THOUGH MISS KANOYA IS DOING THE SAME THING...
...BY CLINGING TO ME TO HIDE FROM HER PROBLEMS...
...I CAN'T DO ANYTHING FOR HER.
OR MAYBE I SHOULD SAY...

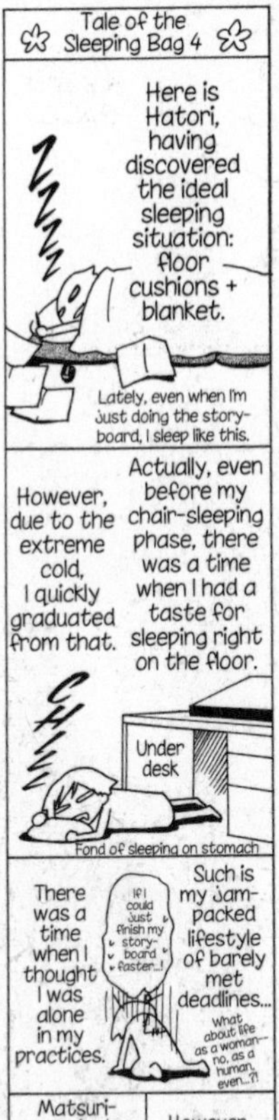
Tale of the Sleeping Bag 4
Here is Hatori, having discovered the ideal sleeping situation: floor cushions + blanket.
Lately, even when I'm just doing the storyboard, I sleep like this.
Actually, even before my chair-sleeping phase, there was a time when I had a taste for sleeping right on the floor.
However, due to the extreme cold, I quickly graduated from that.
Under desk
Fond of sleeping on stomach
Such is my jam-packed lifestyle of barely met deadlines...
If I could just finish my storyboard faster...!
There was a time when I thought I was alone in my practices.
What about life as a woman—no, as a human, even...?!
However, I soon discovered confederates.
Matsuri-sensei, who came to spend the night.
Bisco-chan, I'm sorry. Let me sleep just a little...
Matsuri-san!! I'll put a futon out for you, so please sleep in the tatami room!!
Already finished her work!
KONK
Floor
I'm fine here... Used to sleeping on the floor...
Noo!!
Matsuri-san!! Try the floor cushion! It's nice!!

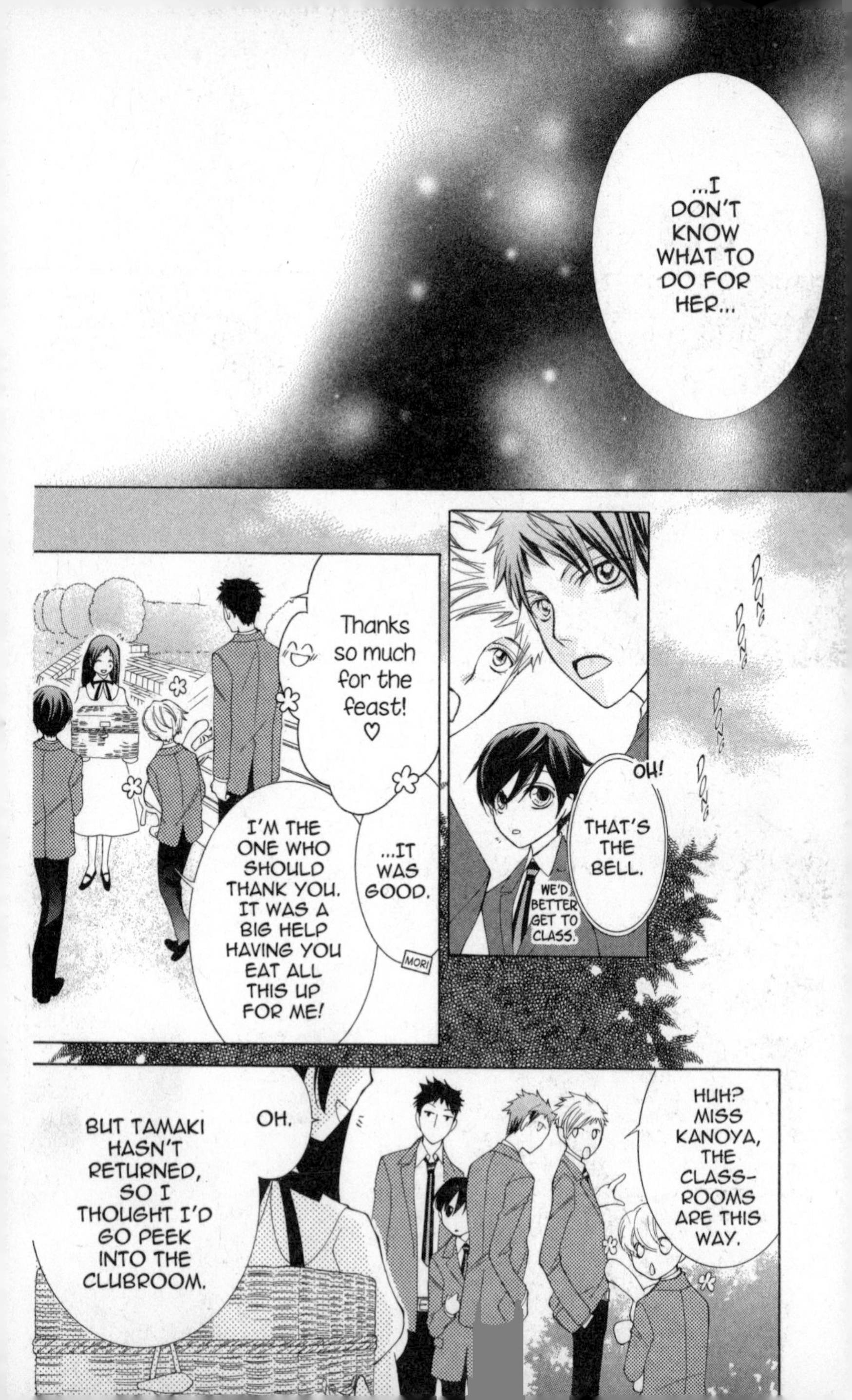

...I DON'T KNOW WHAT TO DO FOR HER...
DONG
DONG
DONG
DONG
OH!
THAT'S THE BELL.
WE'D BETTER GET TO CLASS.
Thanks so much for the feast! ♡
...IT WAS GOOD.
MORI
I'M THE ONE WHO SHOULD THANK YOU. IT WAS A BIG HELP HAVING YOU EAT ALL THIS UP FOR ME!
HUH? MISS KANOYA, THE CLASS-ROOMS ARE THIS WAY.
OH.
BUT TAMAKI HASN'T RETURNED, SO I THOUGHT I'D GO PEEK INTO THE CLUBROOM.

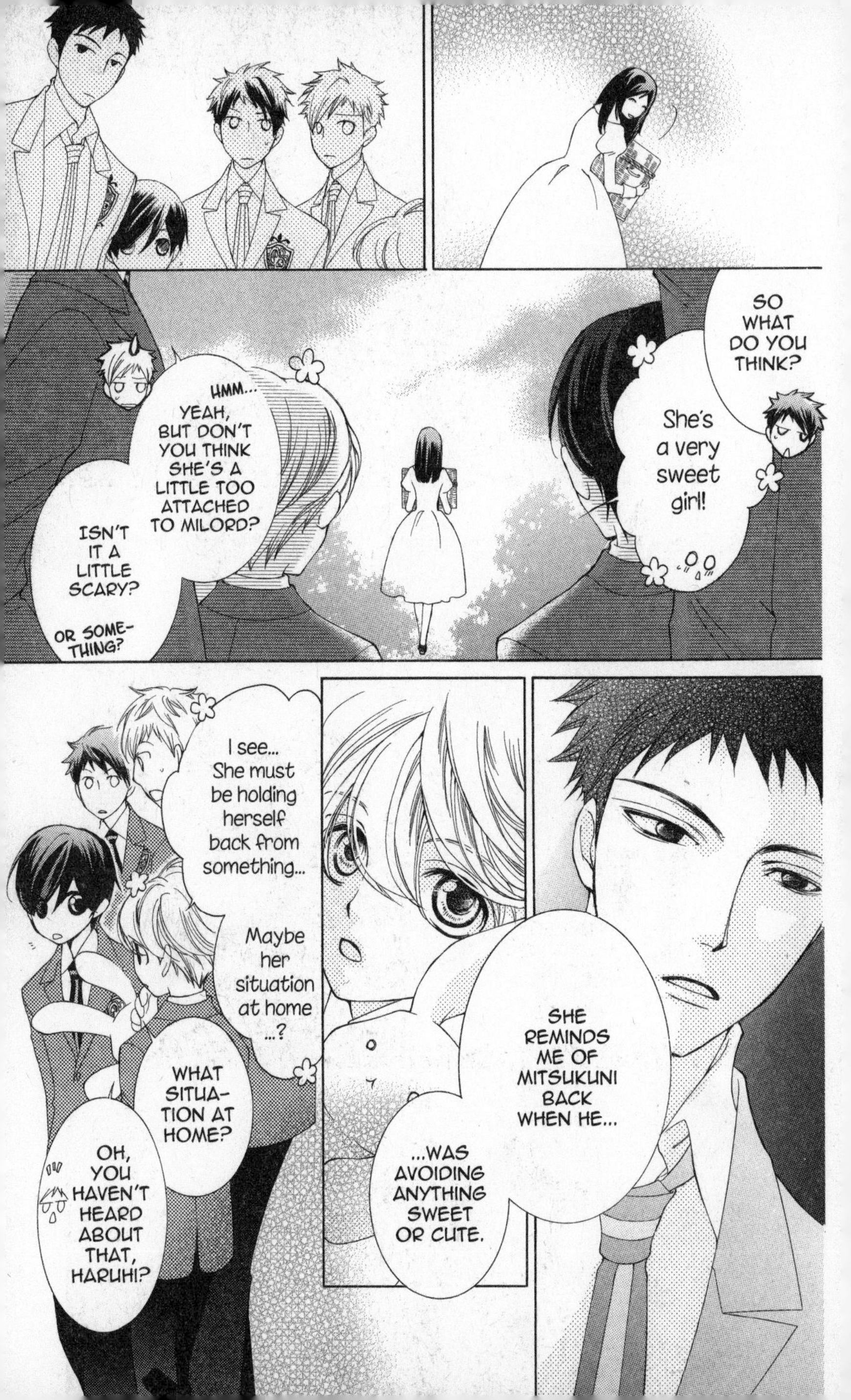
SO WHAT DO YOU THINK?
She's a very sweet girl!
HMM...
YEAH, BUT DON'T YOU THINK SHE'S A LITTLE TOO ATTACHED TO MILORD?
ISN'T IT A LITTLE SCARY?
OR SOME-THING?
SHE REMINDS ME OF MITSUKUNI BACK WHEN HE...
...WAS AVOIDING ANYTHING SWEET OR CUTE.
I see... She must be holding herself back from something...
Maybe her situation at home ...?
WHAT SITUA-TION AT HOME?
OH, YOU HAVEN'T HEARD ABOUT THAT, HARUHI?

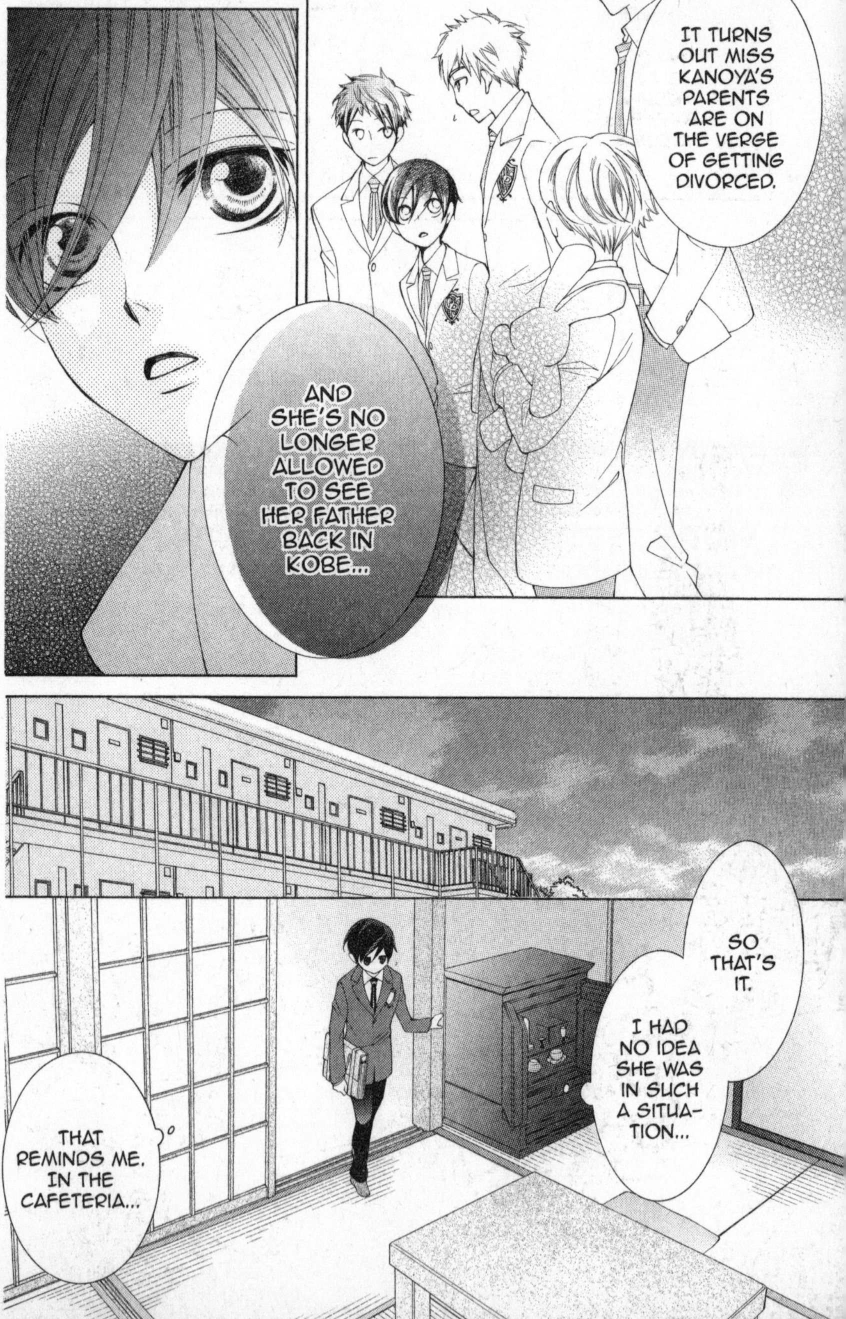
IT TURNS OUT MISS KANOYA'S PARENTS ARE ON THE VERGE OF GETTING DIVORCED.
AND SHE'S NO LONGER ALLOWED TO SEE HER FATHER BACK IN KOBE...
SO THAT'S IT.
I HAD NO IDEA SHE WAS IN SUCH A SITUA-TION...
THAT REMINDS ME. IN THE CAFETERIA...

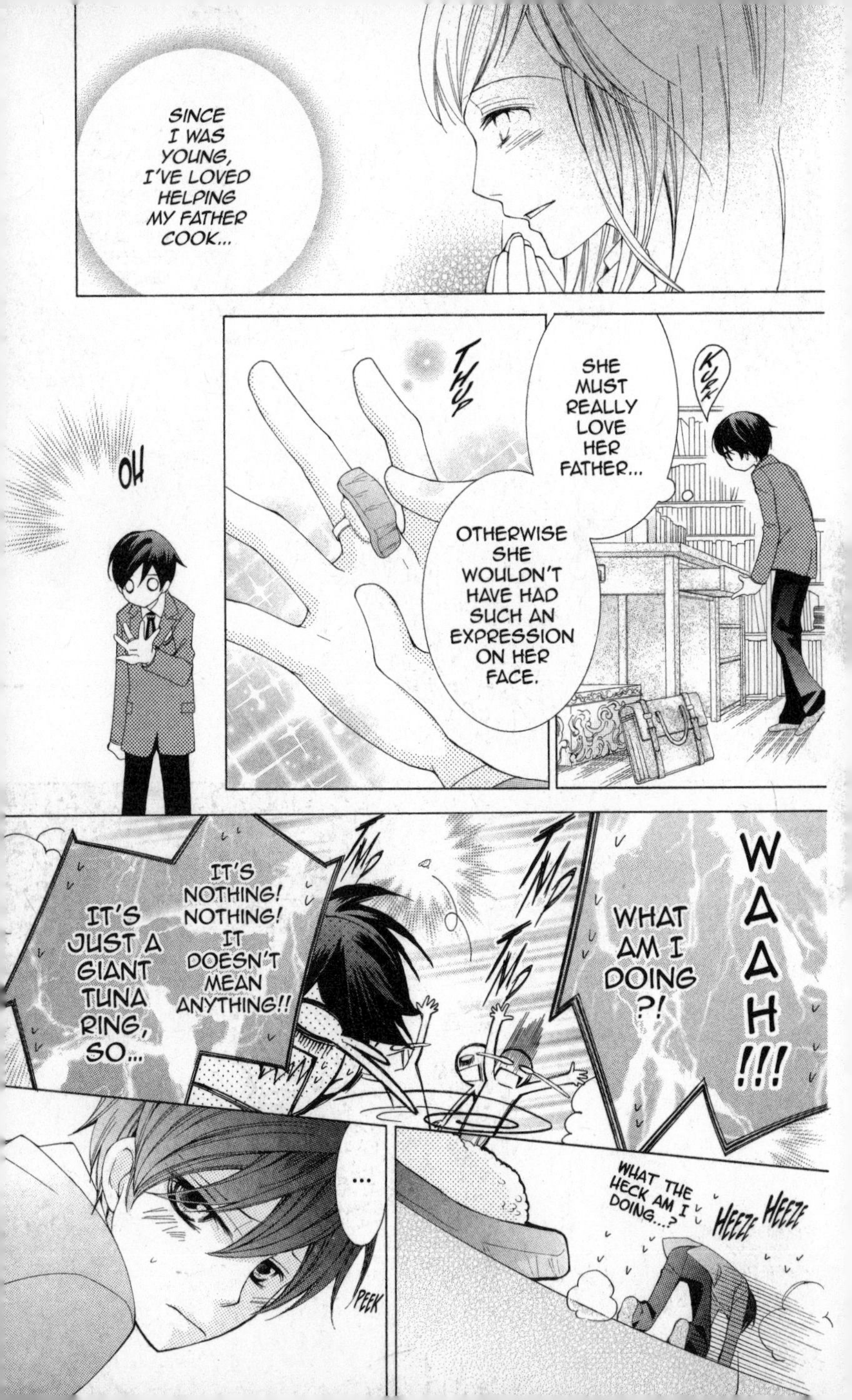
SINCE I WAS YOUNG, I'VE LOVED HELPING MY FATHER COOK...
KURK
SHE MUST REALLY LOVE HER FATHER...
OTHERWISE SHE WOULDN'T HAVE HAD SUCH AN EXPRESSION ON HER FACE.
THUP
OH
WAAH!!!
WHAT AM I DOING?!
IT'S NOTHING! NOTHING! IT DOESN'T MEAN ANYTHING!!
IT'S JUST A GIANT TUNA RING, SO...
WHAT THE HECK AM I DOING...?
HEEZE
HEEZE
...
PEEK

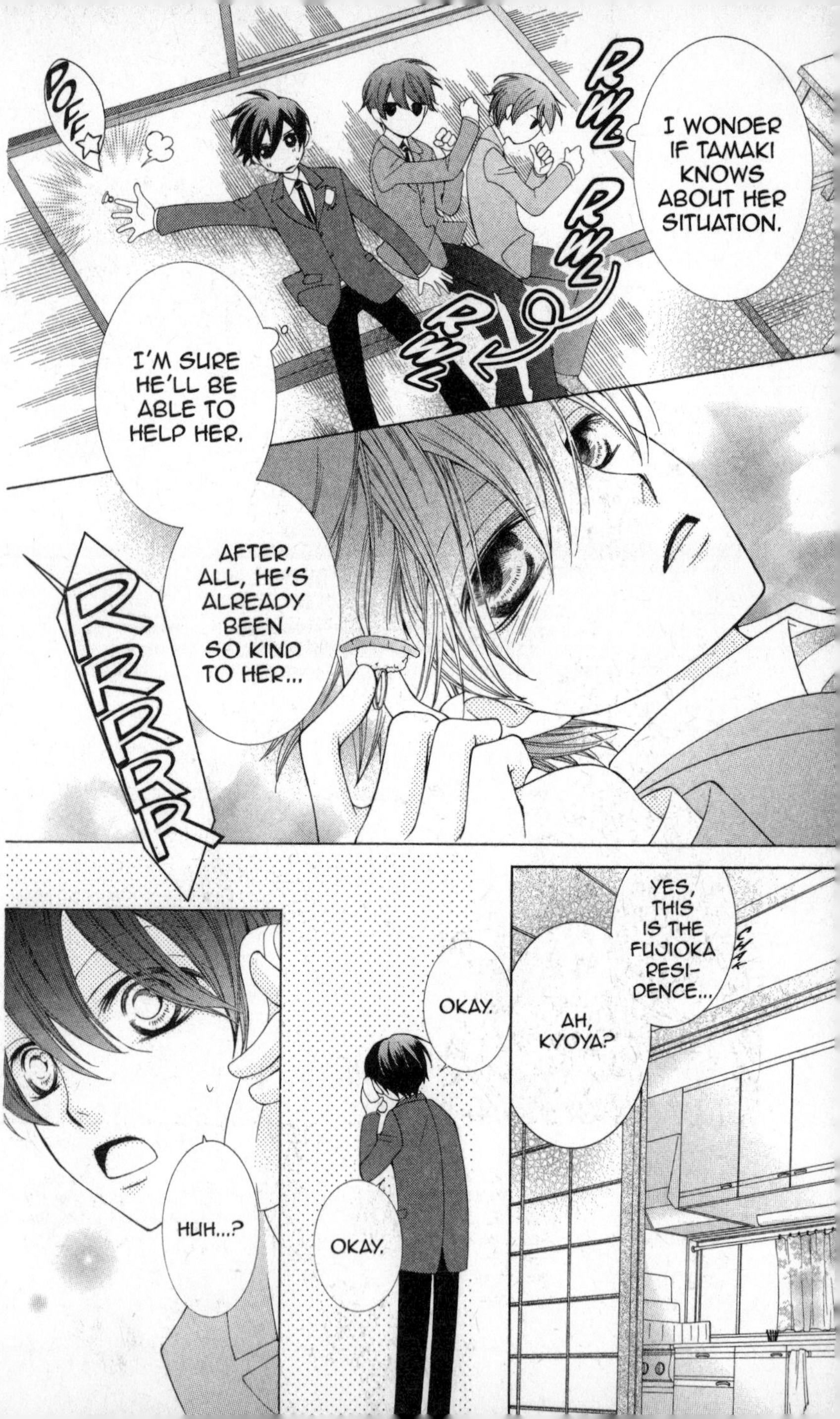

I WONDER IF TAMAKI KNOWS ABOUT HER SITUATION.
RWL RWL RWL
DOFF
I'M SURE HE'LL BE ABLE TO HELP HER.
AFTER ALL, HE'S ALREADY BEEN SO KIND TO HER...
YES, THIS IS THE FUJIOKA RESIDENCE...
AH, KYOYA?
OKAY.
OKAY.
HUH...?

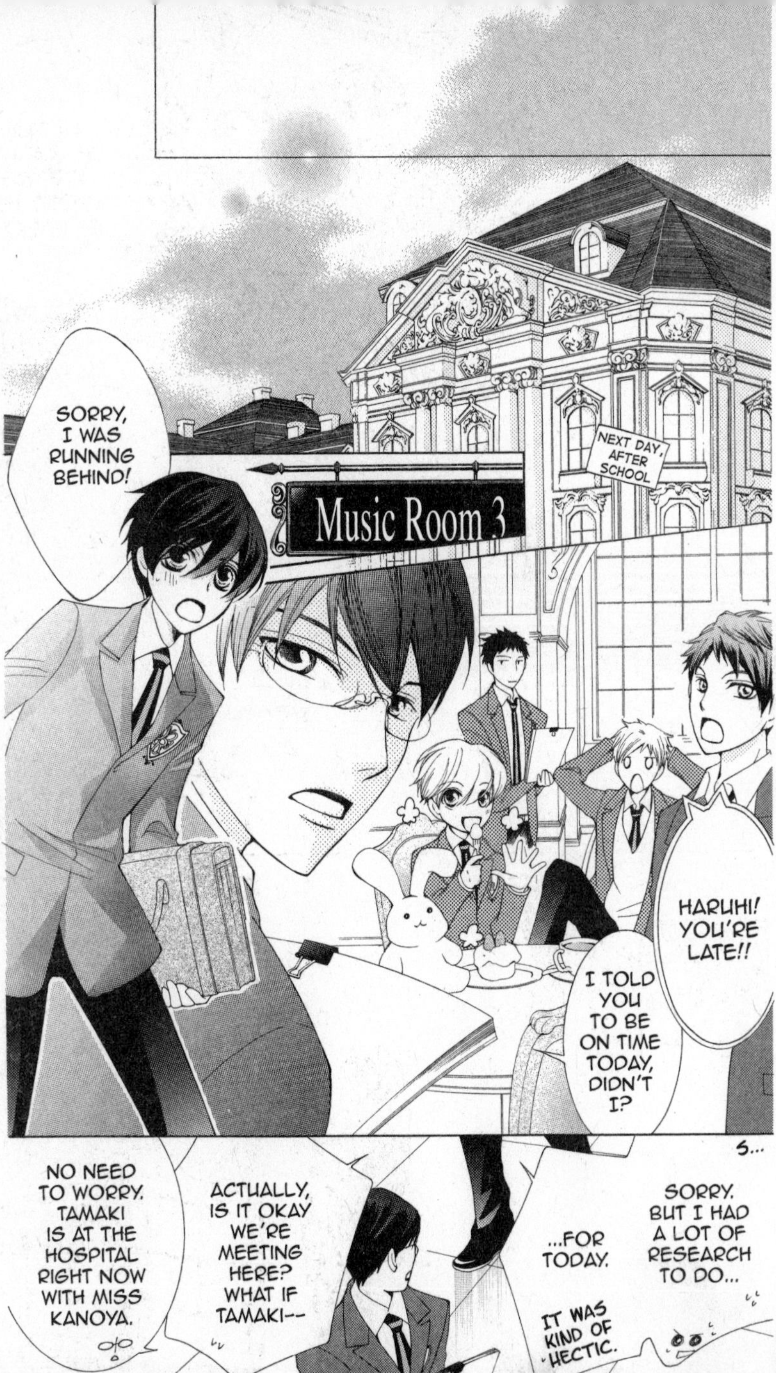
NEXT DAY, AFTER SCHOOL
Music Room 3
SORRY, I WAS RUNNING BEHIND!
HARUHI! YOU'RE LATE!!
I TOLD YOU TO BE ON TIME TODAY, DIDN'T I?
S...
SORRY. BUT I HAD A LOT OF RESEARCH TO DO...
...FOR TODAY.
IT WAS KIND OF HECTIC.
ACTUALLY, IS IT OKAY WE'RE MEETING HERE? WHAT IF TAMAKI--
NO NEED TO WORRY. TAMAKI IS AT THE HOSPITAL RIGHT NOW WITH MISS KANOYA.

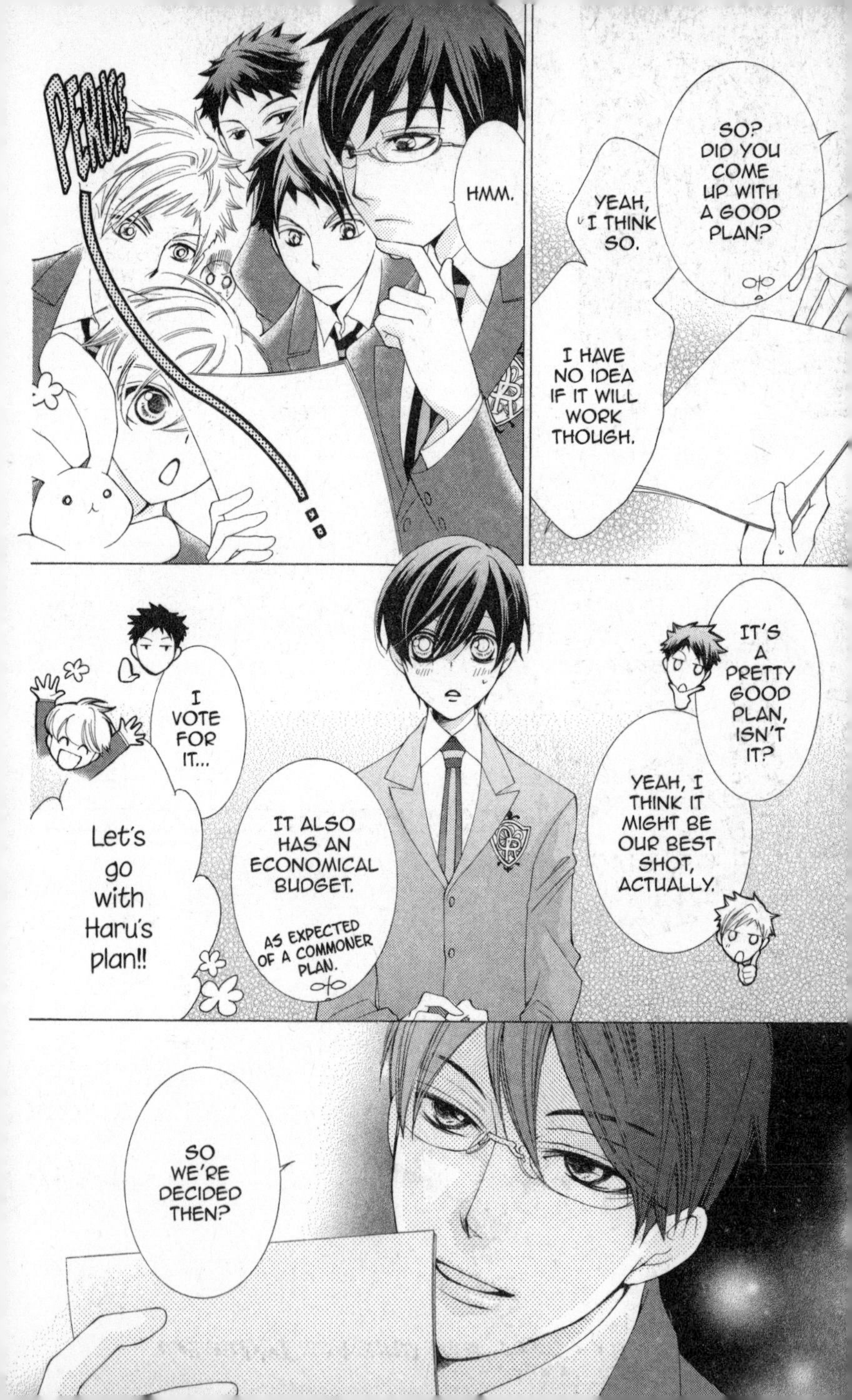
SO? DID YOU COME UP WITH A GOOD PLAN?
YEAH, I THINK SO.
I HAVE NO IDEA IF IT WILL WORK THOUGH.
HMM.
PERUSE
IT'S A PRETTY GOOD PLAN, ISN'T IT?
YEAH, I THINK IT MIGHT BE OUR BEST SHOT, ACTUALLY.
IT ALSO HAS AN ECONOMICAL BUDGET.
AS EXPECTED OF A COMMONER PLAN.
I VOTE FOR IT...
Let's go with Haru's plan!!
SO WE'RE DECIDED THEN?

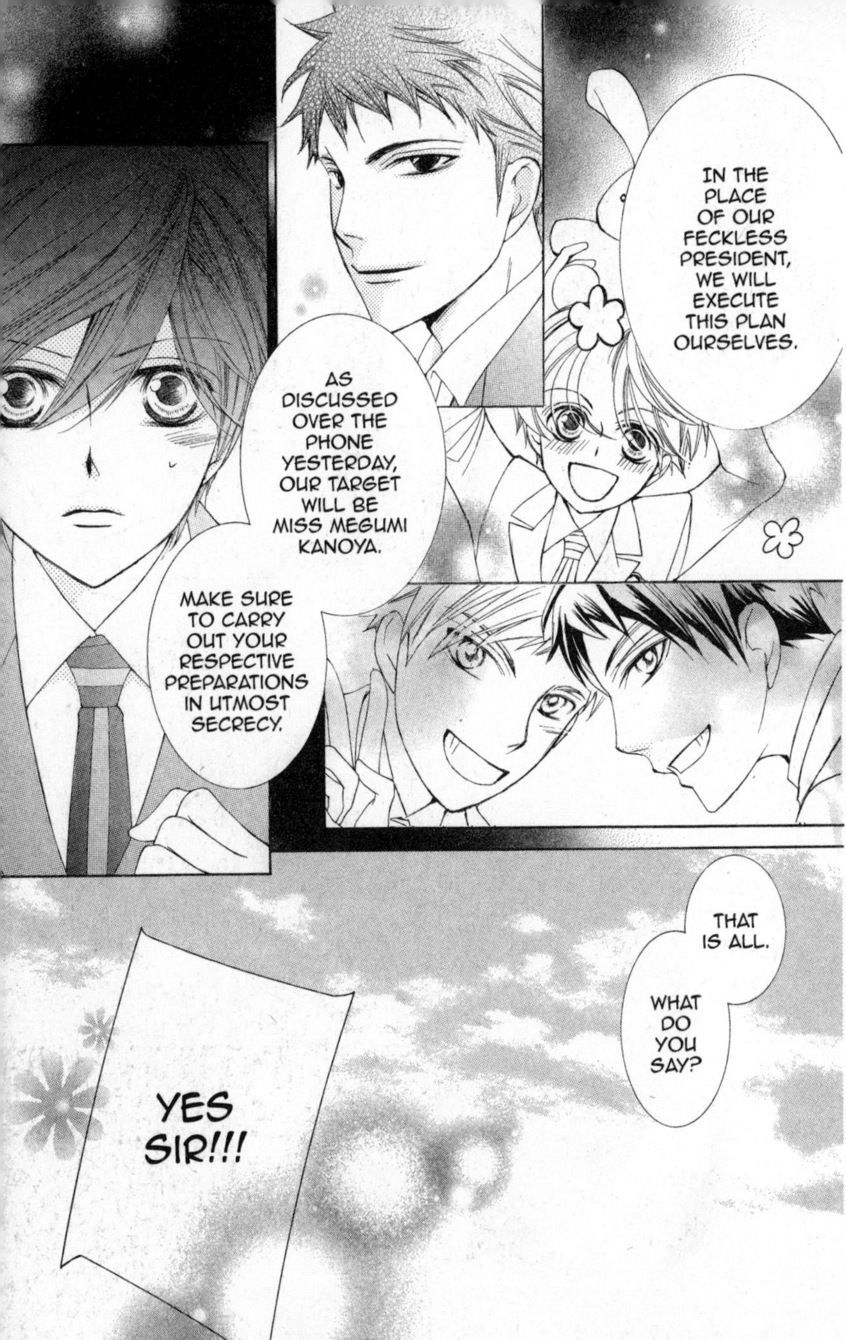
IN THE PLACE OF OUR FECKLESS PRESIDENT, WE WILL EXECUTE THIS PLAN OURSELVES.
AS DISCUSSED OVER THE PHONE YESTERDAY, OUR TARGET WILL BE MISS MEGUMI KANOYA.
MAKE SURE TO CARRY OUT YOUR RESPECTIVE PREPARATIONS IN UTMOST SECRECY.
THAT IS ALL.
WHAT DO YOU SAY?
YES SIR!!!

OURAN HIGH SCHOOL HOST CLUB, VOL. 14/THE END

TEAM ☆ HATORI'S ROOM

SHIZURU ONDA
(FORMERLY KNOWN AS SUBARU AMASAWA)

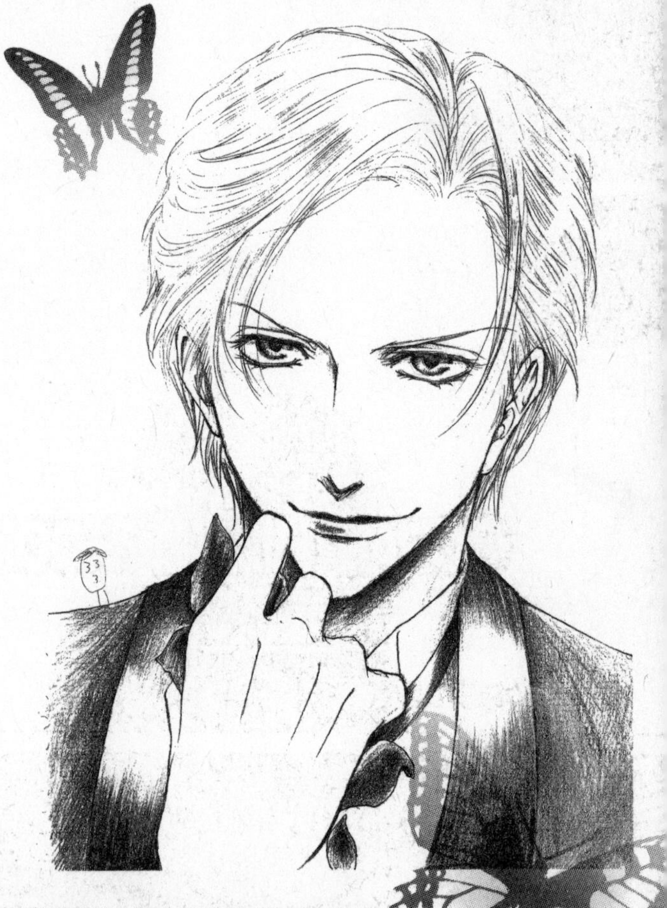

THOUGH SHE DREW ME A NICE SKETCH BACK IN VOLUME 13, THIS TIME SHIZURU-CHAN DREW THIS GORGEOUS TAMAKI!! AND THERE'S A "3 MAN" (A BACKGROUND CHARACTER) SITTING ON HIS SHOULDER! (LAUGHS) SHIZURU-CHAN JUST WON THE DEBUT AWARD FROM *LALA* MAGAZINE THE OTHER DAY. PLEASE MAKE A WONDERFUL STORY TO SEND OUT TO THE WORLD! ♡ CONGRATULATIONS!!

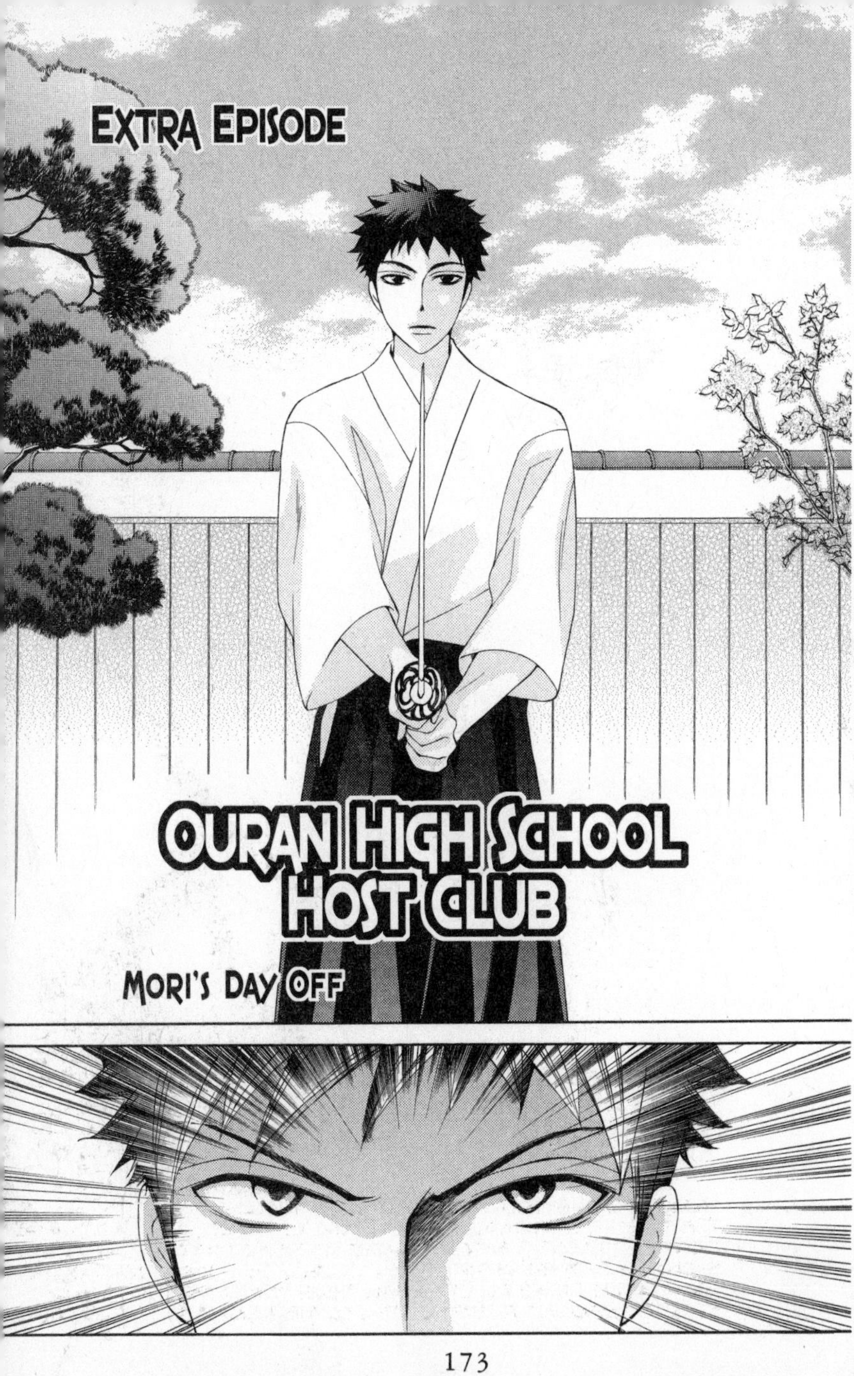
EXTRA EPISODE
OURAN HIGH SCHOOL HOST CLUB
MORI'S DAY OFF

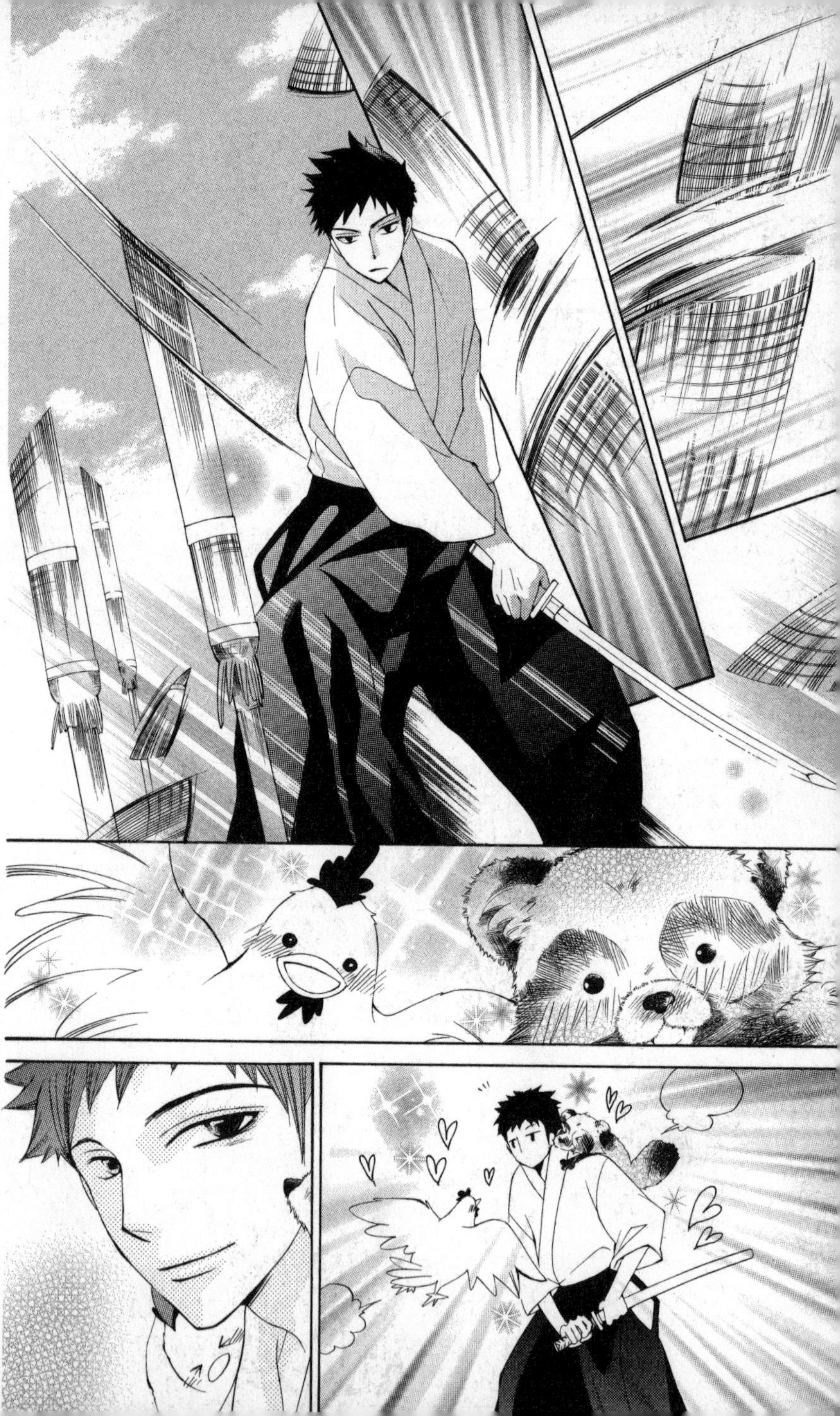

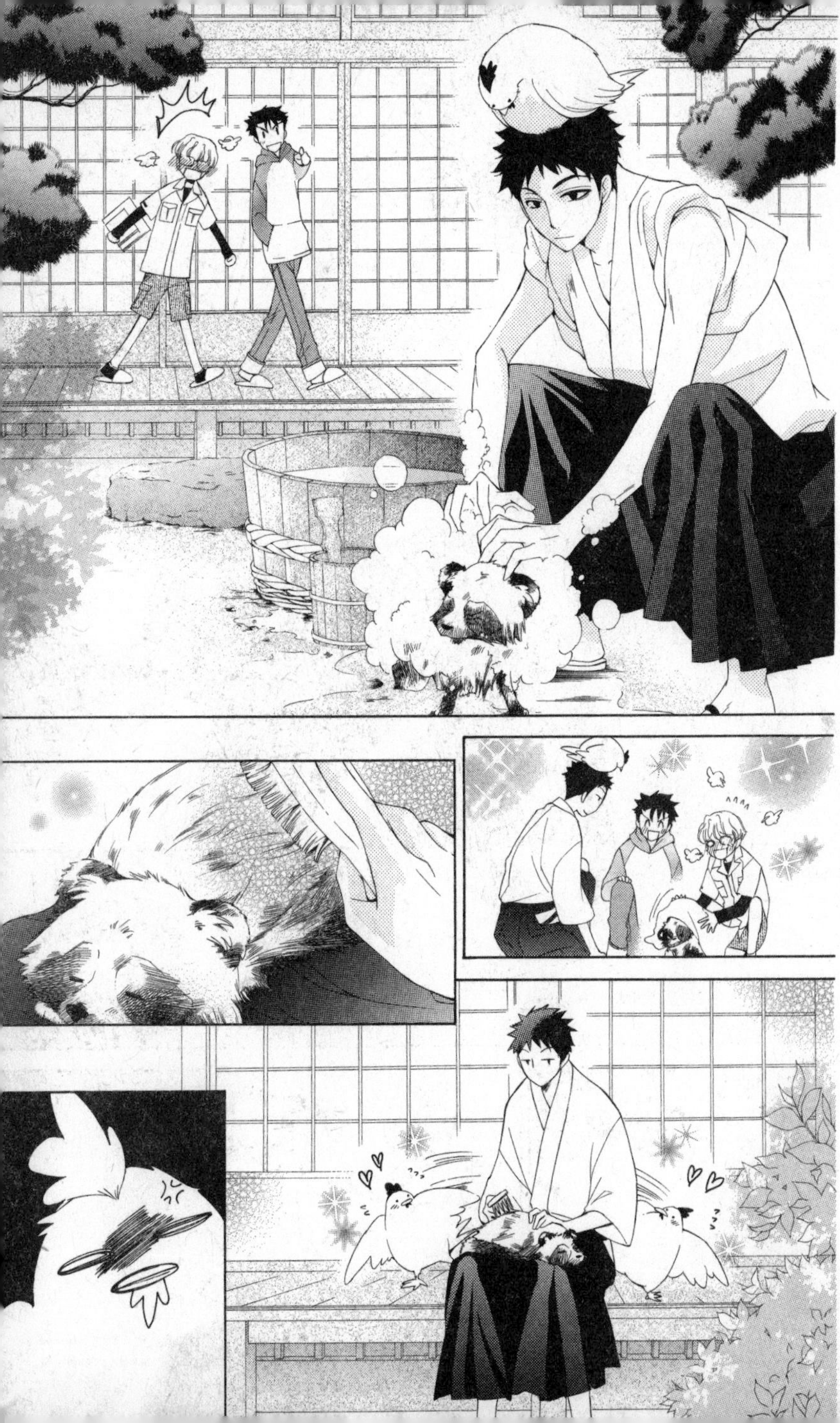

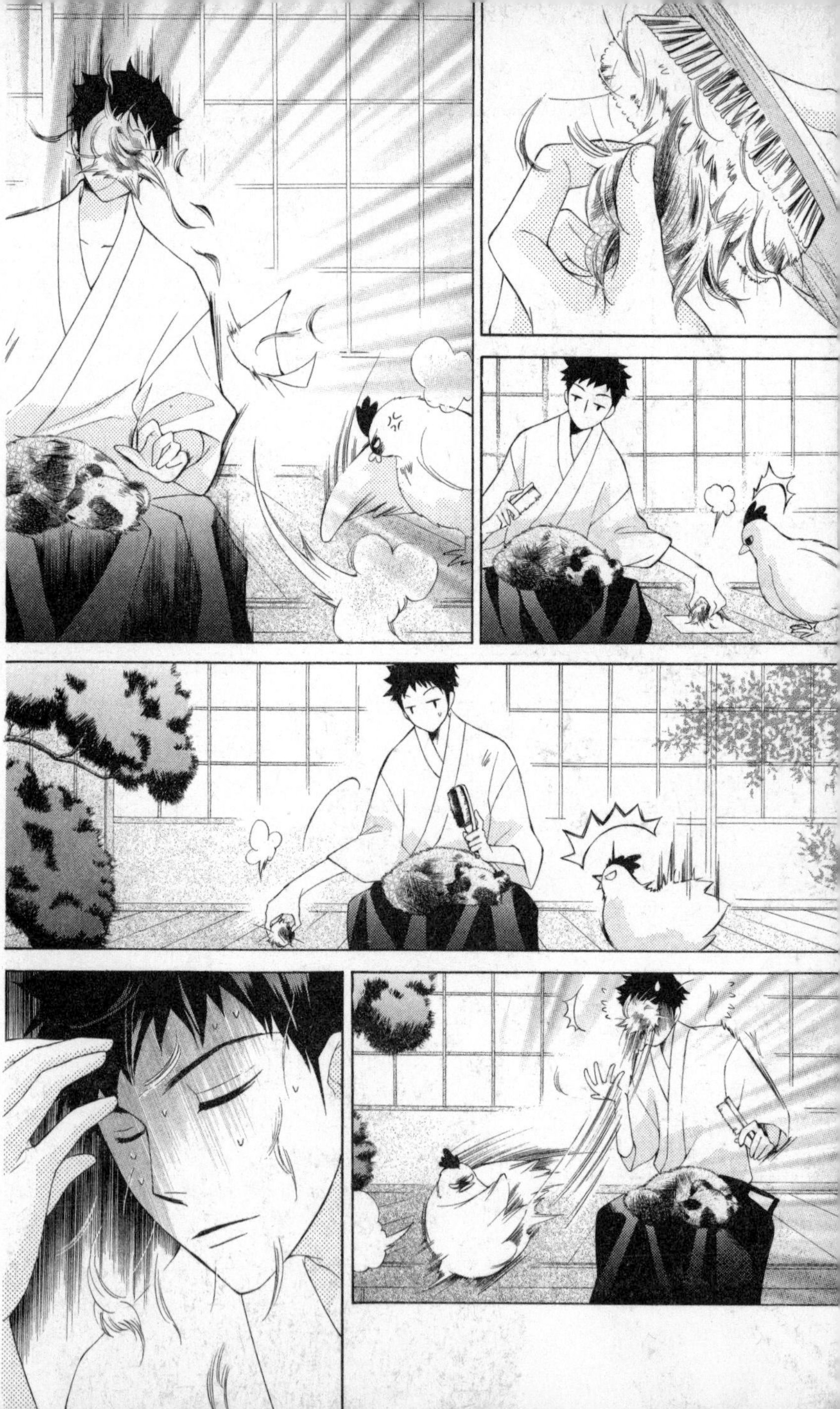

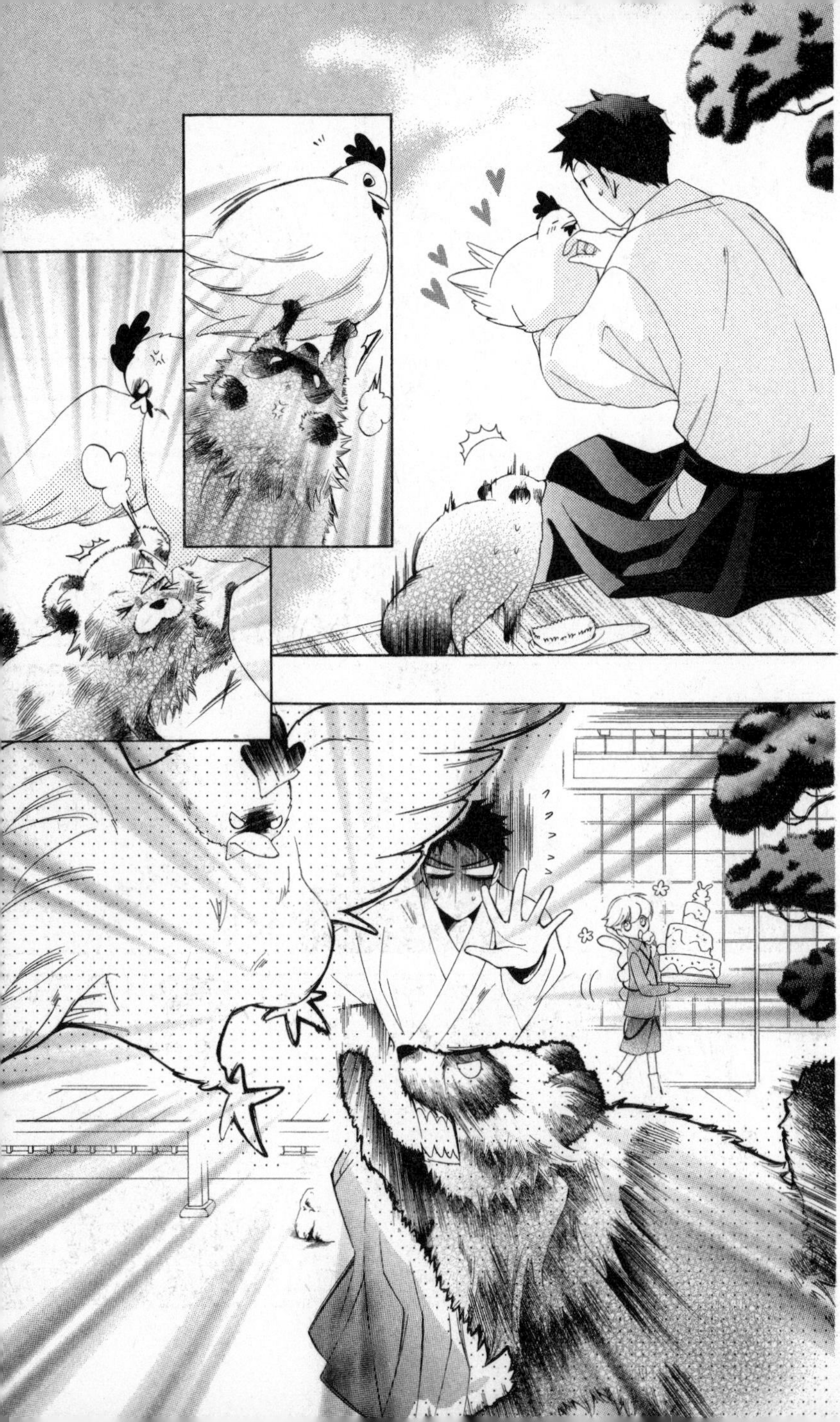

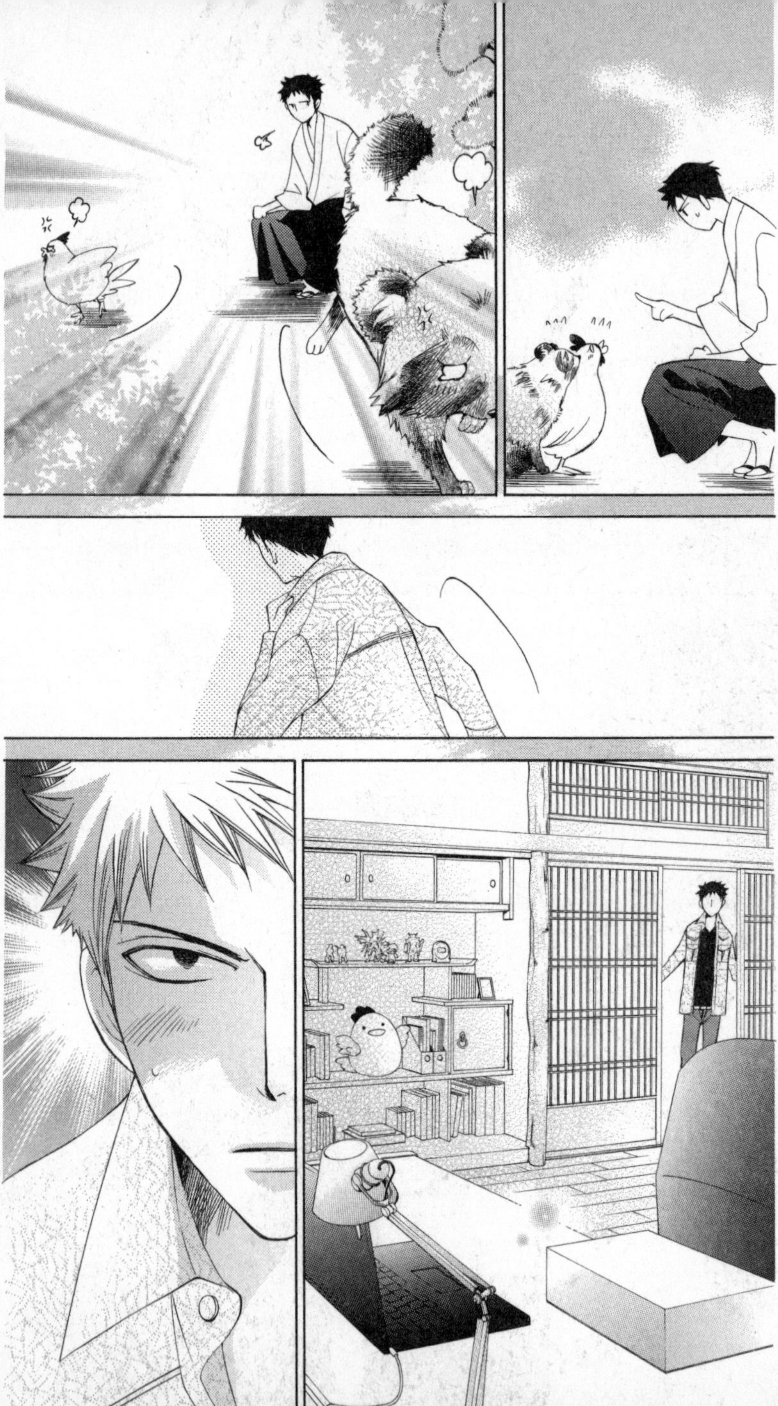

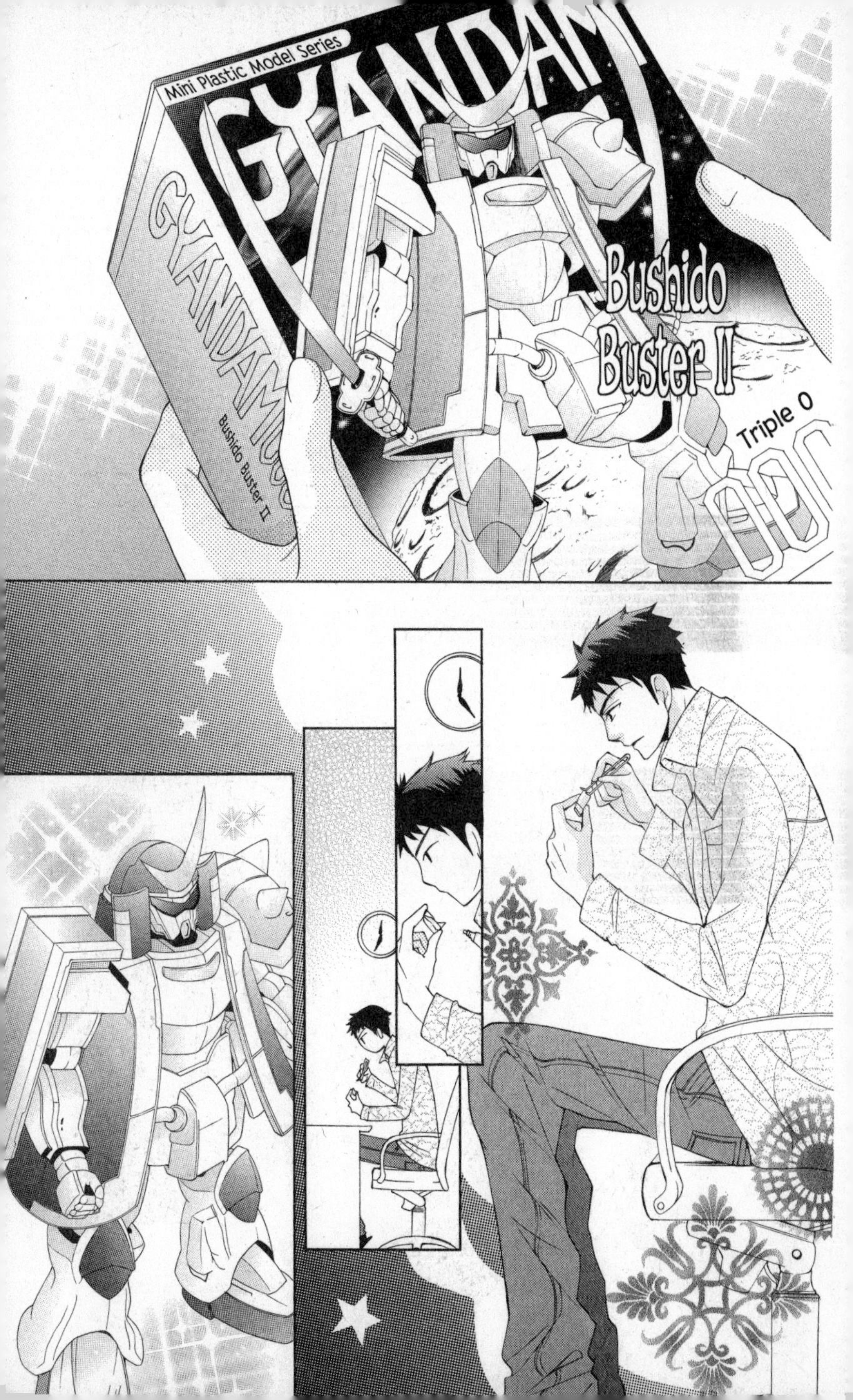
Bushido Buster II
Triple 0
Mini Plastic Model Series
GYANDAM
GYANDAM
Bushido Buster II

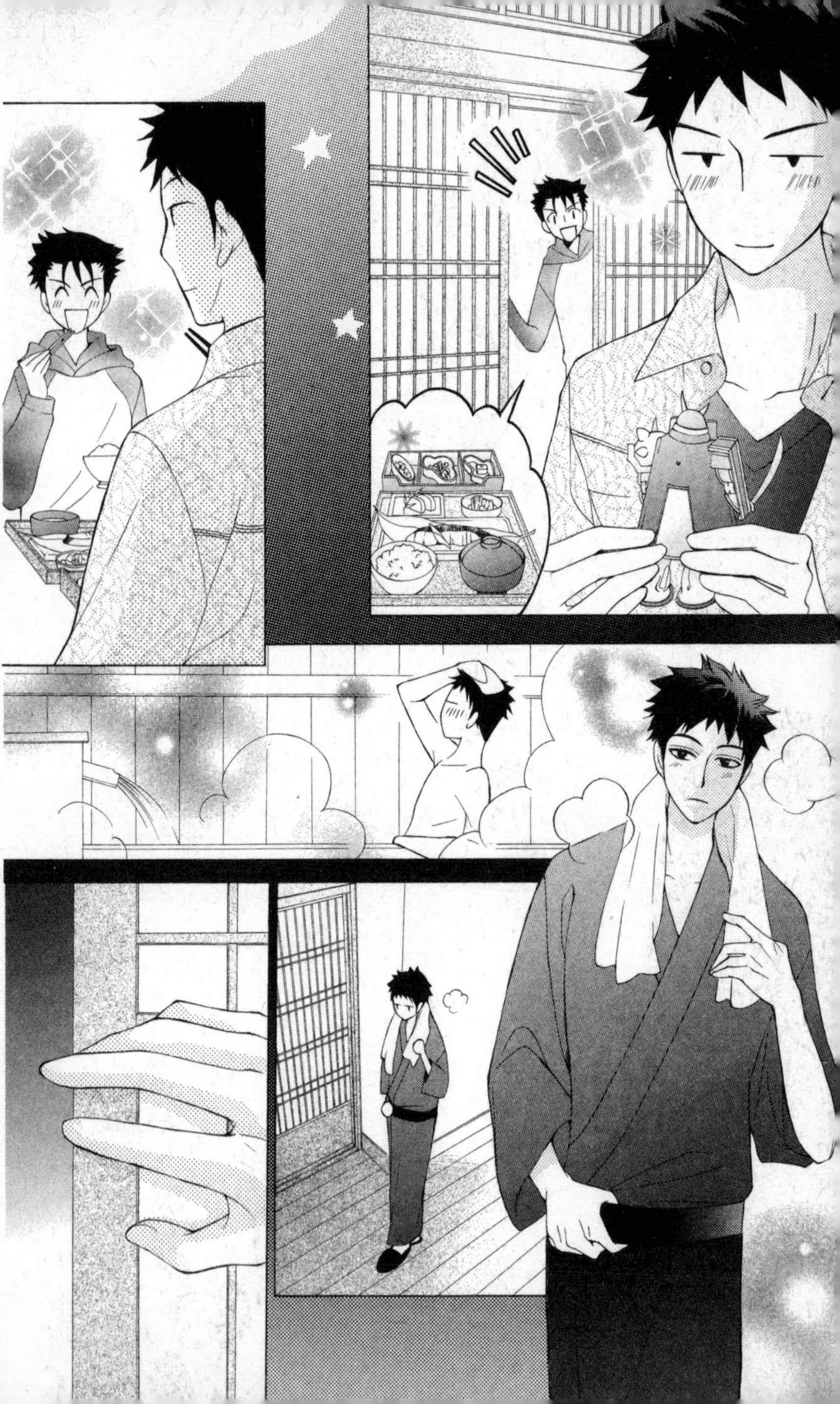

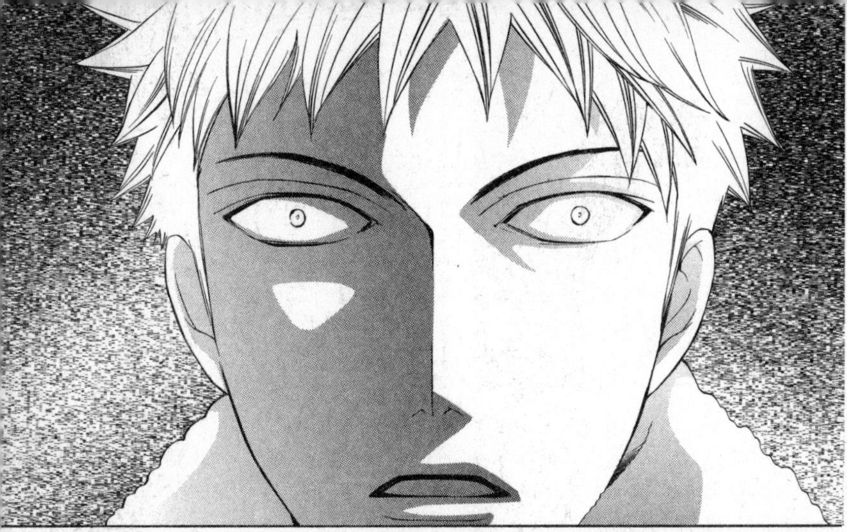
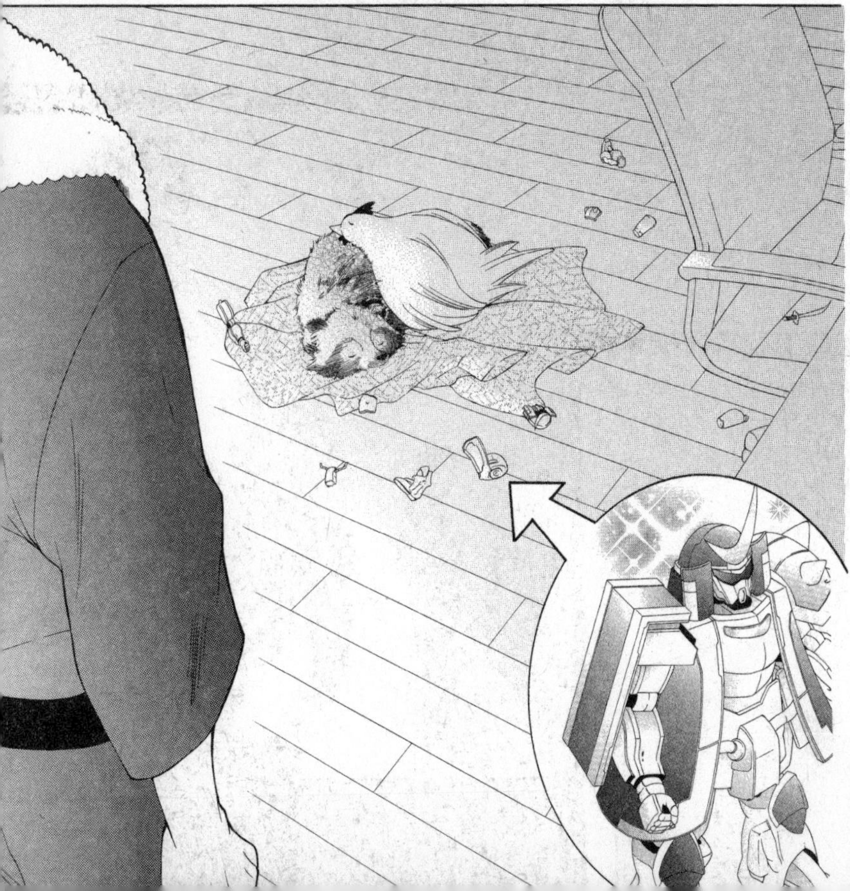

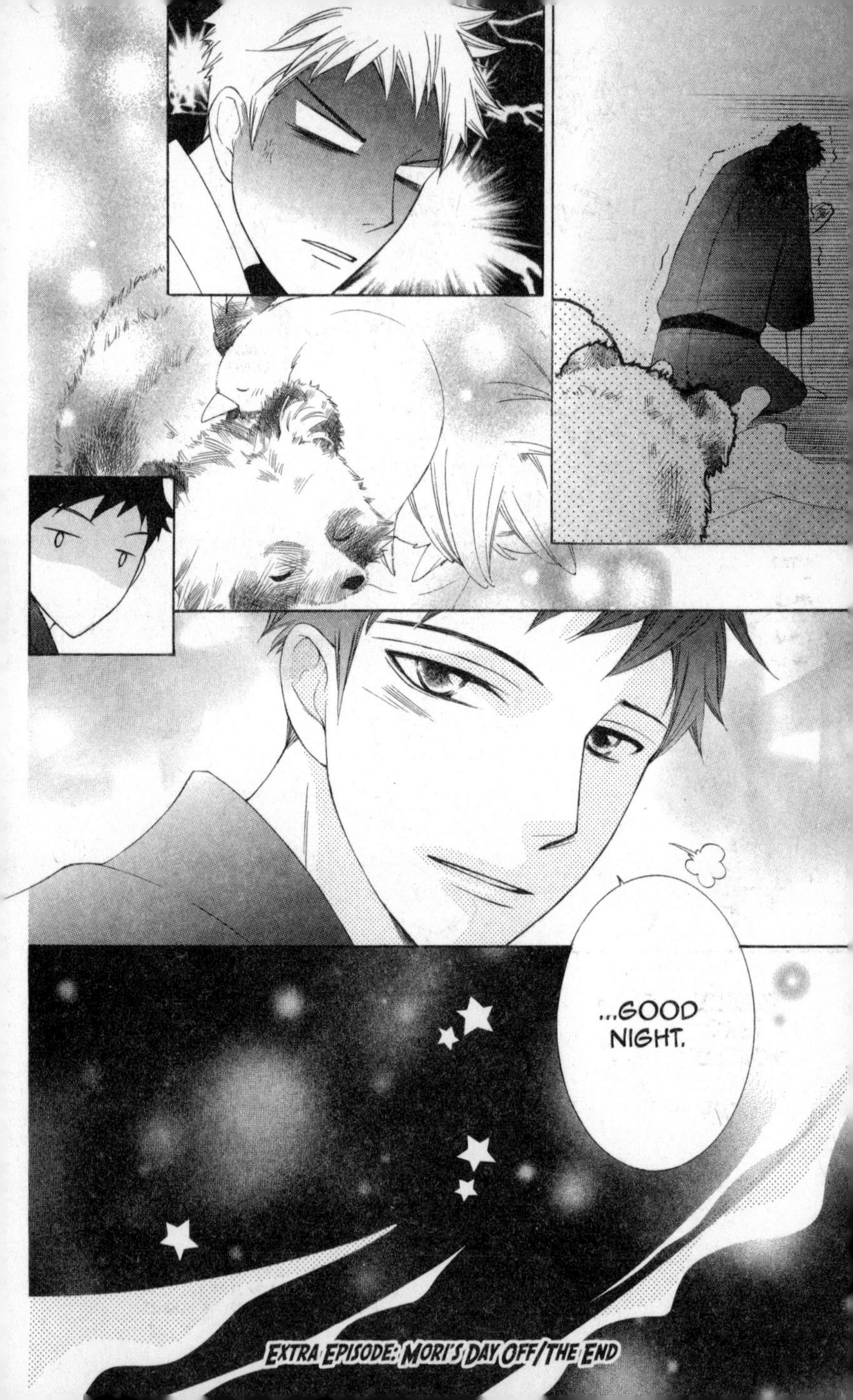
...GOOD NIGHT.
EXTRA EPISODE: MORI'S DAY OFF/THE END

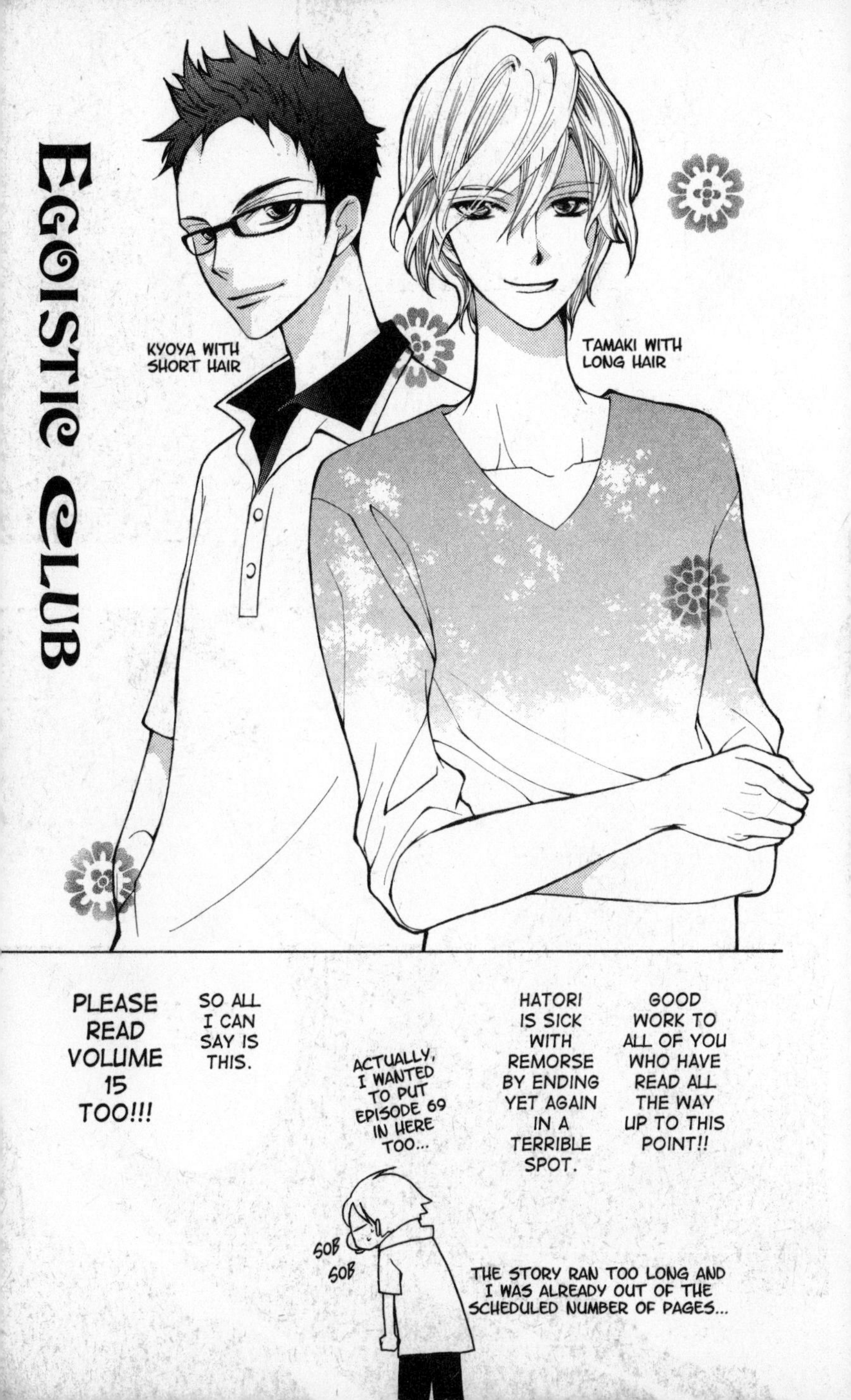
EGOISTIC CLUB
TAMAKI WITH LONG HAIR
KYOYA WITH SHORT HAIR
GOOD WORK TO ALL OF YOU WHO HAVE READ ALL THE WAY UP TO THIS POINT!!
HATORI IS SICK WITH REMORSE BY ENDING YET AGAIN IN A TERRIBLE SPOT.
ACTUALLY, I WANTED TO PUT EPISODE 69 IN HERE TOO...
THE STORY RAN TOO LONG AND I WAS ALREADY OUT OF THE SCHEDULED NUMBER OF PAGES...
SOB SOB
SO ALL I CAN SAY IS THIS.
PLEASE READ VOLUME 15 TOO!!!

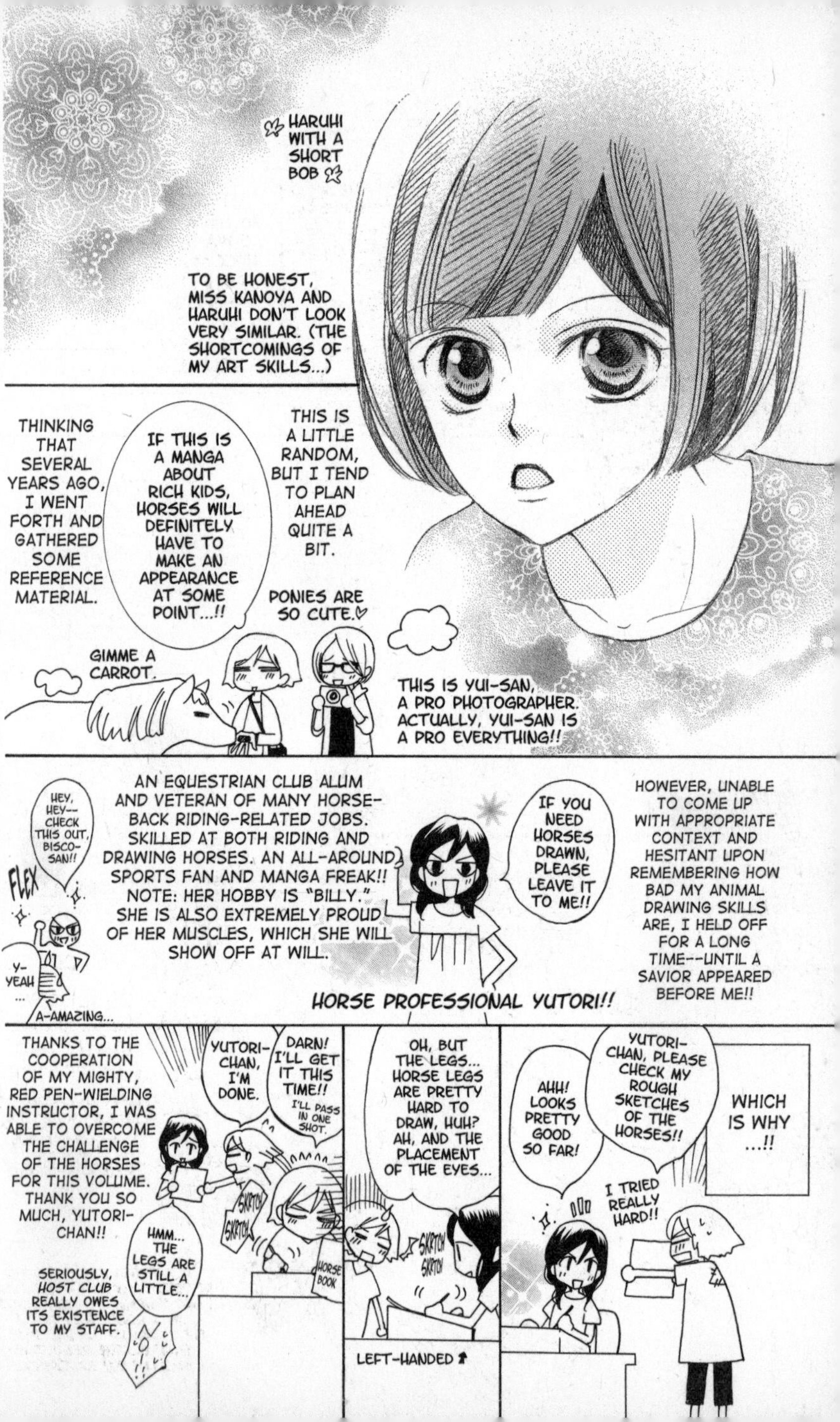
HARUHI WITH A SHORT BOB
TO BE HONEST, MISS KANOYA AND HARUHI DON'T LOOK VERY SIMILAR. (THE SHORTCOMINGS OF MY ART SKILLS...)
THIS IS A LITTLE RANDOM, BUT I TEND TO PLAN AHEAD QUITE A BIT.
IF THIS IS A MANGA ABOUT RICH KIDS, HORSES WILL DEFINITELY HAVE TO MAKE AN APPEARANCE AT SOME POINT...!!
THINKING THAT SEVERAL YEARS AGO, I WENT FORTH AND GATHERED SOME REFERENCE MATERIAL.
PONIES ARE SO CUTE.♡
GIMME A CARROT.
THIS IS YUI-SAN, A PRO PHOTOGRAPHER. ACTUALLY, YUI-SAN IS A PRO EVERYTHING!!
HOWEVER, UNABLE TO COME UP WITH APPROPRIATE CONTEXT AND HESITANT UPON REMEMBERING HOW BAD MY ANIMAL DRAWING SKILLS ARE, I HELD OFF FOR A LONG TIME--UNTIL A SAVIOR APPEARED BEFORE ME!!
IF YOU NEED HORSES DRAWN, PLEASE LEAVE IT TO ME!!
HORSE PROFESSIONAL YUTORI!!
AN EQUESTRIAN CLUB ALUM AND VETERAN OF MANY HORSEBACK RIDING-RELATED JOBS. SKILLED AT BOTH RIDING AND DRAWING HORSES. AN ALL-AROUND SPORTS FAN AND MANGA FREAK!! NOTE: HER HOBBY IS "BILLY." SHE IS ALSO EXTREMELY PROUD OF HER MUSCLES, WHICH SHE WILL SHOW OFF AT WILL.
HEY, HEY-- CHECK THIS OUT, BISCO-SAN!!
FLEX
Y-YEAH ...
A-AMAZING...
WHICH IS WHY ...!!
YUTORI-CHAN, PLEASE CHECK MY ROUGH SKETCHES OF THE HORSES!!
AHH! LOOKS PRETTY GOOD SO FAR!
I TRIED REALLY HARD!!
OH, BUT THE LEGS... HORSE LEGS ARE PRETTY HARD TO DRAW, HUH? AH, AND THE PLACEMENT OF THE EYES...
SKRTCH SKRTCH
LEFT-HANDED
DARN! I'LL GET IT THIS TIME!!
I'LL PASS IN ONE SHOT.
YUTORI-CHAN, I'M DONE.
THANKS TO THE COOPERATION OF MY MIGHTY, RED PEN-WIELDING INSTRUCTOR, I WAS ABLE TO OVERCOME THE CHALLENGE OF THE HORSES FOR THIS VOLUME. THANK YOU SO MUCH, YUTORI-CHAN!!
SKRTCH SKRTCH
HORSE BOOK
HMM... THE LEGS ARE STILL A LITTLE...
SERIOUSLY, HOST CLUB REALLY OWES ITS EXISTENCE TO MY STAFF.

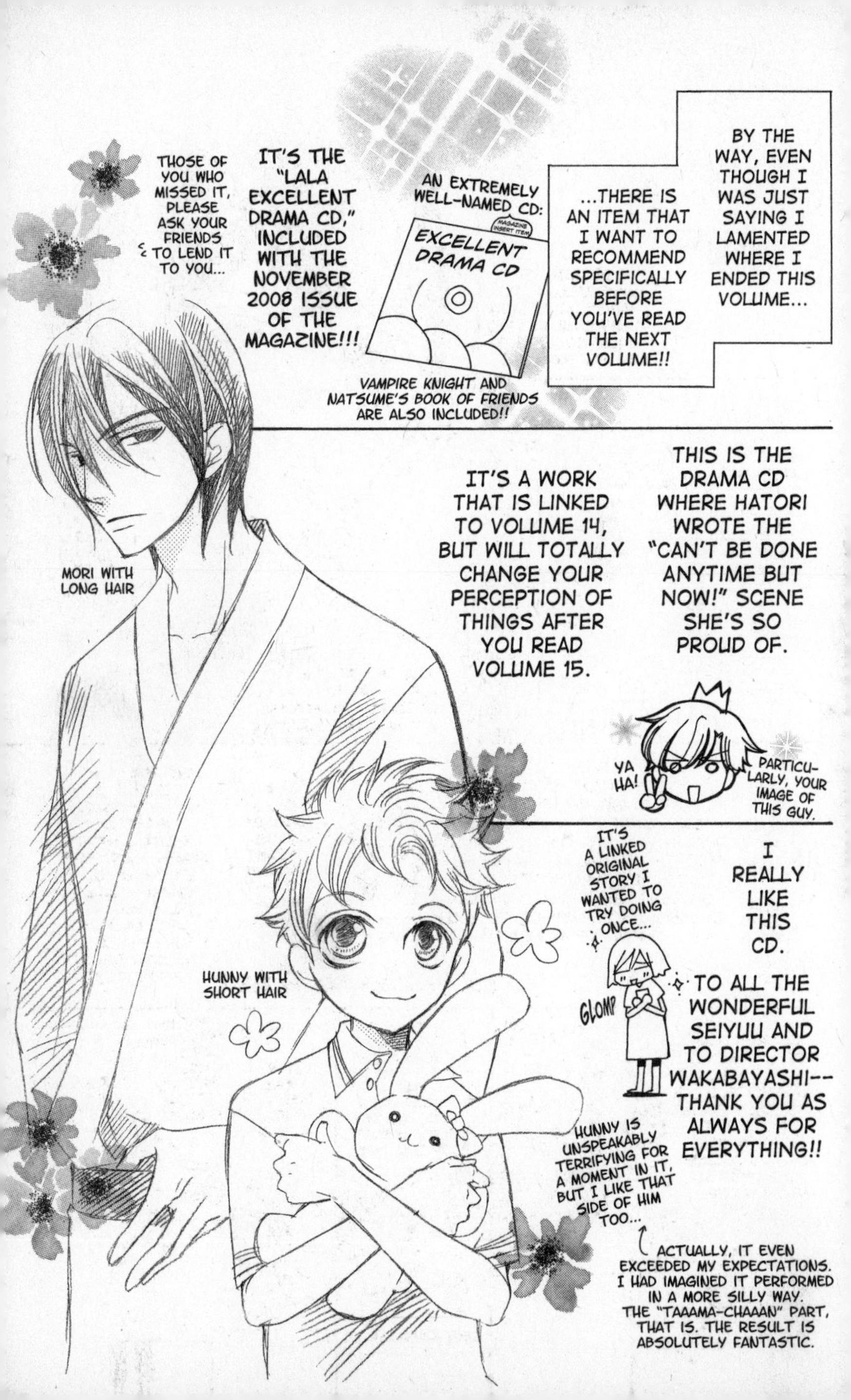
BY THE WAY, EVEN THOUGH I WAS JUST SAYING I LAMENTED WHERE I ENDED THIS VOLUME...
...THERE IS AN ITEM THAT I WANT TO RECOMMEND SPECIFICALLY BEFORE YOU'VE READ THE NEXT VOLUME!!
AN EXTREMELY WELL-NAMED CD:
MAGAZINE INSERT ITEM
EXCELLENT DRAMA CD
IT'S THE "LALA EXCELLENT DRAMA CD," INCLUDED WITH THE NOVEMBER 2008 ISSUE OF THE MAGAZINE!!!
THOSE OF YOU WHO MISSED IT, PLEASE ASK YOUR FRIENDS TO LEND IT TO YOU...
VAMPIRE KNIGHT AND NATSUME'S BOOK OF FRIENDS ARE ALSO INCLUDED!!
THIS IS THE DRAMA CD WHERE HATORI WROTE THE "CAN'T BE DONE ANYTIME BUT NOW!" SCENE SHE'S SO PROUD OF.
IT'S A WORK THAT IS LINKED TO VOLUME 14, BUT WILL TOTALLY CHANGE YOUR PERCEPTION OF THINGS AFTER YOU READ VOLUME 15.
PARTICULARLY, YOUR IMAGE OF THIS GUY.
YA HA!
MORI WITH LONG HAIR
I REALLY LIKE THIS CD.
IT'S A LINKED ORIGINAL STORY I WANTED TO TRY DOING ONCE...
TO ALL THE WONDERFUL SEIYUU AND TO DIRECTOR WAKABAYASHI--THANK YOU AS ALWAYS FOR EVERYTHING!!
GLOMP
HUNNY IS UNSPEAKABLY TERRIFYING FOR A MOMENT IN IT, BUT I LIKE THAT SIDE OF HIM TOO...
ACTUALLY, IT EVEN EXCEEDED MY EXPECTATIONS. I HAD IMAGINED IT PERFORMED IN A MORE SILLY WAY. THE "TAAAMA-CHAAAN" PART, THAT IS. THE RESULT IS ABSOLUTELY FANTASTIC.
HUNNY WITH SHORT HAIR

✿I WASN'T ABLE TO COMMENT FULLY DUE TO LACK OF SPACE, BUT TO HIRO FUJIWARA-SAMA WHO SENT THAT GORGEOUS FAX--THANK YOU SO MUCH!!

THANK YOU FOR THAT IDIOT TAMAKI PICTURE OVERFLOWING WITH LOVE...! I SEE... YOU WERE UNUSUALLY DEXTEROUS THIS TIME, HUH, TAMAKI? (LAUGHS) FUJIWARA-SAN CAME OVER TO FLIRT WITH ME A LITTLE AT THE LALA NEW YEAR'S PARTY. SHE IS AN UTTER BEAUTY WHO IS TOTALLY HATORI'S TYPE! ♡♡

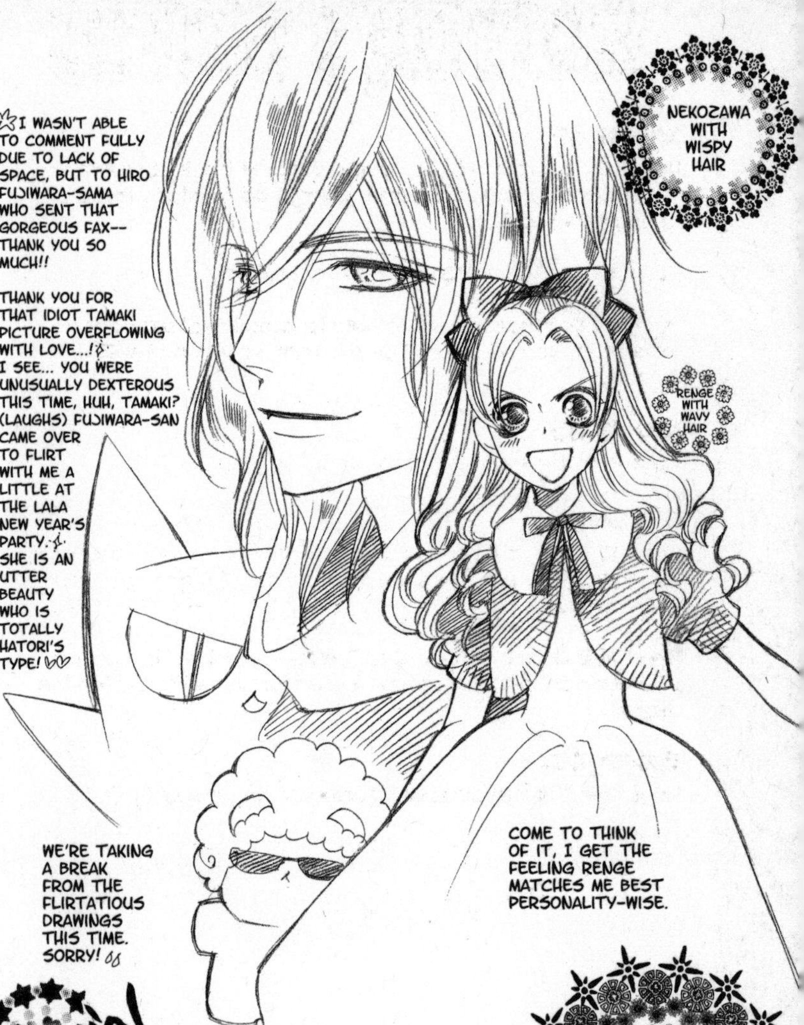
NEKOZAWA WITH WISPY HAIR
RENGE WITH WAVY HAIR

WE'RE TAKING A BREAK FROM THE FLIRTATIOUS DRAWINGS THIS TIME. SORRY!

COME TO THINK OF IT, I GET THE FEELING RENGE MATCHES ME BEST PERSONALITY-WISE.

Special Thanks!!

2009. MAY
BISCO HATORI

✿ T AND EVERYONE AT THE COMPILATION OFFICE

✿ KONAMI KATASE

✿ EVERYONE INVOLVED IN THE PRODUCTION OF THIS BOOK

✿ EVERYONE ON MY STAFF: YUI NATSUKI, RIKU, AYA AOMURA, YUTORI HIZAKURA, SHIZURU ONDA, AND HATORI'S MOMMY

✿ ALL MY EXTRA HELPERS: NATSUMI SATOU, AYA URUNO AND AKIRA HAGINO

AND TO ALL OF YOU WHO READ THIS BOOK!! THANK YOU SO VERY MUCH!

EGOISTIC CLUB/THE END

EDITOR'S NOTES

EPISODE 63

Page 39: *Sugoroku* is a dice game similar to backgammon. *Hanetsuki* is a traditional game similar to badminton played during New Year's.

Page 40: The Meiou Era was from 1492 to1501.

Page 42: Kaminarimon is a famous landmark that serves as a gateway to the Nakamise-Dori shopping street and Senso-ji Temple.

EPISODE 65

Page 104: Rilakkuma is a San-X bear.

EPISODE 66

Page 153: Yashichi is a character on the *Mito Komon* TV series. He is a trained ninja who sometimes helps out the main characters from behind the scenes.

Page 154: Ukkari Hachibe, or "Carefree Hachibe," is another character on *Mito Komon* who is used for comedic relief on the series.

EGOISTIC CLUB

Page 184: "Billy" refers to Billy Blanks, a fitness guru.

Author Bio

Bisco Hatori made her
manga debut with *Isshun
kan no Romance* (A Moment
of Romance) in *LaLa DX*
magazine. The comedy *Ouran
High School Host Club* is her
breakout hit. When she's stuck
thinking up characters' names,
she gets inspired by loud,
upbeat music (her radio is set
to NACK5 FM). She enjoys
reading all kinds of manga, but
she's especially fond of the
sci-fi drama *Please Save My
Earth* and *Slam Dunk*, a
basketball classic.

OURAN HIGH SCHOOL HOST CLUB
Vol. 14
Shojo Beat Edition

STORY AND ART BY BISCO HATORI

Translation/Su Mon Han
Touch-up Art & Lettering/Gia Cam Luc
Graphic Design/Amy Martin
Editor/Nancy Thistlethwaite

Ouran Koko Host Club by Bisco Hatori © Bisco Hatori 2009. All rights reserved.
First published in Japan in 2009 by HAKUSENSHA, Inc., Tokyo. English language
translation rights arranged with HAKUSENSHA, Inc., Tokyo.

The stories, characters and incidents mentioned in this publication
are entirely fictional.

Printed in Canada

Published by VIZ Media, LLC
P.O. Box 77010
San Francisco, CA 94107

10 9 8
First printing, July 2010
Eighth printing, August 2016

www.viz.com   www.shojobeat.com

SURPRISE!

You may be reading the wrong way!

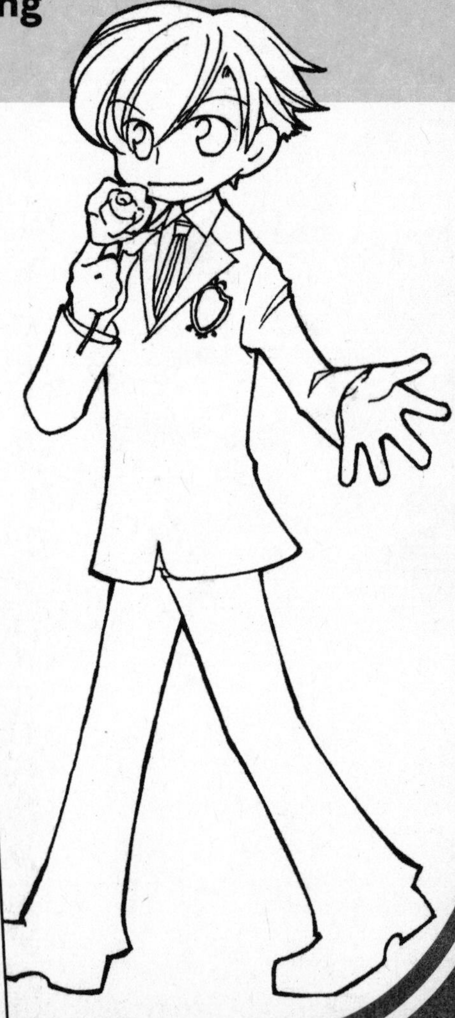

It's true: In keeping with the original Japanese comic format, this book reads from right to left—so action, sound effects, and word balloons are completely reversed. This preserves the orientation of the original artwork—plus, it's fun! Check out the diagram shown here to get the hang of things, and then turn to the other side of the book to get started!

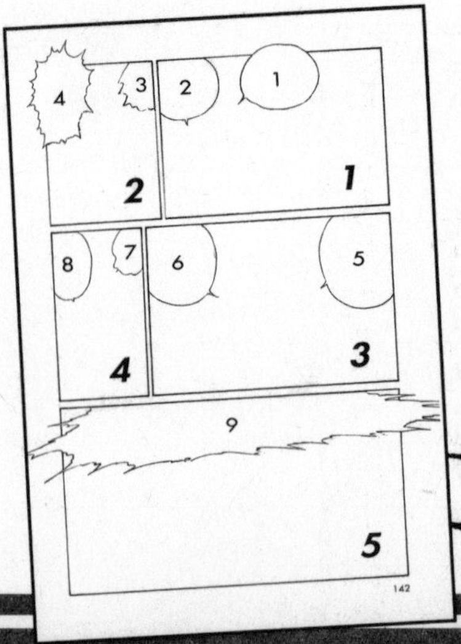